The Way of Divine Love

Or the Message of the Sacred Heart
to the World, and a Short Biography
of His Messenger

Sister Josefa Menendez

Must Have Books
503 Deerfield Place
Victoria, BC
V9B 6G5
Canada

ISBN 9781774645291

Copyright 2023 – Must Have Books

LETTER FROM THE CARDINAL PROTECTOR:

Very Reverend Mother,   April 1938

I have no doubt whatever that the publication of these pages, filled as they are with the great love which His grace inspired in His very humble servant Maria Josefa Menéndez, will be agreeable to His Sacred Heart.

May they efficaciously contribute to develop in many souls a confidence ever more complete and loving in the infinite mercy of this Divine Heart towards poor sinners such as we all are.

These are the good wishes which, with my blessing, I send you and all the Society of the Sacred Heart.

E. CARD. PACHELLI *

* Cardinal Pacelli became Pope Pius XII on March 2, 1939.

TABLE OF CONTENTS

Foreword

This new edition of a translation of Un Appel à L'Amour, is an amplification of the smaller book of the same name which was published in 1938.

On November 13th, shortly before her death, Our Blessed Lord had said to Sister Josefa: "My words will be light and life for an incalculable number of souls, and I will grant them special graces of conversion and illumination." These words have been verified, for as soon as the first small volume appeared it was eagerly seized upon, was reprinted several times, while letters from all parts of the world gave testimony to the profound impression created and to the signal graces that followed on the delivery of the Message.

Within a few months the book had been translated from the original Spanish into French, then into Portuguese, Italian, English, Chinese, and Hungarian - thus fulfilling Our Lord's wish that His call to the way of love should be heard as widely as possible.

The Message, providentially timed to appear before the general conflagration of nations in the World War of 1939-1945, did not suffer any interruption by it. In spite of many difficulties, it passed from hand to hand and continued to be widely read. At the same time, pressing requests for a more detailed biography which would make the bearer of Our Lord's communications better known, were continually being received and have resulted in the present publication.

The Message of Our Blessed Lord, framed as it were, in the life history of Sister Josefa Menéndez, consists mainly in excerpts from her notes. These notes, written under obedience, and carefully preserved, are connected by a running commentary, the testimony of those who day by day assisted at the unfolding of a life which so amazingly carried out the designs of the Heart of Jesus.

In 1926, after careful examination of the writings of Sister Josefa, a Consultor of the Sacred Congregation of Rites concluded his report with these words: "I pray God that these things may become known for the glory of God, and to strengthen the faith of diffident and timid souls, and also that the holy religious of the Sacred Heart who wrote them may be glorified." (From the Italian.)

Without any intention of pronouncing judgment before Holy Church, to whom we submit unconditionally, we think that readers of these pages will be glad to find words of commendation from no less a personage than the Holy Father himself, who as Cardinal Pacelli, and Protector of the Society of the Sacred Heart at the time, gave his blessing to the first edition which appeared in 1938. A facsimile of his letter is reproduced, with his express consent, at the beginning of this volume.

Introduction

On December 29th, 1923, Sister Josefa Menéndez, when thirty-three years old, died a holy death at the Convent of Les Feuillants, Poitiers. She lived as a Sister in the Society of the Sacred Heart only four years, and in so hidden a way that the world ought never to have heard of her, and even in her own community she should soon have been forgotten.

Yet, only twenty years after her death, she is known all over the world. In America, Africa, Asia, and Oceania people are praying to her and are listening attentively to the Message which the Heart of Jesus has given her for men.

In 1938 the substance of the Message, under the title of Un Appel à l'Amour, was published in Toulouse by the Apostleship of Prayer. Cardinal Pacelli, now gloriously reigning as Pope Pius XII, wrote a foreword of recommendation in the form of a letter. Five years later a complete biography was asked for with insistence, since readers were anxious for all the details of a life so rich yet so hidden and in which the very poverty of the human background threw into relief the splendor of Christ's divine action.

This second and complete edition is the answer to that demand. It is drawn from Sister Josefa's notes, written day by day, under obedience, its accuracy confirmed by the very exact reminiscences of the witnesses of her life, namely the Superior and Mother Assistant of the Convent of "Les Feuillants," Poitiers, and her director, Father Boyer, O.P.

The reader will feel a certain curiosity in opening these pages, but their contents will fill him with wonder and admiration, and he will finish the book determined to lead a better life and to love a God who has manifested so intense a love for His creatures.

For every page tells of the wonderful providence of God's love for man. Holy Scripture represents Him in the Psalms as following the sons of men with ever-watchful care, attentive to their every action and answering their least efforts to pray. Turning with love towards His rebel sons, from the beginning He lets His voice be heard through marvels and through His prophets, until the day when He Himself, taking flesh in the womb of the Virgin, tells men in human language of the love that fills His Heart.

Jesus, the Word Incarnate, has transmitted in all its completeness the Message He Himself received from the Father: "Omnia quaecumque audivi a Patre Meo, nota feci vobis" (John 15:15). There is nothing to add to Our Lord's words, and at the death of St. John, the last Apostle, the divine revelation was closed and sealed. Later ages could do no more than draw out its meaning. But its riches are unfathomable, and most men are too inattentive and superficial to sound the depths of the Gospel teaching; consequently, just as under the Old Law Prophets were sent by God to revive the faith and hope of His people, so in the New Dispensation Christ has from time to time given certain chosen souls the mission of interpreting His authentic words, and of revealing their depths and hidden meaning.

Long ago, on Easter morning, He charged Saint Mary Magdalen with announcing His glorious Resurrection to the Apostles. In succeeding ages likewise poor and humble women have been chosen out to transmit His most important desires to mankind.

To recall only the chief instances: Through Saint Juliana of Montcornillon He revived devotion to the Blessed Sacrament, and obtained the institution of the Feast of Corpus Christi; through Saint Margaret Mary a new stimulus was given to devotion to the Sacred Heart; through Saint Thérèse of the Child Jesus He told a world which seemed to have forgotten it the merit and value of spiritual Childhood, and now, He has given a Message to Josefa Menéndez.

The three above mentioned have been canonized by the Church, and so have received, as it were, an official recognition of their mission. Sister Josefa has not had this honor bestowed on her, but while she is not yet called their Sister in glory, she is indeed their Sister in grace, and God has been pleased to seal her testimony. He who treats His creatures with such reverence, "Cum magna reverentia disponisnos" (Wis. 12:18), owed it to Himself to impress a stamp marking His messenger clearly as the bearer of His words.

"His ways are not our ways, nor His thoughts our thoughts," and that there may be no doubt that the communications come from Him and no other, He chooses weak instruments, humanly speaking unfitted for the task in view; so His strength shines forth in their infirmity.

He did not choose the learned and the great in the world's eyes to found His Church, Saint Paul expressly tells us, otherwise the rapid spread of Christianity could have been attributed to their talents and prestige; but He chose the poor and the ignorant, and of these He made vessels of election.

And that the greatness of their mission might not dazzle them and lead to vainglory, He again and again reminded them of their nothingness, their innate misery and their weakness. His gifts are only secure when bestowed on the truly humble of heart. His Providence has always worked in this way. His glory is manifest in man's nothingness. "If I had been able to find a creature more miserable than you," He said to Saint Margaret Mary, "I should have chosen her... ."

And Sister Josefa repeatedly heard the same declaration: "If I could have found a more wretched creature, I should have chosen her for my special love, and through her revealed the longings of My Heart. But I have not found one, and so I have chosen you." (June 7th, 1923).

Soon after we hear Him say: "I have selected you as one utterly useless and destitute, that none may attribute to any but Myself, what I say, ask and do." (June 12th, 1923).

As far as appearances went, nothing signalized Josefa as in any way fitted for so high a mission. If we remember her repeated delays in entering religion, we might be justified in doubting the constancy of her will; then, too, her humble rank in the community, her status as a mere novice, her great love of retirement, and the very real obstacle of her ignorance of the language of the country, all these hindrances combined would at first sight appear insurmountable.In reality they were tokens of God's choice. Though but a lowly little novice, so tender-hearted as to be frequently on the point of yielding to her sensitiveness, she would show later an unconquerable strength of will. In the blinding light of divine revelations, she only crept deeper into her littleness, and the closer God drew to her the more she humbled herself. In spite of the evidence of God's action, she was ever fearful of being deceived herself and of deceiving her Superiors. As a matter of fact, they had rarely met with a more obedient and docile subject, or one more deferential, more eager to submit to control, more ready to sacrifice herself. In her devotions, as in everything else, there was no exaggeration; she was perfectly straightforward and simple. She was mentally healthy and had a well-developed sense of order and proportion. The supernatural, whose weight was often crushing, never disturbed her interior poise, though this equilibrium was kept only at the cost of almost superhuman endurance. All this was in reality the best guarantee to Superiors that her communications were divine in origin.

To Sister Josefa Our Lord said: "You yourself shall be My sign."

Though at first suspicious and reserved in their judgments, both her Director and her Superiors were forced by the evidence of her life to believe that her mission was divine.

JOSEFA'S MISSION

Only very gradually did Our Lord unfold it to her; several times He had told her that He meant to make use of her to "carry out His plans" (February 9th, 1921) for the saving of many souls that had cost Him so dear (October 15th, 1920). On the night of February 24th, 1921 He gave her a yet more explicit call during her Holy Hour. "The world does not know the mercy of My Heart," He said to her. "I intend to enlighten them through you.... I want you to be the apostle of My love and mercy. I will teach you what that means; forget yourself." And in answer to the fears she expressed: "Love and fear nothing. I want what you do not want, but I can do what you cannot." "It is not for you to choose, you have only to resign yourself into My Hands."

A few months later, on Monday, June 11th, 1921, a few days after the Feast of the Sacred Heart, when she had received many graces, He said: "Remember My words and believe them. My Heart has but one desire, which is to enclose you in It, to possess you in My love, then to make of your frailty and littleness a channel to convey mercy to many souls who will be saved by your means. Later on, I will reveal to you the burning secrets of My Heart and many souls will profit by them. I want you to write down and keep all I tell you. It will be read when you are in Heaven. Do not think that I make use of you because of your merits, but I want souls to realize how My Power makes use of poor and miserable instruments." And as Josefa asked if she was to tell Reverend Mother even that, He answered: "Write it; it will be read after your death."

So by degrees Our Lord unfolded His plan: Josefa was chosen by Him, not only to be a victim for souls, especially for consecrated ones, but that through her Christ's Message of love and mercy might reach the world. A twofold mission - Victim and Messenger - and between the two missions there is a close connection. If Victim then Messenger, and because Messenger, necessarily Victim.

JOSEFA AS VICTIM

To be a victim necessarily implies immolation, and as a rule atonement for another. Although strictly speaking one can offer oneself as a victim to give God joy and glory by voluntary sacrifice, yet for the most part God leads souls by that path only when He intends them to act as mediators: they have to suffer and expiate for those for whom their immolation will be profitable, either by drawing down graces of forgiveness on them, or by acting as a cloak to cover their sins in the face of divine justice. It stands to reason that no one will on his own initiative take such a role on himself. Divine consent is required before a soul dares to intervene between God and His creature. There would be no value in such an offering if God refused to hear the prayer.

Already in the Old Testament victims of a certain sort only could be offered to God. To be acceptable they must have special, clearly defined qualities: they were to be spotless, without blemish, males of one year, and above all the offering had to be made by a priest according to a prescribed rite which was to be adhered to rigorously, and which symbolized not only the dispositions of the officiating priest, but also those of the donor of the victim.

In the New Testament a new sacrifice takes the place of the old; Jesus Christ is the sole Mediator, sole Priest, sole Victim, and His sacrifice is no longer symbolic, but real and infinite.

If, then, Jesus Christ wishes to associate other victims with Himself, they must be closely united to Him, and share His feelings, in order to enter fully into His sacrifice; hence they can only be human beings, endowed with intelligence and will.

He Himself chooses these persons, and because they are free He asks them for their voluntary cooperation. Those who accept put themselves at His mercy, and He then makes use of them as by sovereign right.

Assimilated and transformed into Christ, the victim-soul expresses the sentiments of Christ Jesus to God the Father; and to Christ Himself her attitude is one of humiliation, penance, and expiation, sentiments which ought to animate the souls she represents.

And because of this identification with Christ, the victim-soul shares in His dolorous Passion and undergoes, to a greater or lesser degree, and in various but generally superhuman ways, the torments and agonies that were His.

When the suffering is borne for one specially chosen sinner the victim endures the just retribution due to this sinner for his crimes. Every kind of trial is endured, be it illness, or even persecution by the spirits of darkness

11

of which the victim becomes the sport.

With Sister Josefa this was the case to an extraordinary degree. Victim at the express desire of her Lord, not only was her whole being immolated, but the manner of the immolation itself varied according to the particular attributes of God to which she had sacrificed herself.

Saint Thérèse of the Child Jesus offered herself as a victim of merciful love; Marie des Vallées, as a victim of God's Justice; Saint Margaret Mary, of both Justice and Mercy, and so it was with Sister Josefa. Christ told her His wishes in even more explicit terms than He had used with Saint Margaret Mary.

"I have chosen you to be a victim of My Heart" (December 19th, 1920). "You are the victim of My love" (October 2nd, 1920 and November 23rd, 1920). "You are the victim of My love and mercy" (June 30th, 1921). "I want you to be the victim of divine justice and the comfort of My Heart" (November 9th, 1920).

For all these reasons Josefa must suffer. "You suffer in your soul and body, because you are the victim of My Soul and Body. How could you not suffer in your heart, since I have chosen you as the victim of My Heart?" (December 19th, 1920).

As victim of the Heart of Jesus she suffered in order to console the Heart that has been so wounded by the ingratitude of men. As victim of love and mercy she suffered that the merciful love of Jesus might overwhelm with graces the sinner He so loved. As victim of the divine justice she carried the intolerable burden of the divine reproaches, and expiated for guilty souls, who would owe their salvation to her. Her mission exacted perpetual immolation on her part, and Our Lord did not hide it from her. "Love, suffer, and obey," He said to her, "so that I may realize My plans in you" (January 9th, 1921).

On June 12th, 1923 He corroborated the whole of this plan as it affected her. "As for you, you will live in the most complete and profound obscurity, and as you are My chosen victim, you will suffer, and overwhelmed by suffering you will die. Seek neither rest nor alleviation; you will find none, for such is My will. But My love will sustain you, and never shall I fail you."

But before making her endure such piercing and keen agony, He had asked and obtained her consent; for though He is Sovereign Lord and Master, He nevertheless respects the liberty of the creature.

"Are you willing? ... " He said to Josefa, and as she shrank at the prospect before her, He left her. She was heartbroken at His departure, but Our Lady came, and suggested to her child: "Do not forget that your love is free." Several times Josefa tried to escape from the path before her, then Jesus left her, and it was only after she had called Him again and again that He came back to receive from her a willing offering of that which He had suggested only as a possibility. Usually she accepted most generously.

"I offered myself to serve Him in any way He might choose." God knew

Himself free to act in any way He chose, and He said once again: "I am your God, you belong to Me; of your own free will, you have handed yourself over. From now on you cannot refuse Me anything" (July 23rd, 1922). "If you do not deliver yourself up to My will, what can I do?" (April 21st, 1922).

She surrendered; like her Master she would be a willing victim: "Oblatus est quia Ipse voluit." Like Him, too, she would be a pure victim. For how can one expiate another's sins, when one has to expiate one's own? From her birth God had enveloped her in purity, for there cannot be found in her life any fault to which she voluntarily consented. Her greatest infidelities, as she herself owned, were a certain reluctance to respond to the call of grace and indecision in the face of a disconcerting mission; nothing therefore that was a stain on her heart and soul. Jealously Our Lord guarded her: "I want you to forget yourself so entirely and to be so completely given up to My Will that I will not tolerate the slightest imperfection in you without warning you of it" (February 21st, 1921).

Many times when He wanted her to re-state that she was His victim He opened the question by conferring on her a grace of still greater purification. "I want you to suffer for Me, Josefa, but I will begin by letting the arrow of love which is to purify your soul fall on you, for as My victim, you must be all-pure" (June 17th, 1923).

In her pure conscience on which suffering was about to descend there was found no taint of sin, and consequently there was no work of expiation to be done, and that was why the fruits of salvation could be transferred to other souls. Her sufferings bore a twofold character, as is indeed the case with all true victims. As a victim chosen by Christ Himself to continue and complete His redemptive work, she must be very closely united with Christ the Redeemer, and share His Passion by enduring the self-same sufferings as His own; as an expiatory victim for the sins of others, her pains would be proportionate to the sins of the offender for whom she was atoning.

(a) Participation in the Sufferings of Christ

The Passion of Christ being our sole salvation, if we are to be purified and saved, we must of necessity come into contact with the Blood shed by the Lamb. The great cry of the dying Christ is a pressing invitation to the whole human race to hasten to the Saviour's fountains from which all graces flow.

This contact with Christ's Blood is immediately secured by souls that answer His appeal. Others, and alas! they are many, voluntarily keep aloof. It is these that Christ will seek to reach through other souls whom He makes use of as channels of His mercies. They are the most fruitful of all the branches of the mystic vine. Loaded with the sap flowing from Christ Himself, and completely one with Him, by their solidarity with the sinner they stand liable for his sins; so being one with him and one with Christ, in them and by them, grace is communicated. They are victim-souls.

How intimate must be their identification with the Crucified if they are to carry out their part of the contract fully! Full union with Him is implied, whilst He on His part imprints on their souls, hearts, and bodies the living image of His sorrowful Passion.

All His sufferings are renewed in them: they will be contradicted, persecuted, humbled, scourged, and crucified; and what man fails to inflict, that God Himself will supply by mysterious pains, agonies, stigmata, which will make of them living crucifixes.

How great must be the power of mediation of such souls! How efficacious their intercession, when they implore divine mercy, pardon and salvation for their brethren; when in them and through them, the Precious Blood of Christ, infinitely more powerful than that of Abel, cries to the Father!

There is this, however, to notice with regard to some saints, notably Saint Francis of Assisi, that the Passion, as it were, abides in them, God's ultimate plan apparently being to shape them into finished copies of the Crucified. It is God's response to their adoring love of His Passion, and He makes them share both physically and morally in the torments of His Beloved Son.

There is a further purpose with regard to expiatory victims: He seems to dispossess them in favor of other souls, for the Passion of Christ, after marking them with its sign, passes through them, in order to bring about in the sinner for whom they suffer the graces of the sacrifice of Calvary.

They are thus co-redeemers in the full sense of the word; love for their neighbor urges them on, their mission is different from that of others. For whereas God is pleased to allow those other souls of whom we spoke to remain in contemplation of Him, giving glory to His infinite perfections by their love, it is otherwise with victim-souls: when they contemplate Him, He unveils the immensity of His love for souls and the grief with which the loss of sinners fills Him. The sight of this breaks their hearts, and their longing to console Christ is not satisfied with mere words of love; it stirs up their zeal. At whatever price, they will win souls to Him, and He kindles this zeal still more. It is the love of the Sacred Heart Itself, communicated to them, with which they love sinners; love which gives them a superhuman endurance well described by Josefa's own words:

"For the last two or three weeks, I have felt an immense desire for suffering. There was a time when the thought of it frightened me. When Jesus told me that He had chosen me as His victim my whole being trembled; but it is different now. There are days when I endure such agony that if He did not uphold me, I should die, for no part of me is free from pain! ... In spite of this, my soul longs to bear more grievous afflictions for Him, though not without repugnance in the lower part of my consciousness. When these pains attack me I shake with fear and instinctively draw back, but there is granted to my will a strength that accepts, that desires and wants to suffer yet more, so that if the choice between continued pain and Heaven were offered me, I should infinitely prefer to remain in the throes of pain, if by so doing I might console His Heart, though God knows how I long to be forever with Him. I know that this change has been wrought in me by Jesus" (June 30th, 1921).

She was right indeed; the change had come not from herself, but from Jesus, or rather may we not say that it was His strength, His feelings, His desires and sufferings that He had passed on to her?1

"As you are ready to suffer, let us suffer together" (December 19th, 1920), and He gave her His Cross: "Jesus came with His Cross, which He placed on my shoulders" (July 18th, 1920). "I come to bring you My Cross, thus unburdening Myself on you" (July 26th, 1921). "I want you to be My Cyrenean; you will help Me to bear My Cross" (February 23rd, 1922). "Let My Cross be your Cross" (March 30th, 1923).

Innumerable are the times He placed it on her willing shoulders for hours on end, even for whole days and nights. He entrusted her with His Crown of Thorns, which He left in her keeping for long periods, so that like Him she knew not where to rest her aching head. "I will leave you My Crown ... do not complain of the pain ... for by it you share in My pain" (November 26th, 1920). "My Crown ... with it I will Myself encircle your head" (June 17th, 1923). He made her feel the pain of His pierced Side. Our Lady said to her: "This pain is a spark from the Heart of My Son; when it is at its worst, know that it is a sign that some soul is wounding Him deeply" (June 20th, 1921).

He wished her to feel the pain of the nails in both hands and feet: "I am about to give you a new sign of My love. Today you will share with Me the pain of the nails" (March 16th, 1923).

Again He associated her intimately with the agony of His Heart and Soul: "Every Friday, and especially on the First Friday of the month, I will cause you to share in the bitterness of My Heart's agony, and you will experience the torments of My Passion in a very particular manner" (February 4th, 1921).

On March 1st, 1922, He appeared to her, His Face all bloodstained. "Draw near," He said, "come and rest in My Heart; and take part in Its grievous pain."

"He then drew me close to His Heart, and my soul was filled with such anguish and bitterness of sorrow that I cannot describe it."

Like Him, she suffered for others: "I want your whole being to suffer, that you may gain souls" (December 21st, 1920). "There is a soul that is grievously wounding Me ... be not afraid if you feel yourself totally abandoned, for I shall make you share the anguish of My Heart" (September 13th, 1921). "Keep My Cross, until that soul recognizes the truth" (March 24th, 1923). "Take My Cross, My Nails and Crown. I go in search of souls" (June 17th, 1923).

These few examples will suffice; they abound throughout the book. As an atoning victim, Josefa shared in all the torments of Jesus, and her whole person, so to speak, was saturated with unutterable anguish. United with Jesus on the Cross, she was tortured by His sufferings, consumed by His desires; His burning thirst for the salvation of souls urged her to attempt every kind of reparation and expiation within her power.

(b) Diabolical Persecutions

And God allowed trials of every kind to rain down upon her. If illness was not one of them (yet who knows, for she never complained), nor persecution from men (for unlike a Margaret Mary, both her religious and family life appear to have been exempt from these), yet on the other hand, more than many another, she was given over to the fury of Satan. And this is not surprising.

There are few saints in whose lives his rage is not apparent. Christ in the glory of Heaven is beyond the reach of Satan, who as His personal enemy spares no pains to thwart the spread of God's kingdom on earth. The more he knows a soul to be beloved of Christ, the fiercer are his attacks; this, no doubt, in the hope of increasing the number of his unfortunate dupes, but above all, in the perverse hope of snatching from Christ the souls He loves and for whom He has paid so high a price in the shedding of His Precious Blood. Satan, therefore, chooses saints and consecrated souls whom he longs to besmirch, seduce, and dishonor, and flings himself on them. Above all, he abhors victim-souls, so Josefa was particularly hateful to him.

She had joyfully made the sacrifice of the three things she held dearest in the world: her mother, her sister, and her country; she had offered herself for the salvation of sinners, and was, in the event, to snatch a great number from hell-fire. Satan therefore made wanton sport of her. He is permitted by God to have a greater power over victim-souls. Surely this follows from their vocation,1 for as they take on themselves the sins of others, they also assume the consequences which they know will follow. When a man consents to sin, whether he is conscious of it or not, he gives the devil great power over him, the power of seduction and possession. This is not very noticeable, as a rule, for the evil one excels in dissimulation and avoids disturbing those he believes he has in his net. He strengthens what is evil in his prey, multiplies occasions of sin and benumbs the soul, till it sinks into a state of torpor which is absolutely fatal.

When, however, the devil is met by the resolute resistance of the victim-soul who has taken the place of the sinner, unable to make her sin he takes fearful vengeance, using the very powers he has gained over the evildoer in order to torment his substitute.

And this is permitted by God to manifest to all the reality of both the devil and Hell which so many try to forget and to bury in silence and oblivion.

The devil is a reality, and in his dealings with God's saints he shows himself in the undisguised perversity of his vicious and corrupt nature. What must his cruelty be to those souls that are damned and are his forever, if he is so pitiless with those over whom, after all, he has but limited sway? Who would dare affirm that such a lesson is without its use, especially in our days?

God also confounds the pride of the spirit of darkness, who in spite of all his power and rage makes no headway, but meets with constant defeat, which greatly enhances God's glory.

So it was with Sister Josefa.

The devil tried by every possible means to delude and beguile her, disguising himself as an "angel of light," even going so far as to assume the very features of Jesus Christ Himself. Most often however, he tried to turn her from her chosen path by inflicting on her grievous bodily harm.

When Satan, in all his strength, and a frail human being meet in mortal combat, God interposes His power in the conflict and invests the soul with superhuman endurance. He bestows on it unconquerable energy and makes it overcome all temptations and every suffering. The devil's power broke on the frailty of Josefa's resistance, who (though "nothing and misery," as Our Lord called her) with divine help triumphed over the "strong man armed." But God alone knew what it cost her.

Even as a postulant, showers of blows, administered by an invisible fist, fell upon her day and night, especially when she was in prayer and reiterating her determination always to be faithful. At other times she was violently snatched away from the chapel, or prevented from entering it. Again and again the devil appeared to her in the guise of a terrifying dog, snake, or worse still, in human form.

Soon the forcible abductions became more frequent, in spite of the supervision exercised by Superiors. Under their very eyes she suddenly disappeared, and after long search would be found thrown into some loft, or beneath heavy furniture, or in some unfrequented spot. In their presence she was burnt, and without seeing the devil, they saw her clothes consumed and on her body unmistakable traces of fire, which caused wounds that took long to heal.

Lastly, there occurred a phenomenon1 very rare in the lives of the Saints: God permitted the devil to take her down to Hell. There she spent long hours, sometimes a whole night, in unspeakable agony. Though she was dragged down into the bottomless pit more than a hundred times, each sojourn seemed to her to be the first, and appeared to last countless ages. She endured all the tortures of Hell, with the one exception of hatred of God. Not the least of these torments was to hear the sterile confessions of the damned, their cries of hatred, of pain and of despair.

Nevertheless, when at long last she came back to life, shattered and spent, her body agonized with pain, she looked on no suffering, however severe, as too much to bear, if by it she could save a soul from that dreaded abode of torment. As gradually she began to breathe more freely, her heart bounded with joy at the thought that still she could love her Lord.

It was this great love that sustained her, but at times the trial weighed heavily on her. Like Jesus in the Garden of Olives, she spent long hours in anguish and dejection. She realized the vast number of the lost, and was often perplexed as to the use of her descents into Hell and all the tortures that she had endured. But quickly she regained her hold on herself, and her amazing courage did not falter. Then, too, Our Lady helped her: "While you suffer, the devil has less power over that soul" (July 22nd, 1921). "You suffer to relieve Him; is this not enough to give you courage?" (July 12th, 1921).

Then Our Lord showed her the treasures of reparation and expiation she had gained by her repeated ordeals (October 6th, 1922 and November 5th, 1922), and allowed her to witness in Hell the devil's bursts of fury, when there escaped him souls of whom he thought he had a firm hold, but for whom she was offering expiation. The thought that she could console and rest Our Lord and gain souls for Him kept up her heroic spirit and excited her zeal.

Although she instinctively shrank from contact with the devil, for his power and vindictiveness were well known to her by personal experience, yet never did she allow this fear to make her neglect a duty. At one time he carried her off almost daily as she went to her employment; she knew this would happen and the thought of it made her tremble with apprehension, but undaunted she went forward, and on the morrow was still as determined as ever that she would not yield to terror.

In all her heroic fidelity, perhaps the most admirable feature was her conviction that, owing to her fear and occasional repugnances, she was (and this she sincerely believed) ungrateful and unfaithful, and had done absolutely nothing for God.

After nights of unspeakable torment, crushed, yet ever gallant, she rose at the hour of Rule and resumed her ordinary labors, asking no exceptions from common life. She burnt, indeed, with the very fire of the Heart of Jesus, for after all the agonies of Hell and her share in Christ's sufferings, she was neither discouraged nor cast down, but her readiness to suffer only increased.

Like Saint Margaret Mary, she offered herself in sacrifice for religious souls, for priests, for sinners of every description. Docile and abandoned to the divine Will, she asked but one thing, to be able to console Him. She was ready to suffer a thousand martyrdoms to help those who for the most part were utterly unknown to her, but whom she loved in and through Him.

As we pointed out in the beginning, she had to be a victim in order that the Message might be delivered and be listened to by mankind for whom she endured so much.

She who knew the Heart of Jesus and His love for souls, was better qualified than any other to transmit this Message to the world.

THE MESSAGE

It is one of love and mercy. Nowhere is it fully stated, but it is found in fragmentary form all through the book. Its chief points were often reiterated, and with little verbal change.

Here is a short summary of them:

(a) In the first place, the Sacred Heart and the overwhelming charity of Jesus Christ for mankind are brought out in a striking way. It might almost be called a new revelation of the Sacred Heart, confirming and in certain matters completing and perfecting that previously given to Saint Margaret Mary.

More than two centuries and a half have elapsed since 1675, and new currents of devotion have arisen in the Church. At present, the mystical Christ is passionately (and very rightly) cherished by those souls who in their inmost being are conscious of Its reality and Its implications.

The devotion to the Sacred Heart would appear to have grown less, if anything, and to be less well understood;1 to some the devotion appears a mutilation of the worship of the whole Christ, or perhaps feminine with too much sentiment or even sentimentality in it.

Our Lord reacts strongly against this false impression. He reaffirms that there is no mistake, that it is indeed His Heart of flesh, pierced by the lance that He offers mankind; His Heart so full of love and so little loved in return, and of which the gaping Wound cries out how immense is His tender affection for men.

Like all true love, His is consumed by desire for a return in kind, all the more, that only so can man attain happiness here below, and everlasting beatitude hereafter. Let those who reject His love realize the horror of Hell to which they will be condemning themselves.... This was the appeal that, through Josefa, Jesus Christ sent out to the whole world.

(b) That men may be attracted (and herein lie the novelty and force of the Message) ... the Sacred Heart manifests through her His infinite mercy. He loves them every one, just as they are, even the most despicable, even the greatest sinners, one can almost say, especially the most miserable and sinful. He does not ask for their good qualities or virtues, but only for their wretchedness and sins. Far from being an obstacle, their very faults are thus an encouragement to draw near Him.

Such is the gift God asks of His beloved sinners, on the one condition of a true repentance, and a readiness to turn away from their evil ways out of love for Him.

His Heart is there waiting for His erring sons with all the impatience of true love. He assures them beforehand of a free pardon. "It is not sin that most grievously wounds My Heart," He said, "but what rends and lacerates It is that after sin men do not take refuge in It once more" (August 29th, 1922).

What He wants and ardently desires is their trust in His infinite goodness and mercy.

(c) To consecrated and therefore specially loved souls, Jesus offers a share of His redemptive life. He would like them to act as intermediaries for the saving of souls, and that is why He asks of all the spirit of sacrifice in love. As a rule, no great sufferings are to be borne, but He inculcates the importance of ordinary actions however insignificant, if done in union with Him, in a spirit of sacrifice and love (November 30th, 1922 and December 2nd, 1922). He lays stress on the value of the tiniest offerings, which not only can lead them far on in sanctity, but will effect the salvation of many souls (October 20th, 1922). On the other hand, He reminds them of the danger of slackening in their efforts in little ways, which may lead to greater infidelity and finally expose them to hell-fire, where their sufferings will greatly exceed those of less-favored souls

(August 3rd, 1921; December 12th, 1922; March 14th, 15th, 20th, 24th, 1923; September 4th, 1922).

Let consecrated souls therefore re-animate their trust in the Heart of Jesus. "I easily condone their weakness; what I want them to know is that if after their faults and falls they humbly cast themselves into My Heart, I love them always, and pardon them all." He adds: "Do you not know that the more wretched a soul is, the more I love her?" "The fact that I have chosen a soul does not mean that her faults and miseries are wiped out. But if in all humility that soul acknowledges her failings and atones by little acts of generosity and love, above all, if she trusts Me, if she throws herself into My Heart, she gives Me more glory and does more good to souls than if she had not fallen. What does her wretchedness matter to Me, if she gives Me the love that I want?" (October 20th, 1922).

So what the Heart of Jesus demands of His own is humility, trust, and love.

(d) Finally, He repeatedly offers to all the thought of His Passion, for it is the sign of His immense love for mankind and the sole hope of salvation.

His sad and suffering Heart is again and again presented to us; He exhorts and entreats us in virtue of His immeasurable pains to return to Him. How great must have been the love that could bear such agony for us, and at the same time how terrible is the misfortune of those who through their own fault let such a Redemption pass them by! Man has put his sin between himself and God - a chasm impossible to bridge - yet our Jesus comes with His suffering Passion, and oversteps our sinfulness, even veils our crimes with His Blood. The road to salvation is once more opened, but it must and can only be through the Passion. This is the only way to establish contact with God again. The choice lies between the Passion and Hell!

So the work of consecrated souls is to enter into the Passion of Christ and, by personal sacrifices, to pass on its fruits to other souls for whom they pray and immolate themselves.

THE OPPORTUNENESS OF THE MESSAGE

How striking is its actuality today!

Everywhere sin is increasing to an appalling degree. The pride of man leads him to discard his God and attempt to make a paradise of earth. He has so far succeeded only in making it a vestibule of Hell, where impiety, immorality, and the worst passions have free scope; wars rage that are more terrible than any yet heard of, the majority of mankind suffers poverty and slavery, and all without the comfort which faith alone can impart.

The Heart of God inclines in pity towards His forlorn children, and He points out to them the way of happiness, peace, and salvation.

This Message is not only transmitted by Josefa, but reproduced in her life through Christ's operations in her soul, for facts are more calculated to move than are mere words.

If anyone wants to realize the love of the Heart of Jesus for souls, let him read the pages in which Josefa notes down how she listens to the Heartbeats of her Master. "Every heartbeat is an appeal to a soul," He told her (September 25th, 1920).

Surely we cannot doubt the reality of His love, when the flames issuing from His Heart are seen to kindle Josefa's with a love so valiant and intrepid that she braves the sufferings of hell-fire to save the souls He loves. Nor can we doubt the immensity of His love, when for the same purpose she accepts unutterable tortures, and she who knew tells us that her love, "her poor love," is as nothing beside that of her Master, just as the torments she undergoes are but a shadow of those of the Passion (October 28th, 1920). The grief of Jesus at the loss of souls and His joy at their return, which are so plainly shown in Josefa's life, make it impossible for us to doubt the goodness of His love! (August 25th, 1920; December 26th, 1920; August 3rd-4th, 1921; July 29th, 1921; September 3rd, 12th, 25th, 1922). "Help Me," He would say, "help Me to make My love for men known, for I come to tell them that in vain will they seek happiness apart from Me, for they will not find it. Suffer, Josefa, and love, for we two must win these souls" (June 13th, 1923).

We get an inkling of the intense love of the Sacred Heart from that of Josefa for these same souls; it was so real and true that it could have been inspired only by Him.

Infinite Mercy, too, is manifested by Josefa's life. "I will love you," He told her on June 8th, 1923, Feast of the Sacred Heart, "and by the love I have for you souls will realize how much I love them." "Since I forgive you so often, they will recognize My mercy." He even said to her one day: "I love souls even to folly" (September 27th, 1922).

Such a statement surprises us, yet in Scripture do we not read (and Scripture is inerrant): "Can a woman forget her infant, so as not to have pity on the son of her womb? and if she should forget, yet will not I. Behold, I have graven thee in my hands" (Isa. 49:15, 16). "He will put away our iniquities and he will cast all our sins into the bottom of the sea" (Mich. 7:19). "Thou hast delivered my soul that it should not perish, thou hast cast all my sins behind thy back" (Isa. 38:17). "He loved me and delivered himself for me" (Gal. 2:20).

We may well call these statements divine folly!

As to the reality of Hell, again we see the Message lived by Josefa. The sufferings of the Passion which continue uninterruptedly in her, all the demoniacal persecutions and descents into Hell have only one end: to snatch souls from perdition and bring them back to salvation from which they have strayed. We see here exemplified the dogma of the Redemption and of the communion of saints. How, then, would it be possible to deny on the one hand the existence of the devil, of Hell and of Purgatory, and on the other the adequate power of Redemption which suffering has when borne for others? These great supernatural realities we read in the moving pages in which Josefa has them graven in her very flesh and soul.

The Message itself cannot be called a new revelation, but it unveils in a most striking manner what faith has already taught us. Our Lord Himself told this to Josefa: "I repeat to you again that what I have said is not new, but souls need a new impetus to make them advance, just as a flame needs fuel, if it is not to burn itself out."

How great is the force of the appeal which the humble little Sister transmits to us from her Lord!

THE AUTHENTICITY OF THE MESSAGE

We have been enabled to realize how the Message consists not only in the words entrusted to Josefa, but in her whole life. By her very existence, this soul, so beloved of Jesus, speaks to all who will listen, and her life stands as evidence of the divine action upon her.

She alone heard the words of Our Lord, and so is the sole witness; but her life testifies to the truth of the Message, and, moreover, she was closely followed up by qualified observers, who testify to the undeniable virtue of the obscure little messenger of infinite love, and to the reality of her supernatural states, of which tangible proofs were not wanting. All who had to do with her attested her very real virtue; not that she shone in a striking manner, for she was ever more imitable than admirable, but all felt the unconscious influence she exercised around her. No self-seeking, but rather self-denial in everything, unquestioning obedience, gentleness, and patience: all the result of true humility.

"You are the echo of My voice," said Our Lord to her (December 10th, 1922), and, in fact, everything in her was an echo of the divine. Her unaffected virtue led one to a conviction that God was acting on this soul, and this by itself could have provided clear evidence that her supernatural communications came from God. Nevertheless, Superiors and her Director remained for a certain length of time deliberately hesitant and uncertain, and they deserve our thanks for their reserve and wary misgivings, which insisted on proofs.

With her innate candor and honesty, she could never have practiced willful deception. Perhaps one is justified in asking whether she was led astray by her heart or imagination - a not infrequent trait in persons of sincere holiness. But (and this is a good sign) Josefa lived in perpetual fear that such might be the case, and was quite prepared, had Superiors deemed her to be in illusion, to consider all that had taken place as delusion. Such action was characteristic of her.

When she went to Rome to carry a message from Our Lord about the Society of the Sacred Heart to the Mother General, she was suddenly seized with a blinding fear (at the devil's instigation) that all was a dream and that she had no message from Heaven to deliver. Without hesitation or reflection on the harm it might do her cause in the eyes of her Superiors, she confessed her anguish of mind, and the certitude she now felt that all was a chimera of her imagination, and she humbly begged that no credence should be given to anything she might say. That she should have had this anxious concern at such a moment is another proof of the truth of her mission.

She could not have acted so had she not been profoundly humble and self-forgetful; her writings bear the same impress of sincerity.

It was by the express command of Our Lord and of Our Lady that she kept her Superiors informed of all that passed: "You must write," said Our Blessed Lord to her. This, no doubt, was meant to secure that none of His words should be lost (August 6th, 1922), but also His divine purpose may have been that all Josefa's actions should be controlled and witnessed from start to finish. In all she wrote there never occurs a useless word, nor anything false or equivocal; nothing that could be regarded as self-praise nor that betrays a shadow of vanity. All is true, reasonable, moving, and holy.

The same control was exercised over her supernatural states. When she was carried off into Hell, or when she returned to consciousness after an ecstasy, her Superiors were present; they watched with solicitous and maternal eyes her gradual return to life's interests, noting carefully words that escaped her in those impressive moments.

When she had communications with souls in Purgatory who came to ask her prayers, the name, exact date, and place of their death, if given, were always found on investigation to be correct.

No possible doubt exists concerning the forcible abductions of Josefa by the devil; they took place under the very eyes of her Superiors, who were powerless to prevent them. Likewise the effects of fire which burned her were seen on her garments and flesh; fragments of scorched linen are still preserved.

The most convincing feature of these diabolic visitations (visions of Satan, descents into Hell), which to most people would have been terrifying, was that they seemed neither to have troubled her imagination, nor to have disturbed the calm equilibrium of her eminently sane temperament. So also the divinely supernatural, with those simple and homely proofs of affection she received from Our Lord and His Mother,1 must surely have moved her feelings to an extraordinary degree, yet they left her peaceful, silent, and apparently without even the natural desire to talk over her wonderful experience with anyone. The Mothers noticed how very discreet she was, never speaking of the favors she received, except to the two witnesses already mentioned. Finally, all the sufferings (nights spent in Hell, or in bearing the Cross, or in wearing the Crown of Thorns) which might have made her beg for relief, only gave her a greater desire to suffer for love of Our Lord and of souls.

So her writings and her life confirm each other as evidence that all that took place in her was divine in origin. Even the most extraordinary happenings have an aim and significance. There are no useless details, no record of revelations that do not bring out in clearer light and force some dogmatic truth, giving us deeper insight into the Heart of Our Lord, His love, the value of souls, the happiness of Heaven, the irreparable loss of the damned.

Everything in Josefa's life is grace-giving and profoundly moving. The writings of this unassuming Sister, regarded as ignorant in the world's eyes, will, no doubt, be scrutinized and pondered over by theologians and masters of the spiritual life, and as in the case of Saint Thérèse of the Child of Jesus, numerous books will be written to develop the profound doctrine contained in these writings, and to make known the mysteries of love. But better still, the mere reading will bring numberless graces and lead many to conversion and holiness. The world may be astonished at the great things that come from a life so simple; but it is precisely in her nothingness that the overwhelming proof of the authenticity of her Message lies.

In very truth it was countersigned by a Hand that was nothing less than divine.

Digitus Dei est hic

(Signed) H. Monier Vinard S.J.

A Soul's Awakening (1890-1907)

"I want you to be all Mine."
(Our Lord to Josefa, March 17th, 1901)

Spain gave Our Lord the soul He was to consecrate to His Love, though it was in France that He revealed Himself to her.

Josefa Menéndez, a native of Madrid, was born on the 4th of February 1890, and was baptized in the church of San Lorenzo on the 9th of the same month, being given the names of Josefa Maria.

Her father, Leonardo Menéndez, also a native of the same capital, had had a sad youth, for his father died when he was very young, and his mother marrying again, the unwanted boy was sent to school. When only seventeen years of age he lost the mother, whom he dearly loved, and to drown this sorrow and his loneliness, he enlisted in the army. His superior officer was not long in appreciating his marked artistic talents, and he was appointed decorator of the Artillery Museum, where he did so well that ever after he was in constant demand whenever military decorations had to be designed, either in the local cathedral of St. Isidore or at the Royal Palace.

In 1888 he married Lucia del Moral, a devout and conscientious girl who made him an excellent wife and devoted herself to the upbringing of their little family of four girls and two boys, though both the latter died as infants, leaving as the eldest of the family Josefa, who took her responsibilities very seriously.

The father, being energetic and intelligent, was able to provide them with a comfortable home, and the atmosphere of Josefa's childhood was joyous and carefree, and her childish piety developed early. She was only five when she was confirmed and the Holy Spirit took possession of a singularly docile and innocent mind which later on was to be so choice an instrument in God's Hands.

The little girl's confessor, R. F. Rubio, was a great enthusiast for devotion to the Sacred Heart, and he later entered the Society of Jesus. He cultivated her aptitude for prayer, for he was struck by the spirituality of his little penitent. He remained her confessor until her entrance into our Society. At seven she made her first Confession; in later years she used ingenuously to recall the date, a First Friday in October 1897, exclaiming regretfully: "If only I could now feel such contrition for my sins as I had on that day."

Father Rubio gave her spiritual training suited to her age; he taught her how to meditate and use ejaculatory prayer, and Josefa gradually acquired the habit of constant awareness of the divine Presence. When she was able to read, she delighted in El Cuarto de Hora de Santa Teresa, a simple little meditation book which her confessor gave her, and she learned how, after reading a passage slowly, to reflect on it and end with a resolution. She was extraordinarily faithful to the habits thus early acquired.

"I delighted in my little book," she said later, "especially when it spoke to me of the Child Jesus or of the Passion. I found plenty to say to Our Lord and already I planned to devote my life to Him who possessed all my love."

Josefa was by nature both serious and vivacious. She freely asserted her authority over her three little sisters, and often the harassed mother would proudly trust her eldest to replace her. She was no less her father's pet; he dubbed her his "little empress" and could refuse her nothing ... a fact well known and exploited by the younger ones, who always had recourse to her intercession when some favor was hoped for. Every Sunday the whole family went to High Mass, and the father never failed to give each child a few coppers, to teach them generosity in almsgiving; they were known and loved by all the poor of the neighborhood. If the weather was fine, the Sunday afternoons were spent in country walks; if cloudy and wet, they all stayed at home, and father and children enjoyed themselves together till it was time to say the Rosary in common.

Leonardo taught his eldest little daughter himself, and so elated was he with her progress that he fondly hoped to have her trained for the teaching profession. This, however, was not to be, as we shall see; Our Lord had His own and very special designs for her future.

When she was eleven years old the all-important preparation for First Communion began. The very idea of it was an enthralling delight to the thoughtful and spiritual-minded child, who began to attend the instructions given at the Reparatrice Convent. The great day was preceded by a short retreat, and we still possess the "notes" of what she afterwards called the first appeal made to her by the Lover of her soul.

"In my first meditation I reflected on the words 'Jesus wants to give Himself to me, that I may be wholly His.' What joy! I thought, He is the one object of my desires. Yet how is it to be done? I consulted one of the nuns, and she explained to me that I must be very, very good, and that thus I should always belong entirely to Our Lord.

"The subject of meditation on the second day was 'Jesus, Spouse of Virgins, takes delight in the pure and innocent.' This was a great light to me, the solution of yesterday's puzzle; of course I must become His little Spouse, then indeed I should belong entirely to Him, just as Mummy belonged to Daddy. So there and then I promised Our Lord ever to remain a virgin (I did not understand what it meant) that I might always be entirely His. All day long I renewed this promise, and in the evening during Benediction I made a consecration of myself to the Child Jesus, asking with great fervor that I might be wholly and entirely His. That I was soon to receive Him in my heart by Holy Communion filled me with a strange joy, and while I was silently reveling in the happy thought, I heard a voice, that I can never forget, saying to me: 'Yes, little one, I want you to be all Mine.' What happened then it is impossible for me to put into words, but when I left the chapel my mind was quite made up: I would be very, very good.

"Of vocation I had never heard, and I thought nuns were unearthly beings quite apart, but from that time onward something seemed to set me, too, apart, and this feeling remained. It was only long afterwards that I knew it had been a vocation to religious life.

"On the third day of the retreat I renewed my resolution, and on St. Joseph's day, the happy day of my First Communion, I made this offering, and it came from my very inmost being:

" 'On this day, March 19th, 1901, before all Heaven and earth, taking as my witness my Heavenly Mother Mary, and St. Joseph, my advocate and father, I promise Jesus that I will ever safeguard in me the precious virtue of virginity, my only desire being to please Him, and my only fear that of offending Him by sin. Show me, O my God, how to belong wholly to Thee in the most perfect manner possible, that I may ever love Thee more and more and never displease Thee in anything. This is the desire of my heart, on this my First Communion day. Holy Mary, I beg you on this the Feast of your Holy Spouse, St. Joseph, to obtain my petition.

" 'Your loving Child,

" 'JOSEFA MENÉNDEZ.'

"I duly wrote and signed it, and at every subsequent Communion I renewed this offering. When afterwards I told Father Rubio what I had done he explained to me that little girls should not make promises beyond that of being very good, and he wanted me to tear up the paper. I could not, and I continued to repeat: 'Lord, I am Thine forever.'"

This witness of her first oblation was kept by Josefa till her dying day, and the little faded paper, covered with her large childish script, still bears witness to her faithful love.

This first meeting with her Eucharistic Lord initiated Josefa into the divine intimacy which was afterwards to become so powerful and so free. Holy Communion was her greatest happiness and all noticed how solid virtue began to develop in her.

"After Josefa's First Communion," wrote her sister, "one may say that she ceased to be a child. I don't remember seeing her take any part in the amusements she prepared for us with so much zest. Her charity was very great, too, outside the home. If a child she knew fell ill, she never failed to visit her. Her piety and spirit of sacrifice, the result of the good example given us by our parents, joined to her natural qualities, made her the soul of the little family. 'Pepa' as we called her, was a sort of second mother to us, and we never hesitated to confide to her our hopes, our troubles and our childish fears. One day when I was quite small, I was sent to buy something. I did so, but forgot to pay. Great was my apprehension when I became aware of my omission. I dared neither go back, nor bring the money home. I wrapped it in paper and left it beside a doorway in the street. Then I ran to Pepa and told her in secret what had happened. Very sweetly she comforted me, kissed me, soothed me, and herself went and paid for me. We always ran to her in our troubles, for she managed to arrange things so that we were not scolded.

"Thanks to her influence over our parents, Josefa obtained for this same little sister the grace to make her First Communion two years before the time that was then usual.

"Thus Pepa's childhood passed in great simplicity, as was customary in Christian families of our station in life, but already what our eldest sister was to become was foreshadowed."

At about this time her parents apprenticed her to a school of Arts and Crafts (Fomente del Arte),1 where her intelligence and readiness in learning soon attracted attention. Her clever fingers turned out marvels of needlecraft, and she was very successful, securing the diplomas year after year.

When she was thirteen Josefa returned home, for the time had come to see to the education of her little sisters, but an accident had occurred at that time to their father, which determined their admission into the Free School of the Sacred Heart.

It was the year that Catholic Spain was to choose Our Lady under the title of the Immaculate Conception as Patron of her Infantry Regiments. An open-air Mass was to be celebrated on that occasion in the Park of the Royal Palace. Leonardo, watched by the young King Alphonsus XIII, was working at the decoration of the altar. Suddenly he dropped a tool which might have wounded the Prince in its fall, and the abrupt movement he made to avoid this caused him to lose his balance. He fell from the scaffolding and broke his arm. The King, touched by this act which had preserved him, wished to take charge of the education of the children. He offered to place them with the "Dames Anglaises," which was a Royal Institution. But though Leonardo was deeply touched, he would not part with his family and preferred to send them as day-scholars to the Sacred Heart Free School, which was not far from his home. The two little girls were delighted, whilst Josefa was to benefit by the familiar intimacy with the Blessed Sacrament accorded by the Leganitos Chapel. The Blessed Sacrament henceforth became a daily attraction, Our Lord already directing this simple child so dear to His Heart to the Tabernacle where He forever dwells.

Family life continued happy and peaceful. The "little empress" kept her place as the most devoted of daughters and the best of sisters. Everything in the family was simple and joyous, but faith above all reigned supreme.

The great treat of those days was a visit to the Carmel of Loeches, where the children had an aunt. They were received like little princesses and had the run of the Chaplain's quarters, where they discovered a copy of the Carmelite Rule, which they eagerly read. On their return home the great game was to play at being Carmelites. Office was chanted, penances performed, in all of which Josefa was the leading spirit, but it was for her a good deal more than a mere game.

Her parents were proud of her aptitude for dressmaking and held to her completing her training in a millinery establishment. The conversation of the workgirls was not always edifying, but in her daily Communion Josefa drew strength to retain her purity of heart; she wrote in her reminiscences of that time:

"I went through many perils, but God always protected me amid the dangers of evil talk, so common in our workroom. It often made my tears flow to hear things that troubled me, but I never doubted that God meant me to be His own, and this was my comfort and my strength. Nothing and nobody could have altered my resolve or made me doubt its truth."

"On Sunday," her sister tells us, "she often went to a Patronage, of which the president was the daughter of the owner of our house. This lady was wholly given to good works and very charitable. On Sunday, therefore, we spent the afternoon in useful and merry surroundings, and many children found there a shelter which preserved them from sin. Josefa was the life of the little party, and brought all her self-forgetfulness and intelligence into play, and our benefactress, who appreciated her virtue, used to assign her those parts in our little plays that no one else wanted, and these she acted with ready grace and simplicity.

She often accompanied the Senora X in the visits she paid to the poor. Pepa saw how she not only distributed alms, but was glad to render the most humble services to her clients. This greatly attracted her own generous nature. One day Maria secretly confided to Josefa that she had discovered a poor leprous old woman and that she was trying to find among her friends one who would join her in seeing that the poor patient wanted for nothing and was loved. Her name was Trinidad and she suffered very much. Her left side was paralyzed and her face and hands ravaged by the disease; she lived alone and was able to do nothing for herself. Pepa was delighted at this appeal to her generosity, and it was its hidden heroism that she most appreciated. For many weeks she went to feed Trinidad. Once she took her sister with her, thinking she could count on her discretion, but ...

"The impression made on me by the poor leper was such that on my return home it was noticed, and I was questioned. I had to tell. Our mother forbade Pepa ever to go back to the poor invalid; a prohibition which cost her very much."

So her time passed between family life, her work, and the exercise of charity. But Divine Love's austere law was soon to be fulfilled in the sufferings which would try and strengthen her young soul.

"Never doubt the love of My Heart," the divine Friend was to say to her later. "What matter if the wind of adversity blow, I have planted the root of your littleness in the soil of My Heart."

Waiting (1907-1920)

"Let yourself be led blindfold, for I am your Father, and My eyes are open
to lead and guide you."
(Our Lord to Josefa, September 18th, 1923)

Suffering so characteristic of the whole of Josefa's life now first made its
appearance in the home where hitherto it had been unknown. It was
accepted peacefully as the friends of God are wont to accept it. Josefa
learned to suffer as she had learned to love, and her heart opened wide to
sorrow and sacrifice. It was going to do its work in making her will more
flexible, teaching her to overcome her nature, while contact with the cross
strengthened her love, maturing it without destroying its intensity.

In 1907 death came to the happy little home. Carmen, one of the little
sisters, was carried off by sudden illness, and the children's grandmother
followed soon after. The loss of Carmencita was like a death knell to her
parents. They fought against it, but is was more than they could bear.
Both father and mother were laid low, the one by typhoid fever, the other
by congestion of the lungs. Josefa's true worth was at once revealed; she
gave up her work and divided her attention between the two invalids, the
care of her sisters, and the manifold home duties that pressed on her
young shoulders. Medical advice was costly, and soon ran away with all
their savings. Poverty was now added to sickness, yet not for a moment
did Josefa's courage flinch, and for a period of well-nigh seven weeks she
bore unaided the full responsibility of anxiety and privation.

"We three children all slept together on a mattress on the floor," she said.
"Our kind doctor wanted father and mother to be taken to hospital, but I
did not consent, for I was certain Providence would not forsake us, and it
came to our help through the nuns of the Sacred Heart. Oh, I shall never
forget how good they were to us!"

A novena to Saint Madeleine Sophie was begun, and in the course of it the
mother, whose life was now despaired of, called the family to her bedside.
"Do not cry any more," she said. "Mother Barat has just been here to visit
me. She told me that I am not going to die, because you still need me."

"We never heard the particulars," Josefa said afterwards, "but the next day
she was out of danger, and father got well too, but his strength was gone
and he never was able to work again."

The nuns of the Sacred Heart watched discreetly over this interesting
family. Josefa had no sewing-machine, and her slender resources did not
allow her to purchase one. The Superior sent for her and asked her to buy
her one, and to use it for a time to try it, and gave her an order for literally
thousands of scapulars of the Sacred Heart for the soldiers of Melilla.
When Josefa wanted to return the machine to Leganitos the Reverend
Mother refused, saying that the making of the scapulars had more than
paid for it; Pepa was profoundly touched by this kindness; she felt that
such generosity was drawn from the Sacred Heart, and she henceforth
became so attached to the Society that her one desire was to enter there.

Work came to her from various quarters. She already had a reputation for clever dressmaking, and before long had more orders than she was able to attend to, which spelled for her days of uninterrupted labor prolonged far into the night, but her energy and self-denial were equal to the occasion. She organized a workroom and there trained a number of young girls. She rose at six in the morning, and after hearing Mass at the Sacred Heart, returned to her labors till midday. After the meal, which was always followed by a visit to the Blessed Sacrament, the apprentices returned, and all the afternoon was spent in work. They were a happy little band, for Josefa's good temper made all go smoothly, and her girls appreciated her thoughtful kindness, always alive to what could give them pleasure. But she was conscious of her responsibilities, and with gentle firmness insisted on good work and order. Every evening the Rosary was said in common, and Josefa's devotion added many other prayers. On Saturday the two sisters went to Confession, and Father Rubio followed up Josefa with paternal interest.

"On Sundays," this sister tells us, "the whole family rose early, in order to assist at several Masses. In the afternoon Pepa and I went to see the nuns of the Sacred Heart at all three houses in Madrid, and in the evening the whole family assisted at Benediction at Leganitos."

When they were obliged to go out the two sisters accompanied each other; they exchanged thoughts, told each other of their fervent aspirations, and both spoke of vocation, a thing not possible at home, as their mother's tears flowed freely whenever they alluded to the subject, so they resolved not to sadden her by speaking of it in her presence.

"One day," wrote Mercedes, "Josefa told me she wanted to be a nun, but far from Spain, so that her sacrifice might be complete. As I did not agree with her in this, she answered me that nothing was too good to give God."

In spite of her thoughtful character, she was always gay, and whilst this disposition of hers sweetened all contact with her, her efficiency and self-denial were equal to every occasion. Little by little comfort once more returned to the home-circle, but it was of short duration, and in the beginning of 1910 their father was carried off by a heart attack. During his last illness his wife never left him day or night, and spared nothing to give him relief. One day when she had gone out to procure a medicament for him, she saw a statue of the Sacred Heart in a shop window among a quantity of antiques. She was much moved and would have liked to buy it, thinking what pleasure it would give them all at home, and of the love with which they would pray around it. She went in and timidly asked the price, but alas, it far exceeded the small contents of her purse, for she had only enough to pay for the medicine her husband required. She thanked, left the shop, and had already gone some way along the road, when she heard herself called back. "Pay what you can, and take the statue," said the man. Touched and delighted, Lucia gave the money she had with her, carried off her treasure, and returning to Leonardo - "Instead of the medicine," she said, "I have brought you the Sacred Heart." The sick man was pleased beyond measure, for his faith was very great. The statue was placed at the foot of his bed, and he never tired of looking at it. He died, with eyes fixed on it, on the 7th of April 1910, leaving it to his family as a pledge of assured protection. Father Rubio, who had assisted him in his last moments, now constituted himself the friend and adviser of the sorrowing household, while Josefa became the sole support of her mother, and her earnings alone kept the wolf from the door. Her soul lived ever on her one love, and her offering was daily repeated and remained the strength and horizon of her life in the difficult days that followed. Before her father's death she had already made known her secret aspirations and begged leave to enter the Society of the Sacred Heart. For the first time in his life he was angry with Pepa. She dried her tears, but kept her treasured vocation unchanged in her heart.

Later on, a Carmelite Father offered to obtain her admission into his Order. That was not her vocation, and she gratefully refused, but took occasion to tell her mother once more where God called her. She met with no other opposition than tearful appeals not to abandon her, and for the second time she deferred her entrance. Great, however, was her grief when her younger sister obtained their mother's leave and left for the Noviceship at Chamartin (Madrid). Josefa who had trained her with a view to passing on to her the support of the family was deeply disillusioned. Her faith in God was her only support, and her mature virtue once more helped her to forget herself. Her sister wrote on this subject:

"We were inseparable till the day of my entrance into the Noviceship. My departure gave her keen sorrow, but in my youthful thoughtlessness and desire to consecrate my life to Jesus Christ, I hardly realized it. It was only later that I became aware of the sacrifice I had imposed on my beloved sister; then the thought that God had so arranged it alone consoled me."

Josefa continued her devoted life of hard work and made light of her fatigue; she turned her hopes towards the youngest of her sisters, but she, too, in time, was to have a vocation, and three years after Josefa's death entered the Carmelite Convent at Loeches, where she took the name of Madeleine Sophie of the Sacred Heart. She was later sent to Portugal, where the Order was to be restored at Coimbra.

God who was leading Josefa by hidden though sure ways, was more than once to allow her to take the wrong path, thereby teaching her the science of abandonment and the perfection of sacrifice.

Father Rubio, who had followed her up for the last twelve years, did not abandon her, and in February 1912, when she was twenty-two, he thought the moment opportune. The Order of Marie Réparatrice seemed to him one that would suit Josefa; he knew the nuns intimately, and began to direct her vocation towards them. Though her attraction lay in a different direction, Josefa stifled her feelings and asked to be admitted at the Réparatrice Convent. Here she was happy; she appreciated the spirit, and generously embraced her new religious life. The thought of making reparation for the sins of men through the Heart of Mary appealed to her, and no sort of temptation or trouble came to mar the happy months that followed. Gradually, however, and almost in spite of herself, there stole over her soul's consciousness the reawakening of another love - that of the Sacred Heart - her first attraction, and every time she heard the convent bells ringing (for they were close to her convent) the inward struggle was renewed. Our Lady herself intervened and showed her that she had not found her true home.

Josefa had charge of a large room which contained a big statue of the Blessed Virgin, under the title of Our Lady of Sorrows; in accordance with Spanish custom, it was adorned with rich vesture, and in her hand Our Lady held a crown of real thorns. Josefa was surprised one day to see the crown lit up by a shaft of light coming from she knew not where. She did not venture to speak of the marvel, but as the light continued for three or four days, she resolved to investigate its origin. She found that it proceeded from one of the thorns, and at the same time she heard a penetrating voice saying: "Take this thorn, my child; Jesus will give you others as time goes on." Josefa detached the thorn as she was bid, and the response she gave to her Mother's gift was a fresh offering of herself which was before long to receive its seal in suffering.

Her six months' postulantship was over and the day of her clothing fixed, when her mother, who had missed her sorely, came and claimed her again. Father Rubio seconded the mother's request, and so it came about that Josefa's return home was decided, and she left the Novitiate with the feelings we can imagine. She took with her the thorn, whose light, like that in her own heart, was quenched. Its reality, however, had sunk deeply into her inmost being, and this reality was suffering.

Courageously she faced the upward path to God, and resumed the old tasks. This time she was employed very largely by the nuns of the Sacred Heart in making the children's uniforms. Simple, modest, and conscientious in her work, her life was illumined by her constant prayer. She went every fortnight to see her sister, now a novice at Chamartin, and they talked together of what filled her soul. She loved to talk of the life of a Sister in the Society of the Sacred Heart, which she felt fulfilled every aspiration she had.

The nun who was over her in the school linen-room was struck by her devotedness, her love of duty, and the sweetness of disposition that made light of every difficulty and never caused the smallest embarrassment to others. Her tact, her dexterity and judgment, her silent activity all greatly impressed her; she was always on the watch to render service and every spare minute was spent before the Blessed Sacrament. "I feel thoroughly in my element when I am here," she used to say in speaking of Chamartin.

Very different was the story when she was obliged to work for clients outside. Her delicate conscience was many a time outraged by the absence of modesty in dress of those she worked for, and who as Catholics should have known better; it was then more than at any other time that she felt her "banishment" from Convent walls, and she would exclaim: "Since childhood my one prayer has been that 'I might dwell in the House of the Lord,' and the more I see of life outside, the greater is my longing to die, if this wish of my heart cannot be granted."

She lived on her burning hopes, and her daily Communion was fuel to the fire. This was the source of her serenity and of her courage; to others the secret of her cross and of her thorn was never told.

She had few friends, but her example and her counsels had made her the center of a group of working girls on whom her influence was remarkable. She would head a pilgrimage to Avila or to the Cerre de los Angeles,1 where the memorial to the Sacred Heart had been erected in accomplishment of the national vow, and on these and other rare outings her bright cheerfulness and fervor made a deep impression on them.

The months dragged on, and all the time Josefa was watching her opportunity. In 1917 she thought the moment had come, and when she begged her admission at Chamartin she was kindly received and her mother's consent obtained. Her departure was fixed for the 24th of September, Feast of Our Lady of Mercy. Alas, when the long-desired day dawned her mother's tears shook her resolution, and again prevailed ... tender-hearted Josefa yielded at the sight of her distress; her place in the Noviceship remained empty, and she was left to weep over the frailty that had prevented her from keeping her tryst. But He who "works in obscurity, and who nevertheless is light" pursued His purpose and in His own good time brought her out of darkness into light.

The French houses of the Sacred Heart which had been suppressed by iniquitous laws were just at this time taking on a new lease of life, and many were reopening after the expulsions that had marked the beginning of the century. The old monastery of Les Feuillants at Poitiers had been preserved for the Society, and here a Noviceship for Sisters was opened, in the house that had been the first General Noviceship of the Society and was still redolent with memories of Saint Madeleine Sophie. It was here that God called Josefa, and He Himself guided her through the final storms of her vocation.

In 1919 she was already twenty-nine years of age and she felt that she had forfeited her chance of success by her former act. What was she to do? An interior voice urged her to try and try again, but an irrevocable denial met her advances; Superiors mistrusted her long and repeated hesitations.

"On the 16th of September, I felt my courage at an end, and kneeling before my crucifix, I begged Our Lord either to take me out of this life or to admit me into the Society of His Sacred Heart, for I could bear no more. Then it seemed to me that He showed me His Sacred Hands and Feet and said to me 'Kiss these Wounds. Can you indeed bear no more for Me? Have I not chosen you for My Sacred Heart?' I am unable to put into words what then took place in me. I promised - oh, I promised Him to live henceforth only for Him and to suffer ... and begged Him to pity my weakness and wavering."

Two months passed in fervent supplications, till there dawned a memorable day for Josefa; it was the 19th of November.

"That day in my Communion I implored Our Lord by His Wounds and Precious Blood to open to me the doors of the Sacred Heart, which I knew I had closed by my own act."

That morning Josefa went as usual to fetch work at the convent at Chamartin; on her arrival she was told that the Superior wished to see her: a letter had just arrived from Les Feuillants (Poitiers) asking for one or two good vocations to begin the projected Noviceship. Did they know of any, and could they send anyone? The Superior asked Josefa if she felt equal to entering in a French house of the Society. This time there was no hesitation; at once she wrote to offer herself, and kneeling before the Blessed Sacrament, she begged that grace and strength might be given her to triumph over her weakness. This prayer was answered, and she was able to say afterwards: "I felt endued with a power I had never before experienced."

Her brokenhearted mother this time offered no opposition, and in order to avoid painful scenes, Josefa left home without saying good-bye and carrying nothing with her. The Mothers at Chamartin gave her her fare and provided her with all she needed. She reached San Sebastian, the first stage of her journey, and there found a warm welcome in the Sacred Heart.

"Jesus took me," she said, "I still do not know how, but I arrived at San Sebastian without money or strength - with nothing but love, I think ... but I was at the end of my pilgrimage... I, the same as ever, so weak, but He sustained me."

The nuns at San Sebastian who had received her with so much affection prolonged her stay there for a whole month. Full of gratitude, she devoted herself to helping in the household. All noted how silently and deftly she worked, always in deep recollection. However, sad letters from her mother and sister and the realization of the difficulty the French language was going to be to her caused her some misgivings, still she kept her will firmly fixed on her goal, and when asked how she would manage in a country whose tongue she did not know, "God is leading me," she answered simply, and on February 4th she left for Poitiers.

It was a final departure, for she never saw Spain again. But what of that? Was she not obeying the call of One whose sovereign love can never ask too much?

In the Open Heart of Jesus
(February 4th-July 16th 1920)

"For all you give Me, I give you My Heart."
(Our Lord to Josefa, July 15th, 1920)

The old-world town of Poitiers is perched above the valley of the Clain, and from the top of its highest hill the ancient monastery of Les Feuillants dominates the surrounding country. There two centuries earlier, a colony of Cistercians had settled; it was a place of prayer and labor, and though the French Revolution left the hallowed spot desolate it was destined to live again, when the storm had passed and faith had revived, for the monastic buildings were peopled once more at the coming of Saint Madeleine Sophie and her newly-founded Order. Here the Saint opened the first Noviceship of the Society of the Sacred Heart, here she made long sojourns, and here, too, many graces were conferred on her. Ever since, the house, the cloisters, and the garden have been regarded by the nuns of the Sacred Heart as a sort of reliquary and memorial of their holy Foundress.

To this remote and solitary house of prayer Josefa was guided by God, that He might there cultivate her soul and train and associate her with His divine Heart in the work of Redemption.

None who saw Josefa on her arrival at Poitiers could have suspected how great a work was beginning, for from the first days of her postulantship she passed unnoticed, and during the four years of her short religious life remained ever the same simple, silent, laborious, and unassuming religious. There was nothing particularly attractive in her exterior; she was usually serious and seemed at times to be suffering, but a bright, intelligent smile lighted up her face when she was addressed, especially if a service were asked of her. Her large dark eyes alone expressed and at times betrayed her inmost feelings; they were limpid eyes, gentle and ardent, and bespoke her interior recollection.

Her gifts, if hidden, were very real ones: she was swift and capable, active and adaptable to all sorts of conditions; she possessed rare good sense and excellent judgment. These gave her character an earnest and balanced foundation on which grace could build at will. Her heart was both tender and generous; her past sufferings had given her breadth of understanding and the kindliness which self-forgetfulness alone engenders. She brought to her religious formation a maturity which was the fruit of sacrifice and a supernatural understanding of the value of a religious vocation, together with a highly developed interior spirit and an immense love of God.

These gifts were hidden from herself as they were from those around her, and from the day of her arrival till her death she went her way utterly unknown, in the complete effacement of a very faithful and obscure life.

There were few novices at Poitiers; Josefa remained first postulant and eldest novice among the members, who came like herself from various houses of the Society.

The humble hiddenness of the life filled her with enthusiasm; it was modeled on that of Nazareth, and she found in it the fulfillment of her most sanguine expectations. It was in effect just what Saint Madeleine Sophie had defined as her ideal - a great deal of strenuous labor offered for the souls of children, accompanied by the vivifying charity and prayerful atmosphere that result from close union with the Heart of Jesus. Josefa threw herself with her whole heart and soul into the current of life as she found it.

Events were few, and there is little to record of the months of her postulantship and noviceship, and the short eighteen months of religious life that followed after her vows till her death. None of the things that made up her daily life are of any value in the eyes of the world, yet are not the first years of the life of the Man-God all summed up in one short sentence: "He was subject to them"? And so it was with Josefa; the less a Sister is spoken of, the more unnoticed, the truer she is to type. None of those who lived with her knew anything of her mysterious intercourse with the Sacred Heart of Our Lord, and when after her death they were asked to recount all they could recall about her, how little they were able to say! She had passed unnoticed and hidden, simply and faithfully doing her duty - that was all.

In this way Our Lord veiled from all the special graces which He now began to give her; day by day His designs of love were imprinted on the warp and woof of a career so hidden from human eyes that no exterior sign revealed the secret of which God Himself was the guardian.

Certainly it is one of the marvels of this narrative that the exterior and visible was such a contrast to the inner and invisible life she led. Josefa always followed common life and seemed in no way different from her sisters, yet she bore on her soul the weight of the most extraordinary and momentous graces of divine predilection which at one moment delivered her over to the onsets of excruciating physical pain, and again held her captive under the Hand of God; there was a twofold current of love between Him and her: Love Divine, which like the eagle precipitates itself upon its prey, and whose velocity none can stay, and a love frail yet ardent - that of Josefa - whose constant endeavor was to hold herself ever ready to accept all the urgent requirements of God's plan.

These pages are an attempt to narrate something of the mystery of her life. While we unhesitatingly submit to the judgment of the Holy See, sole judge in these matters, it would seem that the silence and shade under which that life was to unfold itself bore the stamp of the Holy Spirit, and we are therefore less afraid of temerity in discerning His Hand in the heavenly prudence which surpassed all human feasibility and succeeded in keeping undiscovered, except by her Superiors alone, the course of Josefa's uncharted ways - for the big household of Les Feuillants remained totally ignorant of the mysterious marvels that were being enacted within its walls, and that to the very end of Josefa's life.

Another sign of God's action, and by no means the least, was the jealous care with which Our Lord kept His instrument lowly in her own eyes, as in those of everybody else. "It is not for what you are that I have chosen you, but for what you are not. So I have found room for My power and My love." He reiterated this to her again and again.

It was fundamentally necessary that the Lord of all Wisdom should begin by sinking deep in her consciousness this capacity for humility in which the predilections of His Heart could, so to speak, engulf themselves. Josefa, whose frail skiff had reached the port of the religious life she so coveted, was soon to be tossed by storms and high winds more perilous than any that had hitherto rocked her little craft. "A fortnight of delicious peace," she noted, "followed on my entrance into the Postulantship."

She soon made acquaintance with the Mothers and Sisters, the house and the garden. Memory still recalls the arrival of the little Spaniard with her big black eyes, who did not know how to express her joy and her gratitude for being there. Simple and good-natured, she soon became quite at home in her new surroundings. The Mother Assistant and several Sisters who had spent long years in Spain and had become familiar with the language were able to greet her in her own Castilian tongue. A few days rest, and the new recruit was sent to help the Sister in the kitchen. Josefa was unaccustomed to that particular kind of work, but she put her whole heart into it and her face beamed with pleasure, showing how little it mattered to her what form the work took, if she was thereby able to prove her love for Him who possessed her whole heart. Nothing, it seemed could cast a shadow over such happiness, but the evil one, who had a presentiment of her future worth, was close by, ready to suggest subtle temptations. God was going to allow him to come on the scene, and Josefa sank into the darkest night of trial.

"Soon," she wrote, "I began to waver at the thought of my mother and sister ... of my home, and of the language that I did not understand. The temptation was so strong in the first months that I felt I could not possibly withstand it. Above all, the sad thought of the pain I was inflicting on my sister seemed intolerable. However, I made up my mind to leave them all to the Heart of Our Lord, to place them in His care, and every time the remembrance of these much-loved ones returned I did as I was advised and made an act of love and confidence.

"One evening in the beginning of April the temptation to leave was stronger than usual. All day long I had been repeating: 'My God I love Thee,' for above all I wanted to be faithful to Him. When I went to bed I put my crucifix under my pillow as I always did. I woke towards midnight, and kissing it, I said with all my heart: 'My God from today on I will love Thee more than ever.' At the same instant I was seized by an invisible force, and a shower of blows, as if from a fist, fell on me; they were so violent that I feared I should die. This torture continued all night, all through meditation and Mass. I was so terrified that I never left hold of my crucifix. I felt exhausted and dared not move. At the moment of the elevation of the Sacred Host I saw a sort of flash pass by me, there was a rapid current of wind, and suddenly all was quiet again, but the pain of the blows lasted several days."

This was but the prelude to a lifelong fight Josefa was to wage with the powers of darkness, but it never affected her work nor her fidelity to the

Rule. Her confidence and obedience to her Mistress of Novices grew, 1 and she went to her in all her troubles, there to get the peace and strength she needed to go on suffering.

"On Thursday, May 7th," she wrote, "being absolutely exhausted by my struggles, I begged to be allowed to go, but the Mother Assistant showed me the note I had written with my own hand, asking that for the love of God, in the name of the Blessed Virgin, of my Father Saint Joseph, and of our Holy Mother Foundress, even if I asked a thousand times to be sent away, that I should be reminded a thousand times that in moments when the light shone I was convinced that God wanted me here.

"From that hour I had not a day of peace, and God only knows what I endured ... "

Five weeks of struggle went by; they were exceptionally hard to bear, and Josefa continued to repeat the words obedience had put into her mouth: "Yes, dear Lord, I will stay here; I love Thee, and I will obey. I can see no light, but in spite of this, I will be faithful to Thee." One evening in May the diabolical assaults became more tangible:

"I was in the chapel for my adoration," she wrote later, "when I was suddenly surrounded with what seemed to be a crowd of spirits, I saw horrible faces, heard sharp yells, and there rained on me a shower of furious blows. I could not call for help; I was so overcome that I had to sit down, and pray I could not, so I just looked at the Tabernacle. Suddenly I was roughly seized by the arm, as if someone wanted to force me to leave the chapel. The power that held me was irresistible, and not knowing what to do or where to go, for I was afraid of meeting someone, I went up to our Blessed Mother's cell.

"When the Mother Assistant found me and asked me what I was doing there, I was unable to answer her. Interiorly I said to myself: 'Even if they kill me, I will go and tell her everything' - but I was once more surrounded by that awful crowd whose screams terrified me. When I reached her door in a flash they all disappeared, and I found such peace that I should have liked to stay there forever... .

"The same thing has often happened since. As soon as I have determined to speak, everything stops as I reach the Mother Assistant's door. I have noticed, too, the rage of the devil when she makes a little cross on my forehead; he seems to stamp his foot in fury, and at other times, if she forgets it, I hear hideous guffaws."

It was after such trials that Josefa's postulantship ended. On the 16th of July she was to take the habit, but so many unexpected sufferings and the thought of future trials left her undecided and hesitant; at one time she made up her mind to embrace God's Will at whatever cost, at another she felt paralyzed and could not accept what must be bought at such a high price. "It was thus," she wrote, "till the day when Jesus made His divine Presence clearly known to me, and since then He has given me so much light and consolation."

On Saturday, June 5th, 1920, after a formidable attack of the devil, Josefa decided to go; she went into the chapel with her Sisters for the evening adoration; there, Jesus was waiting for her. Under the influence of the arch-fiend who dominated her: "No," she said, "I will not take the habit, I am going home." "I said it five times, but could not go on," she wrote later. "My Jesus how good Thou art to me."

All of a sudden she was, as she naïvely expressed it, wrapped in a sweet slumber, from which she awoke in the Wound of the Sacred Heart.

"I cannot explain what happened... Jesus... I want nothing more than to love Thee and to be faithful to my vocation."

In the radiance now illuminating her, she saw all the sins of the world, and offered her life to comfort the wounded Heart of Our Lord. She was seized with a vehement desire of uniting herself to Him, and no sacrifice appeared too great that she might be faithful to her vocation. In the effulgence of the Godhead the night had faded away and desolation had given place to unfathomable bliss.

"It was God who did it," she continued in the notes she wrote under obedience. "I am abashed at so much goodness; I want to love Him to folly... . I have but two requests: love and gratitude to His Sacred Heart... . More than ever I recognize my weakness, but also I shall now find strength and courage in Him... . Never before have I rested in that Divine Wound ... but now I know where to go in moments of tribulation: It is a place of sweetest repose and much love.

"I feel keenly that I have been resisting grace and have been unfaithful, but this has become a further motive of confidence and hope that Our Lord will never fail me, even when I seem to be all alone. That was what made me so afraid before: to be alone, and unfaithful. But now I see that, even though I did not know it, He was helping me. Well, I simply cannot express how much I want to love Him."

When Josefa came out of the chapel, still strongly under the influence of the divine contact, she was a totally changed person.

"And then, I don't know what it is," she added two days later, "but I believe He wants to tell me another secret, because during my prayer yesterday, Monday, June 7th, He made me re-enter that Divine Wound: O my Jesus, how great is Thy love for me ... I shall never be able to respond to so much goodness. It seemed to me that I saw in that Divine Wound a tiny opening, and I wanted to know how to get in ... but He made me understand that it will not be till later."

"Twelve days have passed," she wrote on June 17th, "since the signal grace Jesus granted me. I have had immense consolation during that time, but especially I have been able to study all that this Sacred Heart was teaching me. He showed me clearly, that what pleases Him most is to do little acts out of obedience. I understood that I must direct all my energies to this, for that is how I shall learn to deny myself in everything, and however small the act is, it will still be pleasing to His Sacred Heart... . Oh, I want to be burnt up by love. Oh, what a Heart is that of my Jesus!"

Crushed by the weight of so much grace and such amazing happenings, Josefa continued to jot down on paper the overflow of her heart.

"Today, Wednesday, June 23rd, I was meditating on the kindness of the Heart of Jesus and this thought came to me: that this Heart so full of love for souls and for me, that this same Heart is to become my Bridegroom, if I am faithful. I did not know what to say, and how to thank. 'O my God, I can only pay Thee back with Thyself, for I am Thine and Thou art mine.... . I give myself up to Thee, my life must be solely in God ... and for God... .' I must so abandon self that everything in me may be consumed and obliterated and that all I do and am, may be solely of Him.

"After I had received Him in Holy Communion, I told Him, as I always do, how much I love Him, and want to love Him. Then He made me re-enter my place of refuge; it is the third time I have rested in that Divine Heart.... . I am not able to explain what happens ... except to say that I am too little for so many graces.... . My God, Thy Heart fills with love those who seek and love It.

"During the heavenly moments that I spent in that Wound, Jesus gave me to understand that He is rewarding me for the very little I have done to prove my fidelity. I will never again seek my own interests, but only the glory of His Heart. I will try to be very obedient and very generous in the smallest details, for I believe perfection consists in this, and that it is the one way straight to Him."

"Today, June 24th, I saw in a way impossible to explain what the Heart of Jesus is.... . I asked Him to make me thirst for Him. I cannot set down in writing what I saw ... but it was Himself, Heaven on earth.... . O my God, it is too much, I cannot bear such happiness ... would that I had something I could offer Him ... give to Him, who gives me so much, but I am so little.... . I again promised to be faithful and above all to let myself be guided in everything so as to go more surely to His Divine Heart."

Here Josefa stopped, for she does not allow her feelings to run away with her. She tried to penetrate to the very depths of the Heart of Jesus to discover what He expected of her, and to realize the immensity of His loving-kindness.

"As each moment goes by, I notice two things. First, a greater understanding of the Divine Goodness, for if I certainly have always known that God loves mankind to folly, now I know that it is His Sacred Heart that does so.... . His greatest sorrow is not to find a return of love, and if a soul is wholly abandoned to Him, she can be sure that He will fill her with graces, will make of her His Heaven, and take up His abode in her. I promise in a very special way fidelity, obedience, confidence, and abandonment. The second thing I have noticed is the clearer view I have gained of myself. I see myself as I am (though I am not sure that I do fully): cold, distracted, immortified, and ungenerous.... . O my God, why dost Thou love me so? Thou knowest what I am ... but I will not lose confidence, Lord ... what I cannot do myself, that Thou wilt do, and with Thy love and Thy grace I will go forward."

Jesus, too, was about to take her deeper into His Heart; the graces with which He had overwhelmed her in this month of June were but a prelude. Josefa wrote on the evening of June 29th:

"Meditation today was on the three denials of Saint Peter, and comparing my weakness to his, I resolved to weep for my falls, and to learn to love as he did. How often I, too, have promised fidelity ... but I did so today with more force and decision. Yes, Lord, I will be faithful. I promise not only to refuse Thee nothing, but to go forward to do what I know will please Thee.

"I was thus in converse with my God, when again He made me enter the Wound of His side. The little passage by which I was unable to enter the other day opened, and He gave me to understand the happiness that is to be mine if I am faithful to all the graces He has prepared for me.

"I cannot very well describe what I saw; my heart was being consumed in a great flame. I could not see the bottom of this abyss, for it is an immense space and full of light. I was so taken up with what I saw that I was not able to speak or ask anything... . I spent meditation and part of Mass in this way ... till, a little before the Elevation, my eyes, even my poor eyes ... saw my Beloved Jesus, my heart's desire, my Lord and my God; His Heart in the midst of a great flame. I cannot say what passed; it is not possible... . Would that the whole world knew the secret of happiness. There is but one thing to do: love and abandon oneself. Jesus Himself will take charge of all the rest... .

"I was annihilated in the presence of so much beauty and so brilliant a light, when He said to me in a voice so sweet and grave:

" 'Just as I sacrificed Myself as a victim of love, so I want you to be a victim: love never refuses anything.'

"So this heavenly moment passed, for I can give it no other name. I could only say: 'My God, what wouldst Thou have me do? ... Take and dispose of me, for I no longer belong to myself, but I am Thine.' Then He vanished."

When recording this experience Josefa was unable to contain herself. Already her love had become a consuming zeal, for in drawing her near His Heart, Our Lord allowed the thirst that devours His own to overflow onto hers.

"Jesus," she wrote, "I have but one desire - that the whole world may know Thee, but especially the souls of religious whom Thou hast chosen for Thy adorable Heart. If they know Thee, they will love Thee, for Thou art the one and only Good. Inflame me with Thy Love and that is enough for me... . Inflame all hearts and this, too, will suffice, for where there is love, we run to Thee by the shortest way. As for myself, I ask only to love Thee daily more and more, only Thee! Everything else will be but a path to lead me to Thee. Would that I could bring the whole world to the divine furnace of Thy Heart, even if it cost me my life.

"Jesus has given me such a thirst to make all men love Him that I am ready to offer all, to undertake all that costs me most, to please Him and obtain that others may know and love Him.

"I promised Him to do nothing except what Holy Obedience prescribes, and I understand that it will please Him very much if I am simple and very open with Superiors, so as to allow myself to be guided as a little child."

A few days after "this great and heavenly moment," Our Lord showed Josefa the cost of this thirst for souls that He was beginning to communicate to her. She wrote on Saturday, July 3rd:

"I was working in the Noviceship today and thinking of the happiness it was to be living under the same roof with Him and to have Him as the Companion of all my labors. I don't remember exactly what I was saying to Him, but suddenly He showed me His Heart all surrounded with flames and wreathed with a crown of thorns.... O my God, what thorns! ... they were very sharp and penetrated very deeply, and from each there flowed a great deal of blood.... I should have liked to take them from Him. Then my heart was as it were torn with sharpest anguish, and He placed it next His Own under the thorns. My heart was so small that only six of them pierced it. Then there was silence.... I could not utter a word. He knew that I longed for my heart to be bigger that so I might have freed His from more of the thorns.

"Then in a voice so gentle and yet so full of pain, He said: 'My Heart has suffered all this and infinitely more. But some souls unite themselves to Me and comfort Me, and so make up for those who go away from Me.'

"Oh, how He has suffered.... I understand that some thorns wound Him more cruelly than others. I should have liked to know what to do to console Him, for what I can offer Him is very little, and when compared with His torments, very little indeed - but He did not tell me."

On Sunday, July 4th, Josefa was at Holy Mass as usual, associating herself with the Divine Mysteries:

"To tell the truth," she wrote soon after, "not knowing what to say or do, if not to humble myself, for every day I get a clearer insight into my misery and littleness, I was trying to do this, when I saw before me the Adorable Heart. It was pierced through with a large thorn, which caused much blood to flow. O my Jesus! who is wounding Thee so? ... Is it I? ... What sorrow to see Thy Sacred Blood flow; it pains me more than I can say. My Lord and my God, take me and do with me what Thou wilt, but do not let that thorn transpierce Thy Heart.... Then I saw what looked like a very large nail drawn out, leaving so gaping a wound that I could see deep into that burning brazier, and Jesus replied: 'That large nail is the coldness of My religious, I want you to understand it that you may be all on fire with love and may console Me.'

"On Tuesday, July 6th, while I was at prayer, He again showed me His Heart; It was transpierced by six thorns. My grief was very great, because of His sufferings, and of the impossibility I was in to give Him consolation or to assuage His pain. He made me understand that those six thorns are six souls that are offending Him in a particular way. He said: 'These are the thorns I ask you to draw out by your love and desires.'

"Then He allowed a few drops of His Blood to fall on my heart ... O my God, my heart is too small for so much love, but such as it is, it belongs entirely to Thee."

The next day, once more Jesus made her enter His wounded Heart, and left her this watchword: "Love Me in your littleness; this will console Me."

"Of all the graces that I receive," she concluded at this time, "two things remain deeply engraven on my heart: first, a very great desire to love and to suffer in order to correspond to His love, and this I shall find in fidelity to my vocation; second, an ardent thirst that many souls may know and love Him, especially those He has chosen and consecrated to Himself. This, I think, is to be my path in life: to spare myself in nothing, and offer many little acts to Jesus whom I love to folly, or at any rate desire so to love."

Such were the dispositions in which she waited for the day of her clothing. The retreat which was to bring her through many a struggle to this much-longed-for day began on Wednesday, July 7th.

"Ardent desire to surrender wholly, leaving nothing out and refusing nothing of whatever I know to be God's Will. Be very attentive to the voice of God, so that this retreat may be the foundation of my Noviceship. I will ask especially for a great love of my vocation which is for me the means of union and conformity with the Heart of Jesus."

Such are the opening words Josefa wrote in her retreat notebook. She noted faithfully day by day the result of her efforts, and one becomes conscious as one reads these very simple jottings destined for no eye but her own, how great was the storm and commotion of temptation that had arisen within her.

"I was in great consolation," she wrote, "until the third day of my retreat. But in the meditation on the Judgment, when I suddenly found myself alone before God, as my Judge, my soul was filled with fear, and I lost the peace which had not left me since June 5th. I saw before me all the graces that will one day accuse me, and the sight plunged me into such desolation and solitude that it seemed to me far preferable not to receive them, rather than to have to give an account of them... .

"Several days went by and I decided to go home. My God! What darkness and what anguish... . My mother and sister were expected, and this increased the temptation, as it revived my affection for them and for my home.

"From the very first I had told the Mother Assistant everything, and I constantly repeated the offering she had taught me and which had helped me so much before; I wanted to stay and be faithful, and there were moments when I saw that the whole thing was a temptation. But nothing availed and the day before my clothing, July 15th, the struggle was so great, that I could think of nothing to offer God but the temptation itself: 'O my God, I love my liberty, my family and my home - in a word all that makes up this temptation - I offer it all to Thee, for what else do I want but to be faithful and die... .'

"Then it was that Jesus deigned to console me as I shall relate."

But before telling of these graces, Josefa held to stating explicitly her reply of love:

"Practical result of the first three weeks1 of this retreat:

"I saw that God is calling me to great perfection and it consists in complete conformity to His Heart.

"The means: my vocation and holy Rule.

"God is calling me to a life of intimate union with Himself; He wishes me to live in a state of sacrifice, as a victim.... . He will choose my cross. It is not for me to ask or select; He will give what He pleases. He wants my life to be spent in His Heart, and I know that the cross and thorns are part of it. Such is my life; it must be so, and only so shall I be doing God's Will.

"I do not feel that I can very well explain what took place during the contemplation ad Amorem: I had so ardent a desire to give Him all He asks for, that I said with my whole heart: 'Take, O Lord, and receive all my will; I give Thee all I care for most in the world ... if there is anything else that Thou requirest of me, I give it with joy - take my miseries and consume them, take my heart and my soul, take me, Lord."

The response was immediate:

A stream of the Precious Blood escaping from His Heart submerged Josefa. "For all that you give Me," He said, "I give you My Heart."

"I thought myself no longer on this earth - He was clothed in white, and this made His Sacred Heart stand out in an ineffable manner.... . His face was like the sun.... . O my God, what beauty.... . How entrancing to those who know Thee."

Naïvely Josefa explains in the lines that follow how she required no book in order to meditate on Heaven: "For the real Heaven is in my heart. Love is all I want ... love, love."

Once more before the great day He wished to show her whither He was leading her, and Josefa, who had leave to make a Holy Hour, began it with an act of profoundest humility.

"I adored the Divine Majesty," she wrote, "and then I thought of the graces I had received from God, and of my desire to console Him which was growing ever stronger.

"Suddenly I saw Him standing before me in His gleaming white raiment, and His Heart seemed about to escape from His breast. As I was alone in the tribune, I fell on my face, humbling myself all I could, but unable to speak.

"After a moment of silence, showing me the six thorns, He said in a voice that is so piercing-sweet: 'Daughter, take out these thorns.'

"On Friday, July 16th, the day of my clothing, as I received the white veil

45

and all through Mass, Jesus was present to me, and made me enter the Wound in His Heart. All I was able to say was ... My God, I am Thine forevermore ... "

Vocation of Reparation (July 17th-August 25th, 1920)

"If you love Me, Josefa, remove this thorn."
(Our Lord to Josefa, August 17th, 1920)

The wounded Heart of Jesus was very soon to make a further appeal to Josefa, as to one chosen for a special share in His redemptive work for souls. He reminded her of her vocation as victim, and a few days after her clothing, on Thursday, August 5th, He made her share once more the pain of the six thorns that were wounding Him, and comforted her with the words: "If you are faithful, you shall know the riches of My Heart. You will carry My Cross indeed, but as on a well-loved Bride shall My benefits be heaped upon you."

"This time," said Josefa, "I saw Him surrounded with such splendor that it was not possible to gaze fixedly on that dazzling light. His Heart was all aflame and seemed to be escaping from His breast."

On Tuesday, August 10th, she wrote:

"At meditation I had a great desire to comfort Him. I offered Him all the actions of my day, and begged Him to tell me if there was anything else I could do. I promised not to let Him out of my thoughts for a single instant, and I never stopped telling Him of my love. That evening before going to adoration, I went into the oratory of Mater1 to ask our Blessed Lady to help me to console her Son; when I reached the chapel I suddenly found myself in the presence of Jesus... . He said: 'What else do I want but love? Look at My Heart, Josefa. It alone can make you happy. Rest in It.'

"Then He went on to say: 'I had six thorns. You have taken out five; only one remains and that is the one that wounds Me most. Spare no pains to remove it.'

" 'Lord,' I answered, 'what shall I do?'

" 'I want you to love Me and to be faithful to Me. Remember, no one else can make you happy. I will lay open to you the riches of My Heart. Love Me without measure.'

"And again I was left alone."

The feast of the Assumption came round. Josefa, who loved Our Lady so dearly, spent the day in union with her, and as the remembrance of the thorn deeply embedded in the Sacred Heart haunted her:

"I begged her," she wrote, "to take charge of that soul and to draw out the thorn that Jesus had asked me to remove from His Heart.

"The next day, towards three in the afternoon, while I was at my sewing, I

47

was telling Our Lord that I wanted every stitch to be an act of love so as to comfort Him; hardly had I finished the words than I saw Him standing there.

" 'I have not come to comfort you, Josefa,' He said, 'but to let you share My suffering. Can you not see how that thorn pierces My Heart? Draw it out; that soul is almost forcing My justice to act.'"

The salvation of that soul was to cost Josefa a great deal of suffering. Gradually Our Lord was initiating her into His redemptive work, which later was to occupy so great a part of her life. He continued:

" 'The sins of mankind wound Me deeply, but not nearly so much as those of My religious. That thorn is a religious on whom I have bestowed many talents. She appropriates them ... her pride will be her ruin.'

"That evening I saw His Heart all on fire, the Wound gaping wide, and still that thorn was there. 'I have two measures for every soul,' He said, 'one is of mercy, and already it has overflowed ... the other is of justice, and it is very nearly full. Nothing grieves Me more than the obstinacy and resistance of this soul.... . I will make a last appeal to her heart; if she still resists, I will leave her to her own devices.'

"Here I do not know what He made me understand ... but I would give my life to save that soul.

"As I had permission to make a Holy Hour that evening, I offered myself in union with His Passion. 'Do not look at the sins of that soul, but rather at the Blood that Thou hast shed for it ... and which can cleanse all the sins of the whole world.'

"Then I said the litanies of Our Lady and repeated many times, 'Refuge of sinners, pray for us.' When I got to the words 'Lamb of God who takest away the sins of the world ... ' my soul was filled with anguish. Jesus was silent; He did not seem to be listening; He seemed deaf.

"At the end of the Holy Hour He came, His Heart still pierced by that thorn. I implored Him to have mercy on that soul, and as He did not answer, I said: 'But Lord, wilt Thou not forgive her? ... ' 'I will touch her heart once again, and if she responds she will be the beloved of My Heart. If she still holds out, My justice must act.'"

Many days went by, Josefa's offerings were more and more costly, but as she said, her soul was plunged in unspeakable sadness.

"I think that never before have I understood as I do now what is meant by resistance to grace. I seem to endure something of the grief of the Heart of Jesus when a soul turns away from Him.

"If you are ready to suffer," said Our Lord to her on Wednesday, August 18th, "I will wait for that soul, but unless she herself wills to be forgiven, I cannot pardon her. She was created without her cooperation, but she is free to save or lose her soul."

"A few days later He added: 'When I find a soul that is loving and wants to comfort Me, I am ready to grant whatever she asks, so I will wait, and knock again at the door of her heart; if she is willing, My Heart is ready to forgive.'

"His words left me in agony. He has taught me to repeat often: My God, I will suffer for love of Thee, and to comfort Thy Sacred Heart."

Josefa was oppressed by the suffering she was undergoing, she felt as if the divine anger had fallen on her.

Our Lord's calls pursued her and left her no rest either day or night. The weight of that soul was heavy on her own, without, however, lessening her desire for reparation.

On Wednesday, the 25th of August, after a night of agony and supplication, Josefa, ever faithful to her morning's meditation, began it with the other novices.

"Suddenly," she wrote, "I saw Him... . He, the all-beautiful... . I cannot attempt to describe Him. He was standing upright, vested in white, He held His Heart in His hands, as in a brazier of fire. His whole Person shone with radiant light. His hair was like spun gold, His eyes like brilliants, and His countenance ... what can I say ... I can find no comparison worthy of It... . His Heart surmounted by the cross no longer had any thorn in It. The wound which was open wide, emitted flames ... a very sun... . From the wounds in His hands and feet also came bright flames... . From time to time He opened and extended His arms; all I could say, was, O Jesus! how beautiful Thou art ... how hearts would be ravished could they behold Thee ... and the thorn? ... 'The thorn?... It is gone, for there is nothing so strong as love, and that I find among my religious.'

"His Heart was kindling more and more. I thanked Him for having drawn me to this Society, and begged Him to have compassion on me who am a miserable creature and unworthy to be here: O Lord, do not permit me to be the one blot on this holy group of consecrated souls. Do not allow the graces I receive to be my condemnation, for there is no evil of which I am not capable; I want to be faithful or to die."

It was in this new joy that a few minutes later Josefa assisted at Mass, associating herself with the thanksgiving of the Blessed Virgin.

"After Communion I asked Him to consecrate me His true spouse by fidelity ... but to leave me in the common way, for I should never be able to correspond to His graces.

" 'Leave yourself in My hands, Josefa. I will use you as seems best to Me. What of your littleness and weakness ... no matter ... All I ask of you is to love and console Me. I want you to know how dearly My Heart loves you, how great are the riches it contains, and you must be like soft wax that I may mold you to My liking.

" 'Listen ... I want you to offer Me all, even the smallest things, so as to comfort My Heart's sufferings, especially those I have to endure from consecrated souls in religion. I want you to rest in My Heart without any fear. Gaze on it; cannot this flame burn up all your imperfections? Leave yourself entirely in My hands and be busy only in pleasing Me.'

" 'I want you to tell Reverend Mother in all simplicity whatever I ask of you, and you must have no personal care as to how they use you. Lastly, I repeat: be like soft wax, to which I can give any shape I please... . Remember that I am your Father, your Spouse, your God.'

"Then He vanished. Never had I seen Him so beautiful!

"All this time I was able to talk to Him and listen to Him because I had leave. But from today onward I have been ordered to make no more account of these things, and not to answer anything."

Josefa Under Trial (August 26th-October 8th, 1920)

"I will give a sign in you."
(Our Lord to Josefa, September 20th, 1920)

Towards the end of August 1920, in order to try the spirit that actuated Josefa, she was forbidden to have any communication with the apparition that had so often filled her heart with such joy. She was told to turn away, and to attach no importance to anything she might see or hear.

Was doubt beginning to creep in? Her soul was thereby profoundly unsettled, and she asked herself if she had not all along been the sport of illusion, as others seemed to think. Moreover, the devil had already suggested this to her many times, and she had rejected it as a temptation, so as to remain faithful to what she deemed God's Will in her regard. Oh, where was the truth?

At the same time her mind was tortured by the fear that this path which she had neither sought nor wanted might eventually become an obstacle to her vocation. Her instinctive horror of all that was out of the ordinary, her genuine wish for a life hidden and humble, added to her present confusion of mind.

Already accustomed to the most intimate self-sacrifice and matured by her spirit of faith and obedience, she never hesitated to do as she was told, without allowing herself either to reason or to argue interiorly, and so she entered on the obscure path where her love was to suffer so keenly, as her notes indicate:

"Thursday, September 2nd, I saw at meditation the same Person, so beautiful, with His Heart as before. He asked me twice if I loved Him. I gave no answer, out of obedience, although it cost me immensely, for in spite of myself, my whole soul bounded forward towards Him."

On September 5th Josefa was in the Noviceship ...

"When suddenly," she said, "I saw a brilliant light, in the midst of which was the Person as always with a Heart all on fire. I was so frightened that I fled to our Blessed Mother's cell. I rubbed my eyes and asperged myself all over with Holy Water, but the Vision remained.

" 'Why are you afraid?' said a voice. 'Do you not know that this is the abode of your peace?' A few minutes passed, then the voice added: 'Do not forget that I want you to be a victim of My love.' Then all was quiet again."

The trial continued day after day, Josefa resisting and making no response, but sometimes she was unable to withdraw from an overwhelming attraction - it dominated her, filled her with happiness and heavenly peace.

" 'Come,' said the voice, 'enter in ... lose yourself in this abyss.'"

On Wednesday, September 8th, towards evening, she was praying in the cell of Saint Madeleine Sophie, when like a flash of lightning the burning Heart of Jesus passed before her and she heard: "Which do you prefer, My Will or yours?'

"I understood that to be the answer to what I was asking of Our Lord with all my heart; to be a good religious, solely occupied in loving His Divine Heart, but following common life, for I am so afraid all those things will be an obstacle to my vocation."

Next day, the 9th, at Mass, she saw Him whom for so long she had never doubted. In one hand He held His Heart, and with the other He offered her a chalice:

"I have heard your distress," He said to her. "I know your desires, but I cannot grant them. My love needs to rest in you. Take this Blood which has flowed from My Heart. It is the source of love. Do not fear, and do not abandon Me. I delight in living in you, for so many turn away from Me."

Josefa remained silent ...

"But," she wrote, "I could not help thinking: My God, if I had known, I should never have come here! The idea tormented me, for I thought that if I had stayed in the world, nothing of all this would have happened, and every day my anxiety increased. I will surely go backward, unless God keeps me faithful to Him. But I feel myself bound in a way I cannot understand and the love of my vocation grows and grows. That is what makes me constantly beg the Heart of Jesus to leave me to common life, I mean, with none of these extraordinary happenings, even if it be with no consolation whatever, if that were His Will, provided I can remain faithful in little things and love His Adorable Heart above measure."

This Heart again showed Itself to her on September 16th. She heard:

'To satisfy a love so great, you must try to find souls for Me. You will do so by suffering and by love. You will have to bear many humiliations, but do not be afraid, for you are in My Heart.'

In the face of doubt, she tried to close her eyes, but was unable to distract her mind from the urge to love God which daily increased in her soul.

"The only comfort I can get is in incessantly telling Him of my love," she wrote; "it detaches me from the things of earth. The ardent love I used to have for my family and for many others, though still there, has changed ... nothing of it all can fill my heart now. When I say even unconsciously: 'My God I love Thee'; it satisfies me and helps me to do what otherwise would be impossible.

"Sometimes I am distracted when at work; then suddenly the Heart of Jesus passes before me like a flash, and rekindles the flame of love in my heart."

The crucifying trial increased in severity as time went on, and Josefa's fears grew, but her spirit of obedience kept her faithful, and it gradually became evident how Our Lord, by detaching her from created things, was attaching her more and more to Himself.

On Friday, September 17th, He showed Himself to her at Mass. His face was sad, His hands bound, the crown of thorns encircled His head, and His Heart as always was on fire. He offered her a cross which she had not at first noticed.

" 'Behold the Cross that I give you,' He said. 'Will you refuse it?'

"I was in anguish at not being able to answer," she wrote, "for in spite of myself my heart went out to Him. I burn with longing to love Him; but I am not sure that it is really Himself, and this fills me with acute distress. What I now ask is that once and for all these things should cease."

But He came again:

"On Sunday, the 19th, during my prayer, I was turning over in my mind how to love Him more, for I can think of nothing else. Suddenly I saw Him. His Heart was like a great conflagration ... the Heart that fills me with peace, and makes me able to bear anything."

" 'If you love me,' He said, 'I shall always remain near you. If you follow Me closely, I shall grant you victory over the foe; I shall manifest Myself to you, and teach you how to love.'"

The next day, the 20th, while her mind was still preoccupied with the same trouble, she begged Our Lord to give a sign to her Superiors, that they might know for certain whether or not these things came from Him.

He appeared suddenly and said to her: "A sign? I will give a sign in you. All I ask of you is to surrender yourself entirely to Me."

And so it came to pass, for God was imprinting His sign on the docile and generous heart of Josefa, whose obedience throughout this trial was a proof in itself. In spite of the divine advances, she continued to keep silence. But there came a day ...

"When," she wrote on September 27th, "I cannot say what happened. I found myself obliged to surrender, and give myself up to God's demands, and I was only able to say: 'Yes, Lord, I am Thine; whatever Thou willest, I also will.' At the same moment I saw Jesus in all His beauty, and He said: 'Have no fear. It is I.'"

On Friday, the 29th, she saw Him once more, when again He asked her: "Are you ready to do My Will?"

"My God," she wrote, "I deliver myself over into Thy hands to do whatever is Thy Will, if really it is Thyself. All I ask is that I should not be in delusion and that nothing should prejudice my religious life.

"Then He answered: 'What is there to fear, if you are in My hands? Never doubt the goodness of My Heart, nor the love I bear you.' A flame escaped from His Sacred Heart and wrapped me round. 'All I ask of you is that you should always be ready to console My Heart, whenever I call on you. The comfort given Me by one faithful soul compensates for the coldness and indifference of so many others. You will sometimes feel in your heart the anguish that is in Mine, and that is how you will allay My sorrow. Fear nothing, I am with you.'"

But even so she was not fully reassured, and when the presence had left her and she was once more alone she was again a prey to very great distress. Tossed between an attraction that was at times irresistible and fear of the abnormal, and bound to silence by obedience, she implored Our Lord to leave her to the simple and common life that her love ambitioned, or to give light to her Superiors that would put an end to so many doubts and so much suffering.

She whom no one ever invokes in vain was to come to Josefa's aid.

In the evening of Sunday, October 3rd, the Mother Assistant guessed from Josefa's face of acute agony all that the poor novice was going through, and she sent her to bed early. In the lonely little dormitory where she could not find relief in sleep she prayed to Our Lady.

"I recited the litanies of Our Lady," she wrote, "then with all my heart I prayed, telling her with anguish what I had been saying for many days past: 'O Mother, for the love of God, do not let me be deluded, and make me know whether it is all true or not.'

"At once I heard a light footstep, as of somebody coming, and then I saw, standing by my bedside, a person clothed in white and wrapped in a long veil. Her features were very fine, her hands crossed; she looked at me very tenderly and said: 'My child, you are not mistaken, and Reverend Mother will soon know it, but you must first suffer if you are to win souls for my Son.'

"She disappeared, leaving me in peace beyond all words."

It was the Queen of Heaven, and Josefa never doubted it for a minute, but Mary had said "you must suffer," and Josefa was being asked to give her consent freely to an appeal to cooperate in redemptive suffering.

The following day, October 4th, Our Lord, showing her His wounded Heart, said: "Look at the state to which unfaithful souls have reduced My Heart. They do not know how much I love them, and that is why they forsake Me. Will not you at least do My Will?" A flood of apprehension overwhelmed her soul.

"I did not answer," she wrote honestly, "but everything within me said No. He disappeared. I felt I must have displeased Him, for He vanished like a flash.

"Next day, October 5th, while I was saying the litanies of Our Lady, she came again, stayed quite a long time and then said to me: 'If you refuse to do my Son's Will, you will wound His Heart. Consent to everything He asks of you, but do not attribute anything to yourself. Be very humble, child!' She looked at me with great compassion, then went away."

From now on Our Lady, full of tender compassion and strong kindness, intervenes in Josefa's life. Her Son's part is paramount, she helps only when there is question of reassuring Josefa in her faltering hesitations, of strengthening her in her fears, or of bringing her will into line with God's. She acts as a warning, sometimes as a support; she initiates her into Our Lord's plans and prepares her for His coming; she teaches her how to guard against the snares of the devil and how to repair her failings. She, "as an army set in array," is there to defend her in the perilous combats with the evil one.

This intervention of Our Lady increased in the eyes of Superiors the light beginning to dawn around Josefa; her simple and courageous obedience, her indifference and abandonment, as well as her humble distrust of herself, her fear of an abnormal path, and above all her love of her vocation, which she held in higher esteem than anything else in the world - all pointed to a heavenly origin in her state; and these signs could not be opposed indefinitely. The time seemed to have come to allow full liberty to the divine action, whilst still surrounding Josefa with vigilant control. She was given permission to "offer herself," and that in spite of her acute repugnance to it.

"On Friday, October 8th," she wrote, "at Meditation, I made an act of conformity to the Divine Will. During Mass, a little before the Gospel, I saw Our Lady. I begged her intercession; I told her why I felt such repugnance for those graces, but that I had quite made up my mind to accept all to glorify the Heart of Jesus, to console Him and to win souls for Him. I think she had pity on me, for she said: 'My child, this is the prayer you must say to Our Lord, and His Heart will not resist: "O Father, make me worthy to accomplish Thy Holy Will, for I belong to Thee." '

"Then she added: 'If you are in the hands of a good Father, what more do you want?'

"I implored her to receive my offering and to carry it herself to Jesus.

"That same evening when I went to the chapel I found myself suddenly in Our Lord's presence.

"His face was so beautiful, His Heart encircled with flames; in the midst, in front of the Cross, was an open book. I did not understand what it signified.... . I offered myself once more and promised never to take back my gift. He placed His hand on my head and said: 'If you do not forsake Me, neither will I desert you. Henceforth, Josefa, call me nothing but Father and Spouse. If you are faithful, we shall make this pact together: Bride and Bridegroom, espoused to one another, you Mine, and I yours. And now write what you read in My Heart; it sums up all I want of you.'

"Then I read in the book:

" 'I shall be the one love of your heart, the sweet torture of your soul, and the welcome martyrdom of your body.

" 'You shall be the victim of My Heart through a bitter dislike for all that is not Me; victim of My soul by all the anguish of which yours is capable;

victim of My body, by the denial of all that could satisfy yours, and by your hatred of the flesh which is both criminal and cursed.

"When I had read the book, He made me kiss it, and then He disappeared."

First Steps (October 9th - 28th, 1920)

"Your misery attracts Me."
(Our Lord to Josefa, October 15th, 1920)

Humanly speaking, one might expect that so luminously mapped-out a path would have offered Josefa neither obstacles nor shadows. This would be to forget God's ways with souls He has specially chosen: He draws them, and then hides Himself - He attracts, then baffles them - He fills them with gifts and next leaves them to their native poverty. He carries them in His arms, and then allows them to fall back into nerveless weakness. These are the searching alternatives that confirm them in detachment, abandonment, and humility, and alone can convince the creature of its nothingness, placing the instrument passive and quiescent in His divine hands.

Josefa's notes acquaint us with these vicissitudes, and their moving simplicity and candid sincerity make of them a document of real importance.

From the very first she had been put under obedience to write down all she saw and heard. To begin with, this was a kind of relief to her feelings, but whereas she then threw on paper with burning and naive diffuseness the sentiments she felt incapable of keeping to herself, later she became aware that these notes which she believed to be for herself alone would become a necessary means of control in the hands of her guides, and her habitual self-diffidence and the reserve that had always surrounded her relations with Our Lord reasserted themselves in her writings.

She sacrificed her repugnance by obeying the injunction, but her acceptance was not free from struggle and some wavering, as her notes bear witness, even to the end. Her style changes from now on, and becomes very sober, facts alone are briefly mentioned. We rarely meet with the outpourings of the earlier days, but what is very characteristic is that she never fails to recount her own weaknesses and vacillations, nor her occasional resistance in the face of some particularly crucifying event. No doubt Our Lord meant us to learn from these honest acknowledgments how great is His compassion and how untiring His mercy.

Before recording the contents of Josefa's notebooks it may be well to answer the perfectly legitimate question as to how in general they were written.

From the very beginning of her supernatural intercourse Josefa had been told to ask permission before entering into communication with her celestial visitors, and to give an account of what had passed immediately afterwards. She submitted to this control, which cost her nature very much. This gave her Superiors the possibility of writing down these divine appearances at once, noting the place and time of these messages, in the very words which she used to repeat, as if still under the ascendency of an invisible presence.

In this manner Our Lord's words were accurately recorded - words of which He had said that none of them were to be lost.

During her days of laborious work which left her little leisure Josefa was glad to hand over her papers to the secure keeping of her Superiors. When in the evening her labors were at an end, or during the freer hours of Sunday, she knew that the transcription of her notes was expected of her as part of her obedience. Leaving her needle, her sewing-machine or her broom, as the case might be, she went to her cell to complete this task, which always cost her a great deal. There, oftenest kneeling before a small table, she re-copied in her rapid if unskilled writing the notes that had been left in the care of her Mothers. The only additions she made were of facts which formed the setting to Our Lord's words, a few heartfelt comments and a more detailed avowal of her failings.

All these precious documents have been religiously preserved.

The principal facts of Josefa's life were published in 1938 in Un Appel à l'Amour, but the wish to know more than this slight biography revealed was expressed by many. The time seems to have come to give Josefa's writings more fully to a wider public. Perhaps this is also the best way of fulfilling the wishes of the Divine Heart. He wants the riches of His love and mercy to be known. He wants souls to understand to what an extent He condescends to live their ordinary life with them, so as to transform it into "days of divine life"; He thirsts for a union which our frailty need not interrupt, and above all He longs to let souls know how certain they are of His forgiveness, for all their weakness. But if He seeks their love and trust to this extent, it is because He wants to associate them with Himself by total surrender, that they may with Him carry out His work of love and redemption.

All this imprinted itself day by day and hour by hour on the life of Sister Josefa. If Our Lord imposed on her the duty of writing down in detail all He said to her, certainly it was not for her own benefit, since it entailed nothing but sacrifice. It was in order that many souls might gather from these pages the lessons and appeals of His Heart.

Since October 8th, the day on which she made her offering, Josefa had recovered her peace of soul, together with divine light. Her work had in no way been modified throughout this difficult period, and when Our Lord wanted her He always found her at her duties.

"Today, October 15th, "He said to me: 'Your misery attracts Me. What would you do without Me? Do not forget that the lowlier you become, the nearer I shall be to you. Let Me do as I please.'"

That same morning Josefa had renewed her act of total surrender into His hands by way of preparation for her Communion. No sooner had she done so than Jesus appeared and said: "I forgive you all; you are the price of My blood, and I intend to use you to save the many souls that have cost Me so dear; do not refuse Me anything. See how much I love you."

"As He said these words He enveloped me in the flame of His Heart and gave me great courage, for now I am no longer afraid of suffering; my one wish is to do His Will."

The Blessed Virgin strengthened her a few moments later:

" 'My daughter,' she said, 'you will never forsake my Son, will you?'

" 'No, Mother, never.'

" 'Do not be afraid of suffering, for you will always be given sufficient strength to bear it. Think of this: you have only today in which to suffer and love ... eternity will be all joy.'

"I begged her not to desert me, but to obtain for me from Jesus the fidelity I need. Then I asked her forgiveness, and she answered:

" 'Have no fear, Josefa; leave yourself in the hands of Jesus and constantly repeat this prayer: "O Father, merciful and good, look upon Thy child, and make her so entirely Thine own, that she may lose herself in Thy Heart. May her one desire, O Father, be to accomplish Thy holy Will." This prayer will please Him, for He wants nothing so much as surrender, and thus you will comfort His Heart. Do not fear, abandon yourself. I will help you.'

"It seems to me," commented Josefa, "that all that made me braver, and as I have now given myself over entirely into God's hands, nothing else matters.

"On the evening of Saturday, October 16th, I asked Him why He gave me so many totally undeserved graces. During my adoration I saw Him crowned with thorns and He gave me this answer: 'Have I asked you to merit the graces I give you? What I ask is that you should accept them. I will show you the School in which this lesson can be learned.'"

This School was about to open for Josefa.

"The very next day, October 17th," wrote Josefa, "I saw Him just as He was yesterday, His Heart all aflame and the Wound even wider. I adored Him with deep respect and asked Him to kindle a fire of love in my heart. He said: 'This is the School where you will acquire the knowledge of complete renunciation, and thus I shall be able to do with you what I will.'"

Josefa made a beginning in this science of all sciences; she had yet to learn how to make a complete surrender of herself to her Master, which would leave Him free to use her as He wished.

Two days of great loneliness of soul went by. She asked herself whether she had perhaps displeased Him... . She appealed to Him... . He came... .

" 'I love to hear you calling Me; I thirst so for love.'

"As He said these words, I understood that I had not so much as begun to love Him. I asked Him to teach me how to love Him. He made me listen to the beating of His Heart; then He said: 'If you are resolved to be faithful, I will pour into your heart the flood of My mercy and you will know what My love for you is. But always remember that if I love you it is because you are little, not because you are good.'"

Many a time this lesson of humility would be repeated, and while Our Lord enkindled in her heart a most vehement love of Himself, He constantly reminded her of her utter insignificance on the one hand, and on the other of the souls for whom He thirsts.

"Today at my prayer," she wrote, on Thursday October 21st, "I asked Him that souls may love Him, and I said: 'If it is love that Thou askest, Lord, attract many souls to this Society, for here they will learn to love Thy Heart.'

"During my thanksgiving, first I saw His Heart surrounded with thorns and with flames, which I take to be love; then I saw Him, extending His arms.He said: 'Yes, Josefa, all I ask of souls is their love, but they give Me only ingratitude; I should like to fill their souls with grace, but they pierce My Heart through and through. I call them and they turn away from Me ... if you accept, I will give you charge of souls, and by your sacrifices and love, you will win them for Me.'

"As He said these words, He again drew me close to His Heart; I heard Its mysterious beating; the sound filled me with a kind of agony. Then He went on to say: 'You know very well that I want you to be the victim of My love, but I will never leave you without help. Surrender yourself entirely to Me.'"

On Saturday, October 23rd, in a way peculiarly His own, He told her that her whole life was to be a dwelling in love as in its appropriate atmosphere. Josefa was working in the linen-room when suddenly He stood before her. There happened to be a great press of work at the moment, and she asked Him to allow her to remain at her task, at the same time begging Him to forgive her for the liberty she was taking... .

" 'For I would not willingly pain Thee, my Jesus' ... but He at once vanished. I was rather sorry for having said that to Him, and to comfort Him I kept on telling Him how I loved Him."

That evening she was on her way to the third story to close some windows, and as she walked along she constantly murmured her love for Him the thought of Whom never left her. "Suddenly as I reached the top-story corridor," she wrote, "I saw Him coming to meet me from the other end."

Jesus was surrounded with light so radiant and so lovely that it lit up an otherwise dark passage. He walked rapidly, as if eager to meet her.

" 'Where do you come from?'

" 'I have been closing the windows, Lord.'

" 'And where are you going?'

" 'I am going to finish doing so, my Jesus.'

" 'That is not the way to answer, Josefa.'

"I did not understand what He meant, and He continued: 'I come from love and I go to love. Whether you go up or down, you are ever in My Heart, for it is an abyss of love. I am with you.'

"As He disappeared, He left me in such joy that it is quite indescribable."

This exquisite little incident is remembered at Poitiers, for the dark passage goes by the name of The Corridor of Love.

But rare were the moments of consolation in Josefa's history at this period; she had to learn by experience what was the true significance of self-surrender and the value of souls.

"Wednesday, October 27th, during my evening adoration, she wrote, He came again and said: 'I want you to save souls... . Look at the fire of My Heart; it is the craving to save them that will burn up yours.'

" 'You will gain them by your offerings. Stay still in My Heart and fear nothing.'"

The day after He again appeared to her in the dolorous condition which made her write:

"Oh, how sorry I felt for Him... . He looked at me in such a way that I realized that my pain was but a shadow of His. I then saw behind Him an interminable file of souls, and looking at me significantly He said: 'All these are waiting for you ... you are free in your choice, Josefa, but if you truly love Me, you will not be afraid.'

"I again murmured how afraid I was these things might be noticed.

" 'What matter if they are? If so you can give glory to My Heart.'

" 'But I am only a novice, Lord!'

" 'I know that quite well, but only be faithful, and nothing of this will harm you. Do not fear.'

"Then I offered myself to His service, to be used just as He wills. "

'Yes, I shall make of you a victim, for you must resemble Me if you are to be My Bride, and can you not see what I am like?'

"I have not seen Him again since then."

Daily Precepts and Forgiveness (October 22nd-December 18th, 1920)

"I will seek you in your nothingness, to unite you to Myself."
(Our Lord to Josefa, November 8th, 1920)

Josefa's offering was to carry her still further on the way marked out for her by Our Lord.

More than ever she came to know experimentally what courage and confidence the Divine Will was to ask of her.

"I am so tempted, so cold, so unsettled," she wrote at the end of October, "that my vocation seems to have vanished - no faith left, all is black, and I so unfeeling. I offer this suffering to console His Heart and win Him souls, but this very thought continually brings to my mind what a life of infidelity I have led. When I see what I myself am, it seems presumption to pray for others. How helpless I am!"

It seemed to be Our Lord's will to leave her to herself for a while; though this abandonment was only apparent and nothing abnormal in the spiritual life. Coming as it did after the familiarities of love she had experienced shortly before, it threw her soul into a kind of confused distress to which she was as yet unaccustomed. Nevertheless, she reacted bravely and never ceased affirming a love which it was her determination to maintain faithfully, come what might.

"O my God," she wrote, "I want to comfort Thy Heart ... though I see nothing and feel nothing, yet I believe in Thee and I love Thee, and needless to add, I call on Our Blessed Lady all the time."

A week passed, but the temptation grew as time went on ... on Saturday, November 6th, Josefa woke up convinced that nothing was of any avail and that her vocation was lost. She tried hard to make acts of faith and trust.

"In the midst of this storm," she wrote, "I was able to repeat only these words: 'Jesus, Jesus, forsake me not.'

"My time of prayer was spent in this way. Then Mass; I went to Holy Communion, but could only call on Jesus to help me, and say over and over again: 'I believe that Thou art in the depths of my soul, O my God - indeed I believe it!' Suddenly I heard His answering voice: 'I am there!'

"At once peace returned to my tortured soul, and I saw Him. He was wearing His Crown of Thorns, and some little streamlets of blood coursed down His face. His Wound was wide open and His hands pointed to His Heart. 'O my Jesus, how lonely Thou hast left me ... and for so long ... and I was so tempted.'

" 'When I leave you so cold,' He said, 'I am using your warmth to give heat to other souls. When I leave you a prey to anguish, your suffering wards off divine justice when it is about to strike sinners. When it seems to you as if you did not love Me and yet you tell Me unceasingly that you do, then you console My Heart most. That is what I want: that you should be ready to comfort My Heart every time I need you.'

"I told Him that what most troubles me is the fear of having offended Him, for He knows well enough that I do not mind pain.

" 'Come, Josefa, do not be afraid, for you are never alone... . The lowlier and the more humble you are, the more you must be kept safe.'"

In the face of such divine assurances, Josefa could but repeat how feeble she knew herself to be, how great was her love, how whole-hearted her surrender... .

"I begged Him to give me the virtues I lack, especially humility. He interrupted me: 'I possess humility for your pride.'

" 'I am such a coward, so weak when I have to suffer... '

" 'Am I not strength itself?'

"Finally, I offered myself, keeping nothing back.

" 'That is well said, Josefa: nothing for yourself... you all for Me ... and I all for you. When I leave you alone and in agony, accept My Will, and abandon yourself to Love.'"

The next day, the Master of love further insisted, and repeated whilst showing Himself to her during her prayer (November 7th).

" 'Tell me that you love Me; that is what I like best to hear.'

"I answered that there was nothing that I wanted more than to love Him and that all other things called forth in me but a shadow of love."

" 'Yes, keep for Me the heart I have given you and seek for nothing but love. That is My wish. My Heart longs to burn and consume hearts in the glow of Its fervent love."

Jesus made known to her at the same time what were the exigencies of a love so impassioned as to consume gradually all that was still alive and imperfect in her nature. Her smallest faults seemed to her to be real infidelities, and in her self-reproach she continually implored forgiveness.

"On Monday, November 8th, while I was sweeping the stairs, I was telling Him how sorry I was for a stirring of impatience to which I had yielded in the morning, and which gave me great remorse. Near the bottom of the staircase I saw Him before me and He seemed to be searching for something. I finished the sweeping, then I followed Him to the Noviceship, and there He said to me: 'You must not grieve overmuch at your falls.Why, I could make a saint of you without more ado, but what I do ask of you is that you should never hold out against My Will. Do what

I ask you to do. Humble yourself, I will seek you out in your nothingness, and unite you to Myself.'"

Such clear directives throw ample light on the path Our Lord had chosen for Josefa. Humility was to make it secure and obedience would be her guiding star.

" 'If I give you these graces, it is because I trust in your fidelity and obedience to Myself and to Reverend Mother who represents Me. Abandon yourself to My care; I want you to become the victim of divine justice and the solace of My Love. I will immolate you, but with arrows of love. I will take you prisoner, but with cords of love. Fear nothing. You are deep down in My Heart. Abandon yourself to Me.'"

This divine action on her soul was one of trial, and all Josefa saw was her own frailty. Ten days of brave struggle followed, in which she fought through costly efforts to overcome long, obscure, and difficult temptations from within and without. "However," she commented on Friday, November 19th, "I do not think I offended Him, though the temptations were many."

Notwithstanding, when Jesus appeared to her during her adoration that evening, with His Heart torn and lacerated, she exclaimed:

" 'O my Jesus, is it I that have thus wounded Thy Heart?'

"He did not let me finish: 'It is not you, Josefa, but the coldness of those souls who make no return for My love. If you could but understand My sadness that My love meets with no return.'

"His Heart then became a living flame.

" 'See what your loving heart does to Mine, for though you feel cold and imagine you no longer love Me, it holds back My justice from punishing sinners. One single act of love in the loneliness in which I leave you repairs for many of the acts of ingratitude of which I am the object. My Heart counts and collects these acts of your love as a precious balm.'"

Her anguish was dispelled in the flame that blazed from the divine Wound, and even at times invested her.

"I prayed to Him for all those souls, begging of Him to make many of them know the goodness of His Heart and love Him.

" 'It pleases Me to see you famished for My love and burnt up with longing to see Me loved. That by itself is consolation to My Heart. Yes, pray for the souls of which I have given you charge. A few more sacrifices, and they will return to Me.'"

On Saturday, November 20th, He came to her, as a beggar, destitute and asking for love.

"Many little wounds were lacerating His Heart," she wrote.

" 'Tell Me, would you not attempt the impossible to comfort Me, Josefa?

... Share with Me for a moment the bitterness of My Heart.'

"Then helpless distress seemed to overpower my soul. He was still there, and gradually His Heart lit up, and all His wounds disappeared.

" 'Listen,' He said, 'I want you to give Me souls. Only love in all you do is required. Suffer because you love, work because you love, and above all abandon yourself to love. When I let you feel anguish of spirit and great loneliness, suffer in love. I want to make use of you as a tired man uses a stick to lean upon.... . I want to possess you, to consume you entirely, but all in great sweetness, so that enduring a martyrdom of love, you thirst to suffer more.'"

These visits always brought pain to Josefa, but though they at times baffled her, they never tired her generosity. "For the last few days," she wrote, "my soul is as it were immersed in fear, and weighed down by God's Justice ... shall I ever emerge from this abyss?"

Our Lord sustained her, nevertheless, and He made Himself manifest to her during Mass, on Sunday, November 21st.

" 'I come to rest in you, for I am so little loved,' He said. 'I am in search of love and meet only with thankless neglect. Rare are the souls that truly love Me.'

"I asked Him if this Noviceship did not comfort Him a little. Then to console Him, I offered Him the love of Our Lady, of the Saints, of all faithful souls, and even mine.

" 'Yes, Josefa, love Me and never tire of telling Me of your love.'"

She obeyed His instructions with all her heart, in spite of the dark night of desolation into which it was His Will to plunge her.

"I tried," she wrote next day, "to say over and over again 'My Jesus I love Thee.'

" 'And so do I love you,' she heard Him answer during her prayer.

"He came with no radiance round Him, looking like a beggar; I was silent. But as He continued to gaze sadly at me I ventured to speak, and I told Him how much I longed to comfort Him.

" 'Yes, do comfort Me, today; I will stay beside you all the time, so that you may not forget.'

"At the end of my prayer, as He did not go away, I said to Him: 'Lord, it is time for me to go to my sweeping, but Thou knowest that I love Thee, and that all I do is done solely to please Thee.'

"Twice in the course of my work He asked me again whether I loved Him. 'Say it often, to make up for the forgetfulness of so many.'"

That day, Monday, November 22nd, she spent entirely in that divine company.

"He stayed all the time," wrote Josefa; "we were not separated a single instant. From time to time He stopped me in my work, and once while I was sweeping the old cloister of Les Feuillants, with its primitive tiled pavement, He asked: 'Why are you doing that?'

"He seemed to take delight in the answer He forecast: 'Lord, I do it because I love Thee. See all the tiles of this corridor - as many times I say: I love Thee, Lord.'"

Later on she had to go and fetch some coal from the garden:

" 'What are you going to do?'

" 'I am going to try and prove my love for Thee, by all these little things.'

"He went on: 'Many souls think that love consists in saying: My God I love Thee. No, love is sweet, and acts because it loves, and all that it does is done out of love. I want you to love Me in that way, in work, in rest, in prayer and consolation as in distress and humiliation, constantly giving Me proofs of your love by acts; that is true love. If souls really understood this they would advance in perfection rapidly, and how greatly they would console My Heart.'"

Consciousness of the divine presence made Josefa anxious, lest the novices should notice her absorption when she was at work with them; it seemed to her impossible to give due attention to her work while in the presence of God's Majesty, which captivated and held her. "O my God!" she cried, "what will become of me? I am afraid of forgetting everything."

"A little before midday I asked Him if He would go, because I had to serve the children in the refectory.

" 'But, dear Lord, indeed I shall not forget Thee, while I do it.'"Jesus replied: 'Go and ask Mother what you must do. Tell her that I am with you; let us go together.'"

Docile as usual, she went in search of the Mother Assistant, and explained the case; but it was not possible to free her at that moment. She begged her Master's pardon for the refusal of the request. "It cannot be helped, Josefa, but you have made an act of humility and obedience."

Life together continued that afternoon. If Our Lord thus made Himself visible to Josefa, was it not that later on the faith of many souls should be revivified, that they should realize His invisible presence through grace which is so much more certain and authentic?

As for Josefa, the simplicity of her faith never rested on these favors; she feared them for herself and thought that those around her were bound to notice them. "Lord, how will all this end?" she said. "Thou seest how difficult I find it to attend to anything but Thy presence; something will be noticed... ."

" 'Look, Josefa, if a tiny child finds itself at the foot of a steep hill which it has to climb, and its father is at hand, do you think it will be allowed to fall?'

"These words gave me great confidence, and again I abandoned myself into His hands, that He might do with me whatever He willed."

That evening, Our Lord, who had not left her for a single moment that day, appeared to her during her adoration in the chapel:

" 'It gave Me great comfort today,' He said, 'that you never left Me, and it was your littleness that pleased Me. I must be present to you always, and the more helpless and lowly you find yourself, the surer you can be that I am pleased with you.'

" 'Do not forget that I shall be the divine torment of your whole being, and that you are the victim of My love; but I support you, and will not abandon you, if you are faithful.'

"Then He disappeared."

However, Our Lord did not allow her to rest in the thought of herself. The grace of His habitual presence had for its evident object to make the instrument He was forging adaptable and ready to His hand that He might use her for the salvation of the world. She was to be ever more occupied with souls.

"The next day, Tuesday November 23rd," she wrote, "I asked Him to give joy in His service to all the other novices, as He gives it to me.

"He came at once and said: 'Are you happy in suffering?'

" 'Yes, because it is for Thee that I suffer, Lord.'

" 'Will you carry the burden of other souls?'

" 'Yes, provided they love Thee, Lord.'

" 'Well then, you shall suffer because you are the victim of My love, but it must be in love and joy and peace in everything and always.'"

One day, about that time, Our Lord said to her: "I will join the fidelity of many other souls to yours." And for the first time - always in view of souls - He let her share with Him the pain of the Crown of Thorns.

"I was in the little chapel of Saint Stanislaus," - she wrote on Friday, the 26th of November. "He was asking me to comfort Him and I was thinking what I could do.

" 'I will leave you My Crown of Thorns for a few minutes, Josefa, and you will see what My suffering is.'

"At that instant I felt my head encircled with thorns, which pierced deep into it.

"Many times this same pain was renewed. So terrible was it that I was about to complain, but He said: 'Do not complain, for nothing will cure you of this pain; it is a share in My sufferings.'"

From that time on the Crown of Thorns became part of Josefa's life of reparation. Sometimes it signified her union with Our Lord crucified; at others the quota of pain apportioned to her love; at others again the sign of long-desired forgiveness. There would be times when it never left her forehead. But no outward mark of these mysterious mystical sufferings was visible. The pallor of her face, and the sorrowful expression in her eyes, alone betrayed the intensity of her pain. Her bowed head could find no rest either day or night. Efforts at relief could do no more than help her bear her heavy weight of pain. It was a continuation of her apprenticeship to Christ's redemptive work for which He had selected her. He gradually revealed to her His anxieties about the straying sheep of His fold, and His patient longsuffering which no delays rebut. Towards the end of November He gave into her charge a soul about which she wrote:

"Yesterday He came to the linen-room, where I was working. His Heart was wounded and His countenance was like that of the Ecce Homo.

" 'Till that soul comes back to Me,' He said, 'I shall come to ask you for the love she is refusing Me.'

"At about half-past one I followed Him to the dormitory where I sleep, and with profound respect, I adored Him.

" 'That you may better understand My sorrow, Josefa,' He said, 'I will make you share it.'

"Then my soul became a prey to sadness. Jesus stood there. He was silent. I comforted Him as best I could ... when He left:

" 'You have rested Me,' He said, 'because you have given Me love.'

"On Monday, the 29th," she again wrote, "He said to me during my prayer: 'I am leaving you My Crown of Thorns and you will offer Me the pain of it for that soul. If she delays, we shall unite our burning longings for her return. And this will solace My Heart.'"

But while telling her of His ardent hopes for the return of certain souls, Our Lord allowed her personally to experience the longanimity of His Heart. She knew her frailty, whenever she was left to her own resources.

"Words fail me to express my anguish," she wrote on the 29th of November. "My soul seems far, far from Him ... my body exhausted, my courage gone!"

She asked her Master how He could make any use of her in such a state of powerlessness and distress. "What I want," He answered her, "is that you should live so united to My Heart that nothing whatever can separate you from Me."

Again He appealed to her generosity:

" 'I want to rest in you; do not refuse to give Me what belongs to Me.'

"And there was I so afraid that I should not have time to do my work!

"And I said to Him: 'Lord, I shall be late for my employment.'

" 'Do you not know that I am the Master of your heart and of your whole being?'"

Did she really know it? She tried to escape from His appeal ... Jesus vanished, leaving her to her regrets. Many a time she would fail to take the path He pointed out to her, but these omissions were always followed by fresh forgiveness on His part. It was only through many struggles that she learnt the "science of abandonment."

Her love of common life would be to her to the very end a cause of repugnance and temptation. Her Master left her this battlefield on which to contend, that (so it would seem) He might have the joy of expending on her His longsuffering mercy.

"I have not seen Him again ... but I cannot live without Him ... and since He left me I have never stopped begging Him to forgive me," she wrote. "Yesterday, December 3rd, after my work, I went to the tribune and knelt before the Blessed Sacrament exposed: O my Jesus, I do not deserve to see Thee, but show me that Thou hast forgiven me. I stayed quite still. Suddenly all the temptations of the last few days vanished, and I felt round my head the Crown of Thorns."

This was a sign of coming pardon, to be followed by one of those scenes of loving-kindness, so revealing of the Heart of God.

"The next day, Saturday, December 4th, after my Communion, He stood before me, as a Father awaiting His child: 'Come and tell Me all you are afraid of,' and showing me His Heart: 'When you feel unable to bear pain, come here! If you are afraid of being humbled, come here! If you are seized with apprehension, come closer still!'

"I told Him that these graces frighten me, because I do not deserve them. 'I know you do not deserve them, but I only ask you to accept them.'"

So much compassionate kindness filled Josefa with amazement and desire. She would so like to correspond fully to it, and what she calls her ingratitude filled her soul with sorrow. Our Lady came to comfort her:

"She came," she wrote on Monday, December 6th, "while I was praying for forgiveness and true love.

" 'Daughter,' she said, 'you must not worry like this; you know all that Jesus is to you. Suffer in silence, but without this mental anguish. Love very much, but without introspection and without even knowing whether you love or not. If you fall, do not be afflicted above measure. We are both here to raise you up, and I will never forsake you.'

"I explained to her that my biggest trouble was that I could not follow common life in everything, and that I was so afraid of drawing attention to myself.

" 'Do not forget, Josefa, that it is for souls. If the devil is so desperately determined to make you give it all up, it is because he sees in you, as it were, a rivulet which in its course is going to carry many souls to Jesus.'

"I asked her to bless me and not to leave me all alone, because she can see how weak I am.

" 'Yes, I bless and love you.'"

The next day, December 7th, that gracious Mother came again:

" 'If you want to be a comfort to Jesus, I will tell you what gives Him pleasure: you must offer everything you do for souls, without any personal interest whatever, and act solely for the glory of His Heart.'"

And coming down to particulars, she suggested:

" 'Till I tell you to stop, say every day nine Aves, with your arms in the form of a cross. You must do this, humbling yourself, and recognizing your nothingness; at the same time adore the Divine Will, and leave your Jesus perfectly free to do exactly what He pleases with you. Confide in His Heart and in me who am your Mother.'"

A few minutes later Our Lord Himself once more affirmed the rights which His Mother had pointed out, and reminded Josefa of His plans for her.

"During my thanksgiving, He covered me with the flame of His Heart and said: 'I want you to leave Me to establish a current between your heart and Mine, in such a way that you are in Me, without living in any way for yourself.'

"He stayed for a few moments in silence, consuming my soul in the glow of that flame, then He added: 'I want you to help Me by your littleness and helplessness to snatch souls from the enemy who wants to devour them.'

"About midday, He appeared to me with a radiant countenance: 'Come and rest in Me and share My joy,' He said, 'another soul has come back to Me.'"

So as she went through a whole series of struggles, obscurities, and humble efforts, Our Lord re-animated her courage by showing her the fruits of her conflicts, and how He availed Himself of them.

The Feast of the Immaculate Conception was approaching, and Our Blessed Lady would not let it pass without lighting it up by her loved presence. As soon as it was daylight, as if in haste to comfort her, she appeared to Josefa.

" 'My child,' she said, 'never be afraid of suffering or of sacrifice; such are God's ways. If you want to come out victoriously from the assaults of the devil, pay great attention to two things: first, humble yourself, for you are nothing and deserve nothing ... everything comes to you as a grace from God. Second, when you feel lonely and given up to temptation, when your soul is cold and you have no courage to go on, do not give up prayer. Pray humbly and confidently, and go at once to seek guidance from her whom God has given you for that purpose. Believe me, child, if you do this, you will make no mistakes. Let me bless you, for I am your Mother.'"

Motherly counsels of this nature were the sure forerunners of greater trials, and already the devil was planning to counter God's designs, but Our Blessed Lady came to give her help.

On Friday, December 10th, she brought her the Crown of Thorns after her Communion, as a pledge of Our Lord's special love.

" 'See,' she said, 'I bring it to you myself, that it may be less hard for you.'

"She pressed it right down on my head, and I told her how much I dreaded these graces.

" 'If you refuse them, child, you will endanger your salvation. You will indeed suffer by accepting them, but you will never be left without help. I myself will never abandon you, as I am your Mother, and both of us will come to your aid.'"

The very next day, December 11th, Our Lord was to ask a fresh proof of her love. During her thanksgiving He spoke these words: "Today I will imprison you in My Heart. Look at the fire of My Heart ... but some souls are so cold that even that flame fails to warm them."

"I asked Him how it was that being in contact with His Heart they did not take on Its fire.

" 'It is because they do not come close enough,' He answered.

Then solemnly, so that every word was engraved deeply on her soul, He said: "Love is not loved: think of that, and you will not refuse Me anything I ask of you."

These luminous days were quickly merged in deepest night. That very evening Josefa felt a fresh wave of repugnance and terror rise in her soul for "all those things." Were they not a delusion? This idea took strong hold of her and soon reduced her to the deepest distress.

"From December 11th to the 17th I spent thus," she wrote, after describing the dark tunnel through which she had passed; "that evening I went to the chapel and said to Our Lord with my whole soul, 'Lord, do not allow me to be unfaithful to Thee. Thrust me deep down in Thy Heart, that I may die without ever having been separated from Thee.'

"That same instant Our Lord appeared, His Heart open and surrounded with flames: 'How can I put you deeper in My Heart than you are, Josefa? When you think you are far from Me, I am just thrusting you down deeper into It, that you may be safe.'"

And as if this assurance were insufficient, He revealed to her on the next day, Saturday, December 18th, what her affliction had wrought for souls. He appeared to her after Communion.

" 'I use your helplessness to save souls, Josefa, I want you to be the victim of this Heart. Do not refuse Me anything; comfort Me when I need comfort, and remember that I spared nothing to prove My love for you.'"

Nothing was now wanting to Josefa, surely, except perhaps encouragement from Our Lady, to guide her definitely towards a generosity that refuses nothing and does not spare itself in anything.

She appeared to her a few moments later:

" 'Child of my heart,' she said tenderly, 'I beg of you not to refuse my Son anything He asks of you. Not your happiness only, but that of many others depends on your generosity. Many souls will be the gainers by what you endure, so be faithful and abandon yourself wholly. If you but knew the value of a soul! You are unworthy of so many graces, as I have already said, but if God wishes to use your littleness, have you any right to hesitate?'

"I asked her to bless me; she put her hand on my forehead, and left me."

Invitation to Souls (December 19th, 1920-January 26th, 1921)

"It is My Will to use your suffering for the salvation of many souls."
(Our Lord to Josefa, January 25th, 1921)

Already five months had passed since Josefa had been clothed in the habit of religion, and all this time Our Lord's training had aimed at making her adaptable and supple in His hand. He had shown her the redemptive result of her struggles and suffering, as well as the effects her fidelity had on the salvation of souls.

She was to go forward, henceforth, strengthened by this twofold light and to understand more deeply the interests of the Heart of God.

On Sunday, December 19th, she heard the well-known voice calling: "Josefa!"

She looked about, but seeing no one, went on with her work; however, on reaching the bottom of the stairs near the chapel:

"I felt drawn somehow, and went up to the Noviceship. He was there, and from His Heart there gushed a stream of water. 'This is the tide of love, Josefa, for your martyrdom will be one of love,' He said.

Josefa's one ambition was to love Him and make Him loved, and she cried: "I will never again go back, O my God; I will suffer whatever Thou wilt, provided Thou dost never cast me out of Thy Heart."

" 'You console Me by saying that,' He answered with enthusiasm. 'I want nothing else from you. You may be poor, but I am rich; feeble, but I am strong. But I do ask you never to refuse Me anything.'

"Listen to My Heart beating ... each beat is for a soul I am calling.... I wait and wait in expectation of them. If they heed Me not, I will call again... I will wait for them with you. We shall suffer, but they will come, soon they will come."

So union in a common suffering drew them closer together. Our Lord constantly reminded her of His hopes and wishes, and often He timed His visits in the midst of Josefa's work.

"I was in the dormitory, making the children's beds, and telling Him all the while how much I loved Him," she wrote on Tuesday, December 21st, "when He came to summon me."

" 'Come. I want you.'

" 'I want you to offer yourself as a victim today, and that your whole person may agonize for those souls; humble yourself and ask pardon. I am with you.'"

Then, enveloping her with the fire of His Heart, He added: "Courage. I can give you no better gift than suffering. It is the selfsame road that I trod."

She now seemed to have fully understood the value of the gift, if one may judge from her progress since the day when Our Lord first asked her: "Do you love Me?" Now He was able to say: "Will you suffer?"

The day after He repeated: "Be on the lookout today for what costs and mortifies you most, and make as many acts of love as you can. How different souls would be if they knew this secret ... how dead to self they would become and how they would console My Heart."

Night and day Josefa offered herself for this intention. "I only ask Thee to give me fidelity and courage," she wrote, "for I have not the slightest desire to enjoy myself here below."

"I too ask you for one thing only: fidelity and abandonment."

And then He told her in detail what He required of her. "I want you to be like an empty vase, which I Myself will undertake to fill. Let your Creator care for His creature. As for love, let it be without measure."

That same evening He reminded her why He wanted to be able to count on "a love without measure."

"I was in the linen-room and I heard His voice: 'Josefa! My bride!'

"I could not see Him, but I answered: 'What wilt Thou, Lord?' ... Some time after, in the chapel during my adoration, He called me again: 'Josefa! My bride!'

" 'Why do You call me "bride," Lord? I am only a novice.'

" 'Have you forgotten the day when I chose you, and you chose Me? That day I had compassion on your littleness, and that you might not be left alone, we made a pact of mutual alliance forever. That is why you will have no other love than that of My Heart, and I will ask of you, and give you, whatever I like. Never resist Me.'"

Christmas night was to see the ratification of the divine choice, and Josefa heard for the first time the call that had brought the shepherds to the Crib, and like them she contemplated the "Great Little One" in His Mother's arms.

"During Midnight Mass," she wrote, "I was already in the middle of the chapel on my way up to Communion, when I saw Our Lady coming towards me. In her arms she was holding the Child Jesus, covered with a white veil which she took off as soon as I had communicated. His little garment was white and His hands were crossed on His breast. Then I did not see Him any more... . When I had reached my place in the chapel Our Lady came again quite close to me. She lifted the Holy Child slightly; He was lying in her arms. Little Jesus stretched out His hand and fondled His Mother. Then with His tiny right hand He seemed to be asking me for mine, and I gave it to Him. He seized hold of my finger and held it tight, and all around both of them floated an unknown but delicious aroma. Our

Lady was smiling: 'My daughter,' she said to me, 'kiss the feet of your God, Who will be your inseparable Companion if you wish. Have no fear, draw near, He is all love.'

"I kissed His little feet; He looked at me and then He crossed His hands on His breast and Our Lady wrapped Him once more in her veil. She looked at me and I asked her to bless me, which she did; and then they vanished.

"This time," commented Josefa, who had not lost her eye for dress designing, "Our Lady wore a white tunic, a very pale rose mantle, and a veil of the same color, but it was of much finer stuff; the Holy Child's raiment was of a material I had never seen before; it was as light as foam ... and an aura of radiance surrounded His head, and Our Blessed Lady had the same."

The radiant happiness of Christmas extended over the following days, and after having associated her with His redemptive sorrows, Our Lord made her share in His joys as Saviour.

The very next morning He appeared in all His beauty... and making allusion to the souls to whom He had appealed for a long time... "See my Beloved," He said, "We have saved them! Your pains have consoled My Heart."

A new experience of the predilections of His Sacred Heart still awaited her: on December 27th Saint John, the Beloved Disciple and sharer of graces like her own, appeared to her. During the short span of her religious life he would be several times the bearer of messages to her.

There is little variety in the form of Josefa's notes on these stupendous happenings. At that date we read in her papers:

"I was asking for love ... " (her usual petition) when after Communion Jesus, who always responds to this petition, even amid the gloom of faith (a fact she was quite aware of) today gave her a more tangible proof that He was attentive to her than was His wont:

"Jesus came," she said simply, "and I found myself as once before (on June 5th) in the Wound of His Heart... . He said nothing, but never before had my soul been so steeped in happiness. Then all vanished."

With no transition whatever, she adds: "That same evening Jesus left me all alone."

It is unnecessary to call the reader's attention to the method so often adopted by Our Lord with His little victim: brusquely He detaches her from the delights she has been experiencing, delights both supernatural and very pure. They are but a passing flash, destined to light up the arduous path by which she is rising heavenwards.

"The next day," she continued, "my soul was in such a state of coldness and aridity that I had to force myself to say even a few words to Our Lord. I did my best, and tried to make as many acts of love and confidence as possible. Soon I was unable to hold my own against the temptations which oppressed me."

She noted humbly every detail of these struggles, in the midst of which it seemed to her that her courage must suffer shipwreck. Though the devil's assaults varied little as to their object, being always directed against her vocation, they were nevertheless so acute that she was badly shaken.

"I was thus tempted from December 27th to January 9th," she wrote, "suffering more than I can say. That morning, on awaking, I thought it impossible to go on with the struggle, and the same inexpressible anguish continued during my prayer."

In spite of her distress, she never failed to seek the encouragement she needed in obedience, which alone could defend her, and with touching fidelity she did her best to follow advice which aimed at keeping her safe for God, and relieving her affliction.

"I promised Our Lord to make as many acts of humility as I could, so as to draw down His mercy on me, and during Mass at the Consecration, with all the determination I could muster, I once more made my offering. Suddenly, even before the Elevation of the Chalice, I saw Jesus: His face was so kind, His Heart so ardent. I prostrated myself at His feet to beg His forgiveness and to humble myself.

" 'Love never tires of forgiving!' He said.

"And with gentlest compassion He added: 'But you have not offended Me, Josefa. The blind stumble as you say... . Come, draw near My Heart and rest awhile. I wish you could realize how much you have comforted Me these last days ... and all the time I held you so close to My Heart that had you fallen it could have been only into Its depths.'

"I asked Him why He allowed such darkness and temptations."

" 'It seems to you that you see nothing and that you are about to fall into the precipice. But need you see, if you are guided? ... What you need is to forget self, to abandon your own will and offer no resistance to My plans. Thanks to the acts done in the midst of your sufferings, several of the souls that you will see later have come nearer to My Heart.'"

Our Lord was here alluding to the souls He had been calling when He made her listen to His Heart beating on the preceding 19th of December.

"I then explained to Him that when I am thus tempted and lonely I look everywhere for Him and cannot find Him.

" 'When you cannot find Me, look for Me in your Mother. Follow her directions implicitly, for she will guide you to Me. I gave her to you for that very purpose; and know, Josefa, that if you do what she tells you, you are giving Me as much satisfaction as if you were obeying Me personally. Love, suffer, and obey. So doing you will enable Me to carry out My plans in you.'"

That very evening, in a charming object-lesson, such as He loves to give simple souls, Our Lord renewed recommendations which were very dear to His Sacred Heart.

As she was praying before the Tabernacle, He appeared to her, "holding in His hand," she wrote, "a little chain of brilliants which held three small golden keys, very pretty ones."

" 'Look,' He said, 'one ... two ... three ... they are of gold. Do you know what these keys represent? ... each of them guards a treasure that I want you to secure.

" 'The first is complete surrender of will to all I ask of you, directly or indirectly, steadfastly trusting the goodness of My Heart that always takes care of you. You will repair in this way for the sins of many who doubt My love for them.

" 'The second is a profound humility which consists in knowing that you are nothing, in humbling yourself before all your Sisters, and when I tell you to do so, asking your Mother to humiliate you. Thus you will repair for the pride of many souls.

" 'The third is great mortification in your words and actions. I want you to mortify yourself corporally as much as obedience allows, and to receive with real joy the sufferings I send you. This will repair for the immortification of many, and will console Me in some measure for the sins of sensuality and illicit pleasures of the world.

" 'Lastly, the little chain on which the three keys are strung is an ardent and generous love, which will help you to live abandoned, confidingly trustful, humble and mortified.'"

Josefa never forgot the three symbolic keys. Many a time Our Lord would give her just such a simple object-lesson. They abound in the Gospels, and contain very deep and profound teaching.

But the hours in which Josefa was to find rest became more and more rare. From now on they were seldom granted her, and were of short duration. Our Lord kept before her mind the thought of the souls He had entrusted to her. This work was of prime importance in her life. "Do not tire of suffering," He often repeated. "If you only knew how greatly it profits souls."

Before long He sent her the suffering she most dreaded; she had had it before, and it would often be renewed. "I do not ask Him to take away my pain," she wrote, "but only to give me strength to bear it."

A violent storm of doubt and obsessions clouded her soul. Then, as if it gave her some relief, to hide nothing of her weakness and failings,1 her notes became longer and more circumstantial.

"Monday, January 24th," she wrote. "All day I have been begging Our Lady to deliver me ... and quite suddenly during my adoration in the evening, I recovered my peace of soul."

She stood there, smiling with motherly tenderness.

" 'Here I am, daughter,' she said.

" 'It is right, Josefa, that you should endure these temptations; but love and suffering can obtain anything... . Do not weary of them ... it is for souls.'"

Our Lady disappeared, but her coming had been as the dawn announcing the luminous advent of Jesus, who Himself brought Josefa the assurance that nothing was changed between them.

"On Tuesday, January 25th, He came at the beginning of Mass. I asked Him if I had wounded His Heart. He knows only too well that nothing else matters to me... .

" 'No,' He answered tenderly. 'Ponder this word: "Gold is purified in the fire." So tribulation purifies and fortifies the soul, and the time of temptation is of great profit both to you and to souls.'"

Encouraged by so much compassion, she confided her greatest anxiety to Him: the most painful torment of the days of trial she had undergone. "The fear," she said, "that such struggles would end by putting my vocation in peril."

"Who could doubt of your vocation, Josefa, if you have been able to withstand such tribulations? ... I allow them for two ends," He said, divining the thought that was in her mind. "First, to convince you that when alone you are incapable of anything, and that the graces I give you spring only from My goodness and the great love I bear you; and secondly, because I want to use your sufferings for the salvation of many souls.

"You will suffer to gain souls, because you are the chosen victim of My Heart, but you will come to no harm, for I will not allow it."

To this promise, in which she had perfect faith, she responded by a fresh offering of her whole being. The next day, January 26th, He again insisted on the necessity of suffering:

"During adoration He came," she wrote. "He made me listen to the beating of His Heart. I asked Him to keep me faithful, to teach me to love Him and never to allow me to cause any sorrow to His Heart. He seemed to like that prayer and said to me: 'The soul that loves wants to suffer, for suffering increases love. Love and suffering unite a soul closely to God and make her one with Him.'"

And when she reminded Him of her frailty: "Have no fear, I am strength itself. When the weight of the Cross seems more than you can bear, have recourse to My Heart."

Then He told her where to look for His Heart: "Do you not know where I am to be found, and in complete security? ... Accept the guidance you are given. My eyes are ever on you, fix yours on Me and abandon yourself."

Hidden Life in Fervor (January 27th-February 21st, 1921)

"Tell Me what offerings you can give Me for souls."
(Our Lord to Josefa, February 20th, 1921)

Lent and the Quarant'ore were at hand, and everyone at Les Feuillants felt them to be an invitation to an increase in love and reparation. These latter were becoming more and more Josefa's habitual aim, for Our Lord unceasingly put before her the fact that she was the victim of His Heart; He was now about to give her proofs of it.

The First Friday of February was the anniversary of her arrival at Poitiers. Jesus appeared to her, and showing her His Heart all aglow, He said: "Every Friday, and especially on the first of the month, I will make you share in the bitterness of My Heart, and you shall endure the torments of My Passion in a special way."

" 'In these days when Hell opens to engulf so many I want you to offer yourself as a victim, so as to save the greatest possible number of souls.'

"He stayed a few minutes more, but in silence, and then vanished."

The Sunday of the Quarant'ore, February 6th, He renewed the same appeal to Josefa. From early morning she had offered herself to repair the offenses of sinners, and at about three in the afternoon, Our Lord appeared to her in the chapel.

"What compassion I felt for Him," she wrote. "His face, His arms, His breast were covered with dust, and blood flowed from His head, but His Heart was shining and beautiful.

" 'It is the want of love that wounds Me thus,' He said, 'and the contempt of men who run like madmen to perdition.'

" 'Why then, Lord, is Thy Heart so lovely and so glowing, in spite of the sins of men?'

" 'My Heart is never wounded unless it be by My chosen souls.'"

This answer touched Josefa deeply, and unveiled to her the most intimate of His sorrows; and often He was to ask her to share it and console Him. But today she was made responsible to God's Justice for the flighty and guilty world. She spent before the Blessed Sacrament which was exposed, every minute of leisure left her by her work, and the thought of so many offenses against the Divine Majesty never left her mind.... . Jesus, who had laid this weight upon her, came, however, to uphold her courage, and on February 8th, in the chapel at dusk, she saw Him as if weighed down by a heavy burden.

"The sins committed are so many and so grave," He said, "that the wrath of My Father would overflow were it not for the reparation and love of My consecrated brides.... . How many souls are lost!"

"But one faithful soul can repair and obtain mercy for many ungrateful ones."

These words brought to Josefa's mind the expiatory mission to which, from the first, Love had invited her. But little by little another plan was to become apparent, first intimated to Josefa on Ash Wednesday, which fell on the 9th of February.

Then, for the first time, Jesus entrusted her with His full plan: "The love I bear for souls, especially for yours, is so great that I can no longer contain the flames of burning charity that consume Me, and so in spite of your unworthiness and helplessness, I mean to make use of you to accomplish My plans."

The appeal, with its full implications of the gift of self and total surrender, was to become clear to Josefa only very gradually. But already the Master asked her consent; and a tangible sign was to seal her acquiescence.

" 'Will you give Me your heart?' He asked.

" 'Yes, gladly, and more than my heart, Lord.'

"Jesus took it from me and placed it close to His own. How small it looked beside His! Then He gave it back to me, all on fire.

"Since then I feel within me a consuming flame, and I have to make very great efforts to control myself, lest anything should appear outwardly."

Josefa decided to keep secret this signal grace which she so simply narrates, but Jesus would have no secrets, and on Thursday, February 10th:

" 'Now, listen, Josefa,' He said, 'I do not want you to hide anything from your Mother. She is right; you must tell her all.'"

Two days later He again impressed on her how much He held to her absolute dependence. "Tell your Mother everything," He insisted.

And as she feared even the shadow of hidden self-complaisance in relating such things ... He interrupted her vehemently: "It would be pride if you kept silence. Humility lies in simplicity and lowliness. Know for certain that if I ask you one thing and your Mother asks another, I prefer you to obey her rather than Me."

We find noted on February 12th a long parenthesis regarding her reaction at each of Our Lord's visits:

"In order to obey you, Mother, I will write down what I feel each time Jesus comes: First, an intense desire to humble myself. I always begin by asking His pardon for all my sins, for I see my soul all soiled and besmirched ... and if it were not for an irresistible attraction that impels me forward, I should not dare approach or speak, when in His Divine

Presence. I cannot say how it is that I am drawn ... my soul is in peace ... the more I try to humble myself, the better it seems to please Him. Sometimes, I am not able to utter a word, I am annihilated in adoration. At other times, it is like a torrent of consolation, even when He makes me suffer with Him. My heart as it were expands and loses itself in God. Again, at other times, I feel as if a furnace were kindled within me; Jesus burns me up in the fire of His Heart. At the same time, He makes me see my littleness so keenly that it passes my understanding how a God can love so lowly a creature as I, and my yearning to love Him grows and grows, and I want to gain souls for Him. I feel such a horror of myself that I cannot think what to do to root out my evil inclinations, and repair for my sins and ingratitude. It, so to speak, wrests my soul from earth and I find the greatest difficulty in settling down again to my daily occupations. I wish I could make you understand the agony of finding myself once more in my poor body, for often, when I am with Him, I think this union is going to last forever."

A little later, and still under obedience, she explained how she had accustomed herself to do everything with Our Lord, and to tell Him everything.

"On Monday, February 14th, I was serving in the refectory at midday, as I always do. There was not enough of the first course. I went to the kitchen, and there was no more... . I didn't know what to do ... and as I am accustomed to talk over everything with Him, I said at once: 'My Jesus, there is nothing more to eat.' ... On coming out of the refectory a second time, I suddenly caught sight of Him. He was near the taps in the kitchen; He stretched out His arms and smiled as He said: 'Is it My fault, Josefa, that there is no more?' ...

"He vanished at once, and I don't know how I ever went on serving, for He was so dear, so lovely ... it was like Heaven ...

"That is how I talk to Him of everything that happens. If I am sweeping and drop something: 'O my Jesus ... what a noise. I shall wake Thee.' If I lose my things, I ask Him: 'Where did I leave it, Lord? ... Let us go and look for it together.' When I am tired I tell Him. If I am late for my work, which often happens, for I have to go so many journeys because of all the things that I forget, then I say to Him: 'Come now, Lord! We must hurry today, for it is late and there is much to do,' especially on Saturdays, when I have to distribute the bundles of clean linen and the shoes in the children's dormitories. In short, I tell Him all my fears. There are times when I do not see Him, but I talk to Him, knowing that He is there. Some days I tell Him everything that comes into my head. Sometimes I ask myself if I am not wanting in respect, but I don't think so, because I am so happy, and I find myself at it again in no time.

"Often, too, I call Our Blessed Lady, especially when I sit down to sew: 'Mother, do come and join us two,' I say. 'Jesus is here, so you ought to be here, too.'

"That is how I spend my days. I have explained everything, I think, as well as I can."

These heavenly exchanges did not prevent Josefa from leading the most simple and laborious life with the other novices.

After her Postulantship, during which she had been helping in the kitchen, she was assigned care of the school linen-room. Les Feuillants had not yet completely recovered after its use as an ambulance during the war, so there was little to facilitate the work to which she devoted most of her time and energy. She shared, too, in all the common labors of the house, without ever betraying God's special hold on her true life, which was concealed by her perfect self-forgetfulness.

We must therefore continue to follow her in the obscurity of common life and daily labor.

One little happening which occurred just about this time should not be left unrecorded.

"I was praying before the Tabernacle for my mother and sister. I was sad about them, and should have loved to be able to console them, and I thought of what I would do if I were at home, and I was not counting enough on my Jesus ... when suddenly He came with His Heart glowing, and in a grave, solemn voice He said to me: 'What could you do alone for them?' and showing me His Heart: 'Fix your attention here,' and He disappeared.

On Sunday, February 20th, she wrote: "During Mass, after the Consecration, Jesus came, so entrancingly beautiful (hermosisimo)." She is fond of this superlative, which is the least inadequate expression she can find.

" 'Tell Me what you have to offer Me for the souls I have confided to you. Put it all in the Wound of My Heart, so that your offering may acquire an infinite value.'

"I told Him that He could take everything, for all I do is for these souls.

" 'Tell it to Me in detail.'

"Then I began an enumeration of everything: my Holy Hour, my little mortifications and penances, the suffering of the Crown of Thorns, every breath I draw, my work, my fears, my weakness and nothingness, everything I do and think ... 'It is all for love and for souls, Lord, and it is little indeed.'

"At nine-o'clock Mass He came back, with His Heart aflame.

" 'Look,' He said, 'these souls are safe now, deep in My Heart.'"

The next day, after Communion, Jesus appeared to her, and gazing at her with unbounded love, He told her once again what He wanted of her: "I want you to be so forgetful of yourself and so abandoned to My Will that I shall be able to warn you of your slightest imperfections, for I will allow none in you. You must never lose sight, on the one hand, of your nothingness, and on the other, of My mercy. Never forget that it is from your nothingness that My treasures will be poured forth."

During the morning of Monday, while she was putting the dormitory in order and collecting the children's Sunday uniforms, Our Lord showed Himself to her with His hands bound and His Sacred Head stained with blood from the Crown of Thorns.

" 'Do you love Me?' He asked her eagerly.

"I don't know what answer I gave ... I said a hundred thousand things ... He knows very well that I love Him ...

" 'Listen, Josefa! I want your thirst for souls to grow and I want you to save many of them ... and I want you to be burnt up with this longing.'"

Love's Designs (February 22nd-March 26th, 1921)

"The world does not know the mercy of My Heart! I intend to make it known through you."
(Our Lord to Josefa, February 24th, 1921)

The time for a more solemn appeal had come, and on Thursday, February 24th, during her evening adoration, Josefa heard Our Lord say:
"Tomorrow you will offer My Father all your actions united to the Blood shed in My Passion. Try not to lose sight of the Divine Presence one single instant, and rejoice as far as possible at anything you have to suffer. Do not cease thinking of souls ... of sinners.... . O! how I thirst for souls!"

Already He had told her that He wanted each Friday to be a day of offering and of closer union with His Heart. This was a reminder.

"I offered myself to comfort Him and to win souls ... 'but, O Lord, do not forget that I am the most ungrateful and miserable of them all.'

" 'I know it,' He said, 'but I am training you.'

"He went away ... I made an act of self-surrender, to do all He wished, and I understood that He meant to take me at my word: 'O Jesus, I know that Thou wilt have pity on me, and that Thou wilt give me the strength I need ... ' In the evening, during Holy Hour, I was thinking of sinners and of how many there are ... but also of how much greater His mercy is ... suddenly He stood before me, and with a voice of great majesty, as might be a king's, He said to me: 'The world does not know how merciful I am; I am going to use you to make it known."

Fear took hold of Josefa, and she cried out:

" 'But, dear Lord, do not forget how weak I am, and that the smallest obstacle makes me fall... .'

"As if He had not heard, Jesus continued: 'I want you to be the apostle of My goodness and mercy. I will teach you what this means; forget yourself.'

"I implored Him to have compassion on me, and to leave me without these graces to which I am unable to correspond, and to choose other and more generous souls.

"Jesus only answered by these words: 'Do you forget, Josefa, that I am your God,' and He vanished."

There was no offense to His Heart, however. He knew that in the very depths of her will she was all His, that her very fears were the expression of her humble distrust of self, and with this He was never displeased.

The next day, Friday, February 25th, He returned during Mass:

"He looked at me," she wrote, "and I begged to be left like all the other novices, without any extraordinary happenings, for I cannot exist as things are now.

" 'If you cannot, Josefa, I can.'

" 'But I do not want to,' she ventured to murmur timidly. 'I so want to be like everybody else.'

" 'But I will it to be so. Does that not suffice you?'

"Then He added firmly: 'Where is your love?' ...

" 'Love, and have no fear. I want what you do not want, but I can do what you cannot do. It is not for you to choose, but to surrender.'"

How many struggles this surrender was going to cost Josefa's soul... . God no doubt allowed them to prove the authenticity of His action with greater certainty, and to dispose of any doubts entertained by those around her. It can be truthfully said that Josefa never ceased dreading her mission, and the three years to come would be punctuated by the terrors that assailed her every time she was asked to surrender.

A few days after that memorable date of February 25th, 1921, with confusion she notes that she drew back before the costly act of transmitting the message that Jesus gave her.

Then, she adds, He disappeared... .

The measure of Josefa's sorrow after such a parting is not difficult to imagine. She tried at first to hide it. But the arch-fiend seized his chance of making capital out of the silence that now fell on her soul. He persuaded her that it was all lost and that further efforts were useless. The word "martyrdom" which she used seems not too strong a term to fit the situation - that diabolic influence which God allowed the powers of darkness in that awful hour. "O! Mother, what a martyrdom!" she wrote a few days later. "I could bear no more... had I not been restrained by faith, I know not what I should have done... ."

Then in great detail she related her humiliating struggle and continued:

"The evening of March 3rd I went to ask you to forgive me, as I had already been to Jesus, and I began to see things differently... . I know that He will forgive me again, for I know His Heart... .

"During Holy Hour, for it was Thursday, I threw myself at His feet ... I do not know what I said to Him, but I felt relieved, although my soul remained as cold and stony as ever."

The next day, the First Friday of March, peace and light began to return, though the devil made one last effort which he hoped would settle the matter. Josefa was in the garden, picking flowers for the chapel, of which she was sacristan, when suddenly she was given a violent push, and falling on a glass frame, it broke under her weight. A stream of blood flowed from her right arm, which was deeply lacerated. The hemorrhage yielded to the treatment instantly applied, but her arm remained useless for several days. During that time (ever faithful to obedience) she dictated the notes she was unable to write herself. They were as follows:

"In the middle of my adoration Our Lady came, so kind and so compassionate, with open arms, like a mother. I begged her pardon, and asked her if I should still be able to console Jesus and gain souls for Him." (This was always her first and greatest anxiety.)

" 'For, knowing His Heart, I have no doubt that He will forgive me.'

" 'Yes, daughter, you are forgiven - infernal fury will lay many more traps for you ... but take courage, you will not fall into them.'

"And giving me her blessing, she disappeared."

This celestial visit was again renewed a couple of days later, March 11th:

"I was praying to Our Lady and telling her how much I wished Jesus would forget the past, when suddenly she appeared... . She was all sweetness, her hands crossed on her breast. I knelt down and she said at once: 'Jesus loves you, daughter, just as much as before, and He wants you to gain souls for Him.'"

Then, in allusion to Josefa's wounded arm: "The devil would have killed you, if he had been able to do so, but he was not able."

Jesus Himself came very soon to reassure His child, and to tell her that nothing could change His love or His choice.

Passiontide gave Josefa the chance she coveted of repairing and of participating in the sufferings of her Master.

On March 14th, Monday in Passion Week, He came to her after Communion.

"His glance was penetrating, but full of pity. His way of looking at me made so great an impression on me and said so much... .

" 'I cannot resist your misery any longer,' He said.

"Then, after a moment's silence: 'Do not forget that it is your nothingness and littleness that act as magnets to attract Me to you.'

"That same evening, when I was in the chapel and still under the impression of the look He had cast on me, He suddenly came.

"He had never looked on me like that before, and I think His eyes made me see in one instant all that He had done in me ... and what I had done for Him, alas! so little, returning His love by ingratitude ... but that glance also told me that nothing of it all mattered if I was determined to be faithful, for He was always ready to show me His love and give me fresh graces. All this was present to my mind and I never stopped asking His forgiveness and promising never to resist Him again."

It was the first time that Josefa had drawn special attention to the forceful glance of Our Lord.

" 'See, Josefa, I am still interceding for souls and forgiving them,' He said.

"He glanced at me for a moment with the same searching look as in the morning. It said so much, there was no need for words. Neither did I say anything. After a moment He spoke: 'Do you know all I have done for you?'

"Then I saw again all His graces and my ingratitude. I told Him of my determination to do not only all He asks, but all that I know He would like me to do, and this came from the bottom of my heart. As I spoke, His Heart changed entirely. It expanded, flames issued from the wound and His face shone with bright effulgence. Then He said: 'I will make you taste the bitterness of My Passion and you will suffer in some degree the outrages inflicted on My Heart. You will offer yourself to My Father in union with Me to obtain pardon for many sinners.'

"He looked at me again, as if to give me courage, and departed."

It had become a real necessity for Josefa to implore forgiveness, after her recent failings, and she did so incessantly; Our Lord never resisted these appeals.

"On March 15th, Feast of the Five Wounds, I was still asking Him to pardon me, when, after Communion, as a flash He passed before me, stopped one instant, and said only: 'Love blots out everything.'"

This lesson became more and more deeply imprinted on her mind. She lived on it during her work. That morning, being in the loft preparing linen for the laundry:

"As my one desire is reparation," she said, "I asked Our Lord to save as many souls as there were handkerchiefs to count. I offered my whole day for this object, uniting my sufferings to His Heart and to His merits.

"Towards nightfall, a little before my adoration, I went into the chapel of the Blessed Sacrament, where Our Lord was exposed, and He appeared.

" 'If you concern yourself with My glory,' He said, 'I will look after you. I will establish My peace in you so that nothing will be able to trouble you; I will set up in your soul the reign of My love, and your joy none shall take from you.'

"He came close to me. His wound opened. Then I saw a long line of souls prostrate in adoration, and I understood that all these were the souls I had begged of Him that morning.

The 17th of March, Thursday in Passiontide, was the twentieth anniversary of Josefa's First Communion. This was a date she never allowed to pass unnoticed, and she wrote in her notes: "Twenty years today since Jesus chose me for Himself, and never have I been less worthy of His love."

Then she humbled herself at the thought of so many graces to which she had not corresponded enough, but she added at once:

"I decided that I must make a complete change, and while I was making this firm resolution Jesus, with open arms, appeared before me and in His most endearing voice said to me: 'Yes, Josefa, I did indeed call you that day, and since then I have never forsaken you. I have kept you inseparable from Myself. How often you would have fallen had I not been your support... . Today, I once more reiterate My choice: I want you to belong entirely to Me ... to be faithful to Me ... and to respond to My love. I shall, in exchange, become your Bridegroom and I shall love you as the privileged bride of My Heart. I take on Myself all the labor; you will have only to love and abandon yourself. Your littleness is nothing to Me, and even your falls; My blood wipes them all away. All you need do is to rely on My love and surrender yourself.'"

But the divine predilection always brought Josefa back to one thought, that of the salvation of souls.

On March 22nd, Tuesday in Holy Week, after Communion, Jesus showed Himself to her, His arms extended. She took courage at what she termed "the immense kindness of her Master."

"I should like to ask Thee for many things, Lord," she said.

"Do you not know what is written in My holy Gospel? 'Ask and you shall receive.'"

"Then I implored Him to have compassion on the whole world and to enkindle it with the fire of His own love."

" 'Ah! if only they knew My Heart... mankind is ignorant of Its mercy and goodness: that is My greatest sorrow.'

"I begged Him to set souls on fire with zeal for His glory, to increase the number of priests, and to call many into religious life... . I stopped at last ... but in the silence that ensued I still whispered to Him how much His glance said to me ... and what confidence it gave me. Afterwards He showed me His hands and made me kiss His Wounds. Then He departed."

Such records suffice to show to what extent the burning zeal of the Heart of Jesus already consumed that of Josefa. Souls had become the aim of her life, and her converse with Our Lord in each of these divine visits was always about them.

During meditation on Spy Wednesday, March 23rd, she asked Him in her prayer what exactly He meant by "saving souls."

"He came," she said, "and looked at me with great affection. He replied: 'There are some Christian souls and even very pious ones that are held back from perfection by some attachment. But when another offers Me her actions united to My infinite merits, she obtains grace for them to free themselves and make a fresh start.

" 'Many others live in indifference and even in sin, but when helped in the same way, recover grace, and will eventually be saved.

" 'Others again, and these very numerous, are obstinate in wrongdoing and blinded by error. They would be damned if some faithful soul did not make supplication for them, thus obtaining grace to touch their hearts, but their weakness is so great that they run the risk of a relapse into their sinful life; these I take away into the next world without any delay, and that is how I save them.'

"I asked Him how I could save a great many.

" 'Unite all you do to My actions, whether you work or whether you rest. Unite your breathing to the beating of My Heart. How many souls you would be able to save that way.'"

The last days of Lent associated Josefa more intimately with the sufferings of Calvary. For the first time she followed her Master step by step through the Passion, and on Good Friday, March 25th, she was constantly brought back to His suffering Presence.

"When I had finished my sweeping I went upstairs to visit Our Lady in the Noviceship," she wrote. "I had hardly entered when Jesus came. His hands were bound, and His head crowned with thorns, His face all soiled with blood and bruises. He fixed His eyes on me with supreme sadness, and then vanished."

"At three that afternoon," she wrote, "I saw Him again. He showed me the Wound in His side and said: 'Behold the work of Love.'

"His wound opened and He continued: 'It opens for mankind - for you ... come ... come nearer ... and enter.'"

The Mother of Sorrows put her seal on the graces of the day by one of those revealing words so peculiarly her own. At five that evening Josefa was in the oratory of the Noviceship:

"There, in wordless prayer, I sat at Our Lady's feet and in spirit went through all that I had seen and understood that day. Suddenly I became aware that she was present. Clothed in a very dark purple tunic and veil, she held in her hands the Crown of Thorns, all covered with blood; she showed it to me, saying: 'On Calvary, Jesus gave me all men for my sons; come then, for you are my child. Have you not already realized to what an extent I am a mother to you?'

"I asked her leave to kiss the Crown of Thorns, and as she gave it to me, she put her hand on my shoulder and said: 'O how I love to think of Him as He bequeathed those souls to me.'"

With the morning of Holy Saturday, March 26th, this series of graces came to an end, closed by a heavenly favor that left an ineffaceable stamp on Josefa's soul. "Do you know why I give you these graces in such abundance?" Our Lord asked of her, appearing to her during her prayer, His wounds all glowing. He repeated what He had once said in almost identical terms to Saint Margaret Mary: "I want to make of your heart an altar on which the fire of My love will burn constantly. That is why I want it pure, and that nothing that can stain it should touch it."

"He vanished," said Josefa, "and I went down to the chapel for Mass. After Communion I felt as if in Heaven. I saw within me, as on a resplendent throne, three Persons clothed in white. They were all three exactly alike, and so beautiful! My soul was in such delight that it was like fire which consumed without burning it, pure joy. Then all faded away."

This interior grace was renewed on the 5th of April following. A marvelous peace pervaded Josefa's whole being in the Presence of the Three Persons. She tried to explain, in terms of singular simplicity, what passed in her soul and apparently was ignorant of the import of so signal a grace.

"Ordinarily," she said, "I am enveloped in the Divine Presence, and even when I enter into the Heart of Jesus I am immersed in Him. But on these last two occasions at the moment of Communion it was more like an amazing feast being celebrated within my soul. Jesus entered into me as if into His palace. I cannot explain it... and as I was most determined to surrender myself completely into His hands, to do exactly as He wished with me, it was like Heaven."

It is not difficult to conceive how, after such contacts, Josefa had to do great violence to herself to attend immediately to the work that awaited her. This effort, so impossible to gauge, often gave a loophole to the arch-enemy, and he hastened to avail himself of it.

Opposition from the Devil (March 27th-May 31st, 1921)

"The devil will work assiduously to make you fall, but My grace is more powerful than his infernal malice."
(Our Lord to Josefa, April 6th, 1921)

The months that followed on the Lent of 1921 saw a recrudescence of the devil's attacks. Nothing extraordinary at first revealed his presence. Temptations cleverly exploited Josefa's attractions and repugnances concerning the path into which little by little Jesus was leading her.

His incomparable fidelity and the sway that His Holy Mother held over her continued to protect, pardon, and direct her whenever she swerved from the right way, as undoubtedly she did more than once.But she learnt the searching lesson she was to pass on to us one day: that love knows how to use even our failings for the salvation of souls. Josefa bowed with difficulty to the influence of divine graces, coming as they did in the midst of her very laborious life which she loved so dearly; and on March 27th, Easter Sunday, she wrote:

"This morning at my prayer, I complained a little to Our Lord, because He keeps my mind so concentrated on Himself that I cannot apply myself to my work ... and there is so much work to be got through! I wonder if I should not be more in my own sphere elsewhere."

She had hardly finished her plaint than Jesus appeared with a look of sadness on His face:

" 'Why do you complain, Josefa, after I have drawn you to so special a share in My Heart's work ...

"He spoke these words very forcibly, and vanished."

She had to wait several days before she saw Him again, keeping, meanwhile, the memory of that sadness on the divine countenance which she knew she had caused.

"On Wednesday in Low Week, April 6th, after Communion, He returned with outstretched arms, while I was telling Him how I want really to love Him. He listened in silence, as if He would like me to say it again. I begged Him to forgive me, saying: 'Dear Lord, I surrender myself wholly to Thee.' He looked at me very lovingly and said: 'A soul who truly surrenders herself to Me gives Me so much joy that in spite of her miseries and imperfections she becomes a very heaven of delight to Me and I take pleasure in abiding in her. I will tell you Myself what prevents Me from effecting in your soul the realization of My designs.'

Seeing the anxious look on her face, He added: "Yes, the devil will tempt you assiduously and try to make you fall, but My grace is more powerful than his infernal malice. Trust yourself to My Mother, surrender yourself to Me, and always be very simple and humble with your Mother."

Josefa understood how opportune this recommendation was, for she had a presentiment that the devil was about to attack her; she prayed and renewed her offering:

"I begged Him," she wrote on Thursday, April 7th, "to teach me how to humble myself and how to surrender myself in a way that pleases Him. I think He likes this prayer, for suddenly He came:

" 'You can humble yourself in various ways,' He told me, 'first, by adoring the Divine Will, which, in spite of your worthlessness, uses you to make known God's Mercy. Secondly, by thanking Me for having placed you in the Society of My Heart, though you have done nothing to merit it. Never complain of this.'

"He impressed these words so deeply on my soul that I begged of Him no longer to remember my ingratitude, and I again told Him how much I wished to make amends for the pain I had given His adorable Heart.

" 'You will comfort Me, Josefa, if you often repeat this prayer: "O Divine Heart - Heart of my Beloved - the most tender and sensitive of all hearts, I give Thee thanks that in spite of my unworthiness Thou hast deigned to choose me to spread the knowledge of Thy mercy on souls." '

"He looked at me again and vanished."

That evening, in Saint Madeleine Sophie's cell, where she had gone in the fullness of her heart to beg of her never to doubt her desire to be her true child, Jesus came unexpectedly, and opening His Heart made her enter therein, saying: "Here, you will obtain forgiveness."

Our Lady was watching with maternal solicitude over Josefa, on account of the latter's inexperience. Coming on Saturday, April 9th, she said: "What I chiefly fear is that you may not be open enough with your Mother (Assistant) and that so you will fail to notice the toils of the evil one who tries to ensnare you. Do not relax, Josefa; watch over your thoughts, that temptation may have no hold on you. And should you feel any complacency in yourself, own it at once, humbling yourself. Be very simple with your Mother. This I again recommend to you; it is the only way of protecting you from the wiles of the devil."

Jesus Himself drove the lesson home a few days later. On Monday, April 11th, she repeated the words Jesus had taught her on the preceding Thursday.

"At once He came, and I saw by His look that it pleased Him to hear me say that prayer, so I repeated it again.

" 'Every time you say those words I place them in My Heart that they may become for you and for souls a new source of grace and mercy.'

"I asked Him, or rather I begged Him, to have compassion on me, for none is more in need of it than I.

" 'If through you, Josefa, I will to pour out the treasures of My mercy, do you think that I would not begin by yourself?'"

Then He reminded her to hide nothing from the Mother to whom He had entrusted her.

"You must learn to own to her even what humiliates you most, and in the most costly way. If I had not willed to subject you to obedience," He said with emphasis, "I should have left you in the world, but I led you to My Heart that there you might live only to obey."

Two days later, she was to experience how grace is always hidden in obedience.

"On Wednesday, April 13th, I received a letter from my sister, and the thought that she would very likely enter the Carmelites and leave my mother all alone upset me. However, I never ceased telling Jesus that I would be faithful to Him. The following day the temptation was so strong that I went and told you all, Mother, because I knew it was from you that I should get light. You said one thing that struck me very forcibly: 'The Heart of Jesus loves your mother infinitely more than you do.' I reflected on this, and in consequence resolved to leave everything in God's hands.

"The next day, during my thanksgiving, He who knows my frailty came, full of kindness, and said to me:

" 'If you surrender all, you will find everything in My Heart.'"

It was by such a call to abandon all into His hands that Our Lord prepared her for the stormy days that were about to begin for her.

On Friday, April 22nd, we see in her notes how the devil tried to take away her peace of mind:

"... I went up to the oratory of Our Lady in the Noviceship to implore her not to let me fall. She came, at once, very motherly and said:

" 'My daughter, I will give you a lesson of very great importance: the devil is like a mad dog, but he is chained, that is to say, his liberty is curtailed. He can, therefore, only seize and devour his prey if you venture too near him, and that is why his usual tactics are to make himself appear as a lamb. The soul does not realize this, and draws nearer and nearer, only to discover his malice when in his clutches. When he seems far away, do not relax your vigilance, child; his footsteps are padded and silent, that he may take you unawares.'"

"She gave me her blessing and went away."

Temptation was, indeed, very close to her, and this time Josefa was to learn how strong the devil is, even when allowed only a measure of liberty by God.

"Two or three days later," wrote Josefa, "I was alone and feeling very desolate. The fury of the devil seemed to fall upon me and blind me and tear me from my vocation. I suffered much until Saturday, May 7th, but I did not cease calling on Our Lord and Our Lady for help.

"That evening I went to make my adoration with the other novices, and to help myself I began to read the words spoken to me by Our Lord and which I had written in my little notebook. But instead of being a help, this reading increased my trouble, for I thought that all these graces would lead in the end to my perdition. I tried as well as I could to repeat my offering, but that instant a shower of blows fell upon me. Frightened, I left the chapel to put the notebook away and see if the Mother Assistant was in her cell, so as to tell her what had happened. But when I reached the cloister of Saint Bernard I was violently caught hold of by the arm and dragged to the kitchen, and the idea came to me to burn the notebook. I tried to do so, but was unable to lift the copper. A mother who was there told me to throw the book into the wood bin, and that it would then be burned at once."

Josefa crumpled it up in her hands, threw it into the bin, and went away much relieved in mind, and hardly realizing what she had done. She then went to resume her work in the ironing-room. Gradually, however, the gravity of the action she had been, as it were, forced into came home to her. What would happen if the notebook fell into strange hands and revealed the great undertaking of Love which Our Lord had so formally charged her to keep secret?

"In other circumstances, I should have been desperate," she continued, "but this time I prayed with all my faith to be delivered, and above all to be forgiven... . I went back to the kitchen, hoping that the notebook would not have been burnt, for it was late. But I could not find it, and I implored Our Lady to take charge of it herself... ."

The next day, a Sunday, seemed an eternity to Josefa, who dared not own her fault to the Mother Assistant, and sought to avoid saying anything about it. But when evening came she was unable to bear alone the anxiety it caused her, and she confessed the whole story to the Mother Assistant.

"When I saw her fear of the consequences I implored Our Lady to restore the notebook to her. I hoped with full confidence that this would be done, not for myself, but for her."

Our Lady could not turn a deaf ear to so filial a prayer.

"On Monday, May 9th, I was sweeping the corridor of the cells, and could not take my mind off the thought of the notebook ... but I had lost all hope of finding it again... ."

Suddenly Josefa heard the well-known voice of Our Lady:

" 'Go to the kitchen; there you will find it.'

"I did not pay any attention, and continued sweeping, thinking that I must be going out of my mind, but I heard the same words a second time, and so went up into the oratory of the Noviceship, where a third time the same voice repeated: 'Go to the kitchen; there you will find it.'"

Hastily Josefa ran downstairs, and on reaching the kitchen, there in the wood bin she saw her notebook ... it was wrapped in a piece of very clean white paper, and laid on one side against the edge of the bin. Josefa seized it - with what excited feelings can be imagined.

She spent two or three days in gratitude, not unmixed with shame at so much indulgence... .

On May 13th, during her adoration, Jesus appeared with arms extended:

"I begged His forgiveness, at once," she wrote. " 'Forget it all,' He said. 'My Heart has wiped it out. Do not be discouraged, for My mercy is best shown in your frailty.'"

Then she implored Him not to tire of her and of her frailty and falls.

"Never does My Heart refuse to forgive a soul that humbles itself," He answered, drawing near, "especially when it asks with confidence.

"Do you understand that, Josefa? I shall raise a great edifice on mere nothingness; that is to say, on your humility, surrender, and love."

Our Lady was to have the last word in the closing stages of this trial.

Next day, Saturday, May 14th, she appeared to her child, who was just finishing the Stations of the Cross.

She was more beautiful than ever; her dress gleamed with silvery reflections and she smiled as she told her of the entry into Paradise of a soul for whom many prayers and sufferings had been asked.

"When she was about to go, I thanked her once more for the notebook.

"What did you want to do with it, my child?' she asked.

"In spite of my shame, I told her the truth: 'Alas, I meant to burn it!'

" 'It was I who prevented your doing that,' she said; 'when Jesus speaks, all Heaven listens in admiration to His words.'"

Josefa, who now understood better than ever the value of words from the lips of Jesus, was speechless with sorrow at what she had done.

"I asked her forgiveness and thanked her for not allowing the notebook to be lost.

" 'When you threw it away, I saved it... . The words of my Son,' she said a few days later, 'I leave here below only for the good of souls, otherwise I take them back to Heaven.'"

Josefa never tired of thanking this compassionate Mother who had come to her rescue so mercifully.

"I thought," we read in her notes, "how very much she loves me and how wonderful is her tenderness for me.

" 'Ah! daughter, how should I not love you? ... my Son shed His blood for all men ... all are my children. But when Jesus selects one soul in particular, my Heart rests in her.'"

This oneness of love of Mother and Son was further confirmed by Our Lord; Josefa wrote on the 18th of May:

"After Communion, my soul was filled with such peace that I could not help saying: 'O Jesus, I know Thou art here; I am certain of it ... ' Before I had finished whispering the words, He stood before me. His hands were extended, His face expressed the most loving tenderness, His Heart was escaping from His breast, and His whole Person shone with respendent light. It was as if a fire were burning within Him.

" 'Yes, Josefa, I am here... .'

"I was beside myself... but regained sufficient hold on myself to beg His pardon, and to bewail my failings, miseries, and fears.

" 'If you are an abyss of miseries, I am an abyss of mercy and goodness.'

"Then, stretching out His arms towards me, He said: 'My Heart is your refuge... .'"

Thus ended the incident of the notebook: on Our Lord's part a veritable effusion of mercy.

The devil tried many other ways of destroying the writings to which Our Lord attached so high a price. But he never succeeded.

On May 25th, feast of Saint Madeleine Sophie, who in 1921 was still only a Beata, Josefa recorded the first intervention of this holy Mother in her life. She had a very filial love for her, and notes in very simple words this favor which gave her new life and strength:

"Today, the feast of our Blessed Mother [Madeleine Sophie], I went into her cell many times to whisper a little prayer to her, and once (I was in my blue working apron) I just stood for a moment and said: 'O Mother, once more I ask you to make me very humble, that I may be your true daughter!' There was no one in the room and this little invocation escaped me out loud. Suddenly I became aware of the presence of an unknown nun. She took my head in her two hands, and pressed it lovingly, saying: 'My child, commit all your frailties to the Heart of Jesus, love the Heart of Jesus, rest in the Heart of Jesus and be faithful to the Heart of Jesus.'

"I took her hand to kiss it, then with two fingers she made the Sign of the Cross in blessing on my forehead, and disappeared."

This first meeting was followed by many others. Up and down the cloisters of Les Feuillants which her feet had so often trod, in her cell, in the shadow of the Tabernacle where she had prayed, Saint Madeleine Sophie showed herself to her child, with the same vivacious and ardent expression of countenance she was known to have had on earth, but now stamped with the light of glory. Josefa spoke to her with the same confidence and simplicity with which she had recourse to her mothers on earth. She listened to her counsels, confided all her difficulties to her, and under such motherly guardianship she felt her vocation safe.

However, Our Lord was teaching her humility by the experience of many falls, and did not free her from the natural frailty of her nature. He seemed almost to take pleasure in seeing the little novice prostrate in shame at His feet, so that He might constantly remind her of the mercy of His Heart, and sometimes He made use of the simplest comparisons to bring home to her His favorite lessons. "I begged of Him," she wrote on the Feast of the Blessed Sacrament, Thursday, May 26th, "to give me strength to conquer myself, for I do not yet know how to humble myself as He would like."

This was during her prayer, and at once Our Lord made Himself manifest. "Do not be anxious, Josefa," He said tenderly. "If you throw a grain of sand into a vase which is full to the very top, a little of the water will trickle out. If you throw in a second grain, more drops will come out. In the same way, in so far as I enter into your soul, you will become less and less occupied with yourself. But this will come about gradually and take time."

Three days later, Sunday, May 29th, He amplified this thought and strengthened her for the labor which was to be long and costly.

" 'Why are you afraid? I know well what you are, but I say again: I do not mind your helplessness.

" 'When a little child toddles as it tries its first steps, his mother begins by holding his hand; later she lets go of him and urges him on to the effort of walking alone, but she stretches out protecting arms that he may not fall and hurt himself. Tell your Mother that the feebler a soul is the more it needs support, and is there anyone weaker than you?'

" 'My Heart takes comfort in forgiving. I have no greater desire, no greater joy, than when I can pardon a soul. When a soul returns to Me after a fall, the comfort she gives Me is a gain for her, for I regard her with very great love. Have no fear whatever. As you are nothing but wretchedness, I wish to make use of you. I will supply for all your deficiencies... . Let Me act in you.'"

This continual interchange of mercy on the one hand, and humble, generous love on the other, is repeated on every page of this life, and stands out as an essential lesson to be learned. But He who with such persevering longanimity gave it did not want Josefa to become absorbed in her failings, and everything was to become gain for souls.

Concerning the Souls of Three Priests and a Sinner, and Two Chosen Souls (June 1st-July 1921)

"Do you want to be a comfort to Me?"
(Our Lord to Josefa, June 14th, 1921)

"Some time before the Feast of the Sacred Heart, I no longer remember the exact date," wrote Josefa, "I saw Our Lord; His Heart bore three fresh wounds, and from each there flowed much blood.

" 'See what I want for My feast.'"

And as she expressed her grief at His sorrow:

" 'There are three priests who are wounding My Heart ... offer all you do for them.'

"I said how poor I was that He might supply what is wanting to me. He replied with much love and clemency: 'The greater your helplessness, the more My power will sustain you. I will make you rich with My gifts. If you are faithful to Me, I will take up My abode in you and will take refuge there, when sinners repulse Me. I shall rest in you, and you will have life in Me. Come to My Heart and there find all you need, even if it is what I have asked of you. Have confidence and love.'"

From that moment, suffering of both body and soul rarely left Josefa, till Friday June 3rd, Feast of the Sacred Heart, when the power of prayer and the mercy that responds to it were shown to her.

"During my prayer He opened His Heart for me to enter in: 'Come,' He said, 'enter in, and continue to confide to Me all I have asked of you.'

"He gave me sweet repose after all the anguish of the preceding days. Then He, O! so beautiful ... stayed near me ... as if unable to restrain His joy. I spoke to Him of the three priests. 'Pray to My Heart for them,' He said; 'they have not yet come back ... but they are nearer.'"

Overjoyed at the sight of His beauty, Josefa alluded to the Feast, which she thought would have given Him so much glory.

"His Heart glowed at these words; never before had I seen Him so.

" 'Yes, today is the feast of My love. Souls, those that I love so much ... they delight My Heart, coming as they do to seek strength and remedy in My Heart which so ardently desires to enrich them; that is what glorifies and consoles Me most.'

"He stayed to the end of meditation and then followed me to Mass."

It is the custom in the Society on the Feast of the Sacred Heart for all the nuns to renew their vows before the Sacred Host at the moment of Communion. Josefa could hardly contain herself as she listened to the renovation uttered so earnestly by each of the community in turn.

"O! how happy I am in my dear Society ... " she wrote.

"Suddenly I saw His Heart ... at first, alone, immersed in a blazing furnace; then, as if a few fleecy clouds parted, Jesus Himself appeared. O! what beauty! ... I know not what I said... . How can I thank Him for all He does for me?

" 'I will tell you how, Josefa. Take this Heart and offer It to your God. By It, you can pay all your debts. You know now what I wished to do when I attracted you to this house. I want you to fulfill My plans by the docility with which you allow yourself to be handled, and with which you surrender to My love, which only seeks to possess and consume you. Love will despoil you of self and allow you to think only of My glory and of souls.'

Then with increasing animation, He added: " 'Now pray ... ask all you want ... tell Me your desires.'

"Then I prayed for all I most desire - first for the Society, as is only natural, and at the same time I offered Him all those fervent acts of renovation for the three priests... . All day long I never ceased praying for them ... I cannot say how often I repeated: 'Lord, Thou hast told me that today souls give great joy to Thy Heart and gain many graces ... cannot we gain those three priests? O! let Thy Heart be touched!'"

Towards three in the afternoon she went to the Novitiate, and as she passed the organ tribune she made another flying visit:

"To knock at the door of His Heart," she wrote, "in order that He might no longer resist our supplications. He came at once, and as if He had not heard, He said to me: 'What do you want? Tell Me.'

" 'But, my Jesus, Thou knowest ... what of those three priests? ... I implore Thee, since it is Thine own wish... . Thou alone canst do it.'"

Then with majestic solemnity and divine joy, pointing to His Heart, He said: "Josefa, they have returned to Me!" And, as if gripped by intense emotion, He continued: "If they had refused My grace, they would have been responsible for the loss of a great many souls." And, as prostrate at His feet, she was mute with the joy that filled her, He added: "You will repeat these words every day: 'O Jesus, by Thy most loving Heart, I implore Thee to inflame with zeal for Thy love and glory all the priests of the world, all missionaries and those whose office it is to preach Thy word, that, on fire with holy zeal, they may snatch souls from the devil and lead them into the shelter of Thy Heart, where forever they may glorify Thee.'"

Josefa never forgot that Feast of the Sacred Heart. She had witnessed the infinite joy of the Sacred Heart when His priests give Him all the love they owe Him. The prayer He had taught her became her daily petition and priestly souls the first and biggest intention of her consecrated life. A little secret note found only after her death proves that at this time Our Lord kept the thought of the missions constantly before her eyes.

"It was on June 11th (I was still afraid of betraying myself to those around me), when suddenly I saw Our Lord. I told Him of my fears, and with inexpressible tenderness He answered: 'Remember My words and trust in them. The one desire of My Heart is to imprison you in It, to possess you in My love, and to make of your frailty and littleness a channel of mercy for many souls who will be saved by your means. Later on, I will reveal to you the burning secrets of My Heart, and they will be for the good of many souls. I want you to write and to keep all I say to you. It will be read when you are in Heaven. It is not for your merits that I use you, but that souls may see how My power makes use of weak and despicable instruments.'1

"I asked Him if I was to say even that," she wrote ingenuously.

" 'Write it; they will read it after you are dead.'"

Thus He gradually unveiled to her the great design of His love which was being prepared in the silence and labor of her working days. Of suffering there was to be enough, and Josefa, who advanced courageously towards humility, was not without frequent temptation. The devil tried to change into obstacles acts which she could have done so simply at another time; but Our Lady was there as always to enlighten, guide, and defend her.

" 'I used to tell her all that happened to me," she wrote on the 13th of June, "but I was not expecting to see her, when she came like a loving Mother, so kind.

" 'Listen, daughter, do not pay any attention to what you feel. Believe me, the sharper your repugnance, the greater your merit in the eyes of your Master. Be on your guard about these three points by which the enemy of souls will endeavor to make you fall.

" 'First: Never give in to scruples which he suggests to you in order to make you give up Holy Communion.

" 'Second: When my Son asks anything of you - be it an act of humility or some other act, do it with great love, telling Him all the time: "Lord, Thou seest how much it costs me ... but Thou first, and I afterwards."

" 'Third: Pay no attention to the artifice of the devil who tries to persuade you that the confidence you have in your Mother subtracts something from your tenderness for Jesus. If he is able to master you in this matter, he will have gained everything.

" 'Open your heart in all confidence, and love your Mother without fear; always tell her with great simplicity what you think, all that worries you. Jesus also willed to love on earth those who represented His Father, and He is pleased when you are open and simple with her. But on no account ever omit a Communion: this I particularly recommend to you.'"

Who would not wonder at the thoughtful kindness of such motherly counsels! It was by following them implicitly that Josefa became in the hands of her Master the docile and supple instrument He was forging for His redemptive work.

"Tuesday, June 14th, Jesus the all beautiful came," she wrote. "He bore in His hands the Crown of Thorns and He asked me with an expression of the most gracious mildness: 'Will you comfort Me?'

"Of course, I assented at once ... and He continued: 'I want you to work at bringing back to Me a much-loved soul. Direct your attention and offer all you do for him. Often present My Blood to the Father. Kiss the ground in reparation for this outraged Blood trampled underfoot by the souls I so dearly love. If you obtain leave, I will tell you all you can do for him. I shall not infringe the Rule or any observance.'"

Our Lord's attention to the observance of the Rule kept Josefa ever on the straight path.

"Have you leave from the Mother Assistant?" He said to her after Communion the next day.

"Thou knowest, dear Lord, that her one wish is to please Thee." "I know it, but you must first submit to the will of your Superior, even before you do what I Myself ask you."

Then He laid out a plan for days of oblation:

" 'When you awake, enter at once into My Heart, and when you are deep down in It, offer My Father all your actions united to the beating of My Heart. Unite all your actions to Mine, so that it will no longer be you, but I, that act in you.

" 'During Mass, present this soul that I want to save to My Father, so that He may pour over him the Blood of the Victim that is about to be immolated.

" 'When you go to Holy Communion, offer the divine wealth you then possess to pay that soul's debt.

" 'During your prayer, place yourself beside Me in Gethsemane, share My anguish, and offer yourself to My Father as a victim ready to endure all that your soul is able to bear.

" 'When you take your food, think that you are giving Me that alleviation and do the same whenever you take pleasure in anything whatsoever.

" 'Do not be separated from Me even for one instant. Often kiss the ground. Do not omit to make the Stations a single day. If I need you, I will tell you.

" 'Look solely to My Will in all you do and accomplish it with the greatest submission.

" 'Humble yourself profoundly, but always joining confidence and love to your humility.

" 'Do everything out of love, and do not lose sight of what I suffered for souls.

" 'During the night you will rest in My Heart. Mine will hearken to the beats of yours which will stand as so many acts of love and desire. Thus you will bring back to Me that soul that so offends Me.'

"I asked Him to be indulgent with me, if one or other of these points is not done exactly as He wishes, for I am very weak.

"In the evening, during my adoration of the Blessed Sacrament, He came with bleeding hands and feet, and looking up to Heaven, He said: 'Offer My Father the divine Victim and the Blood of My Heart for that soul.'

"He repeated the same words three times. I told Him of my desire to comfort Him and to carry out all He had explained to me.

" 'Do not be over-anxious; you possess My Heart for all I ask you to do.'"

Josefa was learning how great is the price of a soul's salvation. For many weeks to come she was associated with Christ's offering and redemptive sufferings, and step by step she followed the return of the wandering soul.

For the last few days a violent pain in her left side had been added to the many sufferings that were wearing her down. At times she was hardly able to breathe. Efforts to relieve her were quite ineffectual and the doctor's diagnosis did not reveal anything abnormal. But in her heart she feared that this pain might be an obstacle to her religious life.

Again she turned to Mary and confided to her maternal Heart this anxiety, which far more than the pain oppressed her.

On Monday, June 20th, she was praying in the Noviceship oratory:

"Suddenly Our Lady came, and said sweetly to me: 'Do not be anxious, daughter ... tell your Mother that there is nothing to be afraid of. That pain is a spark from my Son's Heart. When it is more intense, offer it up, for it signifies that at that moment a soul is offending Him grievously. Do not fear pain; it is a treasure both for you and for souls.'

"She gave me her blessing and was gone."

That same evening, in the refectory, faithful to her Master's injunction -

"I was offering up my food to Our Lord as He had taught me to do," she wrote, "when suddenly I saw Him, and He said:

" 'Yes, give Me to eat, for I am hungry ... give Me to drink, for I am thirsty. You know well what I am hungry and thirsty for ... souls ... the souls I love so much. You can give Me to drink.'"

"He stayed all through the meal. Then He said: 'Come with Me ... do not leave Me alone.'"

He was planning for her to follow Him along a path of increased pain, and the next day He manifested Himself to her during her thanksgiving: "Offer everything to My Father in union with My sufferings. I will make you spend three hours every day in the dire distress and anguish of My Cross, and it will profit that soul exceedingly."

Josefa never hesitated to accept these missions of suffering. Though she dreaded the favors, the responsibility of which was ever present to her mind, she was ready to take on herself the Cross which was destined to save souls. This Our Lord knew, and He counted on her, and made further demands on her generosity.

On Thursday, June 23rd, at Holy Mass, He appeared again:

" 'Today, I want you to get leave to make a Holy Hour. You will offer that sinner to the Eternal Father, reminding Him that it was for him that I suffered the agonies of Gethsemane. You will offer Him My Heart and your sufferings united to Mine... . Tell your Mother that these pains are a trifle in comparison with the joy which will be Mine when that soul returns to Me.'

"That night," continued Josefa, "I awoke, as the pain was very severe, and soon after, Jesus came, crowned with thorns: 'I come that we may suffer together.'

"He joined His hands and remained long in prayer. If only you could see how beautiful He is, Mother! His eyes look heavenward, and there is such mournful sadness on His countenance ... a luminous ray fell on His face, a sort of reflection of Heaven."

Many days and nights passed. Josefa noted down visits from her Master, who told her again and again of His thirst for souls and of His hopes. She, so to speak, watched this pursuit of love which tracked the path of a soul in peril. But while He made her responsible before God, Jesus wanted her collaboration with Himself to be entirely disinterested. When she asked Him whether the sinner was nearer conversion, He answered her on Tuesday, June 28th, while she was busy working:

" 'Mark My words, Josefa: if you are really desirous of pleasing Me, do not concern yourself with anything else than suffering, while giving Me all I ask of you, without trying to know the "how" and the "when." '

"That night," her notes continued, "Wednesday, June 29th, at two in the morning, suddenly Our Lady came. I said something about that soul and begged her to ask Jesus to remove from him the occasions of sin and to give him the grace and strength to cast sin away. Her eyes filled with tears and she replied: 'Oh, how low he has fallen ... he let himself be deceived like a lamb... but take courage, do all my Son tells you, and ask Him to load on you the punishment that that sinner deserves. If you do this, divine justice will spare him. Do not shrink from suffering, Josefa, you will never lack the strength you need, and when you can bear it no longer, I myself will give you courage and relief. I am the Refuge of Sinners; that soul will not be lost.'"

The next day, Thursday, June 30th, Our Lord appeared to Josefa after Communion and showed her the Wounds in His hands and feet, and taught her to discover the invisible wound of love. "Look at My Wounds," He said. "Adore them ... kiss them ... they were caused not by souls, but by love."

And as she was mute, not knowing what to say, He repeated: "Yes, they are caused by the love I have for souls ... a love of compassion for sinners... . Ah! did they but know ... "

Then, in silence, Josefa let her Master stamp that invisible wound on her soul, so as to share it with Him, and relieve His pain. "The greatest reward I can give a soul," He continued, "is to make her a victim of My love and mercy, rendering her like Myself, who am the divine Victim for sinners."

On the first of July, Feast of the Precious Blood, and the First Friday of the month, Our Lady came to put her in mind of the redemptive value of His blood, which she must make use of for the sinner.

"Adore the Precious Blood of my Son, daughter," she said to her, "and beg of Him to pour it on that soul, that he may be touched, forgiven, and purified ... "

Thus, as day succeeded day, Josefa was kept face to face with her mission.

"Do not stop uniting your actions to Mine and offering My precious Blood to My Father... ."

"Never forget that you are the victim of My Heart."

But Our Lord was far from confining Josefa's horizon to one soul, and on Friday, July 8th, He entrusted to her two other souls of whom He said: "See how they pierce My Heart and rend My hands."

He returned again during her adoration: "Look at My Heart. It is all love and tenderness, but there are those who do not recognize this."

We can easily conjecture the energy and generosity of effort that were required of Josefa to carry on this twofold life: on the one hand, days and nights passed in contact with the invisible, which entailed so great a sacrifice; on the other, the fidelity with which she kept to her work and to the Rule. With matchless kindness Our Lord allowed her to share in His joys as Saviour.

"He came during my adoration, so beautiful," she wrote on Saturday, July 9th, "and He said to me: 'See, Josefa, one of those two souls has at last given Me what she had so long refused Me, but the other is very near being lost unless she succeeds in seeing her utter nothingness... .'"

"Yes, offer yourself to obtain her forgiveness. A soul will profit even after the greatest sins, if she humbles herself. It is pride that provokes My Father's wrath, and it is loathed by Him with infinite hatred."

"I am in search of those who will humble themselves to repair for this pride."

On Tuesday, July 12th, she wrote:

"At about four in the afternoon He returned. His face was so grave and beautiful, and there was a gaping wound in His Heart: 'Give Me your heart, Josefa, that I may fill it with the bitterness of My own; and offer yourself to repair the pride of that soul. Do not refuse Me anything; I am your strength.'

"Then glancing heavenwards, He said: 'Pride blinds her ... she forgets that I am her God and that without Me she can do nothing. Why does she want to rise in this world? I want you often to fall down in adoration before My Father, and to offer Him the humility of My Heart. Do not forget that without Me a soul is nothing more than an abyss of wretchedness... . I will raise up the humble, and make little of their frailties, and even of their falls, provided they have humility and love.'"

Weeks went by without a moment's respite for Josefa. The pain in her side, the Crown of Thorns, her aching limbs, her soul burdened with the weight of divine anger ... everything reminded her of the charge given her by Love.

But Our Lady came to give her fresh courage.

"It was three in the morning," she wrote on the 22nd of July.

"Suddenly she came, and putting her two hands on my shoulders, she said: 'Child of my heart! I come to aid and assist you, for I am your Mother. Nothing of what you endure is useless. You will have to go through another big trial to save that proud soul. As soon as you feel the approach of temptation, reveal it at once. Then obey, obey, obey ... '

"I told her that these two things are what cost me most at present.

" 'Listen, Josefa; now is the time to submit your judgment to obedience, and so you will be expiating the pride of that soul. The devil has little influence over her while you struggle ... you must suffer for souls, you must be tempted, for, mark you, the archfiend dreads your fidelity ... but take courage.'

"She blessed me and disappeared."

In the early dawn, Our Lord Himself came to confirm His Mother's words. It was after her Communion, purchased by such a hard fight.

"He was so beautiful," she wrote, "although He wore His Crown of Thorns and had many bleeding wounds.

" 'Look at My wounds and greet them with a kiss. Know you whence they come? Love. Know you who opened My Heart? Love. And who crowned Me with thorns? Love. If I have loved you so much as to refuse no suffering for your sake, cannot you, Josefa, suffer without refusing Me anything? ... Abandon yourself to Me.'"

By such words, Josefa's will was linked more strongly than ever to that of her Lord.

The fruit of so much suffering had meanwhile ripened through the long weeks of oblations and struggles, as Josefa was soon to learn.

On July 25th, Jesus reminded her of their mutual promise of August 5th, 1920: "If you are faithful I will make the riches of My Heart known to you. You will indeed share My Cross, but I Myself will be your consolation, for you are My well-beloved."

Then He added significantly: "Never do I break My word."

That same evening news of the sinner came indirectly to Les Feuillants, and they were full of hope.

"I do not know how to thank enough," she wrote the next day, Tuesday, July 26th, "all the more that I was still under the impression left on me by His words: 'Never do I break My word.'

"He came," she continued, "and said to me: 'The work is not yet completed; I shall show that soul still greater mercy. All I ask of you is to be faithful.'"

On Wednesday, August 3rd, towards evening, Our Lord appeared radiant and said: "At last the sinner that has made Me suffer so much is in My Heart, Josefa."

The next day, it was of the soul whose pride wounded Him so grievously that He reminded Josefa: "I want that soul to return to Me as quickly as possible. Are you willing to suffer for her? ... Offer everything you do today for that intention. I will return soon."

"That same evening, Jesus intimated His coming to me," she wrote, "and I went to the tribune of the Noviceship. Instantly He came. His Heart no longer bore the wound that for so long the proud soul He had told me of had inflicted on Him."

" 'Come,' He said, 'draw near and rest. That soul is in My Heart ... '"

It was on August 14th that Our Lord definitely confirmed the salvation of those souls so dearly bought.

That evening Jesus said to Josefa: "That soul left by Me on earth to purify herself is now in Heaven. As for the sinner, My Heart has completely won him. He will comfort Me from now on by responding to My love. And you? ... " He continued. "Do you love Me? ... I have plans for you, plans of love ... do not refuse Me anything."

A Religious Community (August 1921)

"I wish to use you for a great undertaking."
(Our Lord to Josefa, July 26th, 1921)

In August 1921 a work of reparation in which Our Lord had invited Josefa to cooperate came to a successful end. In order to follow it from day to day, we must go back to Tuesday, July 26th, when after Communion Our Lord had asked her: "Are you prepared to follow Me faithfully?"

"I told Him my fears on account of my weakness," wrote Josefa, "but as regards my desires, He knows them well enough.

" 'I am about to make use of you for a great undertaking. You must bring back to My Heart a community that has wandered away from Me. I want these consecrated souls to come back here.'

"And He pointed to His Heart. I asked Him what I could do.

" 'Go on doing what I taught you to do for that sinner; offer all My blood; its price is infinite.'

"He came back towards midday, bearing a heavy cross," continued Josefa.

" 'I come to bring you My Cross,' He said. 'I want to take it off My shoulders and lay it on yours.'

"Then He remained without a cross, and I was weighed down by such intense suffering that had He not given me special grace I could not have borne it.

" 'I have chosen nine souls for this work,' He went on. 'When I leave you, I will go to another, and so I shall always be comforted by one or other of My consecrated souls.'

"He remained in silence for a few minutes; then, as if speaking to Himself: 'It is true that many wound Me by their ingratitude, but there are more souls in whom I can rest and who are My delight.'"

Josefa, thus weighed down, went to her ordinary work. Her Master was still present and He said to her: "Let us work together."

As they were alone at the time, she occasionally knelt to adore Him and offer herself to His good pleasure.

" 'I want you not only to draw these souls closer to Me, but to pay their debt, so that they owe no further reparation to My Father,' He explained.

"It was four o'clock when He said to me: 'Now I am going, and I will come back when your turn comes round again.'

"He took His Cross and vanished ... and all suffering left me."

Henceforward, these long hours of expiation recurred at fixed periods, Our Lord going from one to another of the souls He had chosen to carry His Cross. After Communion on July 27th He appeared to Josefa: "I come to rest with you," He said. "I want you to forget yourself and to comfort Me, to think of Me so much and love Me so vehemently that I alone fill your mind and aspirations. Do not be afraid of suffering.... I am powerful enough to take care of you."

She at once spoke to Him of the work of love begun on the preceding day:

"And as if I had reminded Him of a great sorrow, He answered: 'It is a tepid and relaxed community ... '

"Then, after a moment's silence, He resumed: 'But they will be Mine ... They will return to My Heart. It is to bring them back that I have chosen nine victims. There is nothing of greater value than suffering, when united to My Heart. I shall bring you My Cross tonight. I shall come at midnight, for that is your hour when your turn comes round.'"

That same evening Our Lady came to entrust Josefa with a soul in peril:

" 'Till tomorrow I should like you to put all your enthusiasm into saving a child I dearly love,' she said. 'Jesus, casting His eyes upon her, had given her the treasure of a vocation; but she lost it by her want of correspondence. She will die tomorrow, and what pains me most is that she has thrown away her scapular. How much my heart would be comforted if this child could be saved.'

"She gave me her blessing and disappeared.

"I was unable to sleep all night, for I was in great distress at the thought of this child so near her death. Besides, there was the pain in my side, the Crown of Thorns, and all the accumulated sufferings of each night. Towards midnight Jesus came with His Cross. He stayed beside me, but without the Cross, which I felt weighing on my body as a crushing load, while my soul was oppressed with unspeakable sadness."

The weight of this invisible Cross pressed on Josefa's right shoulder, and doubled her in two, almost crushing her. Her breathing, already so painful on account of the pain in her side, became more and more labored, and efforts to help her were quite ineffectual.

"Suffer with courage," Our Lord said to her, "that My religious may let themselves be pierced by this arrow of love." And from His Heart there issued a ray of fire.

"Kiss My hands and My feet, and repeat after Me: 'Father, is not the blood of Thy Son of sufficient value? What more dost Thou require? His Heart, His wounds, His blood ... He offers Thee all for the salvation of these souls.'"

"I repeated the words after Him," wrote Josefa next day. "There were long pauses of silence. I think He was praying, for His hands were clasped and

He was looking up to Heaven ... At four in the morning He said: 'Now I leave you, for another of My beloved ones awaits Me. You know there are nine of you ... all chosen by My Heart... . I will return tomorrow at one o'clock and will give you My Cross again... . Adieu, I was thirsty and you have slaked My thirst. I shall be your reward.'"

On Friday, July 29th, at one in the afternoon, as He had said, Jesus returned with His Cross. "I have come," He said, "to make you share in the bitterness of My Heart, which is oppressed with sorrow."

He gave her His Cross, which at once plunged her whole being into the pain she had already experienced these last two days.

"Much blood poured from the wound in His Heart," she wrote.

" 'Repeat after Me,' He told her: '"Eternal Father, look upon those souls reddened with the blood of Thy Son Jesus Christ, the Victim which is unceasingly offered Thee. Will this blood which purifies, burns and consumes, be powerful enough to touch these souls? ... " '

"He remained in silence for a few minutes. I repeated the words several times; then He spoke with energy: 'Yes, I want them to return to Me. I want them to burn with love, while I am consumed for them with sorrowful love.'

"Then He added sadly: 'Ah, if souls only understood how ardently I desire to communicate Myself to them! But how few do understand ... and how deeply this wounds My Heart.'

"I comforted Him as best I could, and begged Him to forget for a while the souls that grieved Him, and to think rather of those that love and console Him. His Heart seemed to expand at these words.

" 'I am the one joy of souls. Why do they go away from Me?'

" 'Dear Lord, all do not go away ... and if we often fall, it is because of our frailty... . Thou knowest it well!'

" 'I would condone their falls ... and I am not unmindful of their wretchedness, but what I want is that they should not remain deaf to My appeal and that they should not turn away from the arms outstretched to raise them up.'

"From one to four in the afternoon I spent in offering His blood and all His merits to the Father, and in repeating the prayer He had taught me."

In the silence that surrounded her, Josefa resumed her work as soon as Jesus had taken away His Cross, but her soul still bore the dolorous impress of the secret imparted to her by Our Lady.

Her hour of guard recurred on the evening of Saturday, July 30th:

"I was going up the school stairs, when I met Him with His Cross. He told me that He was waiting for me. After asking His leave to put away the work I was carrying," she continued, "I went to the room where I sleep, and found Him waiting."

Then, she spoke to Him of the soul that had been unfaithful to her vocation, and had been placed in her keeping by Our Lady.

Since the day before, when the fury of the devil had made her suffer much, she knew through Our Lady that this much-loved child had escaped the infernal assaults. But during the preceding night she had appeared to her in the pains of Purgatory, begging her intercession that her sufferings might be shortened. Josefa was much affected by this first contact with Purgatory, and she confided her fears to Our Lord: "Lord, if a person of the world can suffer such torments, what must not a religious endure? That is, if she does not use the graces she receives in such abundance... ."

"Quite true," was the reply.

Then with great tenderness He comforted her:

" 'When one of My religious falls, I am always there to raise her up, if she humbles herself lovingly. A soul's wretchedness matters little provided her one desire is to glorify and console Me. In her very lowliness she obtains many graces for others.

" 'I love humility ... and it is pride that turns so many away from Me.

" 'I want your sacrifices and zeal to draw souls, especially consecrated ones, to My Heart. I want your desire to see Me loved and to gain souls to Me to consume you, and your love to comfort Me.'

"He then kept silence for a long time, and I said everything I could to comfort Him ... and I spoke to Him of a soul that needs His help.

" 'If she does not look for strength in My Heart, where will she find it? Love gives strength, but self must be forgotten.'

"Then I said: 'Lord, forgive us; we are so feeble.'

" 'When a soul ardently desires to be faithful to Me, Josefa, I uphold her in her weakness, and even her falls are a call on My mercy and clemency. But she must forget herself, and make efforts in all humility, not for her satisfaction, but for My glory.'"

We have now reached August 3rd, when Jesus, having conquered the sinner that had cost Josefa so much suffering, appeared, saying: "That sinner is now in My Heart."

That same evening, on going to the dormitory, as she drew back the curtain of her cubicle she found her Master with His Cross waiting for her there.

"Take My Cross," He said. "I come to rest in you. Ah, if religious souls but knew how great My love for them is and how they wound Me by their coldness and tepidity! These souls do not know the dangers they run by neglecting their faults. They begin by a small infidelity and end by relaxation. Today, they grant themselves a slight indulgence; tomorrow, they are deaf to an inspiration of grace, and little by little without realizing it they allow their love to grow cold."

And to make Josefa realize where alone lie the safeguards of fidelity, He gave her this valuable lesson: "I will tell you now, Josefa, how to open your heart to your Mother in all simplicity and humility."

"I want you to be holy, very holy, and you will only become so by the path of humility and obedience.... . I will show you all this by degrees... ."

Before leaving her, He concluded with these words: "I advise you always to keep before your eyes, and rooted in your heart these two important principles. First: God has specially cast His eyes on you, to manifest His power the better, by raising a great edifice on foundations of utter insufficiency. Second: If He wants to lead you to the right and you insist on going to the left, the loss of your soul is assured. Lastly, Josefa, let the result of all this be a deeper consciousness of your own powerlessness and a more complete surrender of yourself into the hands of your God."

This lesson of confidence and humility is so dear to the Heart of Jesus that He will come back upon it many a time yet.

The following counsels found in Josefa's notes and carefully preserved by her are enlightening.

"I wish to make known to you the most intimate attractions of My Heart. I have already told you with what simplicity you must confide in your Mother and open your soul to her without allowing yourself the smallest reservation in your avowals. Today I wish to advise you never to lose an occasion of humbling yourself. When you are free to make or not make one of these costly acts, go and do it.

"I want you to give an account to your Mother of the efforts you have made, and of the occasions you have either made use of or lost. The better you know what you are, the better you will know what I am.

"Never go to rest at night with the slightest shadow obscuring your soul. This I recommend to you with great insistence. When you commit a fault, repair it at once. I wish your soul to be as pure as crystal.

"Do not let your falls, however many, trouble you. It is trouble and worry that keep a soul from God.

"I want you to be very little and very humble, and always gay. Yes, I want you to live in joy, while endeavoring all the time to be something of an executioner to self. Often choose what costs you, but without loss of joy and gladness, for by serving Me in peace and happiness you will give the most glory to My Heart."

This very clear statement kept Josefa in the straight path and at the same time taught her that it was the only one in which, following their Master, the workers of His Redemption must tread.

Thus the "great undertaking" - for this was Our Lord's name for it - went on. Josefa continued to carry the Cross which Jesus gave to the nine chosen souls in turn, so that the consecrated souls He was pursuing might be brought back to fervor. This work was, however, about to be completed.

During Mass on August 5th He came resplendent in beauty:

" 'I want you,' He said, 'to burn with love of Me. I have already made it clear to you that you will find happiness nowhere but in My Heart. I want you to love Me ... I hunger for love ... but I also want you to burn with desire to see Me loved, and this must be the one food of your soul.'

"I said many endearing things to Him, and Jesus continued:

'Every day after Communion repeat with all the fervor of which you are capable: "Heart of Jesus, may the whole world be set on fire with Thy love."'"

It was in this kind of fiery fervor that she spent the day "full of ardent desires" as she herself noted.

Towards nightfall she went up to the dormitory. Jesus was waiting for her: "Take My Cross and let us go and suffer for souls."

After a moment's silence, He added: "If My consecrated souls have reflected that I am all love, and that My supreme desire is to be loved in return, why do they treat Me as they do?"

Then He explained to Josefa how love enhances the smallest acts:

" 'When a soul does a costly act out of self-interest or to please herself, but not out of love, she gains little merit. On the other hand, a very little thing offered with great love consoles My Heart so much that It inclines towards her, and forgets all her worthlessness.

" 'Yes,' He repeated, 'My one desire is to be loved. If souls but knew the excess of My love they would not disregard it ... that is why I go seeking them out and spare nothing to get them to come back to Me.'

"He said all this in a very moving way; it was a veritable cry of Love; then He remained long in silence, as if in prayer. At eleven o'clock, He left me, saying: 'Suffer with great love ... never cease offering My blood for souls. And now give Me back My Cross.'"

Three days passed during which besides the mysterious pains that associated Josefa with the Cross of Christ, a costly offering had been asked of the whole house: the changes usual in all religious congregations now demanded of Les Feuillants the sacrifice of their Superior. Josefa, with all her Mothers and Sisters, shared in this meritorious offering, and Our Lord used it to finish His work.

Monday, August 8th, was to be for Les Feuillants one of those days treasured by the Heart of Jesus when Mothers and Sisters, united in the fervent offering of a costly sacrifice, bid good-bye to one they love.

After Communion Our Lord showed Himself to Josefa: "Those souls must come back to Me without further delay. Pray hard that they may allow grace to penetrate them. Although you can do no more than desire to see Me loved, this is already much. It relieves My Heart. For this longing is love. Those religious are soon going into retreat; offer yourself, that love may pierce them through and through."

That evening at seven o'clock, Jesus returned, this time without His Cross, His Heart and Wounds shining brightly. Josefa hardly dared believe in the hope, which she felt, at the sight of the radiance of His sacred face. She asked for the Cross.

"No," He answered, "these souls no longer wound My Heart. I accepted for their benefit the sacrifice made by this household today, for I found much love here. Tomorrow that religious community will go into retreat, and soon will become for My Heart a refuge of much consolation."

Thus ended this tale of divine mercies. Josefa, too, was about to enter on a new phase of her life.

Fresh Trials (August 26th-October 1921)

"Do not be afraid of suffering. If you could but see how many souls have come back to the Heart of Jesus while you were tempted."
(Our Lady to Josefa, October 24th, 1921)

Our Lord's admirable plan for Josefa's life brought her to a new phase at this time:

At the end of August 1921 a more stringent dependence was imposed on her, and we see this reflected in her notes. She was told not to respond to the appeals of her Master outside the times of common prayer, without a special permission. Perhaps this order indicated a certain doubt about her state in the mind of those over her... . The new Superior of the house who, by the express wish of Our Lord, had been fully informed on her arrival of all that was taking place, felt it to be her duty to spare no pains to guarantee the authenticity of the mysterious path into which God was leading Josefa, and it seemed to her that prudence prescribed a wise delay and much circumspection. Josefa submitted with her whole heart to all the directions of obedience. She knew the Heart of Christ too well to allow a doubt to cross her mind or shake her confidence; she knew too the exacting fidelity her Master expected of her in connection with His great undertaking. No hesitation, therefore, troubled for a moment her supernatural and simple obedience to the decisions of her Superior. But great was the cost to herself, reserved as she was in this domain, to be obliged to speak, explain, answer questions, and henceforth submit all to the twofold control of both Mothers, and feel by the very fact that she was under stricter observation.

Nevertheless, all in Josefa's life was divinely linked together. In that very hour God's action appeared so evident that no lasting doubt about this child of His was found possible. God gave the authentic sign by her fidelity and detachment that nothing was able to impair. Then too the devil, to whom was given the dreaded power of sifting the precious wheat of these acts of divine love, found that Our Lord had surrounded His work with a rampart of protection, which in the event was able to resist all the attacks of the enemy.

Thus a new and unpredictable phase of her life opened for Josefa, which was to end in the happy day of her First Vows.

Les Feuillants was a big household, where children abounded, and there in the midst of a numerous community, although Josefa was the eldest member of the little Noviceship, she remained in complete effacement, laborious and devoted as ever. The Superior and the Mother Assistant alone were the guardians of the secret work accomplished under their eyes. But the sure and vigilant support of Rev. Father Boyer O.P., Prior of the Dominicans, who was appointed by Our Lord Himself to cooperate in His designs, laid many anxious fears to rest, and unmasked the snares of the evil one.

So, enveloped by all these guarantees and safeguards, Josefa was led by Our Lord into the dark night of her greatest trial, one which would end only on the day of her religious consecration (July 1922). It was a baptism of pain which bound her to the redemptive work of which she was to be the witness and collaborator, before becoming its messenger.

The hour of the Prince of Darkness had struck, and Josefa entered the lists against him. She was now to meet him at every turn. But Our Lord fought in her, and was preparing the most humiliating of defeats for Satan. He would make him feel the limit of his efforts, the stupidity of his futile devices and the impotence of his guile. If at times He left the devil an appearance of facile triumph, if He abandoned Josefa to the wiles of an adversary who seemed to master her, if He allowed her descent into the bottomless pit, He nevertheless remained in possession of the soul which He had made His willing victim and sustained her by the fidelity of His love. Never was He more present within her than in the hours of her martyrdom, when alone the divine power could act as a counterpoise of trials and humiliations that escape ordinary human experience. By means of the frail instrument that Josefa was, we can see a combat between God and Satan, between charity and hatred, between merciful love yearning to make its affection known to mankind and the enemy of souls whose awareness of a heavenly scheme made him rage against it with satanic fury.

All the demon's efforts during that long period of nine months were centered and concentrated on the destruction of Josefa's religious vocation before it was too late. He spared nothing to bend her to his will: violent temptations, fear of a crushing responsibility by which he terrified her, perfidious falsehoods that alarmed her conscience, deceptive and menacing appearances, blows, abductions, and burnings ... all were hurled at the frail child, as a tornado, in which it would seem she must suffer shipwreck.

That she did resist with incredible energy, was surely a result of her habitual simplicity in the performance of duty, and still more of her loyalty and obedience in letting herself be guided. Above all, she was sustained by a divine strength which never forsook her, though it was veiled at times, and by the power of the Blessed Sacrament imparted to her by her daily Communions.

During the last days of August occasional celestial visitations were granted to her, bracing her will for the struggle ahead.

On Friday, August 26th, at nine in the morning Josefa, faithful to the instructions she had been given, knocked at her Superior's door. She was wrapt in recollection which gave the impression that she was accompanied by an invisible Presence. In a few words she asked leave to follow Our Lord for a few minutes.

"For," she said, "He is here."

Her lowered eyes, the expression of her face, her prayerful attitude, the effort those few words had cost her, spoke for themselves.

"As I left you, Reverend Mother," she wrote later, "I said to Our Lord: 'I have permission.' He was walking beside me and He led me to the tribune. I began by saying what you had told me to say: 'If Thou art really He whom I believe Thee to be, Lord, deign not to take offense if I am made to ask leave every time, before listening to Thee and following Thee.' He replied: 'I am not offended; on the contrary, I want you always to obey and I also will obey.'

"He looked like a poor man when He said this, then He added:

" 'Your Superiors please Me in ascertaining with so much earnestness whether or no it is I. Remain united to Me all day, and repair for many souls, Josefa.'"

With incomparable sweetness Our Lord consented to submit to the requirements which henceforth surrounded His visits. This fidelity of His Heart, fortifying that of His child, put the seal of divinity on His Presence; moreover, during the months of August and September 1921, while bowing to the restrictions imposed, He changed nothing in His intercourse with Josefa and continued as before to ask her for the help of her offerings for souls.

"On Thursday, September 1st," wrote Josefa, "He came after Communion. When He began to speak His voice was very sad.

" 'I want you to comfort Me,' He said. 'Great is the coldness of souls ... and how many blindly throw themselves into Hell. I should like to leave you My Cross as I used to do.'

"Afterwards, when I had asked leave, He led me to the oratory of Saint Stanislaus and there He said: 'If I were unable to find souls to solace Me and draw down mercy, justice could no longer be restrained.'

"A little later, He continued: 'My love for souls is so great that I am consumed with desire to save them. But O! how many are lost, and how numerous are those who are waiting for the sacrifices and sufferings that are to obtain for them the grace to forsake their evil ways... . However, I still have many souls who love Me and belong to Me. A single one of them can purchase pardon for a great many others who are cold and ungrateful.

" 'I want you to burn with desire to save souls. I want you to throw yourself into My Heart and to make My glory your sole occupation.

" 'I will return this evening, that you may slake My devouring thirst and I shall take My rest in you.'

"At the beginning of the Holy Hour, He returned, as He had said:

" 'Let us go and offer ourselves as victims to My Eternal Father. Let us prostrate ourselves in profoundest adoration in His Presence ... and worship Him, offering Him our thirst for His glory. Make oblation and repair in union with the divine Victim.'

"He said all this very slowly, then a little before the end of the Holy Hour,

He went away."

A few days later Our Blessed Lady appeared to Josefa; she came to encourage her, for Josefa was troubled by many secret conflicts.

" 'You little know how much I who am your Mother, Josefa, want you to be faithful, but not to grieve. All Jesus asks of you is surrender to His Will; He will do the rest.'

"I explained to her how much it cost me to have to tell all those things now, not only to the Mother Assistant, but to Reverend Mother as well.

" 'The more Jesus asks of you, the more you must rejoice, dear child,' answered Our Lady, and, as if to root her in humble distrust of self: 'When we look at a masterpiece, it is not the paint brush that excites our wonder, but the hand of the artist. So, Josefa, if it comes about that great things are wrought through you, do not for a moment attribute them to yourself, for Jesus alone does them - He who lives in you, it is He who uses you. Thank Him for so much goodness ... be very faithful in little things as in great ones, without considering the cost. Obey Jesus, obey your Mothers and be humble and abandoned. Jesus is taking care of your littleness, and you know that I am your Mother!'"

On Thursday, September 8th, Our Lord allayed her fears, and gave her the secret of courage. "Let your sole occupation be to love Me; Love will give you strength."

But love, too, was to keep her ever busy about souls. "There is a soul that greatly wounds Me," He told her on Tuesday, September 13th, "and I come to get comfort from you.... Go and ask leave to stay with Me a little while; I will not keep you long. Do not fear if you feel utterly undone, for I want you to share the anguish of My Heart.... Ah! poor soul ... she is on the brink of the abyss."

"For three hours of the night of the 14th-15th, He left me His Cross and His Crown."

The same thing happened on the following nights, and during several days; Josefa thus cooperating towards the return of the erring soul.

At the close of the night of September 24th-25th, which was spent in terrible anguish and pain ...

"Suddenly," Josefa wrote, "all suffering vanished. A sense of immense peace took possession of my soul. Jesus was there, resplendent in light; His raiment looked as if it were made of gold, and His Heart was ablaze.

" 'We have won that soul,' He said.

"I gave thanks and adored Him with deepest reverence, for all God's Majesty was in Him, and after asking forgiveness for my sinfulness, I begged Him to keep me faithful, for I am so weak.... However, He knows I have no other wish than to console and love Him.

" 'Do not worry about your miseries; My Heart is the Throne of Mercy and the most wretched are the best welcomed, as long as they come to lose themselves in the abyss of My love.

" 'My eyes are upon you because you are little and helpless. I am your strength, and now let us go and gain other souls ... but first rest a while in My Heart.'"

This repose was not to be of long duration, and to gain other souls more than she had ever hitherto had to suffer was to be demanded of Josefa. On the same day, Sunday, September 25th, began the phase of great temptations which at first remained in her silent soul, but which quickly acquired a strange influence on her mind.

This was true: it was a desperate fight. Under the most violent attacks of the devil, Josefa kept repeating: "I will be faithful or die." Soon, however, she imagined herself to be abandoned and repulsed by God.

Two or three times peace was instantly restored to her fevered mind when she remembered certain words of her Master. In these rare moments of truce her whole soul at once recaptured a love so ardent as to be inexpressible. Then, how evident her sincerity became, how well witnesses realized the martyrdom she was enduring and her attachment to the vocation which was costing her so dear and which she loved above all else in the world!

At other times her distress was so poignant that no human aid was capable of helping her. She was crushed with sorrow. Her Communions were bought at the price of a huge effort of faith and courage which at times triumphed only at the very last moment, for the devil sought desperately, though in vain, to deprive her of the Bread of Life for which her soul longed.

A month passed, and no outward sign betrayed the violence of the combat. In spite of the fact that her sufferings continued without a break, she never failed to carry out her duties and all the observances of religious life; and always she could be found, silent and courageous, at her allotted task. But the devil redoubled his attacks.

"I was desperate," she wrote on Monday, October 17th. "It was the feast of Saint Margaret Mary, and after Communion I implored her to obtain for me the grace to be faithful and to die without ever being separated from Him. The whole day I continued a prey to that terrible temptation."

The next day she rose, still under the influence of this diabolic temptation and decided to leave all and go.

"At the hour of Mass I went to sweep the corridor of the cells," she wrote, "when suddenly in a flash I was encompassed with peace, and at the same time came the thought 'could I possibly do without Him?' At that moment all my temptations vanished as if they had never been. I ran to the chapel and was just in time to receive Holy Communion."

Often again in the midst of demoniacal assaults, Josefa was to be suddenly delivered, with a completeness that could be attributed only to heavenly intervention.

But not for long did the devil desist; he prowled around her, seeking to exploit any and every occasion on which her will might waver. On His side Our Lord, who knew what intense struggles still awaited her which she could not sustain unaided, urged upon her total and simple recourse to her guides, which had the effect of keeping her humble, while it doubled her power of resistance. At the same time, He did not hide from her how great were the tribulations still awaiting her.

On Thursday, October 20th, He appeared to her with His Heart burning, and showing her a chalice which He held in His hand, He said: "Josefa, you have drunk only a small portion of it yet, but I am here to defend you."

The prospect of further heavy trials overwhelmed Josefa, and for a moment her courage wavered. How could she accept them? It was but a momentary weakening, yet how painful to her loving heart. She spent four days in very great disturbance of mind, and it was the visit of Our Lady which as usual brought her peace. "Do not fear pain and suffering," she said, "I wish you could see how many souls have come back to Jesus while you were under temptation."

And the Master, ever compassionate and close to those in suffering, answered her call for pity the next day, October 25th: "I am here because I heard your call."

In the confusion of mind into which the devil threw her, Josefa, always fearful of having given in, asked piteously what she could do to repair. "There is one thing that you must do, Josefa: love, love, love!"

Love therefore remained the first and the last word of the battle in which she was about to be engaged.

Open Persecution (November 1921-February 1922)

"I will give you courage for anything I ask you to endure."
(Our Lord to Josefa, November 29th, 1921)

For several weeks more Josefa continued faithfully drawing up the notes of all that happened to her. It was an effort of obedience all the more costly for its sincerity.

"From the 11th of November," she wrote, "I no longer enjoyed a single moment of peace, and both my nights and days were spent in extreme distress."

"I was relieved," she wrote on Monday, November 21st, "by the pact they have made me make with Our Lord, asking Him that each breath and every beat of my heart may be so many acts of faith and love, which will speak to Him of my determination to be faithful unto death. This gave me great peace."

A heavenly ray of light pierced through her dark night. On the morning of Tuesday, November 22nd, she was, as usual, sweeping the rooms of which she had the charge, when:

"Two hands were gently pressed upon my shoulders. I turned and saw Our Lady, in all her loveliness and so motherly. My heart gave a bound of joy, and she said sweetly: 'My daughter, my poor, poor, child!'

"I begged her forgiveness and implored her to intercede with Jesus for me."

This was ever Josefa's first impulse, for the sensitiveness of her conscience always made her fear that when in tribulation she might have wounded the Heart of her Master, even without knowing it.

" 'Have no fear, Josefa,' Our Lady replied. 'Jesus has contracted an alliance of love and mercy with you. You are forgiven, and as I have already told you: I am your Mother.'

"I hardly know what I said, as I was overflowing with happiness; every time she comes I find her more motherly. I thanked her, and begged her to obtain for me from Jesus, the return of His Crown.

" 'Yes, He will give it back to you, and if He does not bring it Himself, I will do so.'

"That evening, during adoration, my beautiful Jesus came. He held the Crown of Thorns in His hands. As soon as I saw Him, I told Him how contrite I was, and added all the tenderest things I could think of, so that He would take pity on me.

"He came close to me and with loving graciousness placed the Crown of Thorns on my head.

" 'I want you to reflect deeply on the words of My Mother: "I have contracted an alliance of love and mercy with you." Does love ever grow weary or mercy come to an end?"'

"Three days later, after Communion, Jesus came in all the Majesty of God," said Josefa on Friday, November 25th. "He showed me His Heart surrounded by flames, the Wound opened, and He said: 'See how My Heart is consumed with love for souls! You, too, must burn with desire for their salvation. I want you to go deep into this Heart today and to make reparation with It. Yes, we must repair,' He repeated. 'I am the great Victim, and you are a very little one, but if you are united to Me, My Father will listen to you.'

"After a moment or two He vanished."

On Saturday, November 26th, Josefa was working with her usual industry at the children's uniforms in the Noviceship work-room, when suddenly Jesus rejoined her.

" 'I want you to ask leave of your Mother that I may stay with you a few moments.'1

"I went at once to ask for it, then on to the Chapel of the Congregations, where He came with His Cross.

" 'I have given you a little rest, Josefa; now let Me repose in you. I should like to give you My Cross for a few minutes. Are you willing?

" 'I have so many who forsake Me and are lost! And what wounds Me most is that they are souls whom I have chosen specially and overwhelmed with gifts. In return, they show Me only coldness and ingratitude. How few souls correspond with My love!'"

Our Lord then gave her His Cross and disappeared without another word.

Monday, November 28th, Josefa noted in a few laconic words the trial that henceforth was to leave her no respite. Fresh power had been granted to Satan, and for the first time she heard the raucous voice that was so often to pursue her, night or day, in the corridors, in the noviceship, in the workroom and dormitory: "You will be one of us ... we shall tire you out ... we shall overcome you ... " She was terrified by it, but bore up bravely.

That evening she wrote:

"During adoration Jesus came with His Cross. I asked Him to let me have it, and He answered: 'Yes, that is why I have come. Give Me rest, and make reparation for all that My souls refuse to give Me. How many are not what they ought to be!'

"He left me His Cross for an hour, and when He took it back He only said: 'I will soon return.'

"That night, I think it was nearly midnight when I awoke. He was there: 'I bring you My Cross, and we shall go together to make reparation.'"

She owned humbly that she felt faint under the weight that was crushing her.

"I begged Him to help me," she wrote, "for He knows very well how small I am.

" 'Do not regard your littleness, Josefa; look rather at the power of My Heart sustaining you. I am your strength and the repairer of your abjectness. I will give you courage for anything I ask you to endure.'

"Then He left me alone and returned about three o'clock. 'Give Me back My Cross, I will soon return to you.'"

At daybreak on Tuesday, the 29th, He brought it back during meditation. It weighed on Josefa's shoulder, while Jesus went with her to her work and to Mass. After Communion He reminded her of the secret of all true generosity: "Now you have life in Me; I am your strength. Courage, then, and carry My Cross."

"I went to work, still carrying His Cross," she said simply.

But soon the Cross of Our Lord was to weigh upon her in quite a different manner.

"Since that day," she wrote, "I suffered many things from the devil."

A new trial was added in the night of December 4th. Pulled violently from her bed, she was thrown to the ground, under the fiendish blows. Long hours were so spent, and the torture renewed on the two following nights. After one such terrible night, she wrote on the morning of Tuesday, December 6th:

"Unable to bear any more, I knelt beside my bed. Suddenly I heard gnashing of teeth and a yell of rage. Then all vanished and before me stood Our Lady, all loveliness.

" 'Do not fear, my daughter; I am here.'

"I told her how terrified I was of the devil, who made me suffer so much.

" 'He may torment you, but he has no power to harm you. His fury is very great on account of the souls that escape him ... souls are of such great worth... If you but knew the value of a soul ... '

"Giving me her blessing, she said: 'Do not fear.' I kissed her hand and she went away."

After this maternal reminder of the great worth of a soul, and of the great price that must be paid for it, the Mother and Son disappeared for a time from Josefa's dolorous path. She wrote nothing more about her daily encounters, through which, by one torment after another, her generous love was ripening and being strengthened.

Although Josefa wrote nothing, the account of this phase of her life was noted day by day, as the facts were revealed. This allows us to glance back over events and endeavor to gauge the poignant reality of her sufferings.

On Tuesday, December 6th, as she was coming out of the Chapel where she had just been to Confession, Josefa was suddenly faced, for the first time, with an infernal vision; a huge black dog, whose open jaws sent forth flames, barred her passage and tried to throw itself upon her. She did not draw back, but braved the oncoming beast, notwithstanding the terror that seized her; grasping her rosary, and stretching it out before her, she went her way.

From that day on the devil appeared visibly to her; sometimes a menacing hound that pursued her in the corridors, at others a serpent coiled up in front of her. Soon the apparition took on a human form, more to be dreaded than any other.

These encounters increased in number from day to day, without succeeding in modifying in any way her fidelity and devotedness; but God knows at what a price, and what courage she displayed!

The hour was about to strike when a more intense trial would call for still greater abandonment.

On Wednesday, December 28th, she was returning in the evening from the work she had been doing with the other novices, when she abruptly found herself face to face with the arch-enemy. With lightning-like rapidity and as though she had been a bit of straw, he carried her off and threw her down in a loft which was difficult of access and at the other end of the house. Josefa never had a moment's peace after that day. The devil seized her, baffling every attempt to guard her, with the one exception of God's care. These abductions became more numerous; under the very eyes of her Mothers, who tried not to lose sight of her, she suddenly disappeared, impossible to say how, for it all happened in a flash. After searching everywhere, they might find her in some remote corner of the house where the demon had carried her to persecute her. But Jesus who loved her so much was aware and watchful. He meant to show that He was the Master, and that He reserved this divine guardianship to Himself. When His hour struck He intervened to claim His rights. The devil with blasphemous execrations relinquished his victim - God's might had made the infernal attempt fail. Then Josefa stood up once more, worn out indeed, but conscious of all; her courage revived and she prayed and resumed her interrupted work. The enemy never succeeded in overcoming her unconquerable energy, and the frail creature, clothed with the strength of God, was sheltered by His love.

The fury of Satan increased tenfold in the face of this unexpected resistance. He tried to reveal to all eyes her sufferings which had hitherto remained secret, but in spite of his efforts no one ever became aware of Josefa's disappearances.

From time to time a bright interval lighted up her dark and murky way, then, out of obedience, Josefa resumed her notes:

"On January 1st, 1922," she wrote, "a little after the Elevation, I heard the voice of a tiny child which filled me with delight: 'Josefa, do you recognize me?'

"At once there stood before me Jesus; He seemed to be a child of a year old, perhaps slightly more, clothed in a white tunic rather shorter than usual. His little feet were bare, His flaxen hair shone like gold... . He was too lovely! I recognized Him at once and said: 'I should think I did know Thee. Thou art my Jesus, my Lord, but how little Thou art!'

"He smiled and replied: 'Yes, I am little, but My Heart is very big.'

"When He had said this He put His tiny hand on His breast, and I saw His Sacred Heart. How can I say all that I felt at such a sight... . O! my Lord, if Thou hadst not such a Heart, could I love Thee so much, but Thy Heart has ravished mine...

" 'That is why I wanted you to know It, Josefa,' He said, with a tenderness quite impossible to render, 'and that is why I have hidden you deep down in It... .'

"I asked Him if all these sufferings were at an end.

" 'No, there will be more for you to suffer. I need loving hearts and souls who will make reparation, and victims for immolation... but above all, souls that are entirely surrendered.'"

Then alluding to the word which more than once in the preceding days had given her strength: "Your Mothers have found the word... abandonment. The devil has no power but what is given him from on high. Tell them that I am supreme."

One last word - a recommendation on the subject of humility - from the divine Child:

" 'You see how I have willed to make myself small, Josefa? It is in order to help you, too, to become very little. If I have humbled Myself to such an extent, it is only to teach you likewise to humble yourself.'

"With His little hand He blessed me, and then I saw Him no more."

Josefa's notes again come to an end. That same evening the trial began again more violent than ever.

On Wednesday, January 11th, her Director, in order to strengthen her, proposed to her to advance her Vows by making a Vow of Chastity.

In an ecstasy of joy Josefa renewed that donation of herself already made on the eve of her First Communion and promised fidelity to Our Lord until death.

The day after, during her thanksgiving, Jesus Himself became manifest to her, and alluding to the vow she had taken the day before, said:

" 'Josefa, My bride, do you know what your Superiors have obtained by that vow? ... They have constrained My Heart to have exceptional care of you. Tell them that it has given Me much glory.'

"I asked Him if the trial was over.

" 'I want you to surrender yourself and to be always ready to undergo the torments of the evil one, or receive My consolations, indifferently.'"

Thus was she kept by Our Lord to the path of abandonment, to go forward with closed eyes, confiding in Him. Father Boyer, who followed her up closely, likewise maintained her in faith and humility. "He recommended me to make myself very insignificant, placing myself at the feet of everyone, and to look on myself as the most unworthy of creatures." Our Lord Himself insisted on this same direction, so entirely in accordance with His Heart's wishes in her regard.

"Josefa," He said to her, "did you quite understand the advice given you by the Father? It is indeed My wish that you should be very, very little. I wish," He added forcibly, "that you should be humiliated and ground underfoot, that you should allow yourself to be made or unmade according to the plans of My Heart."

That same evening Our Lady for the first time gave her an intimation that her earthly life would not be of long duration.

Josefa had expressed the hope that she would never have to take back the sacrifice she had made of her country. Our Lady replied: "You will die in France, in this house of Poitiers, and that before ten years are out; and then ... Heaven!"

"I think," Josefa said a few days later, "that it was the 13th or 14th of January that the devil began once more to assail me. He tried to force me to abandon my vocation. In his increasing fury he even tried to ensnare me by taking on the appearance of Jesus Christ."

Here Josefa's notes again come to an end. From the 13th of the month Satan tried every kind of attack, though he did not succeed in shaking her, and witnesses heard her energetic protestation: "Well, then, kill me." Then, as she related, the devil transformed himself into an angel of light in order the better to seduce her, and appeared even under the lineaments of Our Lord... . At first she was nonplussed, but soon discovered the imposture. The words addressed to her no longer bore the impress of that lofty humility, of the strength and sweetness she was accustomed to hear from her Master's lips. Her soul recoiled before a vision that gave her no sense of security or peace.

More than once this particular trial was renewed. Josefa's humble self-distrust, her confidence in her guides, and her implicit obedience to the directions given her, saved her from this new peril. Her spiritual Director ordered her to renew her vow of virginity (until replaced by those of religion) at any and every appearance. The arch-enemy was not able to endure such acts of faith and love, and his crafty wiles failed in the face of them. He changed his attitude and aspect, became agitated and like an imposter caught in the act of deception he betrayed his guile by a sudden disappearance with blasphemous words. Later on, at the word of obedience, Josefa added to this renovation of her vow, the Divine Praises which she begged her heavenly visitants to repeat after her. Jesus Himself, His Immaculate Mother, and Saint Madeleine Sophie at once paraphrased them with incomparable ardor. The devil with his polluted lips was never able to utter such words of praise and benediction - "for he can no longer love." When unmasked thus, his furious violence was redoubled.

Notwithstanding all this, the spirit that guided her and the love that sustained her became more evident. In the midst of such a life of suffering and humiliation Josefa never exempted herself from the prescriptions of the Rule, of common life or of her allotted work. As soon as her prayer was over and she had heard Mass, she went to her sweeping and housework, and was punctually in her workroom, supervising the ironing, and in the little Auxiliary Chapel acting as sacristan; all her spare time was given to needlework and mending. Little works of supererogation, which abound in a big house like Poitiers, fell to her as of right, and in this devotedness she was of great assistance, being both active and intelligent, and still more, self-forgetful and devoted.

She made no change throughout those difficult months of December and January. As soon as the evil one loosened his hold of her, she quietly resumed her tasks with a courage that was nothing less than heroic.

Seeing her thus, ever even and unruffled, who could have imagined all she had just undergone, or what she might expect to happen at any moment? As a matter of fact, in spite of the efforts of the infernal spirits, nothing outwardly betrayed the dolorous road into which it had pleased God to direct her footsteps, and this safe custody in the hands of God was surely a sign of His presence and action.

As always, Our Blessed Lady's advent brought a gleam of peace into her dark night.

On February 3rd (First Friday) Father Boyer, in order to give greater stability to her vocation, at her request allowed her to add to her vow of virginity a second one, always to remain in the Society of the Sacred Heart, as long as Superiors were willing to keep her. This gave her new courage, and a still firmer determination to suffer as long as this pleased Our Lord.

On Sunday, February 12th, after a morning in which the devil had done his best to overcome her constancy, towards evening she had gone with all the novices to the Auxiliary Chapel, where Benediction of the Blessed Sacrament was to be given. After the Blessing Our Lady appeared, surrounded by light and standing quite close to her. Josefa started at the unexpected joy, thrilled at the sight of her Mother ... She had not seen her for such a long time ... she trembled ... hesitated ... but peace was flooding her soul, and she heard the loved voice she knew so well: "Do not be afraid, daughter. I am the Immaculate Mother of Jesus Christ, the Mother of your Redeemer and your God."

Josefa's whole soul exulted, but faithful to the directions given, and in order to thwart any possible snare of the enemy, she said: "If you are the

Mother of Jesus, allow me to renew before you the vow of virginity that I have made, until such time as I shall have the happiness of making my vows in the Society of the Sacred Heart. I renew also in your hands the vow to remain until death in the Society I so love, and to die rather than be unfaithful to my vocation."

Whilst speaking she was gazing spellbound on the sweet vision before her, which was regarding her with such tenderness. Our Lady placed her right hand on Josefa's head and said: "There is nothing to fear, daughter. Jesus is here to defend you and so am I."

Then, she made the Sign of the Cross on her forehead, gave her her hand to kiss and vanished. Josefa's troubled soul was filled with peace and joy, but her enemy was far from disarmed.

Yet did he not seem to know he was defeated? And though Josefa was shattered, the radiant mental picture of her Mother's smile and glance remained her comfort. For some days there was a cessation of her trials, and on the next day, Monday, February 13th, it was the voice of the Master that she heard calling:

"Come, there is no need to fear; it is I."

"Uncertain if it really were Our Lord ... " her notes continue, "I went to tell the Mothers, and from there to the tribune, where I found He was already waiting.

" 'Yes, Josefa,' He said, 'it is truly I, the Son of the Immaculate Virgin.'"

Never would the devil, in spite of his effrontery have dared to use such words.

" 'Lord, my only love,' I answered," wrote Josefa, " 'If it be Thou, deign to allow me to renew in Thy presence the vow I have taken for Thy sake.' He listened to me with pleasure, and when I had finished, He answered: 'Tell your Superiors that because you have been faithful to do My Will, I too will be faithful to you. Tell them that this trial is over... and O! what glory it has given My Heart ... and you, Josefa, rest in Me in peace, as I reposed in your sufferings.'"

A Break after Trial - The Forty Hours (February 14th - March 3rd, 1922)

"Do not think that I love you more now that I console you, than when I ask you to suffer."
(Our Lord to Josefa, February 14th, 1922)

Josefa had now reached an oasis of peace, a break in a stormy sky, a respite between two storms; we may thus characterize the three weeks which elapsed from February 12th to March 3rd, 1922.

Our Lord resumed His divine and cordial relations with Josefa, but she, who had shown herself so brave in the fight and so abandoned in pain, seemed hardly to come up to His expectations when faced with His appeals. He often stopped her in the midst of her work, and her marked attraction for common life seemed to grow each time she was called upon to sacrifice it. This ever remained the beginning of temptation, but no less the source of her humble contrition and of generous new efforts, by which the Sacred Heart of Our Lord intended to teach the world the riches of His pardons.

Josefa's notes were resumed from now on.

"On Tuesday, February 14th, I was preparing for Holy Communion during Mass," she wrote, "and hungering for His coming. A little after the Elevation, I saw Him and He said to me: 'If you are hungry to receive Me, I, too, hunger to be received by My souls. I come down to them with such joy.'

"After Communion He came."

" 'Do not think that I love you more, now that I console you, than when I ask you to suffer. In any case I cannot leave you without suffering, but your soul must remain in peace, even in the midst of pain.'"

"That evening," she wrote humbly, "I was greatly tempted." The devil, who for a time at least had been beaten, still prowled round his victim. Josefa was very vulnerable. Her repugnance to the painful path before her revived; and she accused herself in detail of this weakness. She spent four days in hard struggle, till Jesus, full of compassion, gave her the light she needed, and with it His forgiveness.

"Poor Josefa," He said on the evening of Friday, February 17th, showing Himself to her, as in all humility she was deploring her frailty. "What would you do if you had not My Heart? ... But the more feeble you are, the more tenderly I love you."

"I entreated Him again to give me a love true and strong," she wrote next day, "for I believe that if I really loved Him in the right way I should be better able to conquer myself. This was during my prayer, and Jesus came and said to me: 'Yes, Josefa, let your food be love and humility. But do not forget that I want you to be always abandoned and happy, because My Heart cares for you tenderly.'

"Then I explained how sad I feel that I cannot conquer myself nor correspond to so much goodness."

" 'Never mind. Cast yourself into My Heart, and follow the guidance that is given you. That will suffice.'"

Next day, Sunday the 19th, after the Elevation at Mass, He showed her His wounds shining resplendently.

" 'This is where I attract My souls, to purify and make them burn in the tide of My love. Here they find true peace and it is from them that I expect real consolation.'

"I asked Him how we can console Him, since we are so full of miseries and weakness. He answered me by pointing to His Heart: 'I make little account of all that,' He said, 'provided souls come to Me with confidence and love. I Myself make up for all their frailty.'"

It was Carnival time, days in which so many sins are committed in the world; consequently the salvation of souls could not but be of first importance in Our Lord's daily appeals.

Thursday, February 23rd, Josefa was ironing with the other novices, when suddenly Our Lord appeared and said: "I want you to come with Me."

Always faithful, she begged to be allowed to ask leave. He followed her to the very door of her Superior's room.

"I knocked twice," she said, "but as there was no answer, I was about to go away, but He insisted: 'Knock once more.'

"When I had obtained permission, I went to the tribune, Jesus walking beside me all the way. I asked His pardon, while we walked, for having let slip so many little occasions of doing the small acts He loves. 'If you want more, Lord, tell me and I will do them.'

" 'Love, Josefa, love consoles Me. Love humbles itself. Everything lies in loving... . During these days when I am so sinned against I want you to be My Cyrenean; yes, you will help Me carry My Cross.'

" 'It is the Cross of love ... the Cross of My love for souls ... you will comfort Me and together we will suffer for them.'"

The next day Our Lady came to confirm her Son's appeal.

"Yes, dear child, if you are docile and generous, you will comfort His Heart and mine, and Jesus will be glorified in your wretchedness.

"Then, laying a hand on my head, she went on to say: 'See how His Heart is outraged in the world. Do not lose any chance of making reparation these days; offer up everything for souls ... and suffer with great love.'"

Hardly a day passed without the sins of the world being brought before Josefa's mind, through the grief of her Master.

On Saturday, February 25th, she was on her way to close the windows of the cloister of the cells, when she saw Jesus weighed down by His Cross in the oratory of Saint Stanislaus.

"I went in," she said, "and He said to me: 'Souls are crucifying Me anew; comfort Me, Josefa. My Heart is steeped in woe ... sinners despise Me and trample Me under their feet ... there is nothing of less value in their eyes than their Creator.'

"He left me His Cross and disappeared.

"That night, at about ten o'clock, He returned, a heavy Cross on His shoulders; He was crowned with thorns and His face was streaming with blood. 'See the state I am reduced to... '1

" 'How many sins are committed,' He said, 'how many souls are lost ... that is why I come to obtain relief from those who live only to comfort Me.'

"He remained a moment in silence and with joined hands. He looked so sad and at the same time so beautiful! His eyes spoke more than His lips.

"After a while, He said to me: 'Souls run to perdition, and My blood is lost for them.'

" 'But souls that love Me are sacrificing and consuming themselves as victims of reparation, and they draw down God's mercy, and that is what saves the world.'

"He vanished. I think it must have been about one o'clock, and I kept His Cross till a little after four."

The days of the Quarant'ore were beginning, always a time for very special reparation. On Sunday, February 26th, before the Blessed Sacrament exposed, the whole household was assembled in prayer: a loving Guard of Honor that longed to compensate Him for the outrages of the world. Josefa's inconspicuous figure was among them, sharing their desires and listening in their name to the secrets of her Master.

"During the nine o'clock Mass," she wrote that Sunday, "Jesus came with a radiant Heart... . It might have been the sun.

" 'Behold the Heart that gives life to souls,' He said. 'The fire of this love is stronger than the indifference and ingratitude of men.

" 'Behold the Heart that bestows on the souls He has chosen a vehement desire to consume themselves, and if necessary, die to prove Me their love.'

"His words were so forcible that they went through and through my soul. Then, glancing at me, He continued: 'Sinners tear Me to pieces and fill

My Heart with sorrow... . Will not you, My chosen little victim, repair all this ingratitude?'

"I asked Him what He would have me do, for He knows my helplessness well.

" 'My Will is that you should enter deeply into My Heart today; there you will find strength to suffer. Do not reflect on your helplessness; My Heart is powerful enough to sustain you. It is yours; take from It all you need. Be consumed in It ... offer this Heart and this blood to the Eternal Father... . Cease to live except a life of love, reparation, and suffering.'

"That afternoon at about three o'clock He returned and said to me: 'I come to take refuge here, for My faithful souls are to Me as ramparts to a city: they defend and console Me.'

" 'The world is rushing headlong to ruin. I am in search of souls who will repair the many offenses that are committed against the Divine Majesty and I am consumed with desire to pardon... . Yes, to pardon these dear souls for whom I shed My blood... . Poor souls, how many are lost ... how many throw themselves headlong into Hell.'"

Faced with this sorrowful eagerness, Josefa did not know how to put into words her own ardent wish to suffer and repair for sin.

" 'Do not torment yourself, Josefa; if only you do not part from Me, My strength will give you strength and My power will be yours.'

"He then vanished, leaving me His Cross."

On the Monday of the Quarant'ore and on the night which followed Josefa bore the Cross of Christ, and pain and anguish were her portion.

The following day, February 28th, she went as usual to her work in the laundry, "but after a few hours, the pain in my side was so excessive, that I could hardly breathe," she wrote. She took refuge in the little attic where her bed was, a place already consecrated by many sufferings and heavenly visits.

"Jesus came at once, beautiful as ever, and His Heart all burning.

" 'How great are the sins of men ... but what distresses Me most is that they blindly fling themselves into Hell... . Do you understand My grief, Josefa? To see those souls that have cost Me My life, lost forever... . It oppresses Me to think that for them My Blood was shed all in vain. Come with Me, and together we shall make reparation to My Heavenly Father for all these outrages.'

"Then I united myself to His Heart and offered Him my pain."

She was particular to notice the humble, petitioning attitude of her Master: His hands clasped, His eyes raised to Heaven, His silence, all expressed His divine and constant offering to His Father.

" 'Tell the Mothers that this house is the garden of My delights,' He continued. 'I come here to seek consolation when sinners offend Me and make Me suffer. Tell them that I am indeed the Master of this dwelling, that it is a beloved refuge to Me and that My heart finds rest in it.

" 'I do not want or ask for great things. What I want and what is a consolation to Me is to find love that prompts good works, and that I find in this house.'"

That evening during Benediction Jesus again manifested Himself, and from His Heart there streamed light. "A little group of fervent souls can obtain mercy for many sinners," He said, "for My Heart cannot resist their prayers... . I sought for one to comfort Me and have found her."

The first days of Lent demanded still more redemptive sufferings from Josefa. March 1st was Ash Wednesday, and at the hour of her adoration Jesus became visible to her, His face disfigured with blood:

" 'Is there on earth any creature so insulted and despised as I am? Poor souls ... it is I who gave them life, and they seek to deal out death to Me. Not only are they oblivious of Me, those souls that have cost Me so dear, but they even make Me an object of contempt and mockery.'

" 'Come near Me, Josefa, rest in My Heart and share Its grief. So many fill It with sorrow, but your love will comfort Me.

" 'Repair, Josefa, for those who ought to but do not make reparation.'"

"At this moment the bell rang for the end of adoration, and I left the Chapel. He walked beside me. 'Go, Josefa, and ask whether I may stay with you while you do your work.'

"When leave had been given me, I went to the tribune just for a moment, and then resumed my work in the linen-room, because I think this pleases Him most. He was still there and spoke now and again:

" 'Ask forgiveness for the sins of the world. O! how they sin ... how many are lost ... souls that once knew and loved Me ... but now they prefer their own enjoyment and pleasure to My Heart... .

" 'O! why do they treat Me thus? ... Have I not given them enough proofs of love? ... And once they responded, but now they trample Me underfoot and ridicule Me, frustrating the designs of My love on them ... where shall I find relief for My distress?'

"I said to Him: 'Why, here Lord, in this house, in our souls ... there are still many everywhere who love Thee.'

" 'Yes, I know, but those are the souls I seek; I love them with a boundless love.'

"Again I offered myself to suffer for them, that they may repent. Jesus did not go away, and from time to time repeated:

" 'Gather up the blood I shed in My Passion.'

132

" 'Ask forgiveness for the whole world ... for those that know Me and yet sin, and offer yourself in reparation.'

"He stayed till about eleven o'clock at night, and then left me His Cross, the pain in my side and grief in my soul. A little before three I was relieved of all pain, and being exhausted, fell asleep."

Alas, temptation was close at hand. It would seem that Josefa could not hesitate after such intimacy with the Heart of the Master. Our Lord, however, left her to her inherent frailty. Apparently it was a clearly defined plan on His part, and the means chosen by His wisdom, to keep her safe amid the many graces she received and the dangers that threatened her, allowing her thus to plumb the very depths of her lowliness and nothingness. Already there were signs that the powers of darkness were coming back to the charge.

On March 2nd we find in her notes a humble avowal that she inwardly resisted Our Lord's desire for comfort, because:

"I had not yet finished my work in the linen-room, having had to sweep the little Chapel.

" 'Go quickly and ask leave,' Our Lord insisted. 'I want victims to make reparation and to console Me, and where else can I go if I cannot find them here?'

"I went to ask leave, but Jesus did not return. Both the Cross and the Crown disappeared at the same time, and my soul was plunged in remorse ... for truly I want to live only to be a comfort to Him, but my weakness is overpowering."

Josefa spent the whole day in an agony of distress. It was the First Friday of March; all day long she begged Our Lord and especially Our Lady to forgive her. "For," she wrote, "they know very well that it is my weakness and not ill will."

Our Lady could not resist her distress. She came and reassured her child, who at the time was just finishing the Way of the Cross.

"Do not be unhappy, my daughter; if you are willing, Jesus will go on drawing comfort from you. He wants it so much, but remember that your love is free."

Then she confessed what she ever afterwards characterized as the greatest sin of her life.

That same night Our Lord came, "all-beautiful," but wearing a look of sadness: "Here are My Cross and My Crown, Josefa, take them. Give Me the rest I need, I am so sinned against ... so many souls are lost ... and I love them so!"

And in response to her petition for pardon and oblation of herself to all He might require of her: "Never refuse Me the comfort I look for from you," He said. "True, there are many who love Me and console Me, but none of them can take the place I have reserved for you, for I have cast a special

133

glance of love on you."

At these words, Josefa, who deep down in her heart could not rid herself of the invincible fear she had of the extraordinary path mapped out for her, felt as if a huge wave of opposition arose in her. She was unable to overcome it; when later she gave an account of that dolorous incident, she characterized the inward recoil as "ingratitude." But Our Lord, to whom all hearts are open, knew well that she was dominated by fear, and that she would never entirely succeed in overcoming her apprehension.... His Heart was full of compassion for hers.

" 'If you knew what sins are committed against Me, you would not refuse My Cross,' He rejoined. 'Do you know what that Cross is? ... It is the freedom you must grant Me to use and take you whenever I want you, without regard to the place, the occupation, or the time. It should suffice you to know that I want you to console Me. If I am with you, what does it matter if the whole world is against you?'

"At this point," wrote Josefa in all sincerity, "I say it for my greater shame, I replied by entreating Him to spare me that path. He looked at me sadly and said: 'I cannot forsake you, for My love for you is boundless, but as such is your wish, be it done to you according to your desire. No one but yourself will be able to close the Wound inflicted on My Heart ... '

"He took back His Cross and His Crown and vanished."

A few days later Josefa wrote as follows:

"It is impossible to say all I have gone through since that day. It is a torture that nothing on this earth can equal. First: I know that I have wounded Him, and next, if He does not return, my life will be a martyrdom, for I myself have thwarted the designs of His love."

She had not yet sounded the depths of that Heart's mercy.... Notwithstanding her vacillations, nothing was changed in the design of His love. It would be gradually unfolded, but on a different plane, which His wisdom had already foreseen, so that on March 3rd a new phase in Josefa's destiny began.

The Bottomless Pit opens to Josefa (March 4th-April 15th, 1922)

Remember, daughter, that nothing happens, unless it be in God's plan.
(Saint Madeleine Sophie to Josefa, March 14th, 1922)

This new phase of Josefa's life was perhaps the most mysterious one of all. At first sight, it looked as if chastisement was being meted out to her as a result of her resistance to Christ's appeal; but it soon became apparent that the design that was being woven on the obscure loom of her destiny was a very different one, unveiling to our eyes Our Lord's divine predilection for Josefa, and disclosing how He took advantage of a momentary weakening of her will to further His great work by giant strides, still in and by her.

Greater power over her was being given to Satan, who opened before her the bottomless depths of Hell itself. She was steeped in agonies never before experienced, and knew by sharp physical pain what the loss of a soul really meant, and how total was the immolation demanded of her for its redemption.

Whilst Our Lord allowed her to be thus crushed by sorrow, He sank her deep in humility and in a faith and abandonment that she could never have acquired by her own personal efforts. Our Lord kept the carrying out of this work in His own hands, and it was accomplished when and how He pleased, by means that defied human foresight.

In an admirable page of her autobiography, Saint Teresa describes the indelible impression left on her soul by a passage through Hell. We have many notes written by Josefa under obedience, describing her long sojourns in the abyss of pain and despair. These records, striking in their very simplicity, take us back after four centuries to the classical narration of Saint Teresa. They sound the same note, one of pain and contrition, of redemptive love and burning zeal. The dogma of Hell, often disputed, and oftener ignored in incomplete spirituality, to the great detriment of souls, and even with danger to their salvation, is brought out with a clarity that admits of no doubt. Who, when reading these pages of what Josefa saw, heard and suffered, can question the existence of an infernal power attacking Christ and His Kingdom with desperate fury? Who can gauge the value of the long hours spent in that prison of fire? ... Josefa, who believed herself shut up in it forever, witnessed the fierce efforts of Satan to snatch souls from Jesus Christ, and felt the excruciating torment of no longer being able to love.

Some extracts from her writings will be useful to souls. They act as a cry of warning to those who have a rough path to re-climb, if they are to recover their friendship with God. Above all, are they not a call from Love to those who make up their minds that they will spare nothing in order to save souls who are in danger of eternal perdition?

It was in the night of Wednesday to Thursday, March 16th, that Josefa made her mysterious descent into Hell for the first time.

From the 6th of March, soon after Our Lord's disappearance, infernal voices had several times caused her great fear and disturbance of mind. Damned souls, invisible to her eyes, came from the lowest depths, reproaching her for her want of generosity. She was greatly perturbed.... She heard cries of despair like these: "I am there where love is banished ... forever ... how brief was the enjoyment ... and the punishment is eternal.... What have I gained? ... hate, and that forever ... eternal hatred!"

"O!" she wrote, "to know that one soul is lost and to be able to do nothing for it! To know that for all eternity a soul will curse Our Lord and that there is no cure ... even if I could suffer every torment in the world ... what terrible sorrow.... It would be better to die a thousand times than be responsible for the loss of one soul."

On Sunday, March 12th, she wrote to her Superior, who was absent from Poitiers on a journey to Rome:

"If you knew, Reverend Mother, with what grief I write. I no longer have any of my jewels [as she calls the Crown of Thorns and the Cross], for I have once more wounded Jesus, who is so good to me.... I still hope that He will have compassion on me, but for the moment I am paying dearly for it, for since the night of the First Friday the greatest of sufferings has taken the place of His visits ... when you return, Reverend Mother, you will know the full extent of my weakness."

And in order not to sadden her Superior, she added with the tact that never forsook her:

"How glad I am of the happy days you are having at the Mother-House; except for me, everybody here is, I think, trying to console Our Lord, and His Heart is receiving what He expects from 'His garden of delights,' as He calls this house. With me things go on as before: my efforts are directed to being kind and faithful, and telling everything to the Mother Assistant, and the rest you know.

"Pray, Reverend Mother, that Our Lady may lay her motherly hands on me and obtain my forgiveness."

This time Our Lord sent Saint Madeleine Sophie as His messenger.

On Tuesday, March 14th, she appeared to Josefa in her cell. After listening to her humble avowals, she gave her fresh courage, and heartened her with the words: "Remember, daughter, that nothing happens unless it is in God's designs."

Josefa told her of her overwhelming grief, and of the sorrow that weighed her down when she realized the consequences of her frailty, which she was convinced were beyond repair.

"But, my child, you can repair your fault," was the quick reply, "if from your fall you draw great humility and generosity."

"I asked her whether Jesus would ever again return. I call on Him, I want

Him, for I cannot believe that through my fault I shall never see Him again ... "

Then interrupting her with motherly impetuosity, our Holy Mother said: "But you must expect His return, my child; the longing and expectation of the bride are the glory of the Bridegroom."

This heavenly visit testified to a love that was unchanged and to forgiveness that never tired. Evidently Jesus meant Josefa, now at the beginning of the great trial she was to undergo, to feel that He was still there, and quite unchanged.

"In the night of March 16th towards ten o'clock," wrote Josefa, "I became aware, as on the preceding days, of a confused noise of cries and chains. I rose quickly and dressed, and trembling with fright, knelt down near my bed. The uproar was approaching, and not knowing what to do, I left the dormitory, and went to our Holy Mother's cell; then I came back to the dormitory. The same terrifying sounds were all round me; then all of a sudden I saw in front of me the devil himself.

" 'Tie her feet and bind her hands,' he cried... .

"Instantly I lost sight of where I was, and felt myself tightly bound and being dragged away. Other voices screamed: 'No good to bind her feet; it is her heart that you must bind.'

" 'It does not belong to me,' came the answer from the devil.

"Then I was dragged along a very dark and lengthy passage, and on all sides resounded terrible cries. On opposite sides of the walls of this narrow corridor were niches out of which poured smoke, though with very little flame, and which emitted an intolerable stench. From these recesses came blaspheming voices, uttering impure words. Some cursed their bodies, others their parents. Others, again reproached themselves with having refused grace, and not avoided what they knew to be sinful. It was a medley of confused screams of rage and despair. I was dragged through that kind of corridor, which seemed endless. Then I received a violent punch which doubled me in two, and forced me into one of the niches. I felt as if I were being pressed between two burning planks and pierced through and through with scorching needle points. Opposite and beside me souls were blaspheming and cursing me. What caused me most suffering ... and with which no torture can be compared, was the anguish of my soul to find myself separated from God... .

"It seemed to me that I spent long years in that Hell, yet it lasted only six or seven hours... . Suddenly I was violently pulled out of the niche, and I found myself in a dark place; after striking me, the devil disappeared and left me free... . How can I describe my feelings on realizing that I was still alive, and could still love God!

"I do not know what I am not ready to endure to avoid Hell, in spite of my fear of pain. I see clearly that all the sufferings of earth are nothing in comparison with the horror of no longer being able to love, for in that place all breathes hatred and thirst to damn other souls."

From that day on Josefa frequently endured this mysterious martyrdom. All was mystery in those long, dark, and gloomy sessions beyond the pale. Each time she was warned of the oncoming of the fiends by the noise of chains and distant yells, but they came nearer and nearer and finally surrounded and overwhelmed her. She tried to fly, to distract her mind by work, to escape the hail of blows which in the end overcame and threw her to the ground. She had just time to take refuge in her little cell before losing all consciousness of her surroundings. She began by finding herself in what she described as a dark hole, faced by the demon who appeared to think that she was definitely in his power forever. He boisterously commanded her to be thrust into her fiery niche; and Josefa, tightly bound, would fall into the chaos of fire, the dolorous abode of rage and despair.

Her notes were written objectively, and in the simplest terms she told things just as she saw, heard, and experienced them.

To those watching only a slight tremor made known her mysterious abduction. Her body instantly became entirely soft and supple, like one whose soul had just departed. Head and members were no longer under her control, though her heart beat normally; she was as one alive, yet dead.

This state was prolonged more or less according to God's Will, who thus delivered her over to the powers of darkness, but held her still in His very sure and strong hand.

At the moment decreed by Him there was a slight, almost imperceptible, tremor once more and her body came back to life.

She was not thereby wholly freed from infernal influence in that dark place where he overwhelmed her with threats.

When at last he relinquished his hold on her she slowly returned to herself. The hours spent in Hell seemed long ages to her, and only by degrees was she able to resume contact with the places and people that surrounded her. "Where am I? ... Who are you? ... Am I still alive?" she asked; her poor eyes once again sought to make contact with a life which at the moment was so distant and remote. At times tears silently ran down her cheeks, and her face bore the impress of a sorrow difficult to describe. At last, and very gradually, she succeeded in realizing the actuality of sensible objects and persons; how could one depict the feelings of intense emotion that overwhelmed her when she suddenly became aware that she could still love God!

Josefa herself described this moment of transport in words of passionate fervor:

"On Sunday, March 19th, 1922, which was the third Sunday of Lent, I once more went down into the abyss, and it seemed to me that I remained there for long years. I suffered much, but the greatest of my torments was in believing that I could no longer love Our Lord. When I come back to life I am simply mad with joy. I think my love has increased tenfold and I feel ready to endure for love of Him whatever He wishes. As to my vocation, I esteem and love it to folly!"

138

A few lines further on she said:

"What I have seen gives me great courage to suffer, and makes me understand the value of the smallest sacrifices; Jesus gathers them up and uses them to save souls. It is blindness to avoid pain even in very small things, for not only is it of great worth to ourselves, but it serves to guard many from the torments of Hell."

Josefa tried her best, under obedience, to recount the history of the descents into the bottomless pit, so frequently made at this time. Not everything can be printed, but a few pages which contain valuable lessons may act as a stimulus to those whose good will urges them to sacrifice self for the salvation of the unfortunate beings, who every day and at every hour stand on the brink of the chasm, and who run such terrible risks in the tragic fight between love and hatred, despair and mercy.

On Sunday, March 26th, she wrote again, "On reaching that abode of horror, I hear yells of rage and devilish exultation because another soul has fallen into everlasting torments... .

"At the moment I am not conscious of having previously gone down into Hell; it always seems to me to be the first time. It seems, too, to be forever, and what an agony that is, for I remember that I once knew and loved Our Lord ... that I was a religious, that He conferred great graces on me, and many means by which to save my soul. What was it, then, that I did? How did I come to lose so many good things?... How could I have been so blind? ... And now all hope is gone... . My Communions, too, come back to my mind, and my noviceship. But the most crushing and overwhelming grief of all is the torturing memory that I once loved the Heart of Jesus so dearly. I knew Him and He was everything to me... . I lived for Him... and how can I now exist without Him ... loveless and with blasphemies and deadly malice on every side?

"It is impossible to put into words the poignant distress to which my broken and oppressed soul is reduced... ."

Not infrequently she witnessed the efforts of the devil and his fierce satellites to snatch from divine mercy the souls that were on the point of becoming his prey. The agony endured by Josefa in those cruel moments seems to have been the ransom of those poor souls, who would owe the final victory to her pangs.

She wrote on Thursday, March 30th:

"The devil is more enraged than ever, for he is after three souls to drag them down to Hell. In strident tones he yells furiously to the others: 'Don't let them escape ... they are getting away... stand your ground ... steady, hold hard.'

"And from a long way off I heard vociferations and unspeakable clamor."

She was witness of the fight for these souls for two or three days in succession.

"I begged Our Lord to do with me whatever He willed, if only these three could be spared," she wrote on her return from the abyss, Saturday April 1st. "I appealed to Our Lady and she gave me great peace, for she left me determined to endure anything, if only they could be saved, and I do not think that she will allow the devil to get the upper hand."

On Sunday, April 2nd, she again wrote:

"I could hear Satan's yells: 'Don't let go of them; be on your guard ... plague them in any way you can ... they must not escape ... induce them to despair! ... '

"It was a ferment of agitation, vociferation, blasphemies, when suddenly with a howl of passionate frenzy he cried: 'No matter ... we shall get the other two ... they must be made to despair.'

"By this I understood that one of them was safe forever.

" 'Hurry ... press on ... ' he roared. 'Those two must not escape ... hold them, seize them ... bring them to despair ... they are escaping us... .'

"Then Hell resounded with the grinding and gnashing of teeth, and in indescribable fury the devil howled: 'O! power and omnipotence of that God... . He is stronger than I. There is only one left and she shall not escape ... ' but by the medley of groans and blasphemous words I understood that all three were safe in the Heart of Jesus. How I rejoiced, though unable to make a single act of love in spite of the longing I felt to do so ... but none of the feelings of hatred manifested by the unhappy souls around me affect me, and when I hear their curses and blasphemies, I feel ready to suffer anything rather than hear Him so outraged and offended. Shall I in time, I wonder, become as they are? What suffering such a thought occasions, for can I ever forget how I once loved Him and how good He was to me?

"I have endured much," she continued, "these last days. It is as if a stream of fire were being poured down my throat, passing right through my body, while at the same time I am pressed between the fiery planks, as I said before. The pain is intolerable, and beyond description; my eyes seem to be starting out of their sockets, wrenched out, my nerves strained, my body wracked and doubled in two, incapable of stirring, and over and around the nauseating and offensive stench, infecting the air.Yet, what is all this in comparison with a soul who knows God's goodness and is forced to hate and revile Him? This suffering is all the greater in proportion to the love she formerly had for Him."

There were other mysteries beyond the pale that were revealed to Josefa during this period of Lent 1922.

Whilst day and night she bore the burden of these terrible persecutions, God put her in touch with another abyss of woe, that of Purgatory. Many souls came to solicit her suffrages and sacrifices in terms of very great humility. At first she was frightened, but by degrees she became accustomed to their confidences. She listened to them, asked them their names, encouraged them, and very humbly recommended herself to their intercession. The lessons they inculcated are worth remembering.

One of them came to announce her deliverance and said: "The important thing is not entrance into religion, but entrance into the next world." "If religious souls but realized the heavy price to be paid for concessions to the body ... " said another, while asking for prayers. "My exile is at an end and I am going to my eternal home... ."

A priest-soul said to her: "How great is the mercy of God, when He deigns to make use of the sufferings of other souls to repair our infidelities; what a degree of glory I might have acquired had my life been different."

It was a nun who, on her entrance into Heaven, confided to Josefa: "How different the things of earth appear when one passes into eternity. What are charges and offices in the sight of God? All He counts is the purity of our intention when exercising them, even in the smallest acts. How little is the earth and all it contains, and yet, how loved... . Ah, what comparison is there between life, however prolonged, and eternity! If only it were realized how in Purgatory the soul is wearied and consumed with desire to see God."

There were also some poor souls, who having escaped through God's mercy from a still greater peril, came to beg Josefa to hasten their deliverance.

"I am here by God's great mercy," one of them said, "for my excessive pride had brought me to the gates of Hell. I influenced a great number of other people, and now I would gladly throw myself at the feet of the most abject pauper.

"Have compassion on me and do acts of humility to make reparation for my pride, thus you will be able to deliver me from this abyss."

"I spent seven years in mortal sin," another confessed, "and three years ill in bed, and I always refused to go to Confession. I was ripe for hell-fire and would have fallen into it if by your present sufferings you had not obtained for me the grace of repentance. I am now in Purgatory, and I entreat you, since you were able to save me ... draw me out of this dreary prison."

"I am in Purgatory because of my infidelity, for I would not correspond with God's call," said another. "For twelve years I held out against my vocation and was in the greatest peril of damnation, because in order to stifle my conscience I gave myself up to a life of sin. Thanks to the divine goodness, which deigned to make use of your sufferings, I took courage to come back to God ... and now, of your charity, get me out of this gloomy prison."

"Offer the blood of Christ for us," said another who was just about to leave Purgatory. "What would become of us, if there were no one to help us?"

The names of these holy souls, who were personally unknown to Josefa, having been carefully noted down with the date and place of their decease, were more than once verified. The assurance thereby gained of the truth of the facts she related remains as a precious testimony of her intercourse with Purgatory.

Lent was drawing to a close while these successive alternations of pain and austere graces continued. Without the special intervention of God Josefa could not have endured such contacts with the world invisible and at the same time lead her even life of devotedness and labor. Such, however, was the spectacle of heroic love she daily gave to the Heart of Him who sees in secret, whereas those about her could not but mistake the value of those externally monotonous days, spent in the plain accomplishment of duty.

Two facts relating to the last days of Holy Week stand out.

In the afternoon on Holy Thursday, April 13th, 1922, she wrote:

"I was in the Chapel at about half-past three when I saw before me a personage clothed like Our Lord, rather taller, very beautiful and with a wonderful expression of peace on his face which was most attractive. His vesture was of a dark reddish purple. He held in his hand the Crown of Thorns just like the one Our Lord used to bring me long ago.

" 'I am the Disciple of the Lord,' he said, 'John the Evangelist, and I bring you one of the Master's most precious jewels.'

"He gave me the Crown and himself placed it on my head."

Josefa was at first rather startled at this unexpected apparition, but she gained assurance through the feeling of intense peace which took possession of her. She ventured to confide in the saintly visitor, telling him of the anguish the ill-treatment of the devil caused her.

" 'Have no fear,' was the reply. 'Your soul is a lily which is kept by Jesus in His Heart - I am sent to make you acquainted with some of the feelings that overwhelmed His Heart on this great day:

" 'Love was about to part Him from His disciples, after it had baptized Him in a baptism of blood. But love urged Him to remain with them, and it was love that made Him conceive the idea of the Blessed Sacrament.

" 'What a struggle then arose in His Heart. He thought of how He would rest in pure souls, but also how His Passion would be carried on in hearts sullied by sin.

" 'How His Heart thrilled at the thought of the moment, then approaching, when He would go to the Father, but it was crushed with sorrow at the sight of one of the Twelve, one specially chosen, who was to deliver Him up to death, and at the knowledge that for the first time His Blood was to prove useless to save a soul.

" 'How His Heart wore itself out in love! But the want of correspondence to grace of those so beloved plunged It into dire distress ... and what of the indifference and coldness of so many chosen souls?'

"With these words he was gone."

This heavenly visitation upheld her courage for a time, as it brought so forcibly before her mind the call to reparation by which the Holy Eucharist appeals to consecrated souls.

But this apparition of peace was but an interval in the storm. That very evening the Crown disappeared, leaving her in great perplexity. The enemy was at pains to sow anxiety and trouble in the soul of his victim.

The old anguished question returned: Was she not being played upon by illusion and deception? ... All those things to do with the invisible world, were they not a mirage of her imagination, caused by an unbalanced mind or unconscious suggestion?

These questions were not confined to herself alone. Yet there was nothing in her that could morally or physically give support to this doubt. But the prudence with which she was surrounded was on the watch, and seeking for an authentic sign that what was taking place was due to the direct intervention of the devil. God was about to give that sign and so remove all hesitation and doubt.

On Holy Saturday, April 15th, Josefa, having spent the last two days in terrible contests, heard the sounds that usually were a premonition of the approach of the evil spirits. She was engaged in needlework; and supported by obedience she resisted with all her might the approach of Satan, but he ended by casting her to the ground. Then, as on former occasions, her body seemed to become lifeless.

Kneeling beside her, the Mothers prayed earnestly, begging Our Lord to remove all doubt concerning the mystery enacted under their eyes.

Presently the usual slight tremor which preceded Josefa's return to life was noticed. The expression on her face betrayed the horrors she had witnessed and endured. Suddenly she clutched at her chest and cried: "Who is burning me?" There was no light or flame anywhere near, and her religious habit was apparently untouched. With a rapid movement she tore open the front of her dress, and at once the cell was filled with the acrid smell and fetid fumes of smoke, and her inner garment was seen to be on fire. An extensive burn remained "near the heart," as she said, attesting the truth of this - the first attempt of the kind made by Satan. Josefa was terrified: "I prefer to go," she wrote in that first moment of shock, "rather than continue to be the devil's sport."

God's fidelity, in thus tangibly manifesting the power of the infernal agents, was hereafter of notable comfort and reassurance in the months that followed.

Ten times in all Josefa was thus set on fire. She saw the devil vomit on her flames of which visible traces were seen not on her clothes only, but on her person. Painful wounds which took long to heal left on her body scars which she carried to the grave. Many of those scorched garments have been kept, and are witnesses to the devil's rage, and to the heroic courage of Josefa, who endured these assaults in order to be faithful to Love's enterprise.

A Short Truce (April 16th-July 8th, 1922)

"I shall be the light of your soul."
(Our Lord to Josefa, April 17th, 1922)

Easter fell this year, 1922, on the 16th of April, and Our Lord granted Josefa a brief truce, His risen Body crushing in its victory Satan's power.

Early that morning Josefa saw Him during Mass. It was for the first time since March 3rd - a day which remained in her mind as one of sorrow and contrition, though she never doubted of Our Lord's forgiveness nor His love.

"His whole Person was resplendent in light and beauty," she wrote, "but I told Him I had no leave to speak to Him.

" 'You have no leave, Josefa?' He answered gently. 'May you look at Me?'

"I did not know what to say... .

" 'Look at Me,' He continued, 'and let Me look at you. That is enough.'

"I looked at Him, and He also fixed His eyes on me with such love that I am at a loss to say all I felt... . After a moment He said: 'When Reverend Mother sends for you, ask her leave to speak to Me.'

"Then He vanished."

Although Josefa met her Superior a few minutes later, she obeyed Our Lord literally and waited to be sent for.

"Reverend Mother sent for me towards half-past eleven," Josefa noted, "and gave me the desired permission. I went to the Chapel and Jesus came at once.

" 'Here I am, Josefa! ... Why did you want Me to come back, even if it were but once?'

" 'O! dear Lord, that I might entreat Thee to forgive me, for I do so want it!'

"Then I told Him the whole story of all my miseries and weakness, and with affection simply indescribable He answered: 'He who never needs forgiveness is not the most happy, but rather he who has humbled himself many times.'"

Then Josefa let her whole soul pour out its tale of woe into the compassionate Heart of her Lord - all the obscurities and troubles of the past weeks; and she did not omit her anxiety about the Crown of Thorns: was it really He who sent it to her on Holy Thursday, and then took it away so unaccountably?

Jesus reassured her:

" 'Yes, it was I who entrusted you with that precious treasure. But it was too much consolation for you, and you comforted Me more by accepting the uncertainty than by wearing My Crown on your head.'

"Then I spoke to Him of the burning last Saturday, and told Him how it disturbs me to be thus the devil's sport. He answered strongly, almost sternly: 'Where is your faith? If I allowed you to be the devil's sport, know that I did it solely to give an unimpeachable proof of the plans of My Heart for you.'"

This Paschal dawn lasted a few days longer:

As once long ago Jesus appeared to His disturbed Apostles to speak words of comfort and reassurance after His Passion, so now - on Monday, the 17th, she wrote:

"The Gospel of today was that of the apparition to the Disciples of Emmaus; as I was saying the words: 'Stay with me, Lord, for the day is far spent,' He suddenly made Himself manifest to me.

" 'Yes, I will stay with you, and will be the light of your soul. Yes, indeed, the day is far spent ... what would you do without Me?'"

On Friday, April 21st, after a night during which the return of the enemy and the torments of Hell had disappointed her hopes that they were over, we find in her notes: "This morning during Mass Our Lord came. I had thought all these torments were at an end, and I asked Him if He would not leave me enough freedom to do a little work."

The answer came in a tone of authority: "Josefa, I have told you already that I want to make use of you as an instrument of My mercy for souls; but unless you surrender yourself completely into My hands, what am I to do? ... There are so many souls that need pardon, and My Heart would like to use victims that will aid in repairing the insults of the world and in spreading My mercies. What does the rest matter to you, if I sustain you? Never do I forsake you. What more do you want?"

Thus the Paschal week ended on a note of warning that many sufferings still lay ahead of her. The devil prowled around her path; the souls in Purgatory continued to beg her prayers and the help of her suffrages. But Our Lord, ever faithful, remained by her side and became, as He said, "the light of her life." "On Saturday, April 22nd," we read in her notes, "He came during Mass ... so gracious. I renewed my vows, and I think that pleased Him, for His Heart blazed ardently."

She expressed her anxieties concerning the souls in Purgatory who came to ask her prayers. Our Lord reassured her with His usual kindness, and gave her to understand how great were the graces obtained at the price of her pain. "If I tell you all these things," He said, "it is that you may not recoil, whatever the cost. Be convinced: the greater your sufferings, and the more acute they are, the more are you comforting Me, and it is when you least think it that you are drawing the greatest number of souls to

Me."

And when she told Him how worn out she was by the weeks of pain she had gone through: "I have no need of your strength, but I do need your surrender," He answered tenderly. "True strength is in My Heart. Remain in peace, and do not forget that mercy and love are at work in you."

It was, therefore, from the Sacred Heart that she would draw the fortitude demanded by the path of total abandonment which was increasingly to be hers.

"For some days past," she wrote on Monday, April 24th, "the devil has dragged me down to Hell at the same hour, and keeps me there for about the same length of time. This worries me, and I wonder if I am responsible for this in any way." When next Our Lord appeared to her after her Communion this was the first thing she asked Him.

" 'Do not be anxious,' He replied, 'there is a soul that we must snatch from the devil's grasp, and that particular hour is one of peril for her, but we shall succeed by dint of suffering. There are so many souls exposed to the danger of perdition ... but there are, too, many who comfort Me, and many who come back to My Heart.'

"Then," she said, "I asked Him what we could do to obtain the conversion of a sinner who had been recommended to our prayers, and who is a cause of great scandal.

" 'You must put My Heart between that sinner and My Father, Josefa. My Heart will appease His wrath and incline divine compassion towards that soul. Adieu, console Me by your abandonment and love.'"

Days of trial succeeded those of grace, for the devil did all he could to reawaken in her a whole flood of repugnances, and at the same time he tormented her with every sort of torture; she met him anywhere, he hit her, burnt her, dragged her down to the infernal regions ... and Friday, April 29th, in sheer terror of his threats, she dared not go to Communion, although the thought of one Communion lost was an immense sorrow to her.

These days of great distress brought back many souls, though she was unaware of this encouraging fact.

Tuesday, May 2nd, as she was sweeping the Auxiliary Chapel, suddenly she saw Our Lord in all the beauty of His glory.

"He was standing in between the benches," she said.

" 'Josefa, shall I come? ... I will not hinder your work.'

"I renewed my vows and told Him I must first ask leave.

" 'Yes, go.'

"He disappeared, and I went at once to tell Reverend Mother. When I came back I saw Him through the open door. He was still in the same place, as if waiting for me ... so full of sweetness ... the tenderness of a Father which no words can render.

" 'I want so much to come to you, Josefa. Are you going to shut Me out?'"

This question like an arrow pierced her through. She acknowledged her fear of the devil, who was doing all he could to prevent her from going to Holy Communion.

" 'Do you not know that he can torment you, but that he cannot harm you? Which of the two is stronger, he or I?'"

On Wednesday, May 3rd, after Communion, He came:

" 'Josefa!'

"I asked His leave to renew my vows; and then each time He comes I want to tell Him all my faults... .

" 'You cannot know how My Heart exults in forgiving faults that are of pure frailty. Have no fear ... it is just because of your wretchedness that I have fixed My eyes on you.'"

This gracious indulgence encouraged Josefa to tell Him of her great desire to be faithful to community exercises in spite of the devil. "Let Me use you as I will. To whom do you think common life gives the greater satisfaction? To you or to Me?"

Thus did the Master of abandonment continue the training of Josefa's soul through all the vicissitudes of her troubled life. A truce was called from time to time, and her notes still contained a few glowing passages:

"That evening during my adoration, whilst O Crux Ave, was being sung - for it was the Feast of the Finding of the Holy Cross - I was seized with an ardent desire of embracing the Sacred Wounds. I kissed my crucifix and begged Our Lady to do it for me.

"She came unexpectedly; her hands were crossed on her breast, and she said very gently to me: 'Daughter, what is it you want?'

" 'O! Mother, I want to kiss the hands and feet of Jesus, and if you will allow me' - here I hesitated a little - 'I want to kiss your hand as well.'

" 'You want to kiss my hand? Then do so ... ' and giving me her hand, she added: 'And you would like to kiss the Wounds of Jesus? ... '

"Before I had time to answer, there stood Jesus Himself, beautiful, and with glowing Wounds.

" 'What do you want, Josefa?'

" 'To kiss Thy Sacred Wounds, dear Lord!'

" 'Yes, kiss them.'

"He Himself showed her His feet, His hands, then His Heart. 'That Wound is yours; it belongs to you.'"

" 'See how I refuse you nothing, and would you refuse Me anything?'

"I told Him that He knew my desires, but that my infirmity is great."

In this way she tried to express the contrast she felt at certain times between her will and her actions.

"That accounts for the way in which I so often promise to refuse Him nothing, but fail to keep the promise when occasion arises.... These failures are followed by feelings of deep contrition at having wounded One who is so good to me.

" 'My Heart indeed loves you, and takes pleasure in your helplessness. Do you know how to comfort Me? Love Me and suffer for souls and never refuse Me anything.'"

These graces of predilection always proved to be the prelude of increased suffering, and Satan, who had not given up his intentions in her regard, made her feel his power more acutely than ever in the days that followed. But before giving her into his clutches again, Jesus wished to confirm His plans of love for her.

"I had told Him how intensely I longed for His coming in Holy Communion," she wrote on May 11th, "for I hunger for Him, and the more wretched I see myself to be, the more I beg of Him to bring me Himself the remedy for so much misery. After Communion He came with outstretched arms."

" 'I am longing to imprison you in My Heart, for My affection for you has no measure. In spite of your failings and weakness, I shall use you to make My love known to many souls. There are so many who do not know how much I love them.... My great wish is to see these beloved ones bury themselves in the abyss of My Heart.'"

This was the second time that her coming mission was revealed to her, and as He read in the depths of her soul what she dared not express, He added for her comfort: "When you feel how vulnerable you are, and that fear oppresses you, come here for strength. Adieu."

This adieu introduces us to the last phase before Josefa's vows. Our Lord no longer showed Himself, but Satan entered in triumph. All the torments of the past months were renewed in order to shake her faith and her fidelity. No efforts were spared by the evil one to destroy a vocation he saw to be so fruitful for the salvation of souls. Josefa had become his personal enemy, and for two months the unloosed powers of Hell fought in single combat with this frail creature, so weak in herself, but so strong in the strength of God.

Days and nights were spent, almost without halt or respite, in a desperate conflict, the violence of which was worse than anything she had yet gone through. It was astonishing that her strength did not fail, that she kept up her usual work without interruption, and that no single human eye was allowed to pierce the mystery of this extraordinary trial.

Jesus and His Mother kept watch over her during these waves of tempest, which at the hour decreed by God broke and dispersed.

Friday, May 19th, the canonical examination for admission to the vows took place in tranquility; the devil did not put in an appearance that day, and Josefa was able to testify, in the joy of her heart, to her determination to follow Our Lord and to be faithful to Him till death. This, of course, increased the infernal fury.

From May 25th, Feast of the Ascension, to Pentecost on June 4th the days went by without a single ray of light to relieve the tempest. On Sunday, the 11th, the post brought the glad news from the Mother House that Josefa was admitted to her First Vows. She received the news of this grace of all graces with immense joy, and could scarcely believe it to be true. The letter bore the date June 5th, a remarkable coincidence, for it was on that day two years before that Our Lord had first made Himself manifest to her.

These graces seemed to exasperate the devil, whose rage was intensified, while with tenacity he repeated again and again: "That day will never dawn.... I will wear you out.... I will torture you.... I will snatch you away from this place."

The month of July began in the midst of these relentless fights. The 16th, Feast of Our Lady of Mount Carmel, had been selected for the ceremony of her vows, and on Friday, the 7th, First Friday of the month, she began her preparatory retreat. That very day the devil assaulted her in the most terrible way she had yet experienced.... She afterwards acknowledged that never had she felt so near losing her soul.

These hours of unspeakable agony did not, however, succeed in wrenching from the depths of her soul her yearning for God. It was the Mother of Sorrows who again ruined Satan's plans.

The culminating point of diabolic striving for her soul was reached on the evening of the First Friday and during Saturday, July 8th.

It was five o'clock in the evening. Josefa, worn out, was seated in her little cell, where she had spent the whole of that terrible day. She did not seem to hear the Aves whispered beside her, appealing to the Virgin Mother, through her Sorrows, to come to the aid of her child. Suddenly there came a change over her face ... its expression relaxed, her lips parted, and gradually she joined in the prayers. Then in the calm which began to steal over her the Mothers tried reading to her a few words which had formerly been uttered to her by Our Lady, and which she had carefully treasured. When they read: "Daughter, you will never abandon my Son, will you?" she cried out vehemently: "No, Mother, never."

She threw herself on her knees, her face lit up, and before her liberated soul stood Our Lady herself, the Immaculate. With a transport of love difficult to describe, Josefa repeated the words again and again.

"No, no, Mother, never."

It was a startling moment when the devil's power crumbled and vanished before the sovereign intervention of the Queen of Heaven.

By an unlooked-for coincidence, which had surely been arranged by Our Blessed Lord Himself, Father Boyer O.P., her Director, was announced at that very moment. So Josefa was able to see him, and his words of encouragement and confidence restored her once more to the arms of God.

Retreat for First Vows (July 8th - 16th, 1922)

"Never will I be separated from Thee, but I will follow wheresoever Thou leadest."
(From Josefa's notes of retreat)

We have followed Josefa into the silence of her retreat, of which no single day has been exempt from the attacks of the devil. Her struggles can be followed in the notes of her retreat, in which her rooted love of God's Will stands out, in spite of the fact that it runs so counter to her own attractions, and demands of her such costly immolation.

"Lord," she wrote on July 8th, which had been a day of dire distress, "Thou seest what I am ... but rather than give Thee up and be unfaithful to the call Thou hast given me, I prefer suffering a thousand times over.

"I begin this retreat devoid of any longings, yet do with me whatever Thou wilt; all I ask is that Thou wouldst so bind me to Thy Holy Will that I may never swerve from carrying out what I know to be Thy good pleasure.

"There was a time when I hailed this day with enthusiasm. It has come at last, but it finds me cold, without strength or love ... but what would become of me had I not my Jesus! I love Him without measure, though this love is unfelt... . I will therefore allow myself to be led; I make the retreat solely because it is His Will, and I know that in spite of the darkness He is preparing my soul to unite it to Himself."

The first three days of the retreat passed in relative peace. The evil one tried in vain to torment her in every possible way. Nevertheless, she faithfully noted down the result of her meditations. These notes, which were not intended for any eye but her own, witness to her simplicity, uprightness and mental equilibrium.

"Jesus has given me my being, my vocation, and the means of serving Him according to His own plans," she wrote. "He has every right over me, and I must surrender with entire submission to His Will. It matters little if the path chosen is a very costly one to myself ... the measure of my abandonment will one day be that of my happiness, and true peace will always be mine if I do His Will completely, putting self out of count... .

"The meditation on death has given me strength to endure, for what a consolation it will be in the end to have suffered for God... . Thou knowest, O Lord, that I long to be united to Thee, and never to be separated from Thee, so it is not death that I fear, but life... . Yet my trust is in Thee; I know that Thou wilt never forsake me, and if suffering is what Thou requirest of me, I am content, provided it comforts Thee... . May my life be loyal and true, that in death I may find only beatitude.

"With the Prodigal I long to throw myself into Thy Heart, and there leave all my miseries... . I am sure of my welcome, for however great my sins, much greater is Thy mercy and the tenderness of Thy Heart."

When she listened to the Master's call, during the meditation on the "Kingdom of Christ," anguish and darkness had possession of Josefa's soul:

"Master! Thou seest my distress. Yet who can contemplate Thee leading the vanguard, and not want to follow? ... I will not be kept back by fear, but will joyfully tread in Thy footsteps. Do with me according to Thy Will for Thou art my King... . I surrender all to find all ... and once more repeat that never will I be separated from Thee, but will follow wheresoever Thou leadest.

"I drew fresh courage from the meditation on the Incarnation. There I see Jesus humble Himself to do the Will of His Father; in the same way I must humbly submit to His Will, whatever it may be ... loving that dependence and subjection. My soul ought to be in the habitual disposition to do all, to suffer all, and to sacrifice everything to God's Will. May I lead a life of absolute poverty in all things, that so He may carry out His holy Will in me."

The contemplation of the Nativity revived in her memories of past Christmas joys:

"Jesus, my life, when I see Thee thus in complete destitution, could I desire to possess anything whatsoever? My little Jesus, how beautiful Thou art! I draw near the Crib where Thou art lying on straw, and kiss Thy little feet and hands ... deign to glance at me with Thy entrancing eyes and let me hear from Thy lips 'Have no fear,' for Thou art my Saviour and lovest me with an infinite love, and hast said: 'My daughter, I want you to belong entirely to Me.' Am I not already Thine, Lord - and forever?"

When, on Wednesday, July 12th, Satan's sombre figure cast a heavy shadow across Josefa's path, suffering and desolation "invaded her soul. That night during a prolonged descent into hell-fire, he placed her in front of the empty niches, destined for the souls she had snatched from him, and there tortured her in revenge. She returned to consciousness crushed and worn out, but ready to suffer anything for the salvation of souls. Such an offering is never made in vain, and Josefa's soul again re-entered shadowy darkness.

Of all her sad days, Thursday, July 13th, was one of the hardest. Her notes bear the impress of the successive waves of overpowering desolation which seemed to engulf her spirit. "Jesus," she wrote, "come to my aid; see the night in which I am sinking ... do not leave me in the hands of my enemies ... "

After the meditation on the Two Standards:

"Thou, O Lord, knowest that for years past I have longed only to belong to Thee, to live for Thee, and to love Thee ... now I am on the verge of giving way. O! look on me, and all will be well. O! do look on me, Lord!

There are only two more days. If I cannot find peace in Thee, where am I to seek it?"

How sad were the words which expressed the memory of her heart's longings!

"Thou knowest how I longed for this retreat for my vows ... and see, my days are spent in terror, in dismay, in trouble and pain... . O! why is so much freedom granted to the devil?"

But thoughts of faith soon replaced these reflections -

"Lord, I await everything from Thy Heart, I wish to belong entirely to Thee, and I affirm it again at the very height of my distress, the worst agony I have ever known, as well Thou knowest!"

And as if to give herself courage in reaffirming her resolution to be loyal to the end, she jotted down broken words like the following:

"Lord, whither can I go, to whom can I give myself, if not to Thee? ... I no longer hope or desire anything, but I will not fail in loyalty... . I am ready to do whatever Thou willest ... to suffer as much as Thou willest, and to follow Thee anywhere, giving myself to Thee with entire generosity, for Thou art my Saviour and my God and hast chosen me... . O! Heart full of mercy and love, have compassion on me ... do not let me fall, give me strength to resist, constancy to persevere, and love to suffer."

Such a cry of distress and love could not but reach Heaven. On the evening of the 13th Josefa began her Holy Hour, kneeling in the oratory of Saint Madeleine Sophie. She was in a state of mind difficult to describe, when suddenly - in a flash - her soul became immersed in the profoundest peace. Once more Jesus had manifested His power. In the ineffable joy of that recovery, Josefa, delivered, transformed, and radiant, renewed the vows that in advance had bound her for eternity to the Heart of Jesus and to His Society. The devil was in flight, and in the expansiveness of her new-found happiness Josefa wrote next day: "Jesus, I thank Thee for having restored me to light and peace. I am ready to do Thy Will in everything."

Then as if speaking to herself, she added: "I have loved Thee all my life, Thee alone my God, but no one knew I belonged to Thee. Now the heavens and the earth will know that we love each other and are espoused for all eternity! ... "

During the last two days of her retreat this deep peace continued; she could hardly believe in her joy, but nevertheless she did not relax in the serious pursuit of perfection, and to the very end the devil tried to deprive her of her happiness.

"Jesus, in the desert, was tempted," she wrote. "The devil was allowed to attack God, to give me courage and to teach me that temptation is the crucible of all true virtue.

"I do not know if Jesus was ever tempted during His hidden life, but He willed to experience this trial at the moment when He was preparing for

His public life.

"When God deigns to make use of a soul He acts in the same way: He first of all keeps her hidden, to strengthen her interior life, but when the time comes to carry out His designs, He exposes her to temptation, in order to build her up, to preserve her from self-love and make her more useful to others by the experience she has gained.

"I must trust the Heart that watches over me; and the measure of my suffering, as He has many times told me, is the future measure of my consolation."

The sight of Our Lord in His Agony, braced and stimulated her will:

"How many lessons Thou givest me, Lord. In temptation and desolation, I must have recourse to prayer if I want relief, but especially to obtain strength to carry out Thy Will.

"How hard would be my heart, if at the sight of His Passion I hesitated to walk in the path He points out: a path of humiliation, denial, and absolute surrender of self."

That Friday evening, after the contemplation of the Crucifixion, she wrote:

"Lord, Thou art on the Cross about to die for me and Thy Heart will be opened for me. Heart of Jesus, show me the way in, then draw me down into Its depth.

"There is my dwelling; there shall I stay hidden - there shall I labor and suffer and lose myself ... the lowlier I am the more I shall be able to sink into Its deepest depths ... what a joy to know that Heart and to be His bride... ."

A little further on she renewed her promises with intense spiritual fervor:

"I am not capable of much, Lord, but I promise to follow where Thou leadest me. If I fail (and it will not be once only), I will not be discouraged, but will love Thee still more because of Thy tenderness for me who lovest me as though I had never sinned ... even if I do fall, I will rise again and fly to Thy Heart."

Saturday, July 15th, eve of her vows, Josefa spent in glad expectation. Her joy was at the same time so fresh and so grave that it must have ravished the Heart of Him who delights in the simplicity and spontaneity of love.

"Day of great peace, while waiting for the hour that is to unite me to Him," she wrote. "When He comes He must not find anything that might be displeasing to Him or hinder His entrance... . I must purify the dwelling of my heart. I am about to become the bride of a King who will bring with Him an abundance of all good things. I must lay aside my poor judgment, I must adopt His thoughts and His Will, and subject myself in everything to His tastes... ."

Towards midday the enemy made a final assault, but in vain ... He was not visible to her eyes, but she heard his raucous voice: "It's not too late, if you want to be happy, go away, or else I will burn you."

But this nefarious cloud cast no shadow over her quiet joy. That evening she noted down in detail all her intentions and hopes:

"So numerous," she said, "that I shall not have time to tell them all to Our Lord tomorrow, so I will put this letter on my heart, and He will read it during my thanksgiving. I shall have just made my vows and He will not be able to refuse me anything."

This paper has been preserved. It bears testimony to Josefa's pure affection for everyone she knew. She noted down name after name of all those dear to her (her writing getting smaller and smaller), running through all her intentions with a charity that extended to the uttermost borders of the earth and took in Holy Church, France, and Spain and the whole universe. She felt that in that most solemn hour of her life she was powerful over the Heart of Jesus, and shared more than ever His unfathomable thirst for souls. She concluded:

"As for me, I give myself up body and soul to Thee, and I have no other desire than the glory of Thy Heart which I so love. May the whole world know Thee... . May those consecrated to Thee love Thee ever more and more... . Nothing will ever separate us, neither life nor death. Enkindle me with Thy love, and give me no other consolation than that of consoling Thy Heart... .

"Receive this missive through the hands of Our Lady. For time and for eternity, I am henceforward Thine.

"MARIA-JOSEFA MENÉNDEZ OF JESUS."

The day ended in the full glow of the presence of Jesus who was near, and the night was spent in desires.

All was ready for the offering that was about to be accomplished.

The Offering (July 16th-August 7th, 1922)

"See, have I not been faithful to you? Now My work is about to begin."
(Our Lord to Josefa, July 16th, 1922)

It was a truly heavenly day for Les Feuillants. In the house, where
ceremonies of Clothing and First Vows were frequent, there was in the air
a renewal of fervor and gladness, which never failed to surround the
privileged few who were about to kneel before the altar and make their
offering. The whole family joined in the festive joy of the day, and never
does the motto of the Society "Cor unum et anima una in Corde Jesu"
take on a more living reality than on such occasions.

On the morning of Sunday, July 16th, no one foresaw the marvels that
were about to become realities in the life of the little novice, Josefa
Menéndez. How jealously God had kept her in the shadow of His face!
He had elaborated His plan, formed her and wrought in her, crushed and
ground her, till the pattern He designed had been fashioned and molded.
He had led her through chosen paths, and confounded Satan's devices. His
mercy had triumphed in her wretchedness and His power in her weakness.
Today He Himself was about to lead her to the accomplishment of His
great plans. The alliance was about to be sealed before Heaven and earth;
and she would become His consecrated bride, not to enjoy Him indeed,
but to aid in Love's enterprise which would consummate the union
between them.

She was the only novice to make her vows that day. The Chapel, bright
with flowers, was filled by the children, and by her Mothers and Sisters in
religion, when at eight o'clock Josefa entered with an air of recollected
joy which was not of this earth. Her beloved mother and her sister Angela
had come from Madrid. She knew they were there, and "these two loves
of her heart," as she called them, were part of the offering she was about
to make. Her other sister, Mercedes, a religious of the Sacred Heart, was
united to them in spirit, in her far-off convent of Las Palmas in the Canary
Islands.

Nothing either in her attitude or face, so calm and radiant, betrayed the
mysterious approach of heavenly visitants.

In the silence of prayer, which the liturgical chant interrupted from time to
time, the usual ritual of the ceremony proceeded. After a short discourse
by the celebrant who alluded to the austere joys of religious consecration,
Josefa advanced to the altar rails, and with a firm voice answered the
questions:

"Is it of your own free will that you renounce the world and all worldly
hopes and expectations? And do you take Jesus Christ for your Spouse
with all your heart?"

Her whole soul exulted in the words: "Yes, Father, with all my heart!"

She then received the crucifix on which is nailed the figure of "Him who must henceforth be your Model and the sole object of your love," and the black veil about which the following is said: "Receive the yoke of the Lord, for His yoke is sweet and His burden light."

Holy Mass began. When the solemn moment of Communion arrived, Josefa, all alone at the altar rails, in the Presence of the Blessed Sacrament held before her by the celebrant, slowly with all the will and love of her heart, pronounced the vows which would unite her forever to the Sacred Heart of Jesus. It was a moving moment to those who knew at what a price the favor had been bought, through what tempests her little bark had reached port, and what miracles of love had opened for her the Heart of Him who had been captivated by her littleness.

Human eyes saw only the simple offering, but another, and this a heavenly, scene was being enacted.

A few hours later Josefa, still deep in glad recollection, noted, so that she might never forget it, what Our Lord had been pleased to do for her.

"After the sermon, I went up to the altar rails to receive my crucifix of vows and black veil. Then suddenly I saw Our Lady present, O! so ravishingly lovely, all bathed in light. She held a veil in her hands, and when I returned to my prie-dieu, she herself put it on my head. All round her and framing her person were a number of radiant little faces which looked like those of tiny children, lit up with joy. With ineffable sweetness she said to me: 'While you, beloved daughter, were suffering, these souls were weaving this veil for you. All those you prayed for have left Purgatory and are safe in Heaven for all eternity. There they will protect you.'

"It was an entrancing sight: Our Lady looked like a queen with her beautiful countenance all purity and tenderness, her golden raiment and her exquisitely molded hands ... and then the souls ... so many little heads - O! it was wonderful to see, and I cannot describe how profoundly it affected me. Besides, I was wrapped in the veil, and had my crucifix. I did not know what to say ... I let the flood of happiness just roll over me ... what else could I do?

"When Our Lady finished speaking, the little faces disappeared, one after the other. She gave me her blessing and disappeared, too. I thought myself in Heaven.

"Then came the moment - how brimming with emotion and joy - to read the formula of my vows and receive Holy Communion ... and then, Jesus Himself came. His Heart was flooded with effulgent light, the Wound open wide, and from It issued a force that drew me into It, and I found myself deep down in Its depths.

" 'Now, I am satisfied,' He said, 'for I hold you prisoner in My Heart. From all eternity I have been yours; now, you are Mine forever. You will work for Me, and I will work for you. Your interests will be Mine, and Mine yours. I have been faithful to you, have I not, Josefa? And now My great work will begin.' And saying this He vanished."

A few hours later Josefa, whose heart was overflowing, wrote in her notes of retreat:

"Jesus has come; we are one ... does He know what a miserable creature I am, and that in spite of my longing to please Him and love Him, I shall disappoint Him more than once, perhaps? ... Yes, He knows it better than I do, but He loves me all the same, and He does not mind. He is ready beforehand to repair all my faults; that is why He has given me His Heart!"

Then she tried to find words which would express in detail the vows that bound her to this Sacred Heart:

"O Jesus, I thank Thee for the incomparable grace of my vows. What does my vow of Poverty mean to me? ... I know that, hence-forward, I have no right to anything: everything I use is given me as an alms. I have given up, too, all that I most cherish, my mother, my sister, my home, my country, to possess only Jesus Christ. But above all I must be despoiled of myself. Jesus will be all in all to me and I shall have no other wish or ambition than for Him. He is my strength and my peace; I want nothing but Him, and nothing except what leads me to Him.

"What of my vow of Chastity? Ah! how happy I am in my religious life and none can deprive me of this treasure. The world no longer exists for me, and I am in a closed garden full of every variety of flower, and in this enclosure, and in the midst of these flowers I shall spend my life, for they are all set apart for the Heavenly Husbandman. He cultivates me and I give Him pleasure. He loves me and I love Him! ... What else matters? O most pure Jesus, Bridegroom of virgin souls, I love Thee, for Thou art purity itself; that is what has attracted me from infancy. Jesus is the Spouse of Virgins! such were the words that attracted me as a child and made me relish the charms Thou reservest for consecrated souls, and ever since my soul has been the little flower that sheds its perfume for Thee, O Jesus! Never allow me to lose the spotlessness of grace or the love of virginity.

"And Obedience? It binds me to all legitimate authority, in which I see Thee and through whom Thou speakest to me and makest known to me Thy Will. But love must go further still; I must not only obey all authority, but listen to the interior voice to which I am sometimes deaf, because I find it too costly to follow its behests, or transmit what it tells me to transmit... . No, Lord, I will obey for love of Thee and will ask for no reasons, nor will I hesitate or complain, for it is not my will but Thine that must henceforth live in me, and all I do must be for Thee.

"All day," she concluded, "I was so lighthearted that I did not know what to say to Jesus and His Mother!"

She seemed in very truth to be wrapped in heavenly peace, and sunk in God, but ever the same, kindly, simple, full of consideration for others. She spent the day giving joy to all around her. She paid visits to the infirm and sick, so as to give them the kiss of peace that she had been unable to give them in the Chapel. Her coming was a ray of sunshine and an expression of charity. All the time she could spare was spent with her mother and sister, for her supernatural tenderness as daughter and sister had suffered no change.

When evening came, in the much-desired silence of a prolonged adoration before the Blessed Sacrament exposed, she repeated her consecration to His Heart.

The following days only strengthened her gift of self, until the time when it was Our Lord's intention openly to discover to her the plans of His Heart, thus realizing the words she had heard on the morning of her vows: "Now, My great work will begin."

"On Tuesday, July 18th," she wrote, "when the last bell rang, I left my mother and sister to go to the Chapel. As I went, I asked Jesus not to mind if I did not speak direct to Him quite so often these days, but to take as spoken to Himself all I shall say to them, for He knows I do it for love of Him."

As she entered the oratory of Saint Madeleine Sophie, Our Lord became visible to her. "Josefa, My bride," He said, "have no misgivings on this head. I am as much consoled as if you were with Me. See Me in them, and live in peace."

On Saturday, July 22nd, at the beginning of Mass, He again appeared - "most beautiful to behold," she wrote. "In one hand He held His Heart and with the other He beckoned to me: "Behold the prison I have prepared for you from all eternity," He said. "In My Heart you will henceforth live lost and hidden forever."

After Communion, He again spoke: "Josefa, My bride, let Me rejoice in you. My greatness will make your littleness disappear; from now on we shall labor together and as one: I shall live in you and you will live for souls."

And when she timidly reminded Him of her frailty: "Let yourself be guided.... . My Heart will do all that is needful, My mercy will be active, My love will annihilate your whole being."

"Yesterday," says a further note, "Our Lady came in the course of the morning."

This peerless Mother seemed anxious lest Josefa should forget the dangers with which her path was beset:

" 'Be in peace, daughter,' she said to me. 'Have no reserves, and be wholly occupied with the present moment. Jesus will lead both you and your Superiors. Keep close to them, remain faithful and submissive to the will of my Son, especially in difficult moments.'"

Then after a few recommendations: " 'My divine Son intends to use this little instrument for His glory and that notwithstanding all the machinations of the enemy.'"

So from Mary's own lips she gathered that the devil had not been quelled for long, for though unable to snatch her vocation from her, he would never cease trying to frustrate the plan he saw divinely inscribed on every page of Josefa's life. She was at first disconcerted to find herself still weak in spite of the grace of her vows, when painful temptations again assailed her.

"On Wednesday, July 26th, I was telling Our Lady of this great disappointment," she wrote, "asking her to obtain forgiveness for me from Jesus, to tell Him the joy it is to me to belong to Him, and how it is my one desire to love Him, but also would He deign to remember my lowliness; and as I was speaking to her so frankly and pouring out my troubles, Jesus Himself appeared. He came close to me and said: 'Why fear? I am your Saviour and Bridegroom. If only souls understood all these two words imply... . That is the work I intend to do by your means. The most ardent longing of My Heart is that souls should be saved, and I want My consecrated ones, especially those of My Heart, to know how easily they can give Me souls. By you, I will let them know what treasures go to waste by their not sufficiently understanding these two words: Saviour and Spouse.'"

On the 27th Our Blessed Lady showed herself to Josefa during night prayers. "My dearest child, do not grieve overmuch at your weaknesses, which will occur again,2 but love will always be there to raise you up, for you are sustained by a Bridegroom who loves you and who is your God."

A few days later she came with a message from Jesus, who was going to bring her His Cross:

" 'This night He will bring you His Cross,' and resting her hand on my shoulder," said Josefa, "she added: 'Do not regard your wretchedness, but look at the treasure that is yours, for if you are all His, He is all yours.'"

A few hours later, during the night, Jesus appeared bathed in radiant light and brought her the Cross which she had not carried for a long time.

" 'Josefa, will you share the Cross of your Beloved?' and He laid it on my right shoulder.

" 'Receive it with joy, and bear it with love, for you do this for the souls I love so much. Is it not lighter than before? That is because now we are united forever, and nothing will ever part us.'"

The Lord who allowed her the day to do her work knew she would be ever ready to console Him.

During the night of August 6th:

"I was already asleep when I heard His voice: ' Josefa, My bride!'

"There He stood, so surpassingly beautiful, bearing His Cross, and all encircled with light. I rose at once.

" 'I come to bring you My Cross.'

"And He unburdened Himself of it, laying it across my shoulder. I told Him what a joy it was to me to relieve Him of it in spite of my weakness.

160

" 'I bring it to you at night, for during the day I give it to other religious.'"

Then Josefa spoke to Him at once about souls and especially those of sinners, for this was a preoccupation that never left her.

" 'Yes, there are many who offend Me and many who are lost,' He answered sadly, 'but those who wound My Heart most are the much-loved ones who always keep something back, and do not give themselves wholly to Me. Yet, do I not show them clearly enough how dearly I love them? Do I not give them My whole Heart?'

"I begged His forgiveness for them and for myself who so often keep back something," she continued humbly, "and I begged Him to accept as reparation the acts and the love of those who want to console Him. He answered gently: 'That is My intention ... to repair the faults of some by the acts of others.'"

That night spent under the Cross was a fitting and immediate preparation for Sunday, August 6th, 1922, a memorable date in Josefa's history, for it opened out new prospects of the great work that awaited her. But the divine Master who can work only through the nothingness of His instruments, wished first of all to emphasize once more this need of His Heart. She wrote:

"After Communion Our Lord came in all His beauty; His Heart was wounded and open wide and He began by looking at me; then with great compassion He said: 'Misery! Nothingness! Such you are... . Little still implies some being, but, Josefa, you are less than that, you are nothingness personified.'

"He said this so lovingly that my heart was unlocked, and I simply poured it out: 'Yes, my Master, how true... . I am nothing and would like to be less than nothing, for nothingness never resists or offends Thee, since it does not exist, while I do resist and do offend Thee.'

"He came back during the second Mass and drawing me close to His Heart, He said: 'Are you, then, quite convinced of your nothingness? From now on, none of the words I say to you will ever be blotted out.'

"I told Him that the thought of His putting His work of love into my unworthy hands causes me great alarm, for in spite of my good will, I have a tremendous capacity for evil.

"From His Heart there sprang a flame that burnt me.

" 'Begin My work, but holding on tight to My Mother's hand the while... . Will not that give you courage?'"

Josefa's heart bounded at these words, for nothing gave her greater security than to be in the hands of Mary whom she so loved. "Yes, Lord," she answered spontaneously, "great courage and great confidence. Tell me what I can do to obtain from this dear Mother that she should never let me fail Thee in Thy work but keep me always faithful to Thy plans, and protect me, and that Thy Heart should sustain me; I desire nothing else."

There was a moment of impressive silence, after which Jesus spoke slowly and reflectingly words of extreme importance.

"As My Heart wishes to use abject instruments to carry out this work, the greatest of My Love, this is what you must do as a beginning during the days that precede My Mother's Assumption. You must ponder on and realize the nothingness of the instruments used. Trust wholly to the mercy of My Heart, and promise most solemnly never to resist or refuse Me what I ask of you, however crucifying it may seem.

"On Thursday you will make a Holy Hour to comfort Me for the resistance I meet with from souls consecrated to Me.

"On Friday, I ask of you an act of reparation for the offenses and sorrows inflicted on Me by these same souls."

That night when writing down Our Lord's words, Josefa was deeply struck at the memory of the grave solemnity with which He had spoken. She dared not go on writing lest she should record them inaccurately, and distort her Master's meaning. He deigned to appear and dictate to her what follows:

" 'It is of no consequence! When you write I will tell you what you have to say. None of My words will be lost. Nothing that I tell you will ever be blotted out. It signifies little that you are so worthless and wretched, for it is I who will do all.

" 'I will make it known that My work rests on nothingness and misery - such is the first link in the chain of love that I have prepared for souls from all eternity. I will use you to show that I love misery, littleness, and absolute nothingness.

" 'I will reveal to souls the excess of My love and how far I will go in forgiveness, and how even their faults will be used by Me with blind indulgence ... yes, write ... with blind indulgence. I see the very depths of souls, I see how they would please, console and glorify Me, and the act of humility they are obliged to make when they see themselves so feeble, is solace and glory to My Heart. What does their helplessness matter? Cannot I supply all their deficiencies? I will show how My Heart uses their very weakness to give life to many souls that have lost it.

" 'I will make known that the measure of My love and mercy for fallen souls is limitless. I want to forgive them. It rests Me to forgive. I am ever there, waiting, with boundless love till souls come to Me. Let them come, nor be discouraged. Let them fearlessly throw themselves into My arms! I am their Father.

" 'Many of My religious do not understand all they can do to draw those steeped in ignorance to My Heart. They do not know how I yearn to draw them to Myself and give them life ... true life.

" 'Yes, Josefa, I will teach you the secrets of My love, and you will be a living example of My mercy, for if I have such love and predilection for you who are of no account whatever, what am I not ready to do for others more generous than you?'

"He allowed me to kiss His feet, and then He went away."

From this time on, whenever Josefa had to transmit a message from the Heart of Jesus to the world, He would be there.... He would speak with all the expansiveness of the most burning love, and Josefa would write at His dictation these appeals, one by one, as they fell from His sacred lips.

In the notebooks, these passages are underlined in red ink to make them stand out as exceptionally important.

"On Monday, August 7th, after Communion," she said, "Our Lord appeared, beautiful as ever.

" 'What is it you want to tell Me, Josefa?'

" 'Lord, may I renew my vows, so that I may be obedient?'

[It will be remembered that many months ago this order had been given her, that the snares laid for her by the infernal enemy might be discovered.]

"Whilst I was renewing them, He looked at me with tenderness and compassion. 'Come, since you are nothing, enter My Heart. How easy it is for a mere nothing to lose itself in that abyss of love.'"

"Then He made me enter His Heart ... " wrote Josefa, but she could not comment on so mysterious a favor.

When at last she emerged from the unfathomable depths of Love's home, He said:

" 'That is how I will consume your littleness and nothingness.

" 'I will act through you, speak through you, and make Myself known through you. How many will find life in My words! How many will take new courage as they understand the fruit to be drawn from their efforts! A little act of generosity, of patience, of poverty ... may become treasure that will win a great number of souls to My Heart ... You, Josefa, will soon pass out of sight, but My words will remain.'1

"Then I ventured to tell Him how fainthearted I feel, for I am always afraid of not being faithful; He looked at me with eyes of unimaginable beauty and clemency, and said: 'Fear not! I will mold and use you as seems best for My glory and for the profit of souls. Give yourself over to love, let yourself be guided by love, and live lost in love.'"

Preliminary Explanation

As soon as Josefa had made her vows it became clear that God had chosen her with a view to a great plan of love. All the grace of her vocation, developed in her soul by divine love, had prepared her for this work.

As Spouse of the Heart of Jesus, she must be for Him a living response of love ... and He had revealed to her the secret of the love that He looks for from His Society: "the most tender and most generous love."

As Spouse of His Heart, she must penetrate into its wound, fathom its depths and unite herself with His sorrow at the blindness and loss of souls... . He had taught her that a life surrendered and united to Him in reparation had redemptive power.

As Spouse of His Heart, chosen by this God and Saviour to be an instrument of His love and mercy for souls whom He loves so tenderly, she must share His intense longing for them ... and He had shared with her the burning zeal of His Heart, by showing her the whole world as the object of their mutual love.

During the years of her religious formation, therefore, she had penetrated deeply into the grace of the special vocation by which every religious of the Sacred Heart is called to live as spouse, victim, and apostle.

Jesus Christ had emphasized, in all His guidance of her, every point of the Rule and had also from the beginning of her religious life made clear to her His idea of this Society "founded on love," as He said one day, "and whose life and end is love." (June 12th, 1923).

But this was still only the preparation for a greater plan.

He had spoken to Josefa many times of these plans. In spite of her fear and resistance, He had led her powerfully though very gently towards unconditional surrender of herself to her mission, which He gradually explained. On the day of her Vows, after reaffirming all His rights over her, did He not say these suggestive words: "And now, I shall begin my work"? (July 16th, 1923).

This work, which He Himself called the greatest of His love, was to become clear and be accomplished during the eighteen months that would complete Josefa's short life on earth.

But He who was guiding her and was at work within her kept her ever conscious that she was a weak and worthless instrument such as God always prefers. This is why Our Lord allowed her to experience her weakness in the daily fight in which she would be faithful to the end: temptation, the devil, Hell itself would ever be the greatest of her sufferings. These God put in the balance against her graces, so that Josefa became rooted in the consciousness of her own lowliness and nothingness. These God used as a goad which gave her no moment of rest in view of the sins of the world, souls to be saved, and the fire that was consuming the Heart of her Master.

Before going on to the last and most important stage of Josefa's life, ought we not to pause for a moment to look at the past and the future? ... The design of this work of love then becomes clearer in a twofold plan which seems to summarize it and at the same time allow us to "admire all its details," as Our Lord said.

What at once stands out in Our Lord's teaching, as in His action on Josefa, is its doctrinal character which sets in relief the guiding principles of our Faith. He seems to have wished to remind souls of these principles by a divine object lesson.

The Sovereign Dominion of the Creator over His creature and what this implies of dependence on the Divine Will and surrender to His guidance appears in the first place as the solid foundation of true love.

At the same time the whole history of Josefa is indeed that of Divine Providence which makes no mistakes in its ways. "As you are very small," Our Lord said to her one day, "you must let yourself be controlled and guided by My fatherly hand which is powerful and infinitely strong" (May 26th, 1923). "I will mold you as is best for My glory and for souls" (August 7th, 1922). "Do not fear, for I am looking after you with jealous care, such care as the tenderest of mothers takes of her little child" (May 3rd, 1923). Magnificent definition of divine fidelity, which can say to us at the turning-point of life, as He said to Josefa: "I never fail My word!"

We are constantly reminded of the presence of Grace giving life to the soul, the foundation of its incorporation with Christ. "I am in her," He said. "I live in her; I delight in making but one thing with her" (December 5th, 1923). But in return He asks her never to leave Him alone ... to consult Him about everything ... to ask Him for everything ... to clothe herself with Him and disappear beneath His life: "The more you disappear, the more shall I be your life" (June 5th, 1923). Is not this a commentary on the words of Saint Paul: "I live, now not I but Christ liveth in me"?

Then light is thrown on the value of this life-giving union with Him, transforming the least activities by gilding them with the supernatural. More than once and in tangible ways Our Lord showed Josefa what love can make of the most insignificant actions when they are united to Him. So, He wished to revive in souls the joy of believing in the wealth at our disposal. "How many souls would regain courage," He said, "if they realized the results of their efforts" (August 7th, 1922). "And how great is the value of a day of divine life" (December 2nd, 1922).

Here we reach the dogma which seems central in this wonderful teaching, participation in the infinite merits of Jesus Christ. Our Lord constantly reminds Josefa of this power over the treasures of His redemption given to the baptized soul. If He asks her to complete in herself what is wanting in His Passion, to repair for the world and to satisfy the Father's justice, it is always with Him, through Him, in Him. "My Heart is yours, take it and repair with it" (October 15th, 1923). Then He makes those offerings all powerful over the Heart of the Father, which Josefa heard and passed on to us: "Good Father, Holy Father, Merciful Father! Accept the Blood of Your Son ... His Wounds ... His Heart! Look upon His head pierced with thorns ... do not allow His Blood to be once more useless" (September 26th, 1922). "Do not forget that the time for justice has not yet come, but that now is the hour of mercy" (February 11th, 1922).

Lastly the great reality of the communion of Saints runs through the warp and weft of Josefa's vocation and forms the background of the picture of her life. Our Blessed Lady, Mediatrix of all Grace and Mother of Mercy, has her special place in the center of this wonderful exchange of graces and merits, between the Saints in Heaven, the souls in Purgatory and the Church Militant on earth.... . Only Hell is excluded. Josefa, a tiny member of the Mystical Body of Christ, learns from Him the repercussions in the world of souls of fidelity, sacrifice, suffering, and prayer.

But beyond these doctrinal lessons which seem already very valuable, the Direct Message which the Heart of Jesus will entrust to her to pass on to the world is an appeal of Love and Mercy. One day she said to her Master: "Lord, I do not understand what this work is that you are always telling me about." "You do not know what My work is?" He answered. "It is love ... I want to use you to reveal more than ever before the mercy and love of My Heart. The words or desires that I give to the world through you will rouse zeal in many souls and will prevent the loss of many others, and they will gain an ever fuller realization that the mercy of My Heart is inexhaustible" (November 22nd, 1922).

"From time to time," He said on another occasion, "I long to make a new appeal of love ... " (August 29th, 1922). "True, I have no need of you ... but let Me ask you for love and let Me show Myself once more to souls through you" (December 15th, 1922).

This great plan of love was, indeed, entrusted to Josefa by means of heavenly conversations carried on with her from time to time during the last months of her life. Jesus would choose the day and the time to meet her in the little cell where so often already He had shown her His Heart or brought her His Cross. She could not foresee His calls. Now He wanted her to be ready to write at His dictation on several consecutive days, now He would give her no more of His message for some weeks. Sometimes He would dictate only a few lines hastily, and at others He would keep her a long while on her knees gathering from His sacred lips the secrets of His Heart.

The book, Un Appel à l'Amour (Soeur Josefa Menéndez, Religieuse coadjutrice de la Société du Sacré-Coeur de Jesus, 1890-1923), has already given these words grouped in such a way that their meaning is brought out. In the present book the natural framework of the day to day writing will make the words themselves stand out more clearly. But it seems good to preface them with a broad preliminary synthesis so that souls may more easily grasp the meaning of this new manifestation of the Heart of Jesus.

He wants to reign in souls by giving them a more secure knowledge of His goodness, His love and His mercy. This is the testimony that He came on earth to give to His Father: Deus Caritas est, and this is what He wants

His followers to know and say of Him.

He wants by this new outpouring of His love to gain not only their love in return for His own but the trust that He values still more because it proves the tenderness of their affection and is the source of the most generous love.

He wants to attract and revivify souls by faith in the merciful kindness of His Heart which is so little understood, and believed in still less.

He wants chosen souls to have their sense of security in His love strengthened by deeper experimental knowledge of His Heart, and He expects them to spread the knowledge thus acquired to those who know Him but little or not at all.

He wants His appeal to waken slumbering souls ... to raise the fallen ... to appease the cravings of the hungry ... and that everywhere, even to the ends of the earth... . And He expresses this desire so positively that one cannot remain insensible to this burning appeal of His love.

At the same time He stresses the fact that in the order of God's Providence His plans depend, in part, on the free cooperation of men, a cooperation which He asks of all who have understood the meaning of His plans, the eagerness of His expectations and the significance of the redemptive means He employs. "When souls know My wishes," He said, "they will spare nothing, neither trouble, nor effort, nor suffering" (December 5th, 1923).

This is exactly how Josefa had understood the divine hunger and thirst which were to consume her life in a very few months.

Our Lord's First Requests (August 8th-September 30th, 1922)

"I want to make a new appeal of love heard."
(Our Lord to Josefa, August 29th, 1922)

The month of August 1922 had just begun, three weeks had elapsed since the graces of July 16th and the days that followed, and yet nothing seemed changed in Josefa's life. She was working with her usual earnestness and fidelity. Perhaps her charity was more expansive and her recollection deeper ... But to all appearances she had just slipped back into the hiddenness of her soul's secret life. God was about to deepen in her the sense of her nothingness as His instrument, a purpose which His love could carry out only in hiddenness and silence.

"I cannot account for the fact that for about a week I have felt that I know myself as I never did before," she wrote on August 10th. It is a sight that fills me with sorrow and shame, especially as Jesus is so good to me."

On Monday, August 14th, eve of the Assumption, she went on:

"While I was at my needlework today, I was struck by the thought: Why am I so ungenerous and always so afraid of pain? ... I understood that I look too much at myself and not enough at Him. This cannot continue, for I shall not live long, and soon I shall be unable to work for His glory. I have asked leave to make a Holy Hour to console Him for my lack of generosity, and a day of retreat to ask Him to teach me how to keep my eyes riveted on Him, His Will, His glory, His Heart, without any self-occupation."

On Tuesday, August 15th, Feast of the Assumption, under the protection of Our Lady, she began this day of solitude. "As soon as I awoke," she wrote, "I took my stand close to Jesus, and asked Him to teach me how to love Him with a true love: this is my one desire."

Our Lord answered her prayer by giving her an overwhelming conviction of her nothingness. He made her realize her nothingness and kept her thus annihilated before His face. "As I made my thanksgiving I prayed to be filled with as great a confidence in His Heart as shame for my sins."

But the Master of love willed that she should delve yet deeper into the knowledge of her littleness. He gave her a very clear, if symbolic view of it, and Josefa endeavored to explain it in the following terms:

"During the course of the morning of the 15th, without exactly knowing where I was, I suddenly found myself in a very dark and foggy place. It resembled a dark and dank little garden full of weeds, of thorny bushes whose stems devoid of leafage were entwined and twisted together... . There then occurred a slight lift in the mist, like a ray of sunlight, and I was able to distinguish the litter of grass and thistles which concealed a murky pond from which arose a fetid odor. Then it all disappeared. I was at a loss to know what it all meant, but I went to the Chapel and thought no more about it. But the one thing I kept on begging of Jesus all day was that I might love Him with a true love and fix my gaze constantly on Him. Suddenly He came before me, O! so wonderfully beautiful, and from His Heart there flashed forth a great light, and He said to me with much affection:

" 'My beloved, I am the sun that shows you your misery; the greater you see it to be, the more must your love for Me increase. Be not dismayed, the fire of My Heart will consume the wretchedness of yours. If your soul is tainted and corrupt and incapable of producing any fruit, I am He who tills it and I will send a ray of sunlight to purify and cleanse it.... I will sow seed in it.... Remain small, very small.... Am I not great enough? I am your God, I am your Bridegroom, and you are the misery of My Heart!'"

The Feast of the Assumption did not end without a visit from the Mother of God, and she, too, reminded Josefa that Jesus meant to make use of her very misery to further His great work.

It was while Josefa and her Sisters were saying the Rosary in the oratory of the Noviceship that she appeared:

"She was clothed," said Josefa, "as on the day of my vows, a diadem crowned her head, her hands were crossed on her breast and a little wreath of white roses encircled her heart.

" 'These flowers will be changed into pearls of great price for the salvation of souls,' she said, looking first at the novices kneeling round her statue."

And then turning to Josefa: "Yes, souls are what Jesus loves most; I, too, love them for they are the price of His Blood and so many are lost forever. Do not resist His Will, daughter, and never refuse Him anything He asks of you. Surrender yourself wholly to the work of His Heart which is none other than the salvation of souls."

She gave her a few personal directions, and added: "Have no fear - the Will of Jesus will be done, and His great work accomplished." Then she disappeared.

Our Lady's words, by throwing light on the work into which God's Will was gradually initiating Josefa, reawakened all her fears. Never to refuse her cooperation with this divine plan would remain to the end of her life a constant struggle for Josefa.

On Saturday, August 19th, whilst she was at her sewing, Jesus came. "Go and ask permission," He said.

Soon after, He followed her to her little cell, where on her knees she renewed her vows. So wondrous was the presence before her that she was at a loss how to express her love. "Yes, say again that you love Me.... I love your misery, Josefa!"

She told Him of the repugnance she could not master, when by obedience she had to tell the Mothers the wishes that He communicated to her. "All I ask you to say, hard as it seems to you, is for the good of souls.... No one will ever know how dearly I love them."

Then He continued: "None of you know how dear this house is to Me. I have cast on it a look of predilection. Here I have found misery which I can use as an instrument of My love. I have placed My Cross in the keeping of this group of souls. They do not carry it alone, for I am with them and I help them. Love is proved by deeds. I have suffered because I love them; it is now their turn to suffer because they love Me."

Two days later Our Lord again reminded Josefa that the spirit of faith would keep her in the safe way of obedience.

It would seem that before confiding to her His dearest wishes for mankind, He wanted to safeguard the authenticity of His declarations by Josefa's dependence on others, which He was to exact from her to the end as a sign of His presence. "I tell you," He said to her on Monday, August 21st, "I Myself direct all that happens and I will never allow you to be led by any path but the one I have chosen. Have confidence, and look only at Me, at My hand which is guiding you and at My tenderness which surrounds you with the love of a Father and Bridegroom."

The days went by, leaving Josefa expectant, not knowing what her Master would do.

On Thursday, August 24th, during meditation, He showed Himself to her and merely said: "Ask leave for Me to speak to you."

Josefa obtained leave, but Jesus did not return. She was not, however, upset by this for she had delivered herself over to His sweet Will whom alone she desired.

On Tuesday, the 29th, whilst she was sitting alone at her sewing in the Sisters' room, a well-known voice startled her: "It is I!"

She threw herself on her knees; it was Jesus. She prostrated herself to the very ground in adoration, and with a full heart exclaimed: "Is it indeed Thou, dear Lord? I have been expecting Thee for the last five days and was beginning to fear that perhaps I had displeased Thee."

"No, Josefa, I take pleasure in the expectant love of My friends. There are so many who never think of Me."

"Go to your cell; I will come too."

In a few seconds Josefa had reached her cell, to find that He was already there:

"I asked Him if it would please Him if I renewed my vows.

" 'Yes,' He answered at once, 'every time you renew them I tighten the bonds that unite you to Me.'

"Then I begged Him never to allow me to resist His Will, nor to let my wretchedness be an obstacle to His work.

" 'Never will your wretchedness force Me to leave you, Josefa. Do you not know that it is on account of it that I have chosen you?'"

After a long pause Our Lord spoke again very solemnly: "Write now how My consecrated ones are to make My fatherly Heart known to sinners."

Then kneeling at her small writing-table, she wrote under His dictation:

"I know the very depths of souls, their passions, their attraction for the world and its pleasures; I have known from all eternity how many of them will fill My Heart with bitterness, and that for a great number both My sufferings and My blood will be in vain.... But having loved them, I love them still.... My Heart is not so much wounded by sin, as torn with grief that they will not take refuge with Me after it.

"I want to forgive, I want the world to know through My chosen ones that My Heart is overflowing with love and mercy and is waiting for sinners."

"Here," Josefa said, "I told Him that they know it already, and that He must not forget how wretched I am, and quite capable of obstructing all His plans... .

" 'I know well that souls do know it,' He answered energetically and kindly, 'but from time to time I must make them hear a fresh call.

" 'And now I want to use you, little and miserable one. You have but one thing to do: love Me and abandon yourself to My Will. I will keep you hidden in My Heart and none shall discover you. My words will not be read till after you are dead.Throw yourself, therefore, into My Heart and with immense love I will sustain you ... Do you not realize, Josefa, My fondness for you? Have I not given you enough proofs already?'"

And as Josefa again humbly put forward her many relapses ... "I have foreseen them from all eternity and that is why I love you," was all His reply.

Two days later, on August 31st, Our Lord made His Will clear: "I want you to write, Josefa," and with more insistence, "I want to speak to you of the souls I so love. I want them always to be able to find in My words a remedy for their infirmities."

However, the next day, Our Lord did not summon her to write, but He set before her generosity one of those long and painful redemptive enterprises of which she had had experience before her vows. This appeal is part of the Message that He wished to transmit to souls through the very life of Josefa.

In this month of September 1922 we must watch Our Lord's pursuit of a "much-loved soul" as He Himself called it, the soul of a consecrated priest. With Josefa, we must enter into the unfathomable grief of Jesus, if we would understand the loving reparation demanded, and the redemptive suffering exacted.

"On the evening of the First Friday, September 1st," wrote Josefa, "as I was about to retire to rest and was kissing my crucifix of vows, my beautiful Jesus showed Himself to me.

"Then He spoke of souls with immense tenderness, and especially of three that had been confided to our prayers a few days before, and as if the thought of them had suddenly become a heavy weight on His Heart, He said: 'Two of them are still far, very far from Me ... but the one that grieves Me most is the third. I cannot let justice operate rigorously in regard of the first two, as they know Me less well, but the other is a priest, consecrated to Me in religion ... one I dearly love... . he himself is opening the abyss into which he will fall, if he continues obstinate in sin.'"

On Sunday, September 3rd, after Communion, Josefa again saw the Master. He shone with incomparable beauty, and resting His eyes on the nuns who were deep in their thanksgiving, He said with deep feeling: "I am enthroned in hearts that I have Myself prepared. My consecrated ones cannot possibly realize how greatly they relieve the sorrow of My Heart by giving Me entry into theirs. No doubt they are small and miserable, but they belong to no one but Me. Their wretchedness I condone, for all I want is their love. Weakness and worthlessness are of small account; what I want is their trust. These are the souls who draw down on the world mercy and peace; were it not for them, divine justice could hardly be restrained ... there is so much sin."

"Then," said Josefa, "His Heart seemed oppressed, and appeared as one great wound... . I tried to comfort Him. He looked at me sadly and continued: 'Innumerable are the sins committed, and innumerable the souls that are damned ... But what wounds My Heart above measure is the sinfulness of those that are consecrated to Me ... that soul sins, I love him, and he despises Me. I have to submit even so far as to descend onto the altar at his command, to allow his polluted hands to touch Me ... and to enter his heart, the hideous home of sin. Let Me hide Myself in your heart, Josefa. Poor, poor soul! if he but realized the agony he is preparing for himself for all eternity.'

"I begged Him to take pity on that soul, and reminded Him how He loves to forgive. I offered Him all the affection of His Blessed Mother, of the Saints, and of all good men on earth, and then the sufferings of this house which are considerable at this moment. He answered: 'My justice will be restrained as long as I find victims who will make reparation.'"

He then told Josefa that He would make her go through the torments of Hell reserved for those who had made vows but been unfaithful to them -

" 'In order to stimulate your zeal,' He said, 'and that later my souls may know the sufferings they risk enduring.'

"Then as if speaking to Himself, He said: 'Ah! soul that I love, why do you despise Me? Is it not enough that worldlings sin against Me, but you who are consecrated to My service, why do you treat Me thus? What an agony My Heart endures when treated with such indignity by one whom I chose with so much love.'"

It was on Monday, September 4th, that Josefa underwent, as the Master had decreed, the torments due to religious condemned to Hell. She had not been in contact with that place of indescribable torture since the month of July. This time she was conscious that she bore on her the mark of one vowed and consecrated, and consequently specially beloved.

"I cannot explain how terrible that suffering was, for if that of a worldling is unspeakable, it fades into insignificance when compared with that of a religious."

Words cannot render what she endured; she noted, however, that the three words Poverty, Chastity and Obedience constantly recurred, impressing themselves on the soul with an accusing power that was fraught with poignant remorse.

"Freely you took your vows, knowing fully what it meant ... you bound yourself ... you yourself willed it ... " and the inexpressible anguish of the soul lies in the fact that it unceasingly assents: "Yes, I did it of my own free will. I could have not done it, but I freely vowed and promised ... I was free ... "

She wrote further:

"The soul constantly remembers that she had made choice of God for her Spouse and that she had loved Him above all things ... that for His sake she had foregone the most legitimate pleasures, and all she held dearest in the world ... that in the beginning of religious life she had enjoyed the sweetness, the strength and the purity of divine love, and now, for indulging an inordinate passion ... she must forever hate the God who had elected her to love Him ...

"This fatal compulsion to hate is like a devouring and parching thirst ... memory gives no relief.

"One of the most acute torments is that of shame ... it is as if all the damned around her continually taunted her with her sin. 'That we should be lost is not extraordinary, for we never had the helps that you had. But you! What more could you have had? ... You who lived in the very palace of the King ... and sat at the board of the elect!'

"All I write is but a pale shadow of the reality, for words cannot declare an agony so extreme."

After her return from the abyss of everlasting woe Josefa devoted herself more than ever to the task of saving souls from its dismal depths. She understood as never before the crime of a consecrated soul's defection, the wound in Our Lord's Heart, and above all His burning desire to save from such torments souls that He loves so tenderly (see Appendix).

On Wednesday, September 6th, Our Lord appeared to her at Mass; she was startled at the sight of His marvellous beauty and deep sadness. His Heart was sorely wounded. She tried to comfort Him, and in replying He assumed the aspect of a mendicant asking an alms:

"I ask you only for your heart, that I may hide therein, and forget the bitterness caused Me by that soul, when I am forced to enter it. O! that it is these very souls whom I love so specially who treat Me so: this is My

173

grief!"

After Communion He repeated:

"You whom I love as the apple of My eye, hide and shelter Me in your heart."

"I answered Him with all the affection of which I am capable; I begged Him to hide in its very depths ... Would that my heart were not so small and that it might afford Him repose.

" 'It does not matter that it is small! I will expand it, but let it be all Mine.'"

Then slowly and with long pauses, to sink her deep in each longing of His Sacred Heart, Jesus helped her to make her thanksgiving.

"Console Me ... love Me ... Glorify Me through My Heart ... Make reparation and satisfy divine justice by It... . Offer It to God the Father as a Victim of love for souls ... and in a special way for those vowed and consecrated to Me... . Live with Me and I will live with you... . Hide in Me and I will sink deep into your heart."

Then He recalled to her mind the union of reparation He wished to realize in her soul:

"We shall comfort one another, for My pain will be yours, and your suffering Mine."

Surely this was the same understanding of that union of vocation which once drew from the soul of the holy Foundress of the Society of the Sacred Heart the prayer: "May there never be any other cross for a religious of the Sacred Heart than the Cross of Christ."

Every night, as had now become usual, the Master brought Josefa His Cross which He asked her to carry for the priest that was causing Him such sorrow.

"Will you carry My Cross?" He asked her.

And instantly she offered herself to take it from His sacred shoulders.

On Friday, September 8th, towards evening He came "as a poor man hungry and begging" she wrote, thus accurately describing the atmosphere of sad appeal that seemed to envelop His whole Person.

"O slake My thirst to be loved by souls, especially to be loved by those I have chosen... . That soul is oblivious of My love," He went on, alluding to the unfaithful priest. "It is his ingratitude that puts Me into this state."

"Then," wrote Josefa, "I begged Him to accept all the little acts done here, the sufferings of the house, and above all the very real desire we all have to comfort and please Him. I asked Him to purify and transform these very little things, and give them some value in His sight.

" 'I do not look at the act itself, I look at the intention,' He replied. 'The smallest act, if done out of love, acquires such merit that it gives Me immense consolation... . I want only love, I ask for nothing else.'"

Our Lady could not keep away when there was question of the saving of a soul. She came at the worst moments to reanimate Josefa's courage. On September 9th:

"Suffer with courage and energy, dear child," she said "Thanks to what you have been undergoing that soul has not fallen into greater sin."

So Josefa kept herself at the disposition of Our Lord's Will, and every morning at Mass she saw Him as a poor man worn out by fatigue and grief.

"Keep Me deep in your heart and share with Me My bitter sorrow," He said, on September 12th, during her thanksgiving after Holy Communion. "I can bear the insults I receive from that soul no longer ... yet I still love him," He added with pity after a moment's silence, "I am waiting for him ... I want to forgive him... . With what affection I would greet him if he returned to Me!

"As for you, Josefa, comfort Me, draw near My Heart and share My grief."

There was silence for a space:

"I am in pain," He said at last, "share that pain for it is also yours."

"On the evening of this September 12th as we were rising from our meal in the refectory, I suddenly caught sight of Our Lord.

"He was standing at the end of the refectory, resplendent in beauty, His white raiment shining in the dusk of evening. His right hand was uplifted in blessing, and as He passed in front of me I heard Him say: 'Here I am in the midst of My beloved ones, for in them I find comfort and rest.'"

She followed Him up to her cell, and there He repeated the same words, adding:

"Courage, a few more efforts and that soul will return to Me."

Others besides Josefa had a share in this ransom: there were at that time at Les Feuillants several nuns who by their acceptance of illness or infirmity were closely united to Our Lord crucified. Speaking of them Our Lord said on September 13th:

"Many are willing to entertain Me when I visit them with consolation. Many receive Me with joy in Holy Communion, but few welcome Me when I visit them with My Cross. When a soul is stretched on the cross, and is surrendered to My Will that soul glorifies Me ... and consoles Me, and is very close to Me."

He then made His meaning clearer still:

"It is because of the sufferings of My religious that that priest has not fallen lower still; but yet more must be undergone for his conversion.

"When he has come back to Me, Josefa," He added, so that she might not lose sight of her mission, "I will tell you the secret of My love for souls, for I want them all to know how great it is."

On the Feast of her Seven Dolours, September 15th, Our Lady deigned to come to tell Josefa more about this love of Our Lord's wounded Heart.

"She was clad in pale mauve, her hands joined on her breast, and O! how lovely ... " wrote Josefa.

"I asked her to console Our Lord herself, for though my one desire is to love Him, I do not know how to, and I need her own Heart with which to love and make reparation.

"My child," said Our Lady sadly, "that priest is wounding my Son's Heart ... but he will be saved"; she added a few moments later, "but not without much suffering. It is not in vain that Jesus has given charge of him to His religious ... Happy are those whom He chooses for so precious a trust."

Days and nights passed during which Josefa had no relief from her sufferings of soul or body.

"Be not dismayed," said Our Lord to her on September 21st, "for that soul will not be lost. He will soon be returning to My Heart, but when a soul is to be saved, much suffering is needed."

This none knew better than Josefa. The devil set himself against her in furious assaults as if he had guessed the redemptive character of her sufferings for the soul he thought to have securely in his clutches. Descents into Hell were added to the other painful expiations she underwent, and night after night the Cross of Jesus lay heavy on her shoulder. On the September 25th, after a more than usually painful night, Our Lord manifested Himself to her:

"His Heart had no wound and was transfused with light and beauty. 'See! ... that soul has come back to Me and has allowed grace to triumph. O love Me, and refuse Me nothing to obtain for Me the love of many other souls.'"

The following day He said to her: "That priest has thrown himself into My arms and his sin is forgiven... . Go on offering your sufferings with Me that he may have the strength to climb the steep ascent to a finish."

A few days later Our Lord told Josefa with overflowing joy: "That soul is seeking Me ... I await his coming with tender longing, and no favors will be too great to bestow on him."

Finally on October 20th Jesus confirmed this conversion so dearly bought: "He is now deep in My Heart, and his own retains only the painful but meritorious remembrance of his fall."

Who on reading this account can doubt that the lost sheep is ever the best loved - the Prodigal Son the most eagerly sought and the most tenderly received?

But Our Lord did not allow Josefa any long respite. Her mission ceased neither day nor night, since souls are in peril and the world is full of sin. Such is the lesson He seems to be teaching us through her, by continually inviting her to new enterprises.

"On the evening of September 26th I met Him near the chapel, His head was crowned with thorns, His face bedewed with blood, but His Heart was all fire.

" 'Josefa,' He said, 'do not forget to make the Stations of the Cross.'

"I obtained leave, and as I ended them, He came back and said: 'We must save two souls from a great danger. Offer yourself as a victim for them.' And stressing all that the word meant to Him, He added: 'That is, leave Me free to do with you whatever I will.'

"Straightway my soul was filled with pain and anguish, and I knew not what to offer for the salvation of those souls."

She obtained leave for certain penances, and unceasingly united herself to the Precious Blood. Towards evening Our Lord joined her in her cell.

"With clasped hands and eyes turned heavenward, He said gravely and impressively: 'Eternal Father, Father of mercies, accept the blood of Thy Son, accept His wounds, accept His Heart for these souls.' He paused, and a moment later repeated the same words: 'Eternal Father, accept the blood of Thy Son, accept His wounds, accept His Heart. Consider His thorn-crowned head. Let not His blood be once more shed in vain. See His thirst to save these souls for Thee ... O Father, do not allow them to be lost ... Save them that they may eternally glorify Thee.'"

The next night was spent in anxiety and prayer, for Josefa could think of nothing but souls in danger.

At dawn on Wednesday, September 27th, Jesus, most beautiful, His Heart on fire, stood by her during her thanksgiving. Ever faithful to obedience, she renewed her vows.

"Tell Me once again of your love. Josefa, I will tell you one of the secrets of My Heart ... O help Me in this undertaking of love.

"Lord," she answered, hardly knowing how to respond to His passionate appeal, "Thou knowest that I have no other desire myself ... I long to give Thee souls ... that they may console Thee ... that Thou mayest be known and loved ... but how can my littleness be of any use to Thee?"

The Master then explained: "There are some souls that suffer in order to obtain for others strength not to consent to evil. If those two souls had fallen into sin yesterday, they would have been eternally lost. The little acts you did obtained for them the courage to stand firm."

Josefa was surprised that such little things could have such vast repercussions.

"Yes, My Heart gives divine worth to these little offerings, for what I want is love! I am in search of love. I love souls and I look for a response of love. What is so wounding to My Heart is that often instead of love I meet with indifference. Give Me love and give Me souls ... unite all your actions to My Heart. Stay with Me who am with you. I am Love and desire only love. O! if souls only realized how I wait for them in mercy. I am the Love of all loves, and it is My joy to forgive."

Thus ended with the month of September these enterprises of reparation and salvation through which Our Lord seems to have wanted to write the preface of His Message. "I will speak by you, I will act in you, and I will make Myself known through you," He had said (August 7th, 1922) and He who in His life on earth began by action rather than by preaching, kept faithfully to the same method now.

Before dictating, and even while He was making her write down the revelations of His love and mercy, He willed that they should be found also one by one and day by day in the ordinary course of Josefa's life.

Thus would souls better understand the significance of the Message that His Heart was about to give them, if they saw it also in the life-history of His messenger.

Appeal to Consecrated Souls (October 1st-November 21st, 1922)

"Do My chosen souls know of what treasures they deprive themselves and others, when they are not generous?"
(Our Lord to Josefa, September 20th, 1922)

As often happened in Josefa's redemptive life, trials quickly followed on the more luminous hours when, together with her Divine Master, she had worked for the saving of particular souls. The devil revenged himself for his defeats by a recrudescence of attacks and the infliction of fresh torments. In reality this was all part of the divine plan. Love was endowing the instrument with new capacity for grace, in order to unite it more closely to Himself and use it at His pleasure.

The opening days of October 1922 passed painfully enough, Josefa meanwhile carried on her usual occupations.

It was at this time that she was entrusted with the making of the school uniforms, and certainly her skill as a dressmaker marked her out as well fitted for the work. This did not prevent her helping when all were called to general work in the laundry, ironing-room, etc. She had care also of the Auxiliary Chapel which was situated at the end of a very large inner courtyard, and was separated from the rest of the house. This she kept exquisitely neat and clean, under the direction of the Mother Sacristan, who greatly appreciated her help. Added to this she had charge of the little oratory which had been the cell of Saint Madeleine Sophie, as well as of the chapel of Saint Stanislaus, in which occasionally the Blessed Sacrament was reserved. At the same time and until the end of her life she looked after an old and infirm nun who could not help herself and whom she treated as she would her own mother, with respectful solicitude, so that the poor invalid forgot the length and weight of her trial.

It is fitting to remind ourselves from time to time how active and incessant was her humble work, that we may be able to judge better how great must have been the effort that enabled her to carry it out uninterruptedly, while her inner life moved on such a different plane. It helps us to understand how a distress of soul, at times overwhelming, was so heroically borne by this generous Sister.

On October 6th, first Friday of the month, she wrote in one of those moments of acute mental agony:

"I was weary of suffering and reflected on the uselessness of these descents into Hell ... when suddenly I saw before me a brilliant light. It resembled the sun and dazzled the eyes, and I heard the voice of Jesus: 'God's Holiness is offended and His Justice demands satisfaction. No, nothing is useless. Every time I allow you to undergo the pains of Hell, sin is atoned for and the divine wrath appeased. What would become of

179

the world if reparation were not made for offenses committed? There are too few victims ... too few... .'

" 'How can I make reparation when my own infidelities are so great? I am full of miseries and faults,' answered Josefa.

" 'No matter, the sun of love purifies you and makes your suffering worthy to be used in reparation for the sins of the world.'"

This assurance strengthened her, but without diminishing the weight of Divine Justice that she bore.

Ten days later, Monday, October 16th, Our Lady came to encourage her by a signal grace, of which she gave the following account:

"It was about ten o'clock and I was working at my sewing-machine. I had put my rosary on the table nearby and whilst working said a few Aves ... My soul was steeped in sadness as on the preceding days, and I felt exhausted by the pain in my head and side ... It seemed as if I could bear no more, and I said to myself: 'What shall I do if things go on like this? ... Suddenly I saw Our Lady standing in front of the sewing-machine; O! how lovely she was, her hands crossed on her breast ... She took my rosary by the cross with her left hand, and holding it thus, she slowly dropped it into the palm of her right hand. Then she pressed the cross on my forehead three times and said: 'Yes, child, you can do still more ... you are suffering for souls and to comfort Jesus.'"

O marvel! At the very moment of this motherly caress three drops of blood were imprinted where the cross had touched the undercap on Josefa's forehead. She was not aware of the fact.

"Without giving me time to reply Our Lady put the rosary back on the table, and leaving me full of courage to suffer, she disappeared."

A few moments later one of the novices who was working beside her noticed the drops of blood and told her of them. Startled, she rose and hurried to her cell... . Full of confusion at what had happened, she would have liked to make this proof of Heaven's favor disappear, but she left it like all the rest to the keeping of her Mothers. The coif still bore on the exterior of the broad hem the three drops of vivid crimson blood, whereas there was no mark whatever on the inner side, which was in contact with Josefa's head. Nor was there the slightest sign of a wound on her forehead.

The next day, Tuesday, October 17th, Our Lord was to say to His favored child:

"You will never know how much I love you. Remember what I did for you yesterday... . Yes, it was My blood, look on this grace as a mark of My Mother's tender affection for you. It is My blood that purifies you and fires you with zeal. In it you will find strength and courage."

That little coif more than once manifested the power of Him whose sign it bore. The devil could not resist a blessing given in the name of this Divine blood. One day, however, in fury the evil one contrived to get possession of the treasure which was kept most carefully under lock and key. On February 23rd, 1923 it disappeared. It could not be found, and the search was given up only when Our Lord came and reassured Josefa two days later, on Sunday, 25th: "Do not fear; it was the devil who took it, but My blood is far from exhausted."

In answer to Josefa's fears at the constant threats of the enemy to burn the books in which she wrote (under obedience) the words of her Master, He said to her: "With diabolic craft, he contrives numberless plans by which he hopes to spirit away My words, but in this he will not succeed, and to the end of time many souls will draw new life from them."

On the evening of March 15th, 1923, the Feast of the Five Wounds, Our Lady renewed the favor of the three drops of blood, and as she pressed the cross of her rosary on Josefa's forehead she said: "Offer yourself to efface the wounds caused by the sins of the world. You know the joy of His Sacred Heart when His consecrated souls offer themselves to comfort Him."

Once again, on June 19th, 1923, through His Blessed Mother Our Lord renewed the same pledge of His loving-kindness. The two coifs, both stained with blood, are carefully preserved, and the following day Our Holy Mother, speaking of this signal grace, said to Josefa: "Let the Society keep both these treasures, and never forget how Jesus left them these precious relics. The day will come when they will be one of the proofs that will accredit the reality of His goodness in this work."

But we have been anticipating, and must now return to the end of October 1922, when Our Lord was preparing to begin officially the great work by dictating the first Message to Josefa.

On Friday, October 20th, towards seven o'clock in the evening, she was just finishing her adoration before the Blessed Sacrament when Jesus appeared bearing His Cross.

"Josefa," He said, "share with Me the flames that are consuming My Heart: I thirst for the salvation of souls... . O! if only they would come to Me! ... If only they had no fear of Me ... if they but had confidence in Me.

" 'I am all love,' He continued, 'and how then could I treat severely those I so love? ... All indeed are dear to Me, but I have a great many whom I very specially favor. I have chosen them that I may find comfort in them and overwhelm them with favors ... I will condone all their miseries ... What I want them to realize is that I love them more tenderly still, if after their weakness and falls they throw themselves humbly into My Heart: then I pardon them ... and I love them still.'"

Josefa was encouraged by such great leniency.

"I asked Him if that is the reason why He loves me so much ... for when I ask His forgiveness immediately after, I see quite clearly that He has granted it, for I receive immediately fresh proofs of affection.

" 'Do you not know Josefa, that the more wretched souls are, the more I love them! ... If amongst all others you have won My Heart, it is on account of your littleness and misery.'

"Then I asked Him for His Cross, and why He bore it on His shoulder today. Was there some soul specially wounding Him?

"He answered: 'I am bearing the Cross because among My chosen ones, there are many that resist Me in little ways, and the sum total of these resistances makes this Cross ...

" 'Do you know why they resist Me? It is because they do not love Me ... yes, they are wanting in love for My Heart ... their self-love is excessive.' Then after a short pause: 'When a soul is generous enough to give Me all I ask, she gathers up treasure for herself and others and snatches great numbers of souls from perdition. It is by their sacrifices and their love that My chosen souls are deputed by My Heart to dispense My graces to mankind.'

"He continued, as if speaking to Himself: 'The world is full of perils ... How many poor souls are dragged towards sin and constantly need a visible or invisible help! Ah! let Me say it again, do My chosen souls know of what treasures they deprive themselves and others, when they are ungenerous? I do not say that by the fact of My choice, a soul is freed from her faults and wretchedness. That soul may and will fall often again, but if she humbles herself, if she recognizes her nothingness, if she tries to repair her faults by little acts of generosity and love, if she confides and surrenders herself once more to My Heart ... she gives Me more glory and can do more good to other souls, than if she had never fallen. Miseries and weaknesses are of no consequence, what I do ask of them is love.'"

Many a time Our Lord will come back to this great lesson, which seems to be the keynote of His Message of Mercy.

" 'Yes,' He continued, 'in spite of its miseries, a soul can love Me to folly ... But Josefa, you must realize that I am speaking only of faults of frailty and inadvertence, not of willed sin or voluntary infidelity.'"

And as she begged Him to bestow on them this love which must be measureless in confidence and generosity: " 'Yes,' He replied, 'keep in your heart this desire to see Me loved. Offer your life, imperfect as it is, that all My chosen souls may realize the beautiful mission that they can carry out through their ordinary actions and in their daily struggles ... Let them never forget that I have preferred them to so many others, not because of their goodness, but because of their wretchedness ... I am all love, and that flame in Me consumes all their weakness.'"

Then addressing Josefa, who had expressed her own fears in the face of so many graces and responsibilities: " 'Do not fear,' He said, 'If I have chosen you who are poor and miserable, it is that all may realize once more that I want neither greatness nor holiness ... but only love. I Myself will do all the rest. And I will again tell you the secrets of My Heart, Josefa ... But the desire which consumes Me is ever the same: it is that souls may know My Heart better and better.'"

So on this 20th day of October 1922 the first lines of the Message of Love were written. From now on these heavenly dictations alternated with direct lessons to herself. They appeared as the combined theory and practice of His teaching.

"Shall I give you My Cross?" said Our Lord the next day, Saturday, October 21st.

" 'Dear Lord, You know that in reality I want only what You want.' Then I talked to Him about souls ... of the many that are lost."

He answered sorrowfully: "Poor souls! Many do not know Me, but a great number do, yet leave Me for a life of enjoyment. There are so many sensual people in the world, and even among My chosen ones, there are so many who seek for pleasure! ... They go astray, for My way is one of suffering and crosses. Only love can give them the strength to follow Me in it, that is why I want love."

He then gave her His Cross, saying: "Comfort Me, you whom I love! It is because you are so little that you are able to creep so deeply into My Heart."

How carefully His least words must be treasured, for they give us "the mind of Christ" of which St. Paul speaks.

On Monday October 23rd, Our Lord came to bring her into close relation with the most secret of His wounds: "There are some souls, dearly beloved by My Heart, who wound Me ... they are not faithful enough to Me, and it is precisely because of the special love I bear them that I suffer so much."

Appeals such as these made Josefa long to repair and compensate His Sacred Heart.

" 'But, dear Lord, Thou knowest me! I am all aspirations and never come to acts.' With ardor such as I cannot express, He replied: 'I hold you so close to My Heart, Josefa, that your longings for souls are the very same that are consuming My Heart! ... It is rest for My Heart to be able to communicate with another. That is why I come to repose in you when a soul is grieving Me, and it is My craving to do her good that I pass into you, and so it becomes yours. It is certain that many do offend Me ... but there are many others also that love Me and from whom I receive comfort.'"

Then returning to those who wound Him, He said:

"When two people love one another, a very small lack of consideration in one of them is sufficient to wound the other. And so it is with My Heart. That is why I want those who aspire to intimacy with Me to train themselves well so that later on they refuse Me nothing."

Many days of intense suffering followed, which Josefa offered up for these unfaithful souls.

The devil tried to delude her, and multiplied his snares and threats and her nights were spent in the torments of the damned. She hesitated to tell all she saw and heard in that abode of sorrow, for her soul was dismayed by its horrors. However, she tried to speak and Our Lady appeared to her on Wednesday, October 25th, and told her that by so doing she was carrying out God's plan:

"My child, I come to tell you in the name of Jesus how much glory you gave His Heart today ... You must understand that all He allows you to see and suffer in Hell is meant not only to purify you, but also that you should pass on the knowledge of it to the Mothers. Do not think about yourself but only of the glory given to the Heart of Jesus, and the salvation of souls."

Night after night she spent almost wholly in these torments, and Josefa wrote in great sorrow on November 5th:

"I saw souls fall into Hell in dense groups, and at times it was impossible to calculate their number."

This left her terror-stricken and exhausted.

"Unless I am given special help from on high, I shall no longer be able either to work or apply myself to anything ... "

On Sunday after one of these terrible nights of expiation Our Lord came to her. She was in dire desolation of spirit, and spoke to Him of the innumerable souls lost forever. Jesus listened and His face betrayed immense sadness. After a few moments of silence, He said: "You have seen the fallen, Josefa, but you have not yet seen those who are saved and go up into Heaven!"

"Then," she wrote, "I saw an innumerable crowd of souls, rank upon rank, and they entered into an illimitable space which was filled with resplendent light, and were lost in its immensity."

The Heart of Jesus was as if on fire and He said: "All those are they who have accepted the Cross of My love, and accomplished My Will with submission."

After a few moments, He came back to the subjects of expiation and reparation which He wanted Josefa to undertake, and He explained their value to her:

"As to the time during which I allow you to undergo the pains of Hell, do not for a moment consider it as lost and useless. Sin is an offense against God's infinite Majesty, which therefore calls for infinite reparation. When you go down into the abyss, your sufferings prevent the loss of many souls, the Divine Majesty accepts them in satisfaction for the outrages received from these souls and they repair for the punishment their sins have merited. Never lose sight of the fact that it is only My great love for you and for souls that permits it."

Josefa would not forget it, and it seemed as if she were coming back to the hardest trials of her Noviceship days in the storms that now assailed her. Foreseeing that now the love of Christ's Heart was to be poured out over the whole world, the devil's fury made him fiercely attack the instrument used by Our Lord, but he was not able to shake her lowliness or her trust.

"I hate you," he said to her, "with all the hatred of Hell, and I will pursue you until I have driven you from that accursed house ... " "How many souls she snatches from me" - he one day acknowledged - "and if she is able to do this now, what will it be later on? ... No, I will put an end to this undertaking, I will get hold of her confounded writings and burn them ... I will use my power ... but she is as strong as death!"

Josefa remained unshakable. "I got back my peace of soul with the Mothers," she wrote simply.

How can the value of Josefa's fidelity to duty which never slackened during days and nights of torture possibly be gauged? We can estimate the importance of the undertaking that was beginning, by the devil's infuriated attempts to prevent it ... Yet these were to be totally unavailing in the face of God's own plans.

On Tuesday, November 21st, 1922, in spite of the devil's threats, Josefa renewed her vows in public for the first time, vows which she had made four months ago. The Feast of the Presentation of Our Lady is one that is very dear to the Society of the Sacred Heart. It is in memory of the first consecration made by their Holy Foundress, St. Madeleine Sophie, that the young religious who have not yet made their final profession each year renew their vows of Poverty, Chastity, and Obedience before the Sacred Host at the moment of Holy Communion. Josefa took part in the ceremony with the others, and rejoiced in some moments of light and peace in the midst of her tribulations. She made her renovation with great joy: She brought to her Lord a clearer conviction of her weakness, but accompanied by still greater trust in His love. We find written in her notes of the retreat:

"November 21st: My Jesus, it is now four months since I made my vows! How often I have failed Thee during that time! ... It was because I thought more of myself than of Thy glory and souls... . O Jesus, I am sorry and with my whole heart beg Thee to forgive me, for my joy in being wholly consecrated to Thee has not changed. I renew my vows today with more joy than when I made them, because I know Thee better and Thou hast more often forgiven me... . Do not mind, dear Lord, when I seem to be ungrateful, for with my will I never cease loving Thee; but the devil deceives me ... still my only desire is to be faithful to Thee till death."

After signing this protestation, she added: "O Jesus, my very life ... would that I were holy and could love Thee more, not for myself, but to give Thee glory and to save many souls."

Here indeed is a true expression of the pure love burning in her heart, and Satan's hatred would only kindle it still more. Jesus knew it, and His loving eyes rested tenderly on the weak creature in whom He saw such love.

The Redemptive Value of Daily Life (November 22nd-December 12th, 1922)

"Love transforms and divinizes all."
(Our Lord to Josefa, December 5th, 1922)

On the morning of Wednesday, November 22nd, just before the Elevation at Mass, like the rising sun after a dark night, Our Lord showed Himself to Josefa, more beautiful than ever. His Heart glowed and seemed as if about to escape from His breast. He carried the Crown of Thorns in His right hand.

"I thought at once that He was going to give it to me," she wrote naïvely, "but I did not dare ask for it. I renewed my vows and said the Divine Praises."

"Josefa," He said, while His heavenly glance rested on her, "Do you recognize Me? do you love Me? and do you know how much My Heart loves you?"

Such questions like arrows wounded and inflamed her heart.

"I know He loves me," she wrote; "but to what extent I cannot understand. I, too, long to love Him without measure ... although I cannot correspond to His loving-kindness ... I told Him how happy I was yesterday at the renewal of vows, and I begged Him to keep me faithful, for He knows all the harm I am capable of."

" 'Fear not, Josefa, for in spite of your littleness and occasional resistance, My work is going well, both in you and souls.'

" 'Lord, I do not understand what You mean by this work to which You so often allude.'"

Then Jesus, as it were recollecting Himself, spoke gravely and with force:

"You say you do not know what My work is? Josefa, it is one of love.I want to use you who are of so little account to disclose to the world the mercy and love of My Heart. That is why I am glorified when left free to do with you and in you what I choose. Already your littleness and sufferings have saved many souls... . But later on the words and wishes that I transmit through you will fire the zeal of many others and prevent the loss of a multitude of souls, and men will get to know ever more how inexhaustible is the love and mercy of My Heart ... I do not ask much from them, but I do ask their love."

"Here," she said, "I begged Him to give me that love ... and I told Him once again how earnest is my desire to leave myself totally in His hands. With inexpressible kindness He placed the Crown of Thorns on my head saying: 'Take My Crown, and may it remind you of your littleness ... I love you, nor will My tender pity for you ever let Me forsake you. Love Me, console Me and abandon yourself to Me.'"

That evening, while she was making the Stations of the Cross, she saw Our Lord at the eleventh Station, and showing her His Cross, He said: "Josefa, My bride ... I bore the Cross for love of you. Tell Me once more that for love of Me you are willing to bear the Cross that My Will offers you."

Next day, November 23rd, He gave her to understand what the Cross He offered to her generosity was to be.

He began by saying: "It is in My Heart that souls who know how to deny themselves find true peace." Then He added: "Ask the Mothers to grant you a few minutes every day in which to write down what I shall tell you."

The time had come when He was about to reveal His secrets through her to the world. On Saturday, November 25th, in the course of the morning, He came to her in her cell. Josefa knelt in adoration of His Majesty, and leaving her thus prostrate at His feet, after a few moments of silence, He said: "As you renew your vows I want you to make an offering of entire submission to Me. I must be free and find no obstacle in your will to Mine. So now, write":

Josefa listened and transcribed the grave and burning words that fell from the divine lips.

"I will begin by speaking to My chosen souls, and to all who are consecrated to Me. They must know Me, so as to be able to teach those I shall confide to their care all the kindness and tenderness of My Heart, and to tell all that if I am an infinitely just God, I am nonetheless an infinitely merciful Father. Let My chosen souls, My spouses, My religious, and priests, teach all poor souls how much I love them! All this I will teach you by degrees, and thus I shall be glorified in your abjection, in your littleness, in your nothingness. I do not love you for what you are ... but for what you are not, that is to say, your wretchedness and nothingness, for thus I have found a place for My greatness and bounty."

Here Jesus stopped: "Adieu, Josefa. Come again tomorrow. I will go on talking to you and you will pass on My words with burning zeal. Leave Me absolutely free, for in this am I glorified, and souls will be saved. Remember that I wish to be served in joy of heart and do not forget the nothingness of the instrument. Only love like Mine could close its eyes to your weakness ... Love Me ardently, so as to correspond to My goodness to you."

When night fell Our Lord brought her back His Cross. "How many sins will be committed tonight," He said, "and how many will fall into Hell."

This thought seemed to oppress His Heart. "You at least, Josefa, comfort Me and make reparation for so much ingratitude. How much I suffer when I consider that all I have done will be useless for so many souls... . Take My Cross and remain closely united to Me, for you are not alone."

He vanished, leaving her His Cross. The hours of the night were passed under its weight, besides that of the many torments of soul and body to which she had now been for so long accustomed.

Towards morning Jesus returned. His countenance was still stamped with the impressive sorrow and beauty that Josefa was powerless to describe:

"Poor souls," He said, "how many are eternally lost ... but how many, too, will regain life. You cannot conceive how great is the reparatory value of suffering... . If you consent, I will often make you share with Me the grievous sorrow of My Heart, and thus you will comfort Me and save many souls. Adieu, think of Me, of souls and of My love."

"Ever since Our Lord had asked the Mothers to give me time every day to write down His words," she noted, "I was told to go to my cell between eight and nine o'clock in the morning. The postulants are at their housework then, so there is nothing to prevent me sewing or preparing their work."

Faithful to these instructions, she repaired every day to her cell. As she waited for the coming of the Master she occupied herself with her needlework. Sometimes He came at once, at other times her waiting was in vain. Our Lord wished her to be pliant and abandoned. If by nine o'clock He had not come, she went back to her ordinary work.

On Sunday, November 26th, although He had arranged it with her the day before, He did not come. She did not allow this to trouble her and, following His counsels, she thought of Him, of souls, and of His love.

That evening as she was at her adoration before the Blessed Sacrament He came, bearing His Cross: "My bride, Josefa, I come to rest in you... . You cannot think how the world treats My Heart; sinners wound Me pitilessly, and not they alone but many others pierce Me with painful arrows."

"I begged Him to come to us, for though we are so wretched (I speak for myself) we so long to love and console Him."

"You know quite well that I already do so, do you not see how I come here to give rest to My Heart?

"Listen," He continued patiently, "when I ask you to be My rest and consolation, you must not imagine that you are the only one who gives them to Me. If you could but understand My joy when souls leave Me free and by their deeds say: 'Lord, Thou art the Master!' Do you realize how much this comforts Me? Do you think that I am not glorified by it?

"Take My Cross," He said, giving it to her, "but do not think that you are the only one to bear it for Me. I find repose and glory in you, but in other consecrated souls as well ... who with so much love and submission receive and adore My Will and have no other interest but My glory.

"Take My Cross, Josefa. Ask mercy for sinners ... light for the blind ... love for hearts that are indifferent ... Comfort Me, love Me, surrender. One act of abandonment glorifies Me more than many sacrifices."

The next day, Monday, November 27th, at eight o'clock, Josefa was in her cell, waiting, but abandoned to His Will.

"First of all I wrote down all He had said to me yesterday," she noted, "then I waited ready to do His bidding." But as Jesus did not come, she was preparing to leave, when suddenly He showed Himself to her.

"Go to your work, Josefa," He said. "Tomorrow I will tell My souls that My Heart is an abyss of love. Think of Me all the time. Souls glorify Me so much when they remember Me."

Josefa went away carrying the Cross which was invisible to all eyes but which she felt weighing heavily upon her. She carried it through all her work, in her generosity preferring this burden to any amount of sweetness.

Early the next day, November 28th, she found Jesus already waiting for her in her cell.

Prostrate on her knees and following her usual bent towards self-reproach she asked Him to pardon whatever, even without her knowledge, might have displeased Him. "Have no fear," He answered her; "I know you ... but I so love you that no wretchedness in you will turn the glance of My love from you."

Then with ardor too intense to be restrained, He began to speak and she gathered up His burning words:

In an admirable epitome of His whole redemptive life, Jesus showed infinite love as the central theme:

"I am all Love! My Heart is an abyss of love.

"It was love that made man and all existing things that they might be at his service.

"It was love that moved the Father to give His Son for man's salvation which through his own fault he had lost.

"It was love that caused a Virgin who was little more than a child to renounce the charms of life in the Temple and consent to become the Mother of God, thereby accepting all the suffering involved in the Divine Maternity.

"It was love that caused Me to be born in the inclemency of winter, poor and destitute of everything.

"It was love that hid Me thirty years in complete obscurity and humble work.

"It was love that made Me choose solitude and silence ... to live unknown and voluntarily to submit to the commands of My Mother and adopted Father. For love saw how in the course of ages many souls would follow My example and delight in conforming their lives to Mine.

"It was love that made Me embrace all the miseries of human nature, for the love of My Heart saw far ahead. I knew how many imperiled souls would be helped by the acts and sacrifices of others and so would recover life.

"It was love that made Me suffer the most ignominious contempt and horrible tortures ... and shed all My blood and die on the Cross to save mankind and redeem the whole human race.

"And love saw how, in the future, many souls would unite themselves to My torments and dye their sufferings and actions, even the most ordinary, with My blood in order to win many souls to Me.

"I will teach you all this very clearly, Josefa, that men may know how far-reaching is the love of My Heart for them.

"And now go back to your work, and live in Me as I do in you."

Josefa then left her cell, and gave the precious pages she had written to the Mothers. She herself never retained them, for she knew herself to be just a go-between, and her supernatural detachment grew as she realized the importance of all that was confided to her. But she kept deep down in her own heart the remembrance of the moments when Love's depths were revealed to her. She was as it were invested with the sacredness of it all and it took all her natural energy of character to throw herself wholeheartedly into the work she shared with the Novices. So was the mystery of her life carried on.

The next day, Wednesday, November 29th, while she was waiting for Our Lord and working, suddenly her cell was filled with a soft effulgent light. It was not the Master who had come but the Apostle beloved of His Heart.

"I recognized him at once," she wrote, "he held the Cross of Jesus in his hands. I renewed my vows and he said:

" 'Soul, loved of Our Divine Master, I am John the Evangelist, and I come to bestow His Cross on you. It does not wound the body, but makes the heart bleed ... May the suffering it will cause you relieve the bitterness in which sinners steep the Heart of Our Lord and God... . May the blood of your heart be as a delicious vintage that will make known to many the sweetness and attractiveness of virginity ... Unite your heart to Jesus in all you do. Keep carefully the precious evidences of His love. Fix your eyes on Heaven, for the things of earth are of no account. Suffering is the life of the soul and the soul that has understood its value lives the true life."

Josefa had already noted on Holy Thursday, 1922, how heavenly was the expression of St. John's countenance. He was a friend from the other world whom she was to see again many times, and whose every visit left her with a sense of peace and security. The Cross brought this day weighed chiefly on her soul.

"Although in peace," she wrote, "my heart and soul are oppressed and in extreme suffering.

"The night of November 29th-30th was particularly crucifying. The Cross, the Crown of Thorns, and the pain in my side banished all sleep and obliged me to spend the whole night sitting beside my bed. On Thursday, November 30th, Jesus appeared at eight o'clock, faithful to His tryst:

" 'Write for My souls,' He said. And with no other preamble He continued:

" 'The soul who constantly unites her life with Mine glorifies Me and does a great work for souls. Thus, if engaged in work of no value in itself ... if she bathes it in My blood or unites it to the work I Myself did during My mortal life, it will greatly profit souls ... more perhaps, than if she had preached to the whole world ... and that, whether she studies, speaks or writes ... whether she sews, sweeps or rests ... provided first that the act is sanctioned by obedience or duty and not done from mere caprice; secondly, that it is done in intimate union with Me, with great purity of intention and covered with My blood.

" 'I so much want souls to understand this! It is not the action in itself that is of value; it is the intention with which it is done. When I swept and labored in the workshop of Nazareth, I gave as much glory to My Father as when I preached during My public life.

" 'There are many souls who in the eyes of the world fill important posts and they give My Heart great glory; this is true. But I have many hidden souls who in their humble labors are very useful workers in My vineyard, for they are moved by love, and they know how to cover their deeds with supernatural gold by bathing them in My blood. My love goes so far that My souls can draw great treasure out of mere nothing. When as soon as they wake they unite themselves to Me and offer their whole day with a burning desire that My Heart may use it for the profit of souls ... when with love they perform their duties, hour by hour and moment by moment ... how great is the treasure they amass in one day!

" 'I will reveal My love to them more and more ... it is inexhaustible, and how easy it is for a loving soul to let itself be guided by love.'"

Jesus was silent. Josefa laid down her pen and for a few instants remained in adoration before Him who thus opened His Heart so widely before her. "Adieu," He said at last, "go back to your work; love and suffer, for love is inseparable from suffering. Abandon yourself to the care of the best of Fathers ... and to the love of the tenderest of Partners."

This was ever the lesson dearest to God Our Saviour. His Cross is a choice gift, surpassing the most precious of favors. On this First Friday He left it to Josefa, who carried it both day and night.

On Saturday, December 2nd she noted simply:

"With great difficulty I managed to go to meditation, for my strength is gone."

At eight o'clock, however, she was at her post, and Jesus soon joined her.

"Write for souls," He said, as on the preceding day.

Josefa knelt at her small table, and Our Lord spoke, standing beside her.

"My Heart is all love and it embraces all souls, but how can I make My chosen souls understand My special love for them and how I wish to use them to save sinners and so many souls who are exposed to the perils of the world? For this reason I would like them to know how much I desire their perfection, and that it consists in doing their ordinary actions in intimate union with Me. If they once grasped this, they could divinize their life and all their activities by this close union with My Heart ... and how great is the value of a divinized day!

"When a soul is burnt up with desire to love, nothing is a burden to her, but if she feels cold and spiritless everything becomes hard and difficult ... Let her then come to My Heart to revive her courage ... Let her offer Me her dejection, and unite it to My fervor; then she may rest content, for her day will be of incomparable value to souls. All human miseries are known to My Heart, and My compassion for them is great.

"But I desire souls to unite themselves to Me not only in a general way. I long for this union to be constant and intimate as it is between friends who live together; for even if they are not talking all the time, at least they look at each other, and their mutual affectionate little kindnesses are the fruit of their love.

"When a soul is in peace and consolation, doubtless it is easier for her to think of Me, but if she is in the throes of desolation and anguish, she need not fear. I am content with a glance. I understand, and this mere look will draw down on her special proofs of My tenderness.

"I will repeat again to souls how My Heart loves them ... for I want them to know Me thoroughly, that they may make Me known to those I place in their care.

"I ardently desire My chosen souls to fix their eyes on Me, and never turn them away ... and among them there should be no mediocrity, which usually is the result of a misunderstanding of My love. No! it is neither difficult nor hard to love My Heart, but on the contrary, it is sweet and easy. They need do nothing extraordinary to attain to a high degree of love: purity of intention, be the action great or small ... intimate union with My Heart, and love will do the rest."

Jesus stopped; then bending down towards Josefa who was prostrate at His feet: "Go," He said, "and have no fear. It is I who cultivate this little flower, that it may not perish! Love Me in peace and joy."

On the evening of this First Saturday of the month Our Lord came to comfort her distress, which was caused by the snares of the devil, who perpetually tried to take away her peace of mind.

"Remember the words I spoke to My disciples: 'As you are not of the world, the world hateth you.' Today I say to you: 'Because you are not of the devil, Satan persecutes you.' But in the midst of these torments My Heart is guarding you and is glorified. Love and suffer, Josefa, it is for a soul."

And once more He charged her with one of His consecrated souls, whose love had grown cold, but to whose generosity He held so much.

"He went away," she wrote, "leaving me His Cross."

This Cross with all its attendant sufferings would weigh heavily on her during the nights and days that followed, while Josefa's mind was fixed on the wound she divined in the Heart of her Lord.

Three days later, Tuesday, December 5th, He was already in her cell when she arrived. She renewed her vows.

"Yes," He began by saying, "I am that Jesus who loves souls tenderly... . Behold this Heart that never ceases calling them, guarding them, and caring for them... . Behold this Heart on fire with longing for their love, but especially for the love of My chosen ones."

Then as if these burning words had relieved His love:

"Write, write more for them.

"My Heart is not only an abyss of love, It is also an abyss of mercy; and knowing as I do that even My closest friends are not exempt from human frailties, I will each of their actions, however insignificant, to be clothed through Me with immense value for the help of those in need and for the salvation of sinners.

"All cannot preach nor evangelize distant uncivilized peoples, but all, yes, all can make My Heart known and loved ... All can mutually help one another to increase the number of the saved by preventing the loss of many souls ... and that, through My love and mercy.

"I will tell My chosen souls that My love for them goes further still; not only shall I make use of their daily life and of their least actions, but I will make use of their very wretchedness ... their frailties ... even of their falls, for the salvation of souls.

"Love transforms and divinizes everything, and mercy pardons all."

After a moment of silence Jesus continued: "Adieu, I shall come back again to tell you My secrets. Meanwhile bear My Cross bravely. If you love Me I also love you. Do not forget this."

As He had said, Jesus allowed her to wait several days, bearing His Cross all the time. Our Lady's consoling presence was granted to her on the Feast of the Immaculate Conception. Josefa had suffered intensely all day. Her heart was in anguish, and that evening after Benediction she called on her Heavenly Mother to come to her aid.

"I entrusted my whole soul to her," she wrote, "and begged her never to let go of my hand. Suddenly she stood there in all loveliness! Her hands were crossed upon her breast and her white veil reflected gleams of gold. She said only these words to me: 'My child, if you want to give much glory to Jesus and save many souls ... let Him do as He likes with you and give yourself up to His love.'

"She gave me her blessing, let me kiss her hand, and vanished."

Josefa with renewed courage faced the offerings and suffering which were required to keep her faithful from one day to another.

But she was obsessed by one anxiety. It seemed to her that her companions had suspicions and misgivings on her account, and her humility and love of self-effacement took fright.

"I wanted to talk over all this with Our Lord during Vespers," she wrote on Sunday, December 10th, "and hardly had I begun than He came: 'Josefa, why are you sad? Tell Me all about it.'"

She renewed her vows and confided her anxieties to Him.

"I have told you that you will live hidden in My Heart, why do you doubt My love? ... let My words reach many souls who need them."

Then, humbling her still deeper in her nothingness: "In any case what does it concern you? When a person talks at the bottom of a large empty space, her voice resounds up to the highest point. So it is with you. You are the echo of My voice, but if I be silent, what are you then?"

Such words rooted her in the conviction of her nothingness and at the same time revivified her trust and peace.

"Is it I, Lord, who prevent your coming ... for now five days have gone by without my seeing you?"

" 'No,' He answered with compassionate kindness, 'you do not prevent My coming, but I love to hear you call Me and long for Me. Soon I shall again come and speak to you of My souls. Besides, if you displease Me in anything, I will make you see your misery and nothingness and will manifest My sovereignty over you.

" 'Adieu. Stay hidden in My Heart and let yourself be trained in Love's own way.'"

As He had said, Our Lord soon resumed the revelations of His Heart to Josefa, and on Tuesday, December 12th, He appeared at the accustomed hour. First of all He insisted on His promise to her:

"You, Josefa, as I told you, you must not give in to sadness, for My love takes care of you. I will not fail to hide you deep down in My Heart, and you must never doubt My love, nor forget that I have often told you what a little and miserable creature, a mere nothing, you are, and you must abandon yourself trustfully into the hands of your Creator, with entire submission to His Divine Will.

"And now, write a few more words for My souls:

"Love transforms their most ordinary actions and gives them an infinite value, but it does more: My Heart loves My chosen souls so tenderly, that I wish to use their miseries, their weaknesses, and often even their faults.

"Souls that see themselves overwhelmed with miseries, attribute nothing good to themselves, and their very abjectness clothes them with a certain humility that they would not have if they saw themselves to be less imperfect.

"When therefore in the course of apostolic work or in the carrying out of duties, a consciousness of their incapacity is forced upon them ... or when they experience a kind of repugnance to helping souls towards perfection to which they know themselves to be still strangers, such souls are compelled to humble themselves in the dust, and should this self-knowledge impel them to My feet, asking pardon for their halting efforts, begging of My Heart the strength and courage they need, it is hardly possible for them to conceive how lovingly My Heart goes out to them and how marvelously fruitful I will make their labors.

"Those whose generosity is not equal to these daily endeavors and sacrifices, will see their lives go by full only of promise which never comes to fruition.

"But in this, distinguish: to souls who habitually promise and yet do no violence to themselves nor prove their abnegation and love in any way, I say: 'Beware lest all this straw and stubble which you have gathered into your barns take fire or be scattered in an instant by the wind!'

"But there are others, and it is of them I now speak, who begin their day with a very good will and desire to prove their love. They pledge themselves to self-denial or generosity in this or that circumstance ... But when the time comes they are prevented by self-love, temperament, health, or I know not what from carrying out what a few hours before they quite sincerely purposed to do. Nevertheless they speedily acknowledge their weakness and, filled with shame, beg for pardon, humble themselves, and renew their promise ... Ah! Let them know that these souls please Me as much as if they had nothing with which to reproach themselves."

The bell was ringing for a community exercise, and Jesus, ever faithful to the first indication of obedience, disappeared in a flash.

Advent and Christmas Graces
(December 13th - 31st, 1922)

"Have you understood My love for souls?"
(Our Lord to Josefa, December 16th, 1922)

The month of December 1922 brought to Les Feuillants a visit which was both a joy and a trial to Josefa.

One of the Mothers Assistant General of the Society of the Sacred Heart came from Rome to visit the houses in France. It was a great happiness to receive her at Poitiers, and her visit proved a source of grace for the house, its works, and its inmates.

Warm-hearted Josefa would have loved to share this joy, unalloyed by any haunting fear, but she felt her Mothers would submit many questions to the Visitor, and that she herself would be interrogated.

Her old fears re-awakened, though she trusted her Master.

"I recognized once again," we find her writing on Wednesday, December 13th, "how faithfully Jesus keeps His promises. Our Mother Assistant General received me for a few moments ... with a kindness I hardly dared expect. Our Lord, however, had told me several times: 'If you are faithful, I shall not forsake you and nothing will do you any harm'; and that I see more clearly every day."

The next day, Thursday, December 14th, He came again to the silence of her little cell: "Do you see how faithful a Father and Spouse I am to you? Never be afraid, even if you feel that the storm is about to break." Then with an eagerness that His love could not restrain: "Tell the Mother that My Heart allows and disposes all things in view of My work ... that owing to the Society many souls will be saved ... that My words will rekindle the fervor of many of My chosen souls... and that many others who do not sufficiently appreciate the value of the smallest actions done with love will find in My words a source of grace and consolation."

After He had answered all that still worried Josefa: "Adieu," He said with overwhelming kindness, "abandon yourself to My care, and never doubt My love. It matters little even if you are often shaken by storms, your lowliness is deeply rooted in My Heart. I will come again to speak to you of My souls," He added before departing, "now comfort Me. You may kiss My feet, if you wish. Later on I will bring you My Cross."

Very soon after, Jesus brought it.

"I was waiting for Our Lord, and occupying myself meanwhile with some needlework," she wrote on Friday, December 15th, "when towards half-past eight He came ... He was bearing His Cross but with no sign of sadness. His Heart and eyes were more beautiful than ever."

She could find no words to express her admiration. His attitude, His resplendent white raiment, and the Cross looming darkly against all this radiance was all so beautiful that she could not give an adequate idea of it.

"I knelt down and renewed my vows. I adored Him, and begged Him to give me true love, and I said to Him: 'How glad I am, Lord, that Thou hast brought me Thy Cross.'"

"Do you want it?" He said at once - and as she offered herself to do His Will in all things - "Take it and console Me. Be busy about My interests, for I will look after you." Then in response to the thought He read in her mind: "Yes, it is true that I have no need of anyone ... but let Me ask you to love Me, and by you, to manifest Myself once more to souls. Let My Heart have free access and find repose in pouring out Its love on this group of chosen souls.

"I want all to know how eagerly I seek them out, how I long for them that I may fill them with happiness.

"Tell them not to be afraid of Me ... and tell sinners not to flee from Me ... Let them come and take refuge in My Heart! I will receive them with the most tender and paternal affection.

"And you, Josefa, love Me, and don't be afraid of your weakness, for I will sustain you. You love Me and I love you, you are Mine and I am yours. What more do you want?"

"He said all this with such passionate fervor," she wrote, "that He left me as it were lost in Him. How can I explain what went on in my soul? I asked Him to show me how to love Him, for I have no other desire on earth: to live and love my so-good Jesus!"

On the following day, Saturday, December 16th, Our Lord taught her the secret of true love.

"Today, you are going to console Me. Enter into the depths of My Heart and offer yourself to My Father with the merits of your Bridegroom. Beg Him to forgive the many souls that are ungrateful. Tell Him that even in your littleness you are prepared to repair for the sins mankind commits against Him. Tell Him what a miserable little victim you are, but that you are veiled in My blood.

"So you will spend the day imploring forgiveness and repairing for sin. I want you to unite your soul to the zeal that consumes My Heart. May souls really grasp that I am their joy and their reward ... May they not flee from Me, for I love them so much ... all of them! but I want My chosen souls especially to know how great a predilection I have for them."

After speaking to her of the Society of the Sacred Heart, He concluded by saying: "And you yourself, Josefa, have you understood My love for souls?"

"Indeed I have, Lord, for You are always occupied about them."

"That is why I love the Society and why My Heart reposes in it ... For it

197

has understood the value of souls and the glory of My Heart. Adieu, Josefa, comfort Me and make reparation."

When leaving her Our Lord always gave her the same watchword: Love. As the days and the months went by, Josefa realized more and more that her life was to be one of reparation and that her vocation bound her to the redemptive Cross of Christ. This Our Lord stressed every time He came to her. He never led her outside the very sure path of her vocation, but urged her towards the true consequences of the total gift of herself to the Sacred Heart.

On Sunday, December 17th, He joined her in her cell a little before the nine o'clock Mass.

"You consoled Me yesterday," He said to her, "because you stayed with Me. So many forget Me and so many others busy themselves about a thousand and one trifles, and leave Me alone for whole days ... many others do not hear My voice ... yet I am always speaking to them ... but their hearts are earthbound and cling to creatures. I will tell you all this later on, and will let you know what consolation is given Me by souls, especially by My chosen ones, when they do not leave Me alone... . You will continue writing that they may know how dearly I love them. Go now ... I will return."

The nine o'clock Mass bell was ringing, she noted. Jesus had gone.

Five days passed, and on each of them Josefa expected the return of the Master who had said: "I will return." But He did not come.

The sovereign freedom He exercised in her regard was not the least proof of His action. No doubt He loved abandonment in her, but did He not by the uncertainty, the suddenness of His coming, wish to give a proof that the visits really were from Him, so putting an end to all doubt on the subject?

On December 22nd, Josefa wrote:

"Five days have passed since Our Lord came, yet He said He would return ... What troubles me is not to know if I have displeased Him in something, for I no longer have either His Cross or His Crown."

Her notes continue:

"Before I went to bed, I knelt down to say goodnight to Him, as I always do, and I added: 'Dear Lord, for five days I have been calling Thee, and Thou hast not come!'"

Hardly had she finished speaking when Our Lord appeared to her in all His radiant beauty: "Is it for five days that you have been calling Me, Josefa? And I, how many are the days, the months, the years, during which I have been calling souls but they give Me no answer. When you call Me, I am not far from you, but on the contrary very near. When I call souls, many do not hear Me ... many go away, but you at least comfort Me by calling Me and longing for Me. Slake My thirst by your desire for Me."

How many souls can read in these words escaped from the burning Heart of Jesus the reason why He keeps them waiting for His advent ... how many, too, will take courage and draw happiness from the thought that they slake His thirst by offering to Him their desires for Him.

This period which had rooted Josefa firmly in her vocation of reparation, and inaugurated the Message she was destined to transmit to mankind, ended at Christmas in a scene of utter loveliness, which Josefa noted down in all its simplicity ... her soul becoming more and more attuned to the littleness of the Infant God. But there was never any talk between them other than that of the redemption of souls. More than ever was this the link of love that bound them. We quote her words without commentary:

"Monday, December 25th, 1922: During Vespers I was telling the Infant Jesus once more how much I loved Him, for in spite of the great temptation of these last days, He knows very well that He is my sole love, my King, my treasure. I cannot live without Him ... He is the joy of my life. I was saying this when suddenly I saw Him; He was quite tiny. He was held up by something I could not distinguish, and wrapped in a white veil which left only His little hands and feet uncovered. He held His little hands crossed on His breast, and His joyous eyes were so lovely, so full of joy, they seemed to speak. His hair was quite short; in fact everything about Him was little, and with the tenderest and sweetest voice He said to me: 'Yes, Josefa, I am your King.'

"I was so overjoyed to see Him thus that I took up His word: 'Yes, my Jesus, Thou art my King, and if my enemies and evil inclinations try to make me fall they will not succeed, for I will fight hard always to remain Thy very own.'

" 'It is just because you fight that I am your King. Be not afraid, the enemy will not take possession of the battlefield, for I will defend you, although I am so small ... I want you to be small too. And now, Josefa, I am going to ask you for a gift. You will give it to Me, won't you?'

"I was afraid of what He was going to ask me," she wrote humbly, "but I answered: 'Yes, Lord, with all my heart, but Thou must give me the strength, for Thou knowest what I am.'

" 'I want,' said the Holy Child, 'I want you to make Me a little tunic adorned with many souls ... those souls My Heart loves.'"

Then coming back to His first idea: " 'You see how small I am? Well, I want you to be smaller still. Do you know how? ... By simplicity, humility, and promptness in obedience. Then, Josefa, My Heart wants the warmth of love which only souls can give Me. Give Me that warmth, and give Me souls. I have prepared a great number for you. Do not delay My undertaking ...

" 'If you give Me souls, I will give you My Heart. Which of us two will be giving the greater gift? ...

" 'I will return soon.... . Meanwhile, begin to fashion My tunic, and give

Me souls by your love! See how many turn away... . Do not let them escape... . Poor souls ... do not let them flee away, Josefa, for they little know where they are going!'

"He said all this," she noted, "with so sweet a voice! When He began to speak He opened His little arms. He was so lovely, so ravishing that I was distressed at not being able to kiss His feet, but I dared not ask Him. He seemed all aglow. Indeed He was so beautiful that I cannot describe Him, and the tender sweetness of His utterance was ineffable."

This entrancing Christmas feast was to have a morrow:

"As I was preparing for Holy Communion," she continued, "on Tuesday, December 26th, I asked our Blessed Lady to give me her Son and to teach me to love Him and console Him. I spoke to her as one speaks to one's mother, with great confidence, and after Communion I begged her to adore Him for me and to teach me how to thank Him.

"Suddenly, she stood there with the Holy Child on her right arm. She was clothed in the same pale rose colored vesture and veil as she wore two years ago and the Holy Child was wrapped in a white veil, as yesterday, only there was nothing to be seen of Him, not even His little head. Then she was so motherly and loving as she said to me:

" 'Look, my child, I bring you your Jesus,' and at the same time she uncovered Him.

" 'Place Him deep down in your heart. See how cold He is! You can warm Him by your love. He is so good, and He loves you so much! Let Him be the sole King of your heart.'

"Whilst she spoke, the Holy Child lay still in her arms, gazing at her and sometimes at me. I told Our Lady how I longed to love Him, but that often I am not faithful enough to all He asks of me, especially when it is a message from Him that I must deliver... ."

This was the perpetual cause of self-reproach to her.

"Then in His sweet baby voice He said: 'Mother, I have asked Josefa to make Me a little tunic adorned with many souls, for so many escape Me ... and you know how many I entrust to those who love Me. If they respond to my expectations, this is the greatest consolation that they can give My Heart.'

"Our Lady at once replied: 'Yes, give Him souls, and do not let any go away from Him ... Look! He is going to weep!'

"I told Him that this is my one desire, but that often unknowingly I sadden Him and resist Him, because I let the devil deceive me.

" 'Do not fear, my child, Jesus asks only for your good will. Try your best and prove your affection in that way. Do you know how to do it? Jesus wants you to be very little ... quite tiny, so tiny that you may be able to creep in here.'

"And with her hand she pointed to the empty space between her heart and the Holy Child who was reposing on it.

"She smiled as she said this," wrote Josefa, "and the Holy Child looked at her and smiled too.

" 'You little know how happy you would be in there,' the Blessed Virgin continued, and Jesus, waving His little arms, called out: 'Just try, Josefa ... and you will see ... '

"As they were both so sweetly kind, I again begged for forgiveness for having resisted ... and for all that courses through my imagination in moments of temptation ... Our Lady answered:

" 'Yes, you are right, there are moments when you are ungrateful... . Do you know why? It is because you are thinking of yourself more than of Him. Do not consider whether a thing costs you or not, prove your love by doing all He asks of you. If He tells you to speak, speak. If to be silent, then keep silence. If He tells you to love, then love. What does anything matter, if He takes care of you?'

"I promised her that I would obey Him, and as she began covering up the Holy Child before going, I asked leave to kiss His little feet.

" 'Yes, kiss them,' she said.

"While I kissed them, Jesus stroked my head very gently with His tiny hand ... I kissed Our Lady's hand too. Then she covered up her Babe saying:

" 'Adieu, my child, do not forget the tunic. Comfort Him and give Him souls.' Then they both went away."

The graces of this exquisite vision ended on Wednesday, December 27th, when, on St. John's feast-day, the friend of virgin souls appeared to her. Josefa described him as best she could:

"He came during my adoration. He was of majestic beauty, his right arm extended and his left hand resting on his heart. He is very tall, rather taller and stronger than Our Lord, and with rougher and more marked features. His eyes are black, and his face pale, with dark chestnut colored hair. He was enveloped in a very pure radiance and when he spoke it was so slowly and gravely that his words sank deep into my soul. His voice was both gentle and strong with something heavenly about it.

"I renewed my vows and then he said at once:

" 'Soul, beloved of the Sacred Heart, since this adorable Master takes delight in pure souls, I come to rekindle in yours the fire that must consume you with love for the Divine Heart.

" 'He loved us first; may our love respond to His, with gratitude, constancy, tenderness, and generosity, without any shred of self-interest. May His loving-kindness be ever present to our minds... . May it be the prime motive of a love that must seek the good and glory of the Beloved.

" 'Soul chosen by Jesus with so much love, take up your abode in His Heart. Let it catch the fire of His consuming love, and may you be purified and intoxicated with heavenly sweetness.

"'May your passage on this earth be as that of the dove who barely touches ground. Like the bee on the flower, may your soul ask nothing of this life but the food that is absolutely necessary to its existence.

" 'The world is but a dark passage to one who loves the Divine Master.'

"He crossed his hands on his breast and was silent. He looked so beautiful that he might have been an angel. I was afraid to speak ... At last I ventured to ask him if Our Lord received consolation from religious, He who so loves virginity ... St. John looked up to Heaven and his face brightened as he replied:

" 'Virgin souls are the dwellings of love, where the Immaculate Lamb takes His rest. But among these souls some are the admiration of Heaven itself. On them, the heavenly Spouse fixes His most pure gaze and imbues them with sweet fragrance from His Heart.'

"Then extending his right arm he blessed me and said:

" 'Let Him possess and consume you. May all your care and zeal be concentrated on increasing His glory and love, and may His peace keep you."

On the evening of this same day the signal grace Jesus had granted Josefa on the same date two years before was renewed.

"Towards eight o'clock He came, O! so beautiful ... the wound in His Heart burning and wide open: 'Come,' He said, 'enter into My Heart and rest there. Later on you will give Me yours to rest in.'

Then He plunged her in that abyss.

"I thought it was Heaven," she wrote, incapable of saying more.

"It is impossible to explain what it means to enter into that Heart!"

After a little more than an hour of this ineffable repose, Jesus reminded her of the end and object of all these favors: "Do not forget that the souls I choose must be victims."

Josefa could not forget it, for the Master's plans were too deeply imprinted on her soul; she knew full well that henceforward their union would be consummated only on the Cross.

But at that moment when He reminded her of it, He willed to show her by a symbolic parable that it would always be love that would sign her with the Cross.

"As He was yet speaking, I saw," she said, "a little pure white dove; her grey wings were extended as if to take flight towards the Heart of Jesus. But she was repulsed in this by a tongue of fire that issued from the wound and fell on her little head which was resplendently white. She bore a small black cross imprinted just below her throat."

Josefa made no comment, but till her death she was from time to time to see this little white dove. However, by then the Master had explained the significance of the vision, which was an image of her soul.

For the moment the light went out, it was not yet time for her to take flight into the Heart of Jesus. A whole year of graces, struggles, trials of all sorts, still separated her from her final entry into this adorable Heart. But the fire of love would hold her captive in torments, that He might continue to reveal Himself to the world through her.

The Via Dolorosa

January 1st-February 17th, 1923

"The work of Jesus must be founded on much pain and love."

(Our Lady to Josefa, January 21st, 1923)

We have reached the opening months of 1923, the year that was to end in Josefa's death. It is therefore a last stage that is beginning, and she knew it. On the preceding December 3rd, during a ceremony of Confirmation in the Convent Chapel, Our Lady had told her that she would have to transmit Our Lord's words to the Bishop of Poitiers, and she added: "You will see him three times before your death."

Heaven was almost in sight, and this gave Josefa courage. She needed this courage, for many shadows were to darken her path, and in the first days of January new trials began. The devil again made his appearance, and renewed his previous attacks. But in the midst of blows and threats, abductions, and long hours spent in Hell ... Jesus engraved His own likeness in her and in the same measure associated her with His redemptive work. She was saving souls and preparing the way for His Message of love. In vain Satan grew infuriated, and if occasionally he thought he had triumphed, when the hour marked by the Master of Heaven and Hell struck, he vanished in a howl of blasphemy ...

On Monday, January 8th, Josefa wrote:

"I had a great longing for Jesus this morning. The moment of Communion is a great alleviation to me in these terrible sufferings. Today, after a night of horror spent in Hell, I had an overwhelming longing for Him. As I was returning from the altar rails, I saw Our Lord, walking in front of me. He turned back and said to me: 'Come, Josefa, My Heart awaits you.'

"At once I renewed my vows, and Jesus repeated: 'Yes, My Heart awaits you.'

"I renewed my vows again, and Jesus went on 'You have given Me rest, it is now My turn to rest you.'

"Then His Heart opened and He made me enter in."

A few moments which Josefa characterized as "moments of Heaven" were passed by her in that divine dwelling ...

"When I came forth again, she wrote, "I told Him of my fear of the devil and his threats ... I begged Him never to allow him to delude me.

" 'Why are you afraid?' Jesus answered, 'Do you not know that I am more powerful than all your enemies? The devil with all his raging fury can do no more than I permit. It is I who allow the souls I love to suffer. Suffering is necessary for all, but how much more for My chosen souls! ... It purifies them, and I am thus able to make use of them to snatch many from Hell fire.'"

And alluding to the vain threats she continually heard:

" 'Do not fear,' He said, 'but trust yourself to My Heart, for I guard you as the apple of My eye. Yes, Josefa, this house is much loved by My Heart ... although I have more than once poured into it the bitterness of My chalice ... I will return soon that you may again write the secrets of My love... . Meanwhile, go on working at My tunic.'"

After thus reminding her of His Christmas present, Jesus disappeared, and Josefa returned to her obscure and stormy path.

Once more, on January 21st, a heavenly light shone on her dark night. Our Lady was ever near her child in such sorrowful hours.

On that Sunday morning with its comparative leisure, Josefa finished her notes. It was a labor that cost her obedience much, especially when she had to recount what she had seen in the bottomless pit, into which at this time she was frequently forced to descend.

"I have done it to obey and to show Jesus my love," she wrote.

Towards evening Our Lady appeared to her in the Chapel, and told her how meritorious the act had been.

"As you overcame your repugnance through love," she said, "Heaven opened today to a soul whose salvation was in great peril. If you only knew how many souls can be saved by those little acts!"

"She was so sweet and gentle that I took courage to confide several things to her," said Josefa, and she answered:

"Jesus wishes His words to remain hidden as long as you live. After your death, they will be known from one end of the earth to the other, and in their light many souls will be saved through confidence and abandonment to the merciful Heart of Jesus."

And as Josefa, ever fearful of such great happenings, expressed her anxiety to this best of Mothers:

"My child," she answered tenderly, "why be afraid? The work of Jesus must be founded on much pain and love ... banish fear; Jesus is almighty and it is He who acts. He is strong and He will sustain you. He is merciful and He loves you."

Then she warned her of further tribulations to be encountered: "He reads the depths of all hearts and it is He who permits circumstances to be as they are. If His plans often seem to you to be hindered, it is because He wants to keep you very humble and very lowly."

Josefa told her that she feared herself to be an obstacle to His plans.

"It is true that you are a very wretched little being," Our Lady said with compassion, "but that is just why Jesus has pity on you and why He hides you in the depths of His Heart so that nothing can possibly harm you. Humble yourself in your littleness and misery, my child. Trust Him, for He loves you and will never forsake you. Let your only ambition be to win many souls for Him, to give Him much glory and much love."

"I asked her to bless me. She made the Sign of the Cross on my forehead with two of her fingers saying: 'Yes, with all my heart I bless you.' And she vanished."

Heaven seemed to close again, and the devil regained power over Josefa both day and night.

However, on Thursday, February 1st, St. Madeleine Sophie appeared to her as the forerunner of peace. She summoned her to the little cell which she herself had once sanctified by prayer and holiness. She told her of the entrance into Heaven of five of her daughters and gave her their names, and as if consecrating her presence in that holy spot, she added:

"You cannot imagine with what joy I see my beloved daughters come here. From Heaven, I bless them with the tenderness of a mother and obtain many graces for them... . My desire is that each should be a home of repose and love for the Heart of Jesus."

A few days later, February 4th, she comforted her, saying: "Do not weary of suffering. Souls who suffer through love will see great things, I do not say here on earth, but in eternity."

On Saturday, February 10th, it was St. Madeleine Sophie again who came to tell Josefa of Our Lord's return after some hard days of trial: "May His peace guard your heart, my child... . He will soon come, comfort Him with complete trust. Do not forget that if He is your God, He is also your Father, and not only your Father, but even your Beloved... . Have no fear and tell Him everything, for He is ever ready to listen to you. O how good our God is ... How compassionate is His Heart."

And as it was the eve of the Quarant'ore:

"Console and love Him," she added, "May His Heart find rest here, and may your littleness save many souls for Him ... "

Then stressing the leading thought of her life:

"Console Him by your humility, for all is well where there is humility; but when it is absent, everything goes wrong."

Then after telling her of some of her motherly wishes:

"Adieu," she said as she blessed her, "refuse nothing to your God."

That same evening the devil, exasperated by the intervention of the Saint, and still more by her advice, exclaimed: "That blessed one will be the ruin of my power, through her humility alone." And as if forced to reveal his infernal secret -

"Ah!" he roared, blaspheming, "when I want to keep strong hold of a soul,

I have only to incite her to pride ... and if I want to bring about her ruin, I have only to let her follow the instincts of her pride.

"Pride is the source of my victories and I will not rest till the world is full of it. I myself was lost through pride, and I will not allow souls to save themselves through humility.

"There is no doubt about it," he cried with a yell of rage, "all those who reach highest sanctity have sunk deepest in humility."

Josefa wrote this diabolic confession with deep feeling, and her filial love rejoiced in the midst of her pains at this unexpected tribute to the humility of her Holy Mother Foundress.

The Quarant'ore had always been for her a special time of reparation. But this year was the last on earth during which Our Lord would summon her to carry the Cross with Him for souls who are lost during these days of unbridled indulgence and sinful pleasure.

Her love had grown considerably in the year that had passed, and it was as His consecrated bride that she now shared the bitterness of the wounded Heart of her Master. She was expecting Him, for St. Madeleine Sophie had prepared her for His speedy coming.

On February 11th, during the Quarant'ore Sunday Mass, He manifested Himself to her. It was a month since last she had seen Him. "Josefa," He said, "will you comfort Me?"

She renewed her vows, and expressed the burning desires of her soul, not however without a certain reticence, "for," she said, "I was afraid of myself, for I grow more wretched every day ... "

"Do not think of what you are," said Our Lord, "I will give you the necessary strength for anything I may ask of you. Remember that I permit your miseries and falls,1 so that in spite of the graces I bestow on you, you may never lose sight of your nothingness."

Then His Heart glowed like fire ...

"And now, let us work for souls ...

"Many are lost, it is true ... but we shall be able to save many others from the ways of perdition, and this will comfort My Heart, in spite of the offenses committed against It. Do you know, Josefa, how sinners rend Me, and how much I need those who will make reparation? That is why I come to rest among those I have Myself chosen. May these souls, by their fidelity and their love, heal the wounds that sinners cause Me. I need victims to repair the bitterness inflicted on My Heart and to relieve My sorrow. How great is the number of sins committed! ... How many the souls that are lost!"

She begged Him to come and rest among His own, and to let them know what to do to console so vast a sorrow.

"I look only for love," He answered, "docile love that allows itself to be led by the Lover ... disinterested love, that seeks neither for pleasure nor for self-interest, but thinks only of the Beloved. Zealous love, burning, fiery and vehement love, that overcomes all the obstacles raised by egoism: that is true love, love that snatches souls from the bottomless pit into which they cast themselves headlong."

Encouraged by such condescension, Josefa plied Jesus with her artless questions.

"How is it," she wrote, "that when prayer is made for a soul month after month there seems to be no result? ... How is it that He who so longs for the conversion of sinners, leaves their hearts untouched, so that many prayers and sacrifices are lost? ... and I spoke to Him of three sinners and especially of two, for whom we have been praying so long!"

"When a soul prays for a sinner with an intense desire for his conversion," Our Lord answered graciously, "his prayer generally obtains the sinner's conversion, though sometimes only at the last moment, and the offense given to My Heart is repaired. But in any case, prayer is never lost, for on the one hand, it consoles Me for the pain sin has occasioned, and on the other, its efficacy and power are applied, if not to that sinner, then to others better disposed to profit by it.

"There are souls who during life and for all eternity are called to give Me not only the glory they owe Me themselves, but also that which other souls who are lost should have given Me... . In this way My glory is not impaired and a just soul is able to make reparation for many others.

"Let this be your constant prayer, Josefa: 'Eternal Father, who out of love for mankind gavest Thy Beloved Son up to death, by His Blood, by His merits and by His Heart, have pity on the whole world, and forgive all the sins that are there committed. Receive the humble reparation offered Thee by Thy chosen souls. Unite it to the merits of Thy Divine Son, so that all they do may be very effective. O Eternal Father, have pity on souls, and remember that the time has not yet come for strict justice, but for mercy.'"Do not refuse Me anything," He said before leaving her, "and do not forget that I need souls to carry on My Passion, that divine wrath may be restrained. But," He added reassuringly, "I will sustain you."

The conversation that had taken place in the morning was continued that evening. Josefa was busy in the Auxiliary Chapel, when suddenly Our Lord appeared to her. "You cannot know how much I count on you," He said graciously.

"But how is it possible, dear Lord, for I do nothing out of the way?"

"Do not be astonished... . In spite of the number of offenses committed by sinners, My Heart is consoled, for I have many who love Me. I do indeed feel keenly the loss of so many souls ... but this sorrow does not cloud My glory. Understand this well, Josefa, when a soul loves Me, she can make up for many who offend Me, and this relieves My Heart."

"I explained to Him how much I would like to be one of those loving souls. What could I do to prove my love? ... This Lent I would try to be very simple and very docile ... and console Him specially by my humility, as Our Holy Mother told me the other day; only I am not sure what to do... ."

Then as a father bends down the better to explain a lesson to his child, Our Lord said to her:

"The humility your Holy Mother spoke to you about does not consist in words or exterior actions exactly, but in the fidelity with which a soul moved by grace follows its inspirations, without letting itself be carried away by self-love. This, of course, need not prevent a soul from helping herself by exterior acts to acquire true and deep humility. That is what your Holy Mother meant.

"And now," He said, "this is what you will do to console Me for the sins of the world ... and especially for those of My chosen souls.

"During Lent, you will recite the Miserere every day with true humility and you will add a Pater.

"You will prostrate three times for the space of an Ave Maria, to beg for mercy and pardon in the name of sinners, and for the same intention you will do whatever penances are allowed you.

Then Our Lord expressed the desire that three times a week between eleven and midnight Josefa should unite herself to His prayer to appease the wrath of the Father and obtain pardon for sinners.

She dared not promise to carry out this last request, "for," she said, "I am not sure of obtaining leave."

"Submit yourself in this as in all else to the decision of your Superiors," answered the Master; "and now I shall continue telling you My secrets ... "

"During Lent, I will make known to you anything that displeases Me in your soul and I will use you to comfort My Heart whenever I need you. Adieu, I will come back soon ... Do not leave Me solitary ... Do not forget Me."

This wish of the Heart of Jesus helped her to endure the painful days that followed. How could she leave Him solitary?... when the sins of men were being multiplied and were forever calling on her thought and spirit of reparation.

On Tuesday of the Quarant'ore, February 13th, she once more came in contact with that supreme agony that she shared with all her soul. Whilst she was making the Stations with her Sisters, Jesus came, His sacred face very sad and all disfigured with blood, but His Heart was on fire. He asked her to stay with Him a few minutes. She went to ask leave, and rejoined Him in the Chapel where the Blessed Sacrament was exposed.

"Look at My face, Josefa, it is sin that has thus disfigured it. The world precipitates itself into pleasures of all kinds; such a multitude of sins are committed that My soul is drowned in bitterness and grief... .Where shall I find relief for My sorrow? I come here seeking shelter and love in order to forget for awhile the ingratitude of men."

"I tried to console Him," she wrote; "and a few minutes later He said: 'Come with Me into your cell. There we shall repair for the many sins and offenses that are being committed.'

"I went out of the Chapel, Jesus walked in front of me ... then He disappeared, but when I opened the door of my cell He was already there. I knelt down and He said: 'Prostrate yourself to the very ground and adore the Divine Majesty despised by sinful men. Make an act of reparation and say with Me: "O God infinitely Holy, I adore Thee. Humbly prostrate in Thy presence, I beg of Thee in the name of Thy Divine Son to pardon the many sinners who offend Thee. I offer Thee my life, and I long to repair for so much ingratitude." '

"Here He stopped ... and I asked Him if these sinful souls wounded Him. 'Yes,' He said, 'very much, but My chosen souls comfort Me.'

"I spoke to Him from time to time, telling Him of my longing to comfort Him ... but what could I do? ... so wretched and incapable ...

" 'That is true,' He replied, 'but do you not know how little your wretchedness matters to Me? ... What I want is to be Master of your wretchedness. Do not trouble yourself about anything else... . My Heart transforms everything. Kiss the ground once more and say with Me: "My Father, God Holy and Merciful, accept my desire to console Thee. Would that I could repair for all the sins of the world ... but as this is impossible, I offer Thee the merits of Jesus Christ, Redeemer of the human race, in order to satisfy Thy justice." '

"After a few moments of silence, I asked Him if the devil would persecute me again tonight as he had done on the previous ones, or whether I could make a Holy Hour with all the others.

" 'Yes, I will let you spend that hour united to the feelings of My Heart which is burning with desire to attract souls to Itself in order to forgive them. Poor sinners, how blind they are! I want only to forgive them, and they seek only to offend Me. That is My great sorrow; that so many are lost and that they do not all come to Me to be forgiven.'"

Then taking advantage of Our Lord's indulgence, for He seemed disposed to answer all her questions, Josefa let them tumble out one after another with the simplicity of a child.

"I asked Him if He remembers our faults after we have been sorry for them and have obtained His forgiveness."

" 'As soon as a soul throws itself at My feet and implores My forgiveness, Josefa, I forget all her sins.'

"I asked Him if people will go on offending Him to the end of the world."

" 'Yes, alas, ... to the end of the world, but I shall also have some who are a comfort to Me.'

"I wanted to know if He does not make His voice heard by souls that are plunged in sin, in order to induce them to change, for I see for myself that when I am in temptation and resist, suddenly I feel within me something that makes me know the truth and at once I am seized with sorrow."

Jesus answered: "Yes, Josefa, I pursue sinners as justice pursues criminals. But justice seeks them in order to punish; I, in order to forgive."

Then as she offered Him as a consolation the desires of religious, which are more than usually ardent during carnival time, He added before leaving her: "My chosen souls are to My Heart as balm to a wound. I will return later, Josefa, go on consoling Me."

For the moment the consolation that He asked of her was fidelity, in spite of the toils in which the devil tried to ensnare her.

Saturday, February 17th, all her gloom was scattered when Mary brought her the token she most valued, the Crown of Thorns of her Son: "It is for you, my child," she said. "Do not worry at all about the lies with which the devil tries to torment you."

And as Josefa told her how sad it made her to be unable to escape so many traps laid for her, Our Lady suggested this remedy to her: "Fix your mind on the Passion and sufferings of Jesus." Then placing the Crown of Thorns on her head: "Take it," she added, as she blessed her; "it will keep you in His presence."

A few hours after, it was Jesus with His peace who came to her: "Come ... come closer," He said to Josefa as she hesitated.

"Promise Me never to let yourself be caught again by the devil's snares."

That was what she wanted, but she did not dare promise, for she was so conscious of her weakness.

"If you fall again. I will come to your help."

Then she artlessly confided to Him the counsel given her by her Immaculate Mother which she had already been putting into practice by fixing her mind from hour to hour on the Passion. "Yes," said Our Lord with great kindness, "think of My sufferings."

And pointing out the direction His Message was to take in future, He added: "Henceforth I will come every day to talk to you about My Passion, so that it may be the subject of your own thoughts and of My secrets to you for souls."

The Secrets of the Passion: The Cenacle (February 18th - 28th, 1923)

"Josefa, spouse and victim of My Heart, we are going to speak of My
Passion, that your soul may constantly feed on the remembrance of it, and
that My souls may find in it food for their hunger and drink for their
thirst."
(Our Lord to Josefa, May 2nd, 1923)

The great love-story of the Passion was about to be unveiled to Josefa
stage by stage from the Cenacle to Calvary, during the Lent of 1923. We
must not look for an account of facts of which the Gospels are, of course,
the official and authorized record. Jesus meant to disclose to Josefa the
secrets of His Heart's depths, spoken to one who would understand and
sympathize with His most intimate sufferings. This revelation was made,
then, to every soul that longs to penetrate into the sacred depths of His
Heart to share Its feelings and to refuse nothing that the Cross may
demand of it.

Josefa was to be the first to enter into this sanctuary, treading in the
footsteps of her Master, and while He discovered Himself to her in the
solitude of her cell, she would continue recording the Message of a
suffering love made manifest to the world.

A few days passed, however, before the divine promise was fulfilled. Our
Lord was making His instrument pliant by keeping her waiting and
abandoned to His Will. Three times every week, Monday, Wednesday
and Saturday, Josefa had permission to offer herself to His good pleasure
before retiring to rest.

After the night from Saturday to Sunday, February 18th, she wrote:

"I offered myself to His sweet will, but as I was afraid of falling asleep, I
asked Him to be kind enough to wake me.

"Hardly had I gone to bed than I fell asleep ... I do not remember what the
time was when I awoke at the sound of His voice calling me. 'Josefa!'

"Stupefied with sleep, I said: 'O, my Jesus, forgive me. What time is it?'

" 'What does that matter, Josefa? ... It is Love's hour.'

"How beautiful Jesus looked. He was bearing His Cross. I renewed my
vows and rose at once, and He continued: 'It is the hour when Love comes
in search of comfort and relief by leaving you My Cross. Let us go and
beg for pardon and mercy for souls... . Take My Cross that I may rest a
while.'

"He gave me His Cross, which weighed me down, and I also felt the pain in my side, and my soul was overwhelmed with anguish.... I longed to be able to comfort Him ... but I felt so unworthy of bearing His Cross....

" 'That does not matter,' He said. 'My Cross will lean upon your misery and I will rest in your littleness.... My Cross will strengthen you and I will support you.

" 'When a soul comes to Me for strength, I do not leave her to herself; I hold her up, and if in her weakness she stumbles, I will raise her.

" 'Now let us ask pardon for souls ... let us repair the offenses committed against the Divine Majesty. Say with Me: "O God most holy and just ... Father of all clemency and of infinite goodness, Thou who didst create man out of love and through love hast made him heir to eternal blessings; if he has sinned against Thee through frailty and if he deserves chastisement, accept the merits of Thy Son who offers Himself to Thee as a Victim of expiation. By those divine merits, forgive sinful men, and deign to reinstate them as heirs of Heaven. O My Father, pity and mercy for souls!'

" 'Josefa, I leave you My Cross, that you may ease My burden; I am your strength, console Me' ...

"Then He left me His Cross and went away."

On Monday evening, February 19th, she renewed the same offering before falling asleep.

"I cannot tell whether it was His voice or His presence that woke me at about eleven o'clock.... Jesus was there, bearing His Cross, and I heard Him say: 'Josefa, do you love Me?'

"Conscious of my misery and that I do not know how to love, I did not dare reply.... I asked Him to forgive me for letting myself be troubled by very small happenings which really are not worth it.

" 'Yes, make use of all these small occasions to win souls for Me.'

"Then with His usual kindness He went on: 'Take My Cross, and we shall repair together the many sins committed at this hour of the night.... If you but knew how many throw themselves into sin.'

"He gave me His Cross and I humbled myself in His presence ... I adored Him, for more than ever I realized my unworthiness in contrast with His greatness. He joined His hands and said: 'Come, let us adore God's Majesty, outraged by so many offenses. Let us repair this multitude of sins!

" 'O God infinitely holy ... Father infinitely merciful, I adore Thee. I long to expiate the insults heaped upon Thee by sinners all over the world and at every moment of the day and night. Would that I could at least repair for those being committed at this hour. O My Father, I offer Thee all the acts of adoration and reparation made by souls who love Thee. Above all, I offer Thee Thy Divine Son, immolated on the altar in every corner of the world ... at every moment of this hour. O Father, infinitely good and compassionate, accept His pure Blood in reparation for all the outrages committed by mankind, wipe out their sins and have mercy on them.'

"Then we remained in silence. Jesus was looking towards Heaven.... My soul was in great anguish and my heart crushed with sorrow.... After a time He spoke again: 'Offer your whole being in reparation for so many sins, and to satisfy the Divine Justice.'

"I told Him that I felt unworthy to do this, as I, too, am a great sinner.

" 'If your unworthiness and your sins are great, come and immerse them in the torrent of My Heart's blood and let yourself be purified. Then accept generously all the sufferings My Will sends you, and offer them up to My Heavenly Father. Your heart should burn with desire to console an outraged God, and repair for so many sins through My merits.'"

As Jesus was about to go, Josefa ventured to remind Him of His promise to speak to her of His Passion.

"Yes, I will come back," He said. "Meanwhile comfort My Heart and do all you can in reparation."

These nights of reparation were renewed regularly, but they never prevented her from resuming her work as soon as it was light. During the night of Wednesday to Thursday, February 22nd, Our Lord again awoke her, for, worn out, she had fallen asleep quickly. "Here I am," He said. "I have come to rest in you."

Promptly she rose, renewed her vows, and offered herself to ease His divine shoulders of the heavy Cross. "Yes, I will give it to you, Josefa, and with it all the pain in My Heart."

"At once," she said, "He gave me His Cross ... and I did my best to comfort Him.... He went on to say: 'Tell Me, do you know a heart more loving than Mine, and any that meets with less response to Its love? Is there a heart to be found that consumes itself with greater willingness to forgive? And yet in payment for so much love I receive only great outrages. Poor souls ... let us go and ask pardon, and repair for their sins.

" 'O My Father, have pity on souls. Do not chastise them as they deserve, but have mercy on them according to the entreaties of Thy Son. I long to make reparation for their sins, and render Thee the glory which is due to Thee, O God, infinitely Holy! But cast Thine eyes on Thy Son, He is the Victim who will expiate all these sins.'

" 'Remain united to Me, Josefa, and accept with entire submission the sufferings that are yours during this hour.' "

Jesus went away and an hour was spent by Josefa crushed by excessive pain. "Suddenly," she wrote, "the devil appeared before me and with a shriek of rage he cried: 'It is my turn now.'"

The rest of that night was passed under his blows, threats, and blasphemies. Exhausted, Josefa recovered only enough strength to drag herself to the chapel to receive Holy Communion. The time had come when, having brought her down to the very depths of her weakness and nothingness, Jesus would stoop, and use her as one uses a perfectly mended instrument. That very morning, Thursday, February 22nd, when she had gone to her cell to snatch a few moments rest in transcribing the prayers she had repeated after her Master the night before, suddenly He stood beside her: "Josefa, spouse and victim of My Heart," He said gravely, "we are going to speak of My Passion, that your soul may constantly feed on the remembrance of it, and that My souls may find in it food for their hunger and drink for their thirst."

"I did not dare interrupt Him," she said. "However, I asked His leave to renew my vows.

" 'Yes, renew them; it gives Me glory when you tighten the bonds that unite Me to you, and I fill your soul with so much grace that not only is it as pure as on the day of your vows, but each time it gains a new degree of merit which makes it more pleasing in My sight. Thus, all souls united to Me by these close and sacred bonds clothe themselves in new merit and draw nearer to My Heart which delights in them, each time they renew their vows.

" 'And now, Josefa, I will begin by discovering to you the thoughts that filled My Heart, while I was washing the feet of My disciples.

" 'Mark how the whole Twelve were gathered together, none excepted: John the beloved was there, and Judas who was so soon to deliver Me to My enemies. I will tell you why I willed to have them all assembled together and why I began by washing their feet.

" 'I gathered them all together because the moment had come for My Church to be manifested to the world, and for all the sheep to have but one Shepherd.

" 'It was My intention, also, to show souls that I never refuse grace even to those who are guilty of grave sin; nor do I separate them from the good whom I love with predilection. I keep them all in My Heart, that all may receive the help required by their state of soul... .

" 'But how great was My sorrow to see in the person of My unhappy disciple Judas the throng of those who, though often gathered at My feet and washed with My blood, would yet hasten to their eternal perdition.

" 'I would have these to understand that it is not the fact of being in sin that ought to keep them from Me. They must never think that there is no remedy for them, nor that they have forfeited forever the love that once was theirs... . No, poor souls, the God who has shed all His blood for you has no such feelings for you!

" 'Come all of you to Me and fear not, for I love you all ... I will wash you in My blood and you shall be made whiter than snow. All your offenses will be submerged in the waters in which I Myself shall wash you, nor shall anything whatsoever be able to tear from My Heart Its love for you.

" 'Josefa, let your soul be seized today by an ardent desire to see all souls, especially sinners, come and purify themselves in the waters of repentance ... Let them give themselves up to thoughts of confidence, not fear, for I am a God of pity, ever ready to receive them into My Heart.'"

Here ended the first of Our Lord's dictated messages. Josefa, who had written rapidly for some twenty minutes, said that He spoke "with such eagerness" that it seemed as if He were pouring out His Heart and taking intense pleasure in thus expressing His feelings. As quickly as she could, she committed to paper His burning words, which were only interrupted from time to time by a brief pause.

He then stopped, gave a long look at Josefa, who had put down her pen and was kneeling at His feet; a word of farewell, and He was gone.

Josefa, steeped in the thoughts evoked by what she had just heard and written down, remained a few minutes spellbound before her open notebook. She did not re-read it, but handed it to her Superiors, who were always present. Then she hurried off to the workroom, where her sewing awaited her, but all day she turned over in her mind the sorrowful secrets that Christ had confided to her.

Our Lord did not leave her long without asking her for more reparation for souls in peril. The evening of that same Thursday, February 22nd, as she was just finishing the Stations of the Cross, He came to remind her that He counted on her cooperation.

This time it was for three souls in peril "who are not only My own dearly loved ones, but especially singled out by My Heart's affection."

"That is why I come here to seek comfort in your midst ... Notice, Josefa," He added, "that what the devil said to you this morning is true: many souls find salvation here."

Then after making His thought clear: "You attract them to truth, souls so loved of My Heart, by your miseries and your love."

Josefa was surprised at these words: "Yes," He continued, "two things predominate here: miseries and love. Love is the reason why so many souls find here new life, and it is misery that fixes the eye of God on this group of religious."

The next evening, Friday, February 23rd, at the end of the Stations of the Cross that Josefa and the Novices had just made, Our Lord became visible to her.

"He was standing in front of the altar rails," she wrote. "He was bearing His Cross and His loving gaze was on us all. He said: 'How much comfort you give Me! Ah! could you but see ... what marvels you would discover... . How your prayers are transmuted into treasure for souls!"

"As He said these words, He came close to me ... and gave me His Cross. I told Him my fears; these last nights the devil had never stopped insulting this house... .

" 'Have no fear, Josefa; he can only threaten you, for you are guarded by Me who am almighty. If he hates you, it is because I love you. Ah, if only you realized the important work that is carried out in this house, and how much is done for My Heart and for souls here... .'

"After having thus poured out His overflowing Heart, Our Lord continued: 'But now My Heart is deep in grief because of those three souls whom I entrusted to you... . I shall come here for consolation as long as they continue to offend Me ... I leave you My Cross; do not leave Me alone.' Then He added: 'Love Me and comfort Me, Josefa.'"

The Cross in its most painful form was to weigh on Josefa, for the devil, who had been given special power at this time, continually vented his rage on her. She was expiating for those souls, Christ's "specially loved ones," who had allowed themselves to be seduced, and she was purchasing the light that would bring them back to the truth.

On Sunday, February 25th, Jesus visited her in her cell very early in the morning.

"Why do you fear?" He said gently to her. "Perhaps, because you have still many imperfections, but there is no question of the sins the devil accuses you of... . Yes, renew your vows strengthening the bonds that unite us... . And now, Josefa, do not forget that you are but a tool, and a very useless and wretched one.

"Kiss the ground and write ... for we are going on with Love's secrets.

"I will tell you My reasons for washing the feet of My Apostles before the Last Supper.

"In the first place I would teach souls how pure they must be to receive Me in Holy Communion.

"I also wished to remind those who would have the misfortune to sin that they can always recover their innocence through the Sacrament of Penance.

"And I washed the feet of My Apostles with My own hands, so that those who have consecrated themselves to apostolic work may follow My example, and treat sinners with humility and gentleness, as also all others that are entrusted to their care.

"I girded Myself with a white linen cloth to remind them that apostles need to be girded with abnegation and mortification, if they hope to exert any real influence on souls... .

"I wished also to teach them that mutual charity, which is ever ready to excuse the faults of others, to conceal them and extenuate them, and never to reveal them.

"Lastly, the water poured on the feet of My Apostles denotes the zeal which burned in My Heart for the salvation of the world.

"The hour of Redemption was at hand. My Heart could no longer restrain its love for mankind nor bear the thought of leaving them orphans.

"So, to prove My tender love for them and in order to remain always with them till time has ceased to be, I resolved to become their food, their support, their life, their all. Could I but make known to all souls the loving sentiments with which My Heart overflowed at My Last Supper, when I instituted the Sacrament of the Holy Eucharist ...

"My glance ranged across the ages, and I saw the multitudes who would receive My Body and Blood, and all the good It would effect... . how many hearts I saw that from Its contact would bud forth virginity! ... and how many others that It would awaken to deeds of charity and zeal! ... How many martyrs of love did I see... . How many souls who had been enfeebled by sin and the violence of passion would come back to their allegiance and recover their spiritual energy by partaking of this Bread of the strong! ...

"Who can describe the overwhelming emotions that filled My Soul? Joy, love, tenderness ... but, alas, bitter sorrow also... .

"Later I shall continue, Josefa. Go now in My peace; console Me, and do not be afraid; the well-spring of My blood is not exhausted, and It will cleanse your soul."

Here Jesus stopped.

"Adieu, kiss the ground. I shall return."

She waited several days for this return. Every morning found her faithfully in her cell, but He did not come; the devil, on the other hand, tormented her ceaselessly.

The Blessed Sacrament and Sinners (March 1st - 11th, 1923)

"The Holy Eucharist is the invention of Love, but how few souls correspond to that love which spends and consumes itself for them!" (Our Lord to Josefa, March 2nd, 1923)

On the First Friday, March 2nd, at about nine o'clock, Josefa, active and alert, hurried to her workroom. She had waited long for the coming of Our Lord in her cell, but once again He had not come. She wrote in all sincerity: "I was rather glad to have the time, for I had a lot of sewing to do... . At times I am haunted by the idea that I do no work at all, and that I am of no use, what with all those things... ."

This was a return of the old temptation which the devil never failed to suggest to her eager and devoted nature.

"On reaching the foot of the 'Saint Michael' staircase, I came face to face with Jesus. He stopped me and said: 'Josefa, where are you going?'

" 'I am on my way to iron the uniforms in the linen-room, Lord.'

" 'Go to your cell,' He said, 'for I want you to write.'"

She smothered the secret wish she had to get on with her work, and went upstairs and found that Jesus had already preceded her.

"Who made you, Josefa?" was His first question after she had renewed her vows.

"Thou, Lord."

"Has anyone shown you more love than I? ... Who has forgiven you so often as I, and who will do so again? ... "

Full of shame, she was at His feet in an instant.

"Yes, humble yourself, Josefa; kiss the ground, and never resist My Will. Now write for My souls:

"I want to tell them of the poignant sorrows which filled My Heart at the Last Supper. If it was bliss for Me to think of all those to whom I should be both Companion and Heavenly Food, of all who would surround Me to the end of time with adoration, reparation, and love ... this in no wise diminished My grief at the many who would leave Me deserted in My tabernacle and who would not even believe in My Real Presence.

"Into how many hearts defiled by sin would I not have to enter ... and how often this profanation of My Body and Blood would serve for their ultimate condemnation... .

"Sacrileges and outrages, and all the nameless abominations to be committed against Me, passed before My eyes ... the long, lonely hours of the day and of the night in which I would remain alone on the altars ... and the multitudes who would not heed the appeals of My Heart... .

"Ah! Josefa, let the thoughts of My Heart sink deep into yours.

"It is love for souls that keeps Me a Prisoner in the Blessed Sacrament. I stay there that all may come and find the comfort they need in the tenderest of Hearts, the best of Fathers, the most faithful of Friends, who will never abandon them.

"The Holy Eucharist is the invention of Love ... Yet how few souls correspond to that love which spends and consumes itself for them!

"I live in the midst of sinners that I may be their life, their physician, and the remedy of the diseases bred by corrupt nature. And in return they forsake, insult and despise Me! ...

"Poor pitiable sinners, do not turn away from Me... . Day and night I am on the watch for you in the tabernacle. I will not reproach you ... I will not cast your sins in your face... . But I will wash them in My blood and in My wounds. No need to be afraid ... come to Me... . If you but knew how dearly I love you.

"And you, dear souls, why this coldness and indifference on your part? ... Do I not know that family cares ... household concerns ... and the requirements of your position in life ... make continual calls upon you? ... But cannot you spare a few minutes in which to come and prove your affection and your gratitude? Do not allow yourselves to be involved in useless and incessant cares, but spare a few moments to visit and receive this Prisoner of love! ...

"Were you weak or ill in body surely you would find time to see a doctor who would cure you? ... Come, then, to One who is able to give both strength and health to your soul, and bestow the alms of love on this Divine Prisoner who watches for you, calls for you, and longs to see you at His side.

"When about to institute the Blessed Sacrament, Josefa, these were My feelings, but I have not yet told you what My Heart felt at the thought of My chosen souls; My religious, My priests ... but I will tell you all this later on. Go, now, and do not forget that My Heart loves you ... and, Josefa, do you love Me? ... "

It was by her courageous fidelity more than by her words of love that Josefa replied to this question of her Master. During the following night, which was more full of pain than ever, she gathered from the blasphemies of the devil that the three souls so specially dear to the Heart of Jesus and for which she had suffered so much during the past fortnight were about to return to Him. This encouraged her.

On the evening of the First Saturday, March 3rd, she was in adoration before the Blessed Sacrament, when Our Lord appeared to her with His Heart all gloriously aflame.

"Josefa," He said with eager voice, "let Me rest a while in you, let Me tell you of My joy: those three souls that I had entrusted to you have come back to Me... ."

And He continued: "My Cross is heavy... . That is why I come here to rest and to give a share of it to each of My well-beloved souls... . My Heart is in search of victims to lead the world to love, and I find them here."

With what joy Josefa joined in her Master's exultation. She offered Him all the desires of the house, which she knew were sincere and ardent, that His Heart might find comfort and that many erring souls might return to Him. Then, as she could not forget what Our Lord dictated to her yesterday, she asked Him if He would not tell her for His chosen souls what He expected of them in the Holy Eucharist.

"Yes," He answered, "I want to tell you this, that My best-loved and specially favored souls, My priests and My consecrated nuns, may learn it through you. If their infidelities wound Me deeply, their love consoles and delights My Heart to such a degree that I, so to speak, forget the sins of many others on their account."

"Then," said Josefa, "He spoke to me at length on that subject, but as we were in the Chapel, I told Him that I could not possibly remember it all so as to write it down afterwards.

" 'Never mind; let Me speak to you and pour out all that My Heart feels.'"

Towards the evening of Sunday, March 4th, just as she was finishing the Stations of the Cross, Jesus appeared.

"If you want to console Me," He said, "now is the time. Tonight, very near here, they are holding a meeting in which I shall be much insulted. Offer yourself as a victim in such a way as to make reparation for the outrages committed by these souls. Poor souls! ... How they sin against Me! ... And afterwards ... How will they manage to keep out of that place? ... "

A few minutes later Jesus joined her in her cell, where already she was in prayer, interceding for those sinners. He gave her His Cross and Himself guided her prayer:

" 'O My Father! whilst these sinners offend Thy Sovereign Majesty and furiously outrage the Blood of Thy Son, look upon this willing victim which united to My Heart suffers and makes reparation. Deign to receive her sufferings in union with My merits, O Father of all goodness.' Then He added: 'Now let Me plunge your soul in the bitterness that is in My Heart.'

"And He vanished, leaving me in unspeakable anguish under the Cross."

Night came down on this state of woe and distress which lasted till the Master returned.

"About ten o'clock," she wrote, "He came back and said to me: 'Give Me back My Cross. You have comforted Me.'

221

"I thanked Him for letting me know that He was somewhat comforted and I promised Him unconditional surrender... .

" 'Yes, whenever I need you, come and dress the wounds that sinners have caused.

" 'You have given Me to drink,' He added finally, 'and I will give you a share in the Kingdom of Heaven.'"

There followed a few days of interruption; then once more on Tuesday, March 6th, Jesus came at eight o'clock in the morning.

" 'Josefa, are you expecting Me?' He asked. 'I am going to reveal to you the greatest mystery of My love ... of love for My chosen consecrated souls. Begin by kissing the ground... . When about to institute the Holy Eucharist, I saw the privileged throng who would be nourished by My Body and Blood; some would find there the remedy for their shortcomings, others consuming fire for their imperfections... . I likewise saw them gathered round Me as in a garden, each separately rejoicing Me with her flowers and their scent... . As a vivifying sun, My sacred Body gave them life, and warmed their cold hearts... . To some I went for comfort, to others for refuge, to others again for rest... . Would that all these cherished souls knew how easily they can console Me, harbor Me, or give rest to Me their God.

" 'It is this infinitely loving God who after freeing you from the slavery of sin has given you the incomparable grace of your vocation and has mysteriously attracted you into the enclosed garden of His delights. This God who is your Saviour has made Himself your Bridegroom.

" 'And He Himself feeds you with His immaculate Flesh, and slakes your thirst with His Blood. If you are sick, He will be your Physician; come to Him, He will cure you. If you are cold, come to Him, He will warm you. In Him you will find rest and happiness, so do not wander away from Him, for He is life, and when He asks you to comfort Him, do not sadden Him by a refusal... .

" 'Alas, what sorrow it is to see so many who have been endowed with My choicest graces become a cause of pain to My Sacred Heart! Am I not always the same? ... Have I changed? ... No, My love is unalterable and will endure to the end of time with the same tenderness and predilection.

" 'That you are unworthy I well know; but not for that do I turn away from you. On the contrary, with anxious solicitude I look for your coming, that I may not only ease your troubles, but also grant you many favors.

" 'If I ask your love, do not refuse it. It is so easy to love Love Itself.

" 'If I should ask you for things that cost, know that at the same time I will give you all the grace and strength you need to conquer yourself.

" 'I hope to find in you My comfort, therefore have I chosen you. Open your whole soul to Me, and if you are conscious of having nothing worthy of Me, say with humility and trust: Lord, Thou knowest both the flowers and fruits of my garden ... come and teach me how I may grow what will please Thee most. To one who speaks in this way and has a genuine desire of showing love, I answer: Beloved, if such is your desire, suffer Me to grow them for you ... let Me delve and dig in your garden ... let Me clear the ground of those sinewy roots that obstruct it and which you have not the strength to pull up... . Maybe I shall ask you to give up certain tastes, or sacrifice something in your character ... do some act of charity, of patience, or self-denial ... or perhaps prove your love by zeal, obedience or abnegation; all such deeds help to fertilize the soil of your soul, which then will be able to produce the flowers and fruit I look for: your self-conquest will obtain light for a sinner ... your ready patience under provocation will heal the wounds he inflicted on Me, will repair for his offense and expiate his fault ... a reproof accepted patiently and even with joy will obtain for a sinner blinded by pride the grace to let light penetrate his soul and the courage to beg pardon humbly.

" 'All this I will do for you if you will give Me freedom. Then will blossoms grow quickly in your soul, and you will be the consolation of My Heart.'

" 'Lord, Thou knowest my readiness to let Thee do with me whatsoever Thou wilt... . Alas, I have fallen and displeased Thee ... wilt Thou forgive me once again? I am so wretched and can do no good! ... '

" 'Yes, My beloved, even your falls comfort Me. Do not be discouraged, for this act of humility which your fault drew from you has consoled Me more than if you had not fallen. Take courage, go forward steadily, and let Me train you.

" 'All this was present to Me when I instituted the Blessed Sacrament, and My Heart glowed with desire to become the food for just such souls. If I have taken up My abode among men it is not merely to live among the perfect, but to uphold the weak, and sustain the lowly. I will make them grow and become strong. Their good resolves will be My solace and I will rest in their wretchedness... .

" 'But are there not some among these chosen souls who will inflict sorrow on Me? ... For will they all persevere? ... Such is the cry of grief that breaks from My Heart... . I want souls to hear it.

" 'Enough for today, Josefa. Farewell. You comfort Me when you entrust yourself entirely to Me. Let Me tell you My secrets for souls, since I cannot speak to them thus every day. Let Me make use of you whilst you are still alive.'"

The very next day, Wednesday, March 7th, Josefa heard the dolorous plaint of His Heart. "Kiss the ground in all humility," He said as was His wont.

She fell down in adoration at His feet, and when she had risen, He spoke: "Write today concerning the pain endured by My Heart, when being constrained by the fire that consumed It, I devised the marvel of love, the Holy Eucharist. And while I looked at those many souls that would feed on this Heavenly Bread, I could not but see also the indifference by which so many others ... consecrated souls ... priests ... would wound Me in this Sacrament. There were those who would grow cold ... gradually yield to routine ... and worse than routine ... to weariness and lassitude, and little by little to tepidity... . Still, I wait all night and watch in the Tabernacle for that soul ... fervently hoping that she will come and receive Me ... that she will converse with Me with all the trust of a bride ... telling Me of her sorrows, her temptations, her sufferings ... asking My advice and begging for the graces she needs for herself or others... . Perhaps she has dependent on her or in her family souls that are in danger and far from Me? ... 'Come,' I say to her, 'let us discuss everything with perfect freedom ... Be concerned about sinners... . Offer yourself to make reparation ... Promise Me that at least today you will not leave Me alone ... then see if My Heart is not asking something more of you to comfort It... .' This is what I hoped to obtain from that soul and from many another... . Yet when she receives Me in Holy Communion she barely says a word to Me ... she is distracted, tired or put out ... her whole mind is absorbed by her occupations ... her family cares ... her acquaintances ... or maybe anxiety for her health ... she does not know what to say to Me ... she is indifferent, bored ... wishes it were time to go... . Is it thus that you receive Me, O soul whom I have chosen and for whom I have watched with all the impatience of love throughout the livelong night?

"Yes, I yearned for her coming that I might rest in her and share her anxieties... . I had prepared fresh graces for her, but she does not want them ... she has nothing to ask of Me, neither advice nor strength ... she just complains to herself without so much as addressing Me... . It seems then that she has come simply out of routine, to go through a customary formality, or perhaps because no grave sin prevented it. But it is not love nor a true desire for close union with Me that has impelled her coming. Alas, that soul does not possess the delicate love I had hoped to find in her. And priests? ... Who can express all I expect from each of My priests... . They are invested with My own power, that they may forgive sin... . I Myself am obedient to their word when they summon Me from Heaven to earth... . I am totally surrendered into their hands; they may confine Me to the tabernacle or give Me to the faithful in Holy Communion... . They are, so to say, My almoners.

"To each I have entrusted souls that by their preaching, their direction and above all their example, they may guide them in the path of virtue.

"What response do they make? ... Do they all fulfill Love's mission? ... Will this My minister at the altar confide the souls of his charges to Me today? Will he make reparation to Me for the offenses I receive, the secret of which has been entrusted to him? ... Will he entreat of Me the strength he needs to carry out in holiness his sacred ministry? ... zeal to work for the salvation of souls... . courage in self-sacrifice, more today than yesterday? ... Will he give Me all the love I expect ... and shall I be able to rely entirely on him as on My dear and well-beloved disciple? ... O what cruel sorrow for My Heart, when I am forced to say: 'The world wounds Me in My hands and in My feet and it sullies My countenance... . My chosen souls and My consecrated religious, My priests, they rend and break My Heart... . How many priests after giving back grace to many souls are themselves in a state of sin! ... How many say Mass thus ... receive Me thus ... live and die thus! ...

"Now you know what anguish oppressed Me at the Last Supper when I saw in the midst of the Twelve the first unfaithful Apostle ... and after him so many more who would follow him in the course of the ages.

"The Blessed Sacrament is the invention of Love. It is life and fortitude for souls, a remedy for every fault, and Viaticum for the last passage from Time to Eternity. In it sinners recover life for their souls; tepid souls true warmth; fervent souls, tranquility and the satisfaction of every longing ... saintly souls, wings to fly towards perfection ... pure souls, sweet honey and rarest sustenance. Consecrated souls find in it a dwelling, their love and their life. In it they will seek and find the perfect exemplar of those sacred and hallowed bonds that unite them inseparably to their heavenly Bridegroom.

"Indeed, O consecrated souls, you will find a perfect symbol of your vow of Poverty in the small, round, white and smooth Host; for so must the soul that professes poverty be: no angles, that is to say no petty natural affections, either for things used nor for her employments, nor for family or country ... but she must ever be ready to leave, or give up, or change... . Her heart must be free, with no attachments whatever... .

"This by no means signifies insensibility of heart; no, for the more it loves the more it will preserve the integrity of the vow of Poverty. What is essential for religious souls, is first, that they should possess nothing without the permission and approbation of Superiors; and secondly, that they should possess and love nothing that they are not ready to give up at the first sign. Later, Josefa, I will tell you the rest."

Several days passed without any mitigation of her suffering state. It seemed to her that several times she had yielded to the violent rebukes of the enemy, and she trembled lest she should have wounded her Master.

"I even lost a Communion," she wrote sorrowfully.

On Laetare Sunday, March 11th, Jesus returned once more, and gave her the full sense of security that she was forgiven.

"Take My Crown and have no fear," He said. "The mercy of God is infinite and never refuses to forgive sinners, and more especially when there is question of a poor little creature like you."

Then alluding to the Communion she had missed: "O, Josefa, if only you had known how I was longing for you to hide Me in your heart!"

She could think of nothing to say to make Him forget that pang.

"You will make amends," He said with the utmost kindness, "by preparing yourself today with very fervent longing for tomorrow's Communion. My Heart is consoled each time you tell Me of this longing ... and then," He went on, "the spirit of faith and blind obedience always.

"Continue now to write for My souls: Tell them how they will find in the small white Host a perfect symbol of their vow of Chastity. For under the species of bread and wine the Real Presence of God lies concealed. Under this veil, I am there whole and entire, Body, Blood, Soul, and Divinity.

"It is thus that one consecrated to Jesus Christ by the vow of Virginity must be hidden under a veil of modesty and simplicity, so that under the appearances of her humanity, a purity like that of the angels may be concealed.

"And understand well, you who form the court of the Immaculate Lamb, that the glory you give Me surpasses incomparably that of the angelic spirits; for they have never experienced the frailties of human nature, and have neither to struggle nor to conquer in order to remain pure.

"You thus acquire a relationship with My Mother, who being a mortal creature was nevertheless of spotless purity ... subject to all human miseries, yet at every instant of her life absolutely immaculate. She has glorified Me more than all the celestial spirits, and God Himself, drawn by her purity, took flesh of her and dwelt in His creature.

"Further, the soul that is consecrated to Me by the vow of Chastity resembles Me, her Creator, as far as it is possible for a human being to do so, for when I clothed Myself in human nature, its miseries not excepted, I lived uncontaminated by the slightest blemish.

"That is how the soul by its vow of Chastity becomes a pure white host, which unceasingly renders homage to the Divine Majesty.

"Religious souls, you will find in the Holy Eucharist the model of your vow of Obedience.

"For hidden and annihilated there, are the greatness and power of God. There, you see Me apparently lifeless, who nevertheless am the life of souls and the support of the world. I can no longer go away or remain, be alone or surrounded: Wisdom, Power, Liberty, all are hidden beneath the Host.... The species of bread are the bonds that chain Me and the veil that covers Me.

"In like manner, the vow of Obedience is the chain that binds a religious soul, and the veil under which she must disappear, so that she no longer has either will, judgment, choice or liberty, except according to the good pleasure of God as manifested to her by her Superiors."

Our Lord then stopped after this long discourse and Josefa allowed her heart to speak:

"This morning there was a ceremony of First Communion," she wrote, "and I reminded Him of the consolation He doubtless felt in these pure and innocent souls.

"His Heart was moved at the remembrance: 'Yes,' He said tenderly, 'it is in souls such as these and in those of My nuns that I take refuge in order to forget the iniquities of the world. The children are like fair rosebuds to Me, where I seek shelter. As for My religious, I hide and rest in them, for they are full-blown roses who defend Me by their thorns, and comfort Me by their love. And you, Josefa, give Me that love. Be ready to follow Me to Gethsemane. There I will teach you how to suffer, and I will strengthen you by the sweat of blood drawn from Me by the sins of men. Meanwhile console Me by your desire to hide Me in your heart. In that way you will repair for that lost Communion.

" 'Adieu, do not forget Me. Long for Me as I long for you... . Love Me as I love you... . Seek Me as I seek you... . You see that I never forsake you.'"

Gethsemane- (March 12th - 15th, 1923)

"Stay close to Me in Gethsemane and let My Blood water and strengthen the root of your littleness."
(Our Lord to Josefa, March 12th, 1923)

The very next day, Monday, March 12th, Our Lord called Josefa to Gethsemane. He began by reassuring her, for the night before Satan had multiplied his threats about her Communion, to which she had so eagerly looked forward on the preceding day.

"Have no fear," He said, "the power of the evil one is not greater than Mine. It pleases Me to hear you call Me, and I am so consoled that every desire of your heart cries out to Me; it is as if so many who do not communicate, went to Communion.

"Humble yourself, kiss the ground, and then come with Me ... let us go to Gethsemane, and may your heart be immersed in the feelings of bitterness and sadness with which Mine was submerged.

"After having preached to great crowds, healed the sick, given sight to the blind, raised the dead ... after having lived three years with My Apostles to train them and teach My doctrine to them ... I finally willed to teach them by example how to love one another, to put up with one another, and how mutually to serve each other; and this I did by washing their feet and making Myself their food.

"The hour had come for the Son of God made man, Redeemer of the human race, to shed His blood and give His life for the world. And that I might surrender Myself to My Father's will I forthwith betook Myself to prayer.

"Dearly loved souls, come and learn from your Model that the one thing necessary, whatever the revolts of nature, is surrender to God's Will in humble submission and by a supreme act of the will to accomplish the Will of God whatever the circumstances may be. Learn also from Him that all important actions should be preceded and vivified by prayer, for only in prayer can a soul obtain the strength needed in life's difficulties. In prayer God will communicate Himself, will counsel and inspire, even if His action be unfelt.

"I withdrew into the Garden of Gethsemane, that is to say into solitude. God is to be sought within, away from distraction and noise. To find Him the soul must enforce silence on all the disturbances by which nature often fights against grace; on interior arguments prompted by self-love or sensuality. These constantly tend to stifle the inspirations of grace and keep her from finding God within... .

After these words, Our Lord continued:

"Adore His Will for you, whatever it is ... and humble yourself as befits a creature before its Creator... .

"It was thus I offered Myself to carry out the Redemption of the world.

"At the same moment I felt all the torments of My Passion burst overwhelmingly upon Me: the calumnies and the insults ... the scourging and the Crown of Thorns, the thirst ... the Cross... . All these sufferings thronged before My eyes and pressed upon My Heart, while at one and the same time I saw all the offenses, sins and crimes that were to be committed throughout the ages ... I not only witnessed them all, but was invested in them ... so that under the burden of their ignominy I was constrained to present Myself before the face of My all-holy Father and implore Him to show mercy.

"And there burst upon Me the wrath of an angry and offended God, and in order to appease His Majesty I offered myself as security for sinful man, I, His Son, to calm His anger and satisfy His Justice. But so great was the anguish and so mortal the agony of My human nature under the strain and weight of so much guilt, that a bloody sweat poured from Me to the ground.

"O sinners who thus torture Me ... will this blood bring salvation and life, or will it be shed in vain for you? How can I express My sorrow at the thought of this sweat, this anguish, this agony, this blood ... useless for so many souls.

"That is enough for today, Josefa. Console My Heart; tomorrow we shall go on... . Adieu. Remain close to Me in Gethsemane that My blood may fertilize and strengthen the root of your littleness."

How was it that Josefa succeeded after such confidences in adjusting herself to the ordinary give and take of common life? Yet she was seen to be ever the same, working from morning till night. Only a very special grace could thus keep her present to all, whilst she was at the same time oppressed by those momentous disclosures from the divine lips.

That night from the 12th to 13th of March, Jesus returned with His Cross. It was her right, ratified by obedience; and while still reminding her of her unworthiness, Jesus entrusted her with this treasure which they shared.

"I rest in your nothingness," He said, "but I find comfort and relief as well in the midst of My consecrated nuns, for though they are unaware of it, I entrust them too with souls who are saved and return to Me... . Keep My Cross, and tomorrow I will tell you more of My secrets."

The night as usual was spent in diabolic attacks, and early next morning Jesus resumed His narrative.

"Kiss the ground," He said to His messenger, whom He liked to see thus lowly at His feet. "I am not attracted by your merits but by My love for souls."

"Yes," He continued, "I have come to reveal to you the feelings of My Heart, and also to rest among you all. Ah! how happy I am when souls receive Me with joy ... for I come either to console them or to seek in them My consolation. But they do not always recognize My presence, especially when it is accompanied by suffering.

"And now let us continue our prayer in Gethsemane:

"Draw near Me, and when you see Me submerged in an ocean of grief, rise, and go with Me to the three disciples whom I had left a stone's throw away.

"I had chosen them that they might share My agony, pray with Me and by their company afford Me some consolation... . What were My feelings to find them asleep? O the pang of loneliness, and to have none to share in My sorrow... .

"How often My Heart suffers this same grief ... how often, hoping to find solace among the souls It loves, It finds them slumbering! ...

"It is useless for Me to attempt to awaken them, to make them leave themselves and their preoccupations, their vain and fruitless conversations ... too often the reply that reaches Me in act if not in words amounts to: 'I cannot now, I am too busy ... too tired ... I need repose.' Then gently insisting I say to this soul 'Come for a little while. Come and pray with Me, I need you, do not be afraid of sacrificing your rest for Me; I will be your reward... .' And the same answer is repeated... . Poor sleeping souls who cannot watch one hour with Me... .

"Beloved souls, learn from this how useless it is to seek comfort in creatures. How often you will receive only an increase of distress because they are asleep and respond neither to your hope nor love.

"I went back to My prayer, and again falling on My face I worshipped My Father and implored His help... . I did not call Him 'My God' but 'My Father.' It is when harrowed with pain that you too must call God your Father. Beg for His help, expose your woes ... your fears, your longings ... and let your cry of anguish remind Him that you are His child. Tell Him that your body is exhausted ... your heart is sorrowful even unto death ... that your soul is experiencing what seems a very sweat of blood. Pray with a child's confidence and expect relief from your Father's Heart. He Himself will comfort you and give you the strength necessary to endure the tribulation or suffering, whether it be your own or that of the souls confided to your care.

"My soul, already shattered and a prey to sadness, had to endure still more deadly grief, for crushed by the weight of the sins of men, and in return for so much suffering and love, I saw only outrages and ingratitude. The blood now pouring from My body and which I was soon to shed from countless wounds would be in vain for so many souls ... many would be lost ... a still greater number would sin against Me ... and myriads would not so much as hear My name ... I would pour out My blood for all, offer My merits to each soul... . Blood of a God ... infinite merits ... yet to be in vain for how great a number!

"Yes, I will shed My blood for all and all will be loved with great love ... but for some that love will be more tender, more intimate, more ardent ...

so from these chosen souls I will expect more consolation and love, more generosity and abnegation ... in a word, a fuller response to My loving-kindness.

"Alas! At this moment I see how many will turn away from Me ... some will not listen to My call ... others will hear but will not follow Me ... others will respond for a time with a certain amount of generosity to the call of My Heart, but then will gradually grow drowsy and one day will say to Me by their deeds: 'I have worked enough ... I have been faithful to every detail of my duty ... I have overcome nature ... I am no longer a child ... so many privations ... so much vigilance are no longer necessary ... I need no longer endure this restraint, etc... .'

"Poor soul! is this how you begin to go to sleep? ... soon I shall return and as you are asleep you will not hear Me ... I shall offer you My grace and you will not receive it ... Is there any hope that later on you will be roused? Must one not fear that you will grow weak through lack of food and be unable to throw off your lethargy? ...

"Beloved souls, know that death has stolen upon masses while they were thus sleeping soundly! ... Where and by what means have they been awakened? ...

"I saw all this and felt it in My Heart. What should I do ... turn back, ask My Father to free Me from this torment? ... Show Him the uselessness of My sacrifice for so many souls? ... No! again I surrendered Myself to His holy Will and accepted this chalice, to drink it to the dregs.

"O souls that I love, I did it to teach you not to faint under your burdens. Never count them as useless, even if you are unable to reckon the result; submit your judgment and leave the divine Will free to do with you whatsoever it wills.

"I Myself would neither go back nor escape, and knowing that My enemies would come and seize Me in that very Garden, I stayed where I was.

"Tomorrow we shall continue, Josefa; be on the alert, that I may find you awake if I need you."

A full hour passed in silence in the cell where Josefa, still on her knees, had not stopped writing for a moment. At last she ended her task and Jesus looked down at her and said: "Kiss My feet and remain in My peace. I am always with you even when you do not see Me."

He went away, but not for long, and early on Wednesday morning, March 14th, without further introduction, He resumed His narrative:

"After having been comforted by an angel sent by My Father, suddenly I saw Judas coming, one of the Twelve, and with him those who were come to take Me prisoner. They carried staves and stones, chains and ropes to seize and bind Me. I arose, and drawing near, I said to them: 'Whom seek ye?' Then Judas, putting his hands upon My shoulders, gave Me a kiss. Ah! Judas, what are you doing? ... Why do you betray Me with a kiss?

"To how many souls cannot I also say: 'What are you doing? ... What does this kiss mean?'

"Beloved soul, you who come to receive Me, so often assure Me of your affection ... and you have hardly left Me than already you have betrayed Me to My enemies! You know very well that in that company you find so attractive there will be conversations that wound Me, you who communicated this morning and tomorrow will do so again ... these are the occasions in which you lose My costly grace... .

"And why do you carry on transactions of doubtful integrity? I say to another. Do you not know these are unlawful gains, unlawful this rise in social position ... this wealth? ... In so doing you receive Me as Judas did with a kiss, for in a few moments, a few hours at most, you will give My enemies a sign by which they will recognize Me and so lay hands on Me. Now I speak also to you Christian souls: you betray Me by this dangerous friendship, you cast stones at Me and cause another likewise to betray Me. Why do you do this? You who know Me and so often have gloried in your almsgiving and church-going? ... These acts which might be highly meritorious are but a cloak of your malice... . O soul whom I love ... why are you enslaved by passion? ...

"Friend! whereto art thou come? ... Judas, dost thou betray the Son of Man with a kiss, your Master and your Lord! He who loves you and is ready to forgive again ... one of My Twelve! ... who sat at My table and whose feet I have washed? ...

"How often must I speak thus to the souls I love most dearly?

"I do not ask you to free yourself, for I know it is not always in your power, but what I do ask of you is to keep up the struggle against your passions... . What are passing pleasures ... if not the thirty pieces of silver for which Judas sold Me, and what did he gain? The loss of his soul.

"How many have sold Me and will sell Me for the low price of a passing pleasure? ... Alas, poor souls, whom seek ye? Is it I? This Jesus whom once you knew and loved ...

"Listen to My words: 'Watch and pray, fight your evil inclinations and suffer them not to grow into confirmed habits.'

"The grass in meadowlands has to be mown every year, and in some cases even at every recurring season. The ground needs to be ploughed up, manured, and freed from weeds, and so must work be carried on in souls and evil tendencies carefully corrected. Do not imagine that it is always a serious fault that leads to the worst sins. The greatest faults are often the result of neglect of little things: a small satisfaction indulged in, a moment of weakness yielded to, a consent to do a thing in itself lawful but immortified, a pleasure not sinful, but ill-advised here and now... . All these things recur unheeded, and little by little the soul is blinded, grace loses its power, passion increases and finally triumphs.

"Ah! how infinitely sorrowful for the Heart of God, whose love is boundless, to see so many insensibly approaching nearer and nearer the abyss... .

"That will suffice for today, Josefa. Do not forget that My Heart is drawn here not by your merits, but by your misery and the compassion I feel for you."

Late next night, Josefa awoke at the call of her Master. He brought her His Cross, as had been agreed, and only said: "Take My Cross and be afraid of nothing. Never will it be beyond your strength to bear, for I have measured and weighed it in the balance of love. Ah! do you know the depth of My love for you and for souls? ... It is for them that I use you, for little as you are, and worthless, yet I make use of your littleness by keeping it united to My merits and close to My Heart.

"Keep my Cross, and suffer for souls and for love of Me."

This nightly endurance of pain, so dear to the Heart of Jesus as also to Josefa, continued till dawn. Jesus was thus preparing her for the tryst He had not failed to keep for many days.

No sooner had Josefa reached her cell on the morning of Thursday, March 15th, the Feast of the Five Wounds, than He joined her. Standing before the table in front of which she knelt after having renewed her vows, He said as usual: "Kiss the ground and humble yourself, Josefa."

By this act she each time offered herself once more to do His Will.

"I have told you, Josefa, how those who offend Me gravely deliver Me over to My enemies to put Me to death, or rather they make themselves My enemies and the arms they use against Me are their sins.

"But it is not always a question of grave lapses ... there are souls and even highly favored ones that are false to Me by habitual faults, by evil tendencies acquiesced in, concessions to immortified nature, failings against charity ... obedience ... silence, etc. And if sin and ingratitude from worldlings are hard for My Heart, how much more grievous when inflicted by those I dearly love... . If the kiss of Judas caused Me so much grief, this was because he was one of the Twelve, and from him I expected more love, more consolation, more sympathy!

"O chosen souls, marked out by Me for My home of rest, the garden of My delights, from you also I expect more tenderness, consideration and attentions prompted by love, than from others who are not so closely united to Me.

"You can be a healing balm to My wounds, you can cleanse My defiled and disfigured countenance ... you can help Me to enlighten blind souls who in the darkness of night seize Me to bind Me and lead Me to death.

"Leave Me not alone ... awake and pray with Me, behold the enemy is at hand.

"When the soldiers came forward to seize Me I said to them: 'It is I.' Such, too, is the word I utter when a soul is about to yield to temptation: 'It is I.' You come to betray Me and to deliver Me up... . No matter, come, for I am your Father, and if you consent, then it will not be you that bind Me with chains of sin, but I that shall bind you with chains of love!

"Come, it is I who love you, it is I who have poured out all My blood for you... . I pity your weakness, I long to open My arms and clasp you in Love's embrace!

"Come, My chosen one, come My priest ... I am infinite mercy ... do not fear that I shall punish you... . I shall not repulse you, but shall open My Heart to you and love you with even greater tenderness. I shall wash away your sins in the Blood of My wounds. All Heaven will rejoice and wonder at your regained beauty, and My Heart will find rest in yours.

"Alas, how sick at heart I am when after words so tender there still remain some who would bind Me and lead Me to My death... .

"After he had given Me the traitor's kiss, Judas left the Garden, and realizing the gravity of his crime, gave way to despair. Who can measure My sorrow at the sight of My Apostle casting himself into Hell! ...

"The hour had come, so yielding to the soldiery I meekly gave Myself up as a lamb into their hands. At once they dragged Me to the house of Caiphas, where they heaped insults and mockery on Me and where one of the soldiers struck Me a blow in the face.

"The first buffet... . Mark My words, Josefa, do you think it gave Me more pain than the scourges of the flagellation? Doubtless no, but I saw in this first blow the first mortal sin of many souls who until then had lived in My grace... . And after the first, how many more ... and how great the number of souls who would follow that example and fall into the same danger ... perhaps into a like misfortune: death in mortal sin... .

"Tomorrow we shall continue; meanwhile, Josefa, spend the day in reparation and prayer that many souls may realize where their dangerous path is leading them."

The Feast of the Five Wounds was not to pass without the favor of a visit from Our Lady, and the gift of the drops of blood, which has already been related. The visit, however, was a brief one, and when Josefa timidly asked if she might state some of her difficulties, she answered: "I will return, and then you can ask me whatever you like."

The Flight of the Apostles (March 16th, 1923)

"I will make My plaint resound by My Apostles of the past and by My chosen souls of today."
(Our Lord to Josefa, March 16th, 1923)

Our Blessed Lord came, anticipating His Mother, on the morning of the 16th of March, and Josefa thanked Him for the signal grace conferred on her the day before.

"If you are faithful in your love," He answered, "shall I not be faithful, too, in consoling you? I am preparing another proof of My love for you. Yesterday, Josefa, you received a few drops of My Heart's blood, today you will share the pain of the nails... . I will leave you My Cross, that you may bear it all day and that your love may comfort Me. I will sustain you, for I also do not cease loving you. Do you not see that I give you proofs of My affection? I shall go on doing so till the day when I take you to Heaven with Me.

"Now continue writing for the sake of souls:

"My disciples have all fled; Peter alone, impelled by curiosity, but full of fear, slinks in among the soldiery. All around Me are false witnesses uttering lie upon lie calculated to increase the anger of the iniquitous judges. They call Me a seducer, a profaner of the Sabbath, a false prophet, and the servants and menials, stimulated by these accusations, utter cries and threats against Me.

"Where then were you, My disciples and Apostles, witnesses of My life, of My doctrine, and of My miracles? ... And all those from whom I had every reason to expect help and protection - none was there to defend Me. I was alone, accused of the worst crimes, surrounded by soldiers no better than ravening wolves.

"They all ill-treat Me; one strikes Me in the face, another spits upon Me, a third makes a laughing-stock of Me... .

"And while I offered Myself to be thus ill-used for the sake of souls held captive by sin, Peter, whom I had constituted Head of My Church ... Peter, who but a few hours before had vowed to go with Me to torments and to death ... Peter, who has the opportunity of giving testimony of Me, answers a simple question, first by a denial ... and when the question is repeated, as fear takes an ever stronger hold of him, he swears that he has never known Me and has never been My disciple... .

"Ah! Peter, do you swear that you do not know your Master? You not only swear it, but at a third question you deny Him, uttering horrible imprecations...

"O My chosen followers ... can you fathom the pain of My loving Heart when My own chosen ones deny Me? When the world revolts against Me, when so many souls pour scorn upon Me, ill-treat Me, seek My death, and then turning to My own, I find nothing but loneliness and desertion... . What sorrow, what bitterness for My Heart!

"To you as to Peter I say: 'Have you forgotten the proofs of love I have given you ... the links that bind you to Me ... the oft-repeated promises of fidelity given to Me, and of defending Me even to death itself?' ...

"If you are weak and afraid of yielding to human respect, have recourse to Me for strength to conquer yourselves. Do not trust yourselves, but come to Me confidently, for I will sustain you.

"All you who live in the world in the midst of perils and occasions of sin, be on your guard against danger, for would Peter have fallen, if resisting courageously he had not yielded to vain curiosity?

"All of you who labor in My harvest-field or in My vineyard, if at some time you feel yourselves drawn to work by the attraction of a merely human enjoyment, fly. But if obedience, zeal for My glory or the good of souls, imposes a duty on you, have no fear; I will defend you, and you will pass victoriously through the danger.

"While the soldiers were leading Me to prison, I saw Peter in the crowd and I looked at him ... turning, he looked at Me and forthwith began to weep bitterly for his sin... .

"It is thus that I look on guilty souls - but they? ... Do they look at Me? ... Do our eyes meet? ... Alas, how often I look in vain ... that soul does not see Me, for he is blind! I urge him gently, but he does not respond... . I call the sinner by name, but receive no answer... . I send the trial that might awaken him, and still he slumbers... .

"Beloved souls, unless your eyes are turned heavenward, you will in time become like animals that have no reason. Lift up your heads, gaze on your true fatherland which awaits you. Seek your God. You will find that He returns your earnest look and in His glance are peace and life.

"Here we stop for today, Josefa; tomorrow we shall continue. Keep My Cross and comfort Me."

It was now three weeks since Our Lord had begun to reveal to Josefa for souls the secrets of His Passion.

So forcibly did she become associated with His feelings that her life was saturated by this mysterious participation, and she was unable to detach her thoughts from it. She went about, she worked and prayed and devoted herself, without for a moment losing sight of the sorrows that each morning were imprinted on her soul.

Nights of reparation had their place in this consecrated life, continually bringing to Josefa's mind the fact that she had been chosen not only to transmit a Message to souls, but to cooperate effectively in their salvation. The unity of this twofold mission was inscribed by Our Lord on every page of her life. She is victim, she is apostle, such is the true meaning of her vocation.

On March 16th Our Lady responded to Josefa's request of the day before, and gave her a fresh proof of her motherly love.

"You wanted to ask me something yesterday?" she said kindly, when that evening she came while Josefa was at her needlework. "What was it?"

Josefa answered that she wanted to know how best to pray to Our Lord so as to give Him pleasure.

"I shall tell you," was Our Lady's reply, "but go up to your cell, where you can write."

She had hardly reached her cell when she was joined by Our Lady.

"What pleases My Son most is love and humility - so write: 'O sweet and dearly loved Jesus, wert Thou not my Saviour, I should not dare to come to Thee, but Thou art both my Saviour and my Bridegroom, and Thy Heart loves me with the most tender and burning love, as no other Heart can love. Would that I could correspond with this love of Thine for me. Would that I had for Thee, who art my only love, all the ardor of the Seraphim, the purity of the angels and virgins, the holiness of the Blessed who possess Thee and glorify Thee in Heaven.

" 'Were I able to offer Thee all this, it would still be too little to honor Thy goodness and mercy. That is why I offer Thee my poor heart such as it is, with all its miseries, its weakness and good desires. Deign to purify it in the blood of Thy Heart, to transform and inflame it Thyself with an ardent and pure love. Thus the poor creature that I am, who can do no good but is capable of every evil, will love and glorify Thee as do the Seraphim who in Heaven are consumed with adoring love.

" 'Lastly, I ask of Thee, O gentle Jesus, to give my heart the very sanctity of Thy Heart, or rather to plunge it in Thy Divine Heart, that in It I may love and serve and glorify Thee, and lose myself in Thee for all eternity. I beg this same grace for all those whom I love. May they render Thee for me the glory and honor of which my sins have deprived Thee.'"

Then Josefa shyly asked this most kind and indulgent Mother to tell her of an ejaculatory prayer that she could repeat over and over again while at her work.

"Say these words which He will love: 'O my Beloved, who art also my God, make my heart a flame of pure love for Thee.'

"And every evening before you fall asleep, say with much respect and confidence:

" 'O Thou who knewest all my misery before Thine eyes were fixed on me - Thou didst not turn away from my wretchedness ... but because of it Thou didst love me with a love more sweet and tender. I beg pardon for having corresponded so little to Thy love... . I beg of Thee to forgive me, and to purify my actions in Thy Divine Blood. I am deeply grieved at having offended Thee, because Thou art infinitely Holy. I repent with heartfelt sorrow and I promise to do all in my power to avoid these faults in the future.'

"After which in all tranquility and joy take your rest."

The day came when Our Lord matched the gentle courtesy of His Mother, but in order to recount this sequel of divine condescension we shall have to anticipate, and go on to August 26th of this last year of Josefa's life.

"Josefa," He said to her that night, "is it true that you would like something to say to My Mother that would please her? Write what I tell you."

"Then in ardent, burning, even enthusiastic words," she noted, He said this prayer:

" 'O tender and loving Mother, most prudent Virgin, Mother of my Redeemer, I come to salute you today with all the love that a child can feel for its mother.

" 'Yes, I am indeed your child, and because I am so helpless I will take the fervor of the Heart of your Divine Son; with Him I will salute you as the purest of creatures, for you were framed according to the wishes and desires of the thrice-holy God.

" 'Conceived without sin, exempt from all corruption, you were ever faithful to the impulses of grace, and so your soul accumulated such merit that it was raised above all other creatures.

" 'Chosen to be the Mother of Jesus Christ, you kept Him as in a most pure sanctuary, and He who came to give life to souls, Himself took life from you, and received nourishment from you.

" 'O incomparable Virgin! Immaculate Virgin! Delight of the Blessed Trinity, admiration of all angels and saints, you are the joy of Heaven. Morning Star, Rose blossoming in springtime, Immaculate Lily, tall and graceful Iris, sweet-smelling Violet. Garden enclosed kept for the delight of the King of Heaven ... you are my Mother, Virgin most prudent, Ark most precious containing every virtue! you are my Mother, most powerful Virgin, Virgin clement and faithful! you are my Mother, O Refuge of sinners! I salute you and rejoice at the sight of the gifts bestowed on you by the Almighty, and of the prerogatives with which He has crowned you!

" 'Be blessed and praised, Mother of my Redeemer, Mother of poor sinners! Have pity on us and cover us with your motherly protection.

" 'I salute you in the name of all men, of all saints and all angels.

" 'Would that I could love you with the love and fire of the Seraphim, and this is too little to satisfy my desires ... and to render you filial homage constant and pure for all eternity.

" 'O incomparable Virgin, bless me, since I am your child. Bless all men! Protect them and pray for them to Him who is almighty and can refuse you nothing.

" 'Adieu, tender and sweet Mother; day and night I salute you, in time and for eternity.'

"Now, Josefa, praise the Mother with the words of the Son, and the Son with those of His Mother."

"Never," said Josefa, "had I seen His Heart so resplendent, nor heard in His voice such burning enthusiasm!"

From the Prison to the Scourging (March 17th - 21st, 1923)

"Look at My Wounds! Has anyone else suffered so much to prove His love?"
(Our Lord to Josefa, March 21st, 1923)

"It is twenty-two years today," wrote Josefa (Saturday, March 17th, 1923), "since I heard the voice of Jesus for the first time, when I was preparing for my First Communion. I was reminding Him of this during my thanksgiving when suddenly He appeared ... such loveliness! His garment seemed of gold and His Heart one blaze of fire... . How can I describe It?"

" 'Josefa,' I said to you then, 'I want you to be all Mine.' Today I can say to you: 'You are all Mine.' Then I was preparing to attract you to My Heart ... today you are imprisoned in It. Come ... enter and rest therein, since It is your dwelling."

Then He opened His Heart to admit Josefa... . "It was like Heaven," she wrote, "and I thought myself no longer on this earth ... "

These ineffable moments were of short duration; every time that she enjoyed their strength and peace she knew it to be but a pause between two phases. Such were Heaven's designs.

A few hours later she was at her post of waiting, till it pleased Him to lead her still further into His sorrowful Passion:

"Contemplate Me in the prison where I spent the greater part of the night. The soldiers came and, adding words to injuries, insulted Me, mocked Me, outraged Me, and gave Me blows on My face and on My whole body.

"Tired of their sport, at length they left Me bound and alone in the dark and noisome place, where, seated on a stone, My aching body was cramped with cold.

"Compare the prison with the Tabernacle ... and especially with the hearts that receive Me.

"In the prison I spent only part of one night ... but in the Tabernacle, how many days and nights?

"In the prison I was insulted and ill-treated by soldiers who were My enemies. In the Tabernacle most often it is they who call Me their Father who treat Me thus, but how unlike that of children is the treatment! ...

"In the prison I endured cold, sleeplessness, hunger and thirst, pain, shame, solitude, and desertion. And there passed before My mind's eye all the Tabernacles where in the course of ages I should lack the shelter of love ... the icy-cold hearts that would be as hard and unfeeling as the stones of the prison floor were to My numbed and wounded body.

"And how often should I wait for this or that other soul to visit Me in the Blessed Sacrament and receive Me into his heart ... how many nights should I spend longing for his coming ... but he would let business or carelessness or anxiety for his health get the better of him ... and he would not come!

"How often should I hunger for souls ... for their fidelity ... for their generosity ... would they satisfy that eager hunger by a little victory over self or by a slight mortification? ... Would they comfort Me in My sorrow by their tenderness and compassion? ... In some hard moment would they endure the pain ... neglect ... scorn ... opposition ... grief of soul or family ... would they come to Me and say: 'This I offer Thee to console Thy sadness, to keep Thee company in Thy solitude.' O! if they would thus unite themselves to Me, with what peace would they face difficulties ... how much fortitude they would win and how they would gladden My Heart!

"In the prison what shame I felt at the obscene words of those around Me ... and My distress was increased by the thought that like words would one day fall from lips I love.

"When blows and buffets were rained upon Me by the filthy hands of the soldiery it recalled to My mind how often those who would receive Me into hearts fouled by unrepented sin would shower reiterated blows on Me by habitual and willed sin.

"And in the prison when they pushed Me and let Me fall to the ground bound and helpless, so many were present to My mind who would prefer a moment's satisfaction to Me, would load Me with chains by their ingratitude, would push Me back and again cause Me to fall, by leaving Me alone.

"O you who are consecrated to Me, draw near to the Bridegroom of your souls in His prison. Gaze steadfastly upon Him during that night of pain and see that sorrow continued in the loneliness of countless Tabernacles and the coldness of many hearts.

"If you are desirous of proving your sympathy, open your hearts and let Me find a prison therein... .

"There bind Me with chains of love... there clothe Me with loving attentions... . Appease My hunger by your generosity... . Assuage My thirst by your zeal... . Comfort Me in My sorrow by keeping Me faithful company and wiping away My shame by your purity and uprightness of intention.

"If you wish Me to take My rest in you, prepare for My coming by acts of self-denial ... master your imagination and calm the tumult of your passions ... then in the stillness of your soul you will hear My voice speaking gently within you: Today you are My repose, but for all eternity I shall be your rest... . Tenderly and with love you have harbored Me in the prison of your heart. I shall be your reward exceeding great and you will never regret any sacrifice you have made for Me during your life!

"Let us end, Josefa, and let Me spend today in the prison of your soul. Keep it in deep silence, that you may hear My words and respond to the wishes I shall confide to you."

Three days were spent in this contemplation, not without bringing to Josefa the grace of tribulations through which she kept watch with the Divine Prisoner. She was unconscious of the role assigned to her, which one would have expected would always be nothing but a delight to her. But the kind of love her Master demanded was of a sterner sort, fed on strife, humiliation, and suffering: "It is good for you," Our Lady had once said to her, "to love without knowing or feeling it."

Throughout this history this will be the one lesson Jesus and His Mother never cease inculcating on those chosen souls who are to be the instruments of His infinite mercy and of His redeeming love.

In the evening of Tuesday, March 20th, while she was hanging out the linen in the garden, suddenly Josefa met Our Lord, who looked at her with compassion.

"Go up to your cell," He said. "I want you to write."

Hardly had she reached it than He rejoined her. He was bearing the Crown of Thorns on His head, and she begged Him to give it to her.

"Yes, I will give it to you with great love.... Take it and let us write for My souls.

"After having spent the greater part of the night in the damp, obscure and sordid prison ... after having been subjected to outrages and ill-treatment by the soldiery ... to the insults and mockeries of the servants, who were curious to see what would become of Me ... when My body was already exhausted by so many torments ... listen, Josefa, to the burning desires of My Heart:

"What filled Me with love and made Me long for more suffering was the thought of so many who would follow in My footsteps.

"I saw them faithfully imitating Me and learning from My Heart not only to accept suffering and contempt with patience and serenity, but also to extend their love to those who would persecute them.

"Like Me they would rise to the height of offering themselves up in sacrifice for those who ill-treated them.

"I saw them, strengthened by grace, answer the divine call, become religious, imprison themselves in solitude, bind themselves with chains of love, give up all they cared for, endure courageously rebellions of nature, accept willingly misjudgments, contempt, slander, the condemnation of their life as foolishness ... and throughout all this keep their hearts intimately united to their God and Lord.

"So, in the midst of outrages and infamous treatment this prospect enkindled Me with a burning desire to carry out the Divine Will in all things. Hence, alone and in much pain, but in close union with the Will of My Father, I offered Myself to make amends to His outraged glory.

"You, O religious souls who live in the prison chosen by Love, often deemed useless and even dangerous in the eyes of the world, have no fear; in your solitude and moments of stress, let the world rant against you ... only join your heart yet closer to God, the one object of your affections, and do all you can to repair for the sins and the outrages of mankind.

"At dawn the next day, Caiphas ordered Me to be taken to Pilate, that he might condemn Me to death.

"Pilate questioned Me shrewdly, hoping to discover a true cause for My condemnation, but finding none, his conscience soon told him of what a grave injustice he would be guilty ... so to evade the responsibility He sent Me to Herod.

"Pilate's soul is typical of those who, tossed between the impulses of grace and the allurements of their own passions, blindly yield to human respect and excessive self-love; for if they are faced by a temptation or a dangerous occasion of sin, they blind themselves and argue, until they gradually persuade themselves that there is no harm, no peril in it ... they are wise enough to decide for themselves and have no need of advice ... they are afraid of seeming ridiculous in the eyes of the world ... they lack energy to overcome themselves, and not making use of grace they fall into one occasion of sin after another, until, like Pilate, they deliver Me up to Herod.

"When it is question of a religious, there is perhaps no intention of offending Me gravely. But to resist, a humiliation would have to be accepted, or some annoyance borne ... and if, far from following the inspiration of grace, and honestly manifesting the temptation, this soul in self-interrogation decides that there is no reason to avoid this danger or to refuse herself this satisfaction, she will soon fall into graver peril... . Like Pilate, she will be blinded and lose the courage to act with straightforwardness, and gradually, if not soon, she will come to delivering Me to Herod."

Jesus stopped, and addressing Himself to Josefa, said: "Remain in peace and in the consciousness of your miseries and nothingness. It takes so little to shake you ... but have no fear; My mercy and love are infinitely greater, and your weakness will never surpass My strength."

This principle Our Lord never grows tired of repeating. He wants through Josefa to teach other souls of whose wretchedness He is fully aware, but whose humble trust and brave hearts rejoice His; they will learn that nothing interferes with His plans, and that weakness does no more than hinder them for a moment.

At eleven o'clock He came again, but He was not bearing His Cross, which at once made Josefa anxious.

"For," she said, "He always brings it at night, and I have the permission of my Mothers to wait for Him at this time only in order to comfort Him... . I care nothing for my own rest; I only want His."

Jesus read this in her heart - He loved the simple and very true protestations of the affection which He knew so well. "Have no fear," He said. "Where I am, there is My Cross." And suddenly she felt its weight upon her shoulder. Jesus continued:

"Carry it with reverence and affection for the salvation of many souls that are in peril."

After a few minutes of silence spent in an attitude of intense supplication, He united her with Him in prayer and said gravely:

"Offer to My Eternal Father the sufferings of My Passion; say with Me:

"O Heavenly Father! look upon the wounds of Thy Son and deign to accept them, that souls may accept Thy grace.

"May the nails which pierced His hands and feet pierce those hardened hearts, and His blood touch them and lead them to repentance. May the weight of the Cross on the shoulders of Jesus Thy Divine Son obtain for them the grace to unload themselves of their sins in the confessional.

"I offer Thee, O Heavenly Father, the Crown of Thorns of Thy beloved Son. By the agony it caused Him, grant true contrition to souls for all their sins.

"O Father! O God of mercies, I offer Thee the abandonment of Thy Son on the Cross, His thirst and all His pain, that sinners may recover peace and consolation in sorrow for their sins.

"Lastly, O God of all compassion, in the name of the persevering prayer of Jesus Christ Thy Son for the very men who were crucifying Him, I beg and implore Thee to grant to souls love of God and perseverance in well-doing.

"And just as the torments of Thy beloved Son ended gloriously in eternal bliss, so may the sufferings of penitent souls be crowned by the everlasting reward of your glory."

"Keep my Cross, Josefa - remain united to My sufferings and continually offer to God the Father the wounds of His Son."

After a few moments' pause Jesus departed, leaving Josefa alone with the weight of the Cross on her shoulder.

On the morning of March 21st He returned and resumed the same subject as on the previous day:

"Go on writing, Josefa."

"To all Pilate's questions I answered nothing, but when he said 'Art Thou the King of the Jews?' then gravely and with full responsibility I replied: 'Thou sayest it; I am King, but My Kingdom is not of this world.'

"So, when an occasion of conquering human respect and accepting bravely either humiliation or suffering (even if it could easily be avoided) presents itself, a soul should answer: 'My Kingdom is not of this world,' for that reason I do not seek human favor; I go to my true fatherland, where rest and joy await me. Meanwhile I will do my duty faithfully and make no account of the opinion of the world. If for this I must seek humiliation or suffering, I will not draw back; I will listen to the voice of grace and disregard that of nature. If I am unable to do this alone, I will ask advice, for I know how often self-love and passion blind me and entice me into the paths of evil."

"Pilate therefore, overcome by human respect and the fear of shouldering his responsibilities, ordered Me to be led to Herod, a perverse man who sought only to satisfy his unruly passions. He was glad when he saw Me appear before his Court because he hoped for entertainment through My words and miracles.

"Consider My repulsion when brought face to face with so vicious a man, whose questions, gesticulations, and movements filled Me with shame.

"O virgin souls and pure ... come near Me and defend Me... . Listen to the false witnesses ... see the implacable desire of this crowd avid for scandals and before which I am made a laughingstock. Herod expected Me to reply to his sarcastic remarks, to justify and defend Myself, but I opened not My lips and kept the most profound silence in his presence.

"This silence testified to My sovereign dignity, for the obscene comments of so perverted a man were not worthy of exchange of words with the All-pure.

"During this interview My Heart was closely united to My Heavenly Father. I desired ardently to shed the last drop of My Blood for souls whom I love so much, and I was all inflamed with love at the thought of those who would follow My example and My generosity. Not only did I rejoice during this terrible interrogatory, but I was urged from within to hasten the moment of My suffering on the Cross.

"After undergoing these ignominies in complete silence, I allowed Myself to be treated as a fool and arrayed in a white garment, the sign of derision, and thus was I led back to Pilate amid the jeers of the multitude.

"Look at Pilate! See how afraid and disturbed he is; he is at his wits' end in order to calm the fury of the people who demanded My death; he orders Me to be scourged.

"Such is the soul that has not enough courage and generosity to break energetically with the world's demands, her nature or her passions. Instead of obeying conscience and making short work of temptation which she knows does not come from the good spirit, she yields to one fancy or another, to a slight satisfaction ... if she overcomes herself on one point, she gives in on another, which would need greater effort; if she does some mortification, she hesitates about others which would ensure her fidelity to grace or the Rule, but would deprive her of some small pleasure. She allows herself half of what nature or passion demands and so soothes her conscience.

"We will suppose that there is question of divulging some fault, real or imagined, that she has found in another. It is neither fraternal charity nor zeal for the general good that prompts her, but a hidden envy, the result of passion, which is her true motive. Grace and conscience alarm her, and act as a warning of the spirit inspiring the injustice she is about to commit. There may be a moment of interior struggle, but immortified passion soon deprives her of the light and courage to reject so diabolic a purpose. Then she contrives a way of suppressing part of what she knows, but not all, consoling herself with the thought that it is right that such things should be known... . I will confine myself to a hint ... etc.

"Like Pilate you give Me up to the scourges! Do not think you will satisfy passion thus ... today so much, tomorrow more... . And if you have given in on only a small provocation, how will you act when temptation is violent?

"Contemplate Me, O My beloved, being led away as a meek lamb to the shameful and terrible punishment of the scourging.

"Blow after blow is discharged by the executioners on My body, already covered with bruises and broken with fatigue... . With whips and knotted cords they strike Me with such violence that My very bones are shaken and I am torn with innumerable wounds ... bits of My divine flesh are rent off by the scourges ... blood flows from every limb, and I am reduced to such a state of pitiable disfigurement as no longer to resemble a human being.

"Can you contemplate Me in this sea of sorrow and remain unmoved? Pity I did not expect from My executioners, but from you, O My chosen souls, I do look for compassion!

"See My wounds! who has suffered for love of you as I have? Then addressing Josefa, Jesus continued:

"Contemplate Me in this state of ignominy, Josefa."

Jesus was silent and Josefa raised her eyes to the Master she so loved... . He stood there before her in the woeful state to which the scourging had reduced Him. For a long time He kept her eyes on that sorrowful sight as if to imprint it forever on her soul. Breaking silence at last:

"Tell Me," He said, "will not My wounds give you strength to conquer and resist temptation? ...

"Tell Me if you find not in them generosity wherewith to hand yourself over and sacrifice everything to My Will?

"Yes, Josefa, gaze on My wounds and let yourself be guided by grace and by the desire to comfort Me who am the victim of sin.

"Do not be afraid that your torments will ever equal Mine... . My grace will help you to do whatever I ask of you.

"Adieu, keep Me thus before your eyes!"

Our Lord then disappeared, and Josefa, her eyes closed, remained motionless, with an expression of unspeakable emotion on her face. Silence reigned in the little cell where such an amazing scene had just been enacted. Jesus had reminded souls that "it is not for nothing" that He has loved them with a love we can only call "frighteningly serious." Little by little Josefa came back to herself; her tears began to flow freely ... speech was impossible ... but she remembered that she was merely the instrument to carry a Message, a witness to the excesses of this love, and that souls had a right to receive from her the message of boundless love.

She took up her pen, and still trembling, wrote:

"I saw Him in the state in which the scourging had left Him. This sight has filled me with such compassion that it seems to me that I should have courage to endure any suffering, however intense, to the end of my life... .

"No pain could come anywhere near His agony... .

"What struck me most was the expression of His tortured eyes - those eyes usually so beautiful and so expressive ... today they were closed, swollen and filled with blood, especially the right eye. His hair damp with blood fell over His face, eyes and mouth. He was standing, but bent and bound to something ... but I saw nothing but Him - His hands were tied together at the height of His waist and covered with blood. His body was furrowed with wounds and dark bruises, the veins of His arms all swollen and blackened. From His left shoulder hung a fragment of torn flesh about to detach itself, and the same was the case in several other parts of His body. His garments lay at His feet, crimsoned with His blood. A very tight cord held a rag of cloth round His waist, but its color was quite indistinguishable, so impregnated was it with blood."

Here Josefa stopped; she was unable to go on ... "I cannot give an account of what I saw ... for words fail me ... "

The whole day passed under the unspeakable sensations caused by what Josefa had witnessed, which her face expressed in its deep sadness. Nothing else, however, betrayed this consuming inner life.

Who would have imagined that on this Wednesday in Passion week Our Lord would have deigned to manifest His wounds to the most obscure and hidden of His consecrated religious? No doubt His divine eyes were fixed on the many souls who would read in this account the proof of His infinite love, and who, with faith reanimated at the thought of such tortures endured for love of them, would, like Josefa, draw courage to refuse Him no sacrifice.

From the Crowning with Thorns to the Despair of Judas (March 22nd - 25th, 1923)

"Be attentive, O souls that I love, to the sufferings of My Heart."
(Our Lord to Josefa, March 24th, 1923)

Josefa had not seen Our Blessed Lady for several days, but it was she, who in the night of March 21st-22nd, brought her the Cross.

"I was awakened by a slight noise," wrote Josefa, "and at once I saw her standing by my bed. She was bearing the Cross on her right arm:

" 'It is I, daughter,' she said, 'and I come to entrust the Cross of Jesus to you, that you may comfort Him, for a great many sinners are offending Him. But one in particular is causing Him intense grief.'"

Then after reminding her that the first and best way of repairing was to allow herself to be used according to His Will, she concluded: "Now keep this precious treasure and pray for souls... ."

Her prayer for souls, begun thus under the Cross of Christ, was continued in the pains of Hell, where for some time past she had nightly "fulfilled that which was wanting in the Passion of Christ."

On Thursday, March 22nd, Our Lord appeared to her just as she was preparing to leave her cell at nine o'clock in the morning. "Kiss the ground," He said, "and let your whole soul be penetrated with what I am about to confide to you."

Humbly she threw herself at His feet; she rose, to write rapidly the sorrowful confidences that escaped the divine lips.

"When at last, exhausted by their exertions, these hard and cruel men desisted, they wove a crown of thorns and drove it deep into My head, and as they filed before Me, they mockingly cried out: 'We salute Thee, O King!' Some insulted Me, others savagely struck Me on the head, and each and all added new agonies to those which already racked My body.

"O you whom I love, contemplate Me condemned to death, given over to the insults and profanations of the mob, scourged at the pillar, and as though all this were not sufficient to reduce Me to the most humiliating condition, now crowned with thorns, clothed in a purple rag, and derisively hailed as mock king ... and treated as a fool... .

"I, the Son of God, who hold the universe in the palm of My hand, willed that in men's eyes I should appear as the last and most contemptible of all. Far from flying from such humiliations, I willingly endured them to expiate man's pride and draw souls to follow in My footsteps.

"I expiated by this painful crowning the pride of those who refuse to accept anything that lowers them in the eyes of the world.

"I allowed My shoulders to be covered by that cloak of mockery and Myself to be treated as a fool, so that many souls would not scorn to follow Me in a way that the world holds as vile and humiliating and which to them might seem beneath their condition.

"No path is contemptible or humbling when it is once marked out by the Will of God. You who feel interiorly drawn to this way ... do not resist, do not try by the arguments of pride to do God's Will while you follow your own. You will not find peace and joy in a position more or less brilliant in the eyes of men, but only in the accomplishment of God's Will and in entire submission to all He may require of you.

"There are also in the world a number of souls who are bent on settling their future here on earth. Perhaps one or other feels drawn by a secret attraction towards someone in whom she finds good qualities, honor, faith, and piety, conscientiousness in business matters, a sense of duty to his family, all that she longs to see in one she loves... But suddenly pride takes possession of her mind. Doubtless in this way the longings of her heart will be satisfied, but not her vain ambition to shine in the eyes of the world. Then this soul turns away, looking for what will gain for her more attention from creatures by making her appear richer and nobler. How deliberately she is blinding herself... . No, indeed, you will not find the happiness you seek in this world; and God grant, that although you put yourself in such grave danger, you may find it in the next.

"And what shall I say to those whom I call to a life of perfection and love and who turn a deaf ear to My voice? How exposed to illusions are those who imagine themselves ready to do My Will, to follow Me and unite themselves to Me ... and yet thrust deeply into My head the thorns of My crown... .

"There are souls whom I desire for My own; I know them intimately, and loving them as I do with infinite tenderness, I draw them in the direction in which My wisdom has prepared the most sure way of sanctity for them. There I propose to unveil My Heart to them, there they will give Me most love ... and most souls, too... .

"But what resistance and what disappointment! How many of them, blinded by pride or the desire to satisfy nature or paltry ambition, their minds filled with vain thoughts, end by turning away from the path marked out by love.

"O souls specially chosen by My Heart, do you think that in following your inclinations you are giving Me the glory I expect of you ... or doing My Will when you resist the call of grace or refuse through pride to follow Me in the way of love?

"Ah! Josefa, how many souls are blinded by pride! Today will you multiply acts of humility and submission to the Divine Will, to win for many souls the grace of following the way I have prepared for them with so much love.

"Tomorrow, Josefa, we shall come back on this essential point."

Early on the morning of March 23rd, Friday in Passion week, Josefa was waiting, but her Master did not come; she therefore took her needlework and sat by the table on which her notebook lay open. Suddenly He appeared: " Josefa, are you expecting Me?"

"Yes, Lord," was her answer.

"I have been here some time, but you did not see Me. Kiss the ground, and kiss My feet, too. We are going to make souls understand how many allow themselves to be deceived by pride.

"Crowned with thorns and clothed in the purple mantle, and amidst overwhelming insults and mockeries, I was brought back by the soldiers to Pilate... . Finding in Me no crime worthy of death, he questioned Me again and asked Me why I did not reply, seeing that he had power to crucify Me or release Me.

"Then breaking silence I said: 'Thou wouldst have no power over Me unless it were given thee from above, but the Scriptures must needs be fulfilled.' After which I resumed My silence, surrendering Myself wholly to God.

"Pilate, meanwhile troubled by a message from his wife, and worried by the remorse of his conscience, and fearing that the people might turn against him if he refused to sentence Me to death, sought for a pretext to release Me. So, presenting Me to the people in the pitiable plight to which I had been reduced, he offered to free Me and condemn instead Barabbas the thief. But the multitude cried out angrily with one voice: 'Let Him die! ... He must die and let Barabbas be set free.'

"O all ye who love Me, consider how I was compared to a thief ... or rather valued lower than a degraded criminal, one of the wickedest of men. Hear their cries of rage against Me and their vociferous clamors for My death.

"Far from seeking to escape this affront, I lovingly accepted it for love of souls, for love of you ... desirous of showing you that My love was leading Me not only to death, but to contempt, ignominy and hatred of those very men for whom I should shed My blood in such profusion.

"I was treated as a disturber of the peace, as insane, a madman, and I accepted it all with the utmost meekness and humility.

"Do you think that in My human nature I felt no repugnance and grief? ... I willed to know experimentally all that would have to be undergone by you, that you might draw strength from My example for all the circumstances of your life. So I did not free Myself, though this would have been easy, I accepted all lovingly, that thus fortified you might understand how to sacrifice every repugnance in order to accomplish the holy Will of God, My Father ... repair His glory ... expiate the sins of the world and win the salvation of many souls.

"Here I once more address Myself to the souls to whom I spoke yesterday.

You who are called to a life of perfection, who parley with grace, and answer thus: 'How can I live in continual obscurity? ... I am not accustomed to that kind of life ... to such lowly work ... my family and friends will think me ridiculous ... for I am gifted and could be more useful elsewhere, etc.'

"To you I make answer: 'When I was to be born of poor and humble parents ... far from My own country and home ... in a stable ... in the severest season of the year and the coldest of nights ... did I hesitate? did I refuse?'

"During thirty years I knew the hard toil of an obscure workshop, bearing the contempt and indifference of those for whom My father St. Joseph worked ... nor did I disdain to help My Mother in the humble and hidden occupations of her poor household. Had I not more knowledge than was needed for the humble trade of a carpenter - I who at twelve years of age taught the Doctors in the Temple? But such was My Father's Will and consequently it was in this way that I gave Him glory... .

"From the beginning of My public life, I could have made Myself known at once as the Messiah and Son of God, so as to attract the attention and veneration of men to My teaching. I did not do so, because My one desire was to follow in all things My Father's Will.

"And when the hour of My Passion had struck, see how in spite of the cruelty of some, the insults of others, the desertion of My own, the ingratitude of the crowds ... the unspeakable martyrdom of My body and the intense repugnance of My human nature, I embraced with ever more love that holy Will.

"Thus when you submit yourselves generously to the Will of God in spite of natural interior opposition to it ... the resistance of your family ... the judgments of the world ... when you have given yourself generously to the Will of God, then shall you be closely united to Him and taste ineffable sweetness.

"What I have said to souls who experience this keen repugnance to a humble and hidden life, I repeat to those called on the contrary to spend themselves in the service of the world, when their whole attraction is for a life of solitude and hidden labor.

"O chosen souls, your happiness and perfection do not lie in following your attraction, nor in living known or unknown to the world, in using or hiding the talents with which you have been endowed, in being thought much of or little ... in having good health or not ... but only and solely in embracing with love God's Will, and being in perfect conformity with it in all it requires of you for His glory and your holiness.

"Enough for today, Josefa; we shall go on tomorrow. Love and carry out My Will with joyful alacrity, since it will mark out the path of love for you in all things."

That evening, Josefa made the humble avowal that her Master's recommendation was very much to the point. He wanted her through self-conquest to obtain a like grace for souls very much in need of it. We can learn His valuable lesson from her words.

"I again feel in myself," she wrote, "a sort of revolt at this extraordinary kind of life. It disturbs my peace, I should so like to be allowed to work hard... ."

But Our Lord took no notice of this revulsion of feeling in her which changed neither His Will nor hers, and on Saturday, Passion week, March 24th, He was once more there to keep His tryst with her.

"Let us now return to the Passion," He said to her, as if to drag her away from her own thoughts. This is undoubtedly the means of self-forgetfulness that Jesus offers to all souls.

"Meditate for a moment on the martyrdom of My supremely tender and loving Heart at finding Barabbas preferred to Me, and how, at seeing Myself so scorned, I felt cut to the quick by the cries of the crowd urging My death.

"I called to mind the sweet caresses of My Mother when she pressed Me to her heart ... the toils of My adopted father, and the care with which he surrounded My life... .

"I reviewed in spirit the benefits so liberally bestowed by Me on this ungrateful people ... how I had given sight to the blind ... health to the sick ... healing to the lame ... how I had fed the multitude in the desert ... and even raised the dead to life ... and see now to what a contemptible state I am reduced ... more hated, too, than perhaps any man has ever been ... condemned to death as an infamous thief ... the multitude has demanded My death... . Pilate has now given sentence. O all ye who love Me, attend and see the sufferings of My Heart!

"After the betrayal in the Garden of Olives, Judas wandered away, a fugitive, a prey to the reproaches of his conscience which taxed him with the most execrable of sacrileges. And when he heard that I was condemned to death, he gave himself up to despair and hanged himself.

"Who can measure the deep and intense grief of My Heart when I saw this soul so long taught by love ... the recipient of My doctrine, one who had so often heard from My lips words of forgiveness for the most heinous crimes, finally throw himself into Hell fire?

"Ah! Judas, why not throw yourself at My feet that I may forgive you too? If you are afraid to come near Me because of the raging mob that surrounds Me, at least look at Me... . My eyes will meet yours, for even now they are lovingly intent upon you.

"O all you who are steeped in sin, and who for a time more or less long have lived as wanderers and fugitives because of your crimes ... if the offenses of which you have been guilty have hardened and blinded your hearts ... if to grant satisfaction to one or other of your passions you have sunk into evil ways ... Ah! when the motives or accomplices of your sin have forsaken you, and you realize the state of your soul, O then, do not yield to despair! For as long as a breath of life remains a man may have recourse to mercy and ask for pardon.

"If you are still young, if already the scandals of your life have lowered you in the eyes of the world, do not be afraid.... . Even if there is reason to treat you as a criminal, to insult and cast you off ... your God has no wish to see you fall into the flames of Hell.... . On the contrary He ardently desires you to come to Him so that He may forgive you. If you dare not speak to Him, at least look at Him and let the sighs of your heart reach Him, and at once you will find His kind and fatherly hand stretched out to lead you to the springs of pardon and life.

"Should it happen that you have spent the greater part of your life in impiety and indifference, and that the sudden approach of the hour of death fills you with blinding despair.... . Ah! do not let yourself be deceived, for there is still time for pardon. If only one second of life remains to you, in that one second you can buy back eternal life!

"If your whole life has been spent in ignorance and error ... if you have been a cause of great evil to other men, to society at large, or to religion, and if through some set of circumstances you have come to realize that you have been deceived ... do not allow yourself to be crushed by the weight of your sins and of the evil of which you have been the instrument; but with a soul penetrated with deep contrition throw yourself into an abyss of confidence, and hasten to Him who awaits your return only to pardon you.

"The case is the same for a soul that has been faithful to the observance of My law from childhood, but who has gradually cooled off into the tepid and unspiritual ways of an easy life. She has so to say forgotten her soul and its higher aspirations. God was asking of her greater efforts, but blinded by habitual failings, she has fallen into tepidity worse than actual sin, for her deaf and drowsy conscience neither feels remorse nor hears the voice of God.

"Then, perhaps, that soul awakens with a shock of realization: life appears to have been a failure, empty and useless for her salvation.... . She has lost innumerable graces, and the evil one, loath to lose her, makes the most of her distress, plunges her into discouragement, sadness and dejection ... and finally casts her into fear and despair.

"O soul whom I love, pay no heed to this ruthless enemy ... but as soon as possible have recourse to Me, and filled with deepest contrition implore My mercy and have no fear. I will forgive you. Take up again your life of fervor, and you will have back your lost merits, and My grace will never fail you.

"Finally, shall I speak to My chosen souls? Supposing that one has spent long years in the constant practice of the Rule and of her religious duties ... a soul that I have favored with My grace and instructed by My counsels ... a soul long faithful to My voice and to the inspirations of grace ... and now this soul has cooled in her fervor on account of some petty passion ... occasions of faults not avoided ... some yielding to the claims of nature and a general relaxation of effort ... and in consequence has fallen to a lower level ... to a commonplace kind of life ... then lastly, to give it its true name, tepidity. If, for one cause or another, you awake from this torpid state, the devil will instantly attack you in every way, jealous of a soul he hopes to claim. He will try to persuade you that it is too late, and that any effort is useless, he will accentuate your repugnance to make an avowal of your state of soul ... he will, so to speak, throttle you to prevent you from speaking and accepting the light ... he will do his best to stifle trust and confidence in your soul.

"But listen rather to My voice, and let Me tell you how to act: As soon as your soul is touched by grace, and before the struggle has even begun, hasten to My Heart; beg of Me to let a drop of My blood fall on your soul... . Ah! hasten to My Heart ... and be without fear for the past; all has been swallowed up in the abyss of My mercy, and My love is preparing new graces for you. The memory of your lapses will be an incentive to humility and a source of merit, and you cannot give Me a greater proof of affection than to count on My full pardon and to believe that your sins will never be as great as My mercy, which is infinite.

"Remain hidden, Josefa, in the abyss of My love, praying that souls may be filled with the same sentiments."

Passion week was to close with a sorrowful appeal in which the tender and strong compassion of the Heart of Jesus for souls once more became apparent.

It was some days since the night of March 21st, when Our Lady had brought Josefa the Cross of Jesus and told her: "Many sinners are grievously offending Him, but one especially is filling His Heart with sorrow."

Such words were never wasted on Josefa. Anxiety about souls was an ever present appeal for her prayer, her work, her sufferings. But when she knew of some soul in need of her special acts of reparation, because it was causing Him sorrow, she could scarcely distract her mind from it.

On Saturday, March 24th, Our Lord appeared to her at half-past eight in the evening, just as she was coming out of her cell. He stopped her and said: "Josefa, are you willing to comfort Me for that soul that is wounding Me?"

He was carrying His Cross, and His face was sad but full of beauty. Prostrate at His feet, she instantly offered herself to do whatever He wished.

"Take My Cross and help Me to bear its weight," He said. "Let us go and beg of My Heavenly Father to give her a ray of light to enlighten her and help her to repel the danger that threatens her. Let us present ourselves before Him as intercessors, that He may have compassion on that soul... . Let us beg Him to help her, to enlighten her, to sustain her, that she may not fall into temptation. Repeat with Me these words:

" 'O most loving Father! God, infinitely good, look upon Thy Son Jesus Christ, who placing Himself between Thy divine justice and sinners implores Thy pardon.

" 'O God of Mercy, pity human frailty. Send Thy light upon wandering souls that they may not be seduced and entrapped... . Strengthen souls that they may avoid the snares laid for them by the enemy of their salvation, and with fresh fervor return once more to the paths of virtue.

" 'O Eternal Father, look on the sufferings which Jesus Christ Thy divine Son endured in His Passion. Behold Him as a victim offered up to obtain for souls light and vigor, pardon and mercy.'

"Josefa, unite your sorrow with Mine, your anguish with My anguish, and offer them to My Eternal Father together with the merits and sufferings of all just souls. Offer Him the agonies of My Crown of Thorns to expiate the perverse thoughts of that soul. Say with Me once more:

" 'O all-holy God, in whose presence the angels and saints are not worthy to stand, forgive all the sins committed by thought and desire. Receive in expiation of these sins the thorn-crowned Head of Thy Son. Accept the blood that flows so copiously from His wounds. Purify minds that are sullied ... enlighten and illumine the darkness of their understanding, and may this blood be their strength, their light, and their life.

" 'Receive, O Holy Father, the sufferings and the merits of all who, united to the sufferings and merits of Jesus Christ, offer themselves to Thee, with Him and by Him, that Thou mayest extend Thy pardon to all mankind.

" 'O God of mercy and love, be the strength of the feeble, the light of the blind, and may all men love Thee.'

"A long time was spent thus in prayer," Josefa wrote. "Jesus was silent from time to time. The heavy weight of the Cross was on my shoulder and I endured keen suffering both of body and soul. He said again: 'Repeat with Me:

" 'O God of love, Father of all goodness, by the prayers and sufferings of Thy Beloved Son give that soul the light she needs, that strengthened by Thee she may reject evil and with energy accomplish Thy holy Will. Do not allow her to be the cause of so much evil both for herself and for other pure and innocent souls.'

"It was getting late. Jesus said: 'Now, Josefa, keep My Cross till that soul has realized the truth and has opened her heart to admit true light.'

"Then He went away, and I remained suffering much, till morning dawned."

These mysterious sufferings were of great intensity; Josefa bore them humbly and with singular courage, uniting herself to her Master. She knew that He alone gave them a reparatory value and could render them efficacious to transform that poor soul.

She spent the whole of Palm Sunday in painful intercessory prayer, and while she offered herself as a victim, Jesus was drawing, detaching, touching and once more taking possession of that wandering soul. O marvelous exchange of the communion of Saints!

That evening the Good Shepherd with exulting Heart would bear the lost sheep home, while Heaven rejoiced in Love's victory.

Holy Week (March 25th-April 1st, 1923)

"You will adore Me, you will humble yourself to the dust, you will comfort Me, and all this in a spirit of zeal to obtain that many others may do the same."
(Our Lord to Josefa, March 25th, 1923)

Whilst Josefa was in adoration before the Blessed Sacrament exposed on Palm Sunday, March 25th, Our Lord showed Himself to her. He came to outline all He expected of her during the great week about to begin, the crowning of so many graces received during Lent.

"This," He said, "is My wish:

"You will devote these days to adoring My divine Person outraged by the torments of the Passion. I will keep you constantly in My presence. I will manifest Myself to you, now with the Majesty of the Deity, again with the severity of a Judge, and oftenest covered with wounds and the ignominies of My Passion. Thus in your adoration, profound humility, and reparation of every moment, I shall find relief for My great sadness and bitterness."

Hardly had a few minutes elapsed than Josefa witnessed this triple manifestation of Jesus: as God, as Judge, as Saviour.

"I suddenly saw Him again," she wrote, "unchanged as to features, but surrounded with such Majesty that my soul was crushed with extreme reverence and confusion. I wanted nothing so much as to hide myself, and disappear from His presence. After renewing my vows, I begged Him to purify me that my nothingness might bear the sight of His Majesty. He replied to me in tones that were grave and awe-inspiring:

" 'Humble yourself before the Majesty of your God, and repair thus the pride of human nature, which is so often rebellious against the rights of its Creator.'"

Then Josefa felt, weighing her soul down to the very earth, the pressure of Divine Justice, and filled with terror she prostrated herself at His feet.

"I reminded Him," she wrote, "that He is my Saviour, my Father, and my Beloved, and that He can, if He so wills, forgive all my sins and consume my wretchedness. Jesus, when answering me, spoke kindly but with great authority. 'You speak rightly. I am your Saviour, your Father and your Beloved, and it is My intention to consume your miseries in the burning flame of My love. But I wish you to understand, Josefa, how greatly you must humble yourself, annihilate yourself, and retire into nothingness in your will and whole being, so that God's Will may reign and triumph, not only in your person, but in many other souls. They must acknowledge their sinfulness and misery, and they, too, must humble themselves by yielding entirely and wholly to the Divine Will.

" 'That is what I expect of you this week; you will adore Me, you will humble yourself to the dust and will comfort Me and do all this in a spirit of zeal to obtain that many others may do the same.

" 'Adieu. Later on I will tell you what I want of you.'"

These holy days thus dawned on Josefa's attentive soul. Step by step her Master would lead her through the rugged ways He had assigned her, and in which she was to follow Him.

MONDAY IN HOLY WEEK

On the Way to Calvary (March 26th, 1923)

"The procession winds its way to Calvary; Josefa, follow Me still."
(Our Lord to Josefa)

Early on Monday in Holy Week, March 26th, 1923, Our Lord summoned Josefa to meet Him in her cell, for He had other secret sorrows to confide to her.

"Kiss the ground and acknowledge that you are nothing," He began. "Adore the power and majesty of your God, but do not forget that if He is infinitely just and powerful, He is also infinitely merciful.

"And now let us go on, Josefa. Follow Me, bowed under the weight of the Cross, to Calvary.

"While the loss of the soul of Judas was filling Mine with sadness, the executioners, devoid of every feeling of humanity, now placed a hard and heavy Cross upon My lacerated shoulders. I was to consummate on the Cross the mystery of man's redemption. "Angels of Heaven! look on the God before whom you are ever prostrate in adoration ... See the Creator of all the world's wonders going to Calvary carrying that holy and blessed Cross on which He is to die.

"O souls who desire to imitate Me faithfully, gaze on Me likewise: wearily I dragged Myself forward, for My body was broken by many torments and bathed in sweat and blood. I suffered, but there was none to compassionate Me. The crowd followed Me, the soldiers pitiless as ravening wolves surrounded Me, no one had pity on Me. So great was My exhaustion and so heavy the Cross that I fell on the way... . See how roughly the inhuman soldiery raised Me to My feet once more ... one seized an arm, another My garments which clung to My open wounds ... a third grasped hold of Me by the neck ... and another by the hair. Some showered blows on Me with their clenched fists and others brutally kicked My prostrate body... . The Cross which fell upon Me crushed Me with its weight. My face bruised and torn, mingled the blood which covered it with the dust of the highway, blinding My eyes and adhering to My sacred face. I became the vilest and most contemptible of all creatures!

"Come a little further with Me... . There you will see My blessed Mother, whose heart is pierced with grief.

"Consider the martyrdom of these two Hearts. What does this Mother love more than her Son? ... And far from being able to help Him, she knows that the sight of her anguish increases His.

"And I, what do I love more than My Mother? Not only can I offer her no comfort, but I know that the terrible plight in which she sees Me pierces her heart with a sorrow like My own; for if I suffer death in the body, she suffers death in her Heart.

"See those eyes fixed on Mine, as Mine dulled and blinded with blood are fixed on hers! No word is spoken, but what a world of intercourse our two Hearts exchange in one heart-rending glance... ."

There was silence... . Jesus appeared absorbed by the memory of His Mother's agonized look... . Josefa was penetrated by this long silence, which at last she broke timidly by asking Him if Our Lady knew of His sufferings during those dreadful hours?

"Yes," He answered, "My Mother was present in spirit at all the torments of My Passion by divine revelation. Some of the disciples, though afar off for fear of the Jews, also tried to find out what was going on in order to report it to her. As soon as she knew that My death sentence had been pronounced she came forth to meet Me and did not leave Me any more till I was placed in the tomb.

"Meanwhile the procession advanced on the way to Calvary... .

"Fearing that I might die before crucifixion, those wicked men inspired by hatred, not compassion, looked around for someone to help Me carry the Cross, and for that purpose, offering a small reward, seized on a man of that neighborhood, called Simon... .

"This is enough for today, Josefa; we shall continue tomorrow. Go and ask whether you may make a Holy Hour every day this week and also whether I may be free to call you whenever I want you."

Josefa felt an instinctive hesitation rising within her at these words, but her Master spoke forcibly: "Do not forget that I have every right over you. Your Superiors alone who represent Me can dispose of you, and they grant Me full liberty."

"Full of confusion," wrote Josefa humbly, "I fell at His feet and begged His forgiveness."

The cause of this momentary weakness was never the fear of suffering but her vehement desire to work and to serve - a desire she was never quite able to extinguish. To the very end, this would be to her a source of renunciation and food for her love.

That evening, according to Our Lord's desire a series of magnificent Holy Hours was inaugurated, and during them His Heart again revealed Itself to souls.

He was waiting for her at nine o'clock in the little tribune of St. Bernard. His whole appearance bore the impress of one under the burden of overwhelming sadness. His face was covered with dust and blood.

"Josefa," He said, as soon as she had renewed her vows, "I want you to keep Me company during this hour, and share My sorrow in the prison. See Me in the midst of that insolent group.... Look into and penetrate My Heart deeply ... watch It, consider how It suffers from loneliness, for all have forsaken Me.... My friends have all abandoned Me.

"O Heavenly Father, I offer Thee the sadness and solitude of My Heart, that Thou mayest deign to be the companion and support of those who are facing the passage from time to eternity."

"I adored Him," she wrote, "and then begged Him to let me have His Cross.

"Yes," He said, "I will give it to you and your heart will be pierced with the same sadness as Mine.

"O how great is your littleness, Josefa, when you are one with Me.... Fill your heart with sentiments of humility, of zeal, of submission and of love, just as I did when bearing the affronts to which I was subjected during My Passion. My only object was to glorify My Father, to give Him the honor of which He had been deprived by sin, and to repair for the many offenses committed against Him. That was why I lowered Myself in such profound humility, by submitting to all that His good pleasure demanded and full of zeal for His glory and of love for His Will, I accepted such suffering with complete resignation."

Again there was a long pause, then Jesus continued:

"My God and My Father, may My dolorous solitude glorify Thee! May My patience and submission appease Thee. Restrain Thy just wrath against sinful souls and look upon the face of Thy Christ.

"See His hands bound by the chains with which His executioners loaded Him. In the name of the admirable patience with which He bore such tortures, forgive sinners, support them, permit them not to fall under the weight of their iniquities, be with them in the hour when they suffer imprisonment, and give them the grace to bear up under the miseries and misfortunes of this life, perfectly submissive to Thy holy Will."

After a long silence, Jesus finally said: "Go now, Josefa; take My Cross and do not leave Me alone this night, but keep Me company in My prison."

"How shall I manage, Lord?" she asked diffidently. "I am afraid of falling asleep and of not being able to think of Thee any more."

With divine condescension Jesus replied:

"Yes, Josefa, you must sleep and you can do so without leaving Me alone. When souls are unable to remain long hours in My presence as they would like to, either because they must take their rest or go to preoccupying work which takes up all their attention, there is nothing to prevent their making a convention with Me, for when love is ingenious it can prove its worth in this way even more than by the ardor of its devotion when free and tranquil.

"So go to rest as you must, but before doing so, lay on the powers of your soul the obligation of rendering Me all night the worship of your love. Set the tenderest affections of your heart free, that through the slumber of your senses, they may not cease to remain in presence of the only object of your love. One instant is enough to say to Me: 'Lord, I am going to sleep or to work, but my soul will keep Thee company. Its activity alone will rest tonight, or is engaged in this work, but all my powers will still belong to Thee and my heart keep for Thee its tenderest and most constant affection.'

"Go in peace, Josefa, and may your heart remain attached to Mine."

This direction, carefully preserved by Josefa, was to be one of her great comforts during her last months here below. Her wording is perhaps unskillful, but faithful souls will know how to draw from these lines the value that lies in intention when it is directed to the ever-present Guest within, who in all the wealth of His life dwells there. Hours that otherwise might seem to be wasted will acquire, through union with Him, full redemptive significance.

TUESDAY IN HOLY WEEK

Simon of Cyrene (March 27th, 1923)

"When a soul loves truly, she neither measures what she does nor weighs what she suffers."
(Our Lord to Josefa)

On Tuesday morning in Holy Week Our Lord resumed the dictation that had been interrupted the day before.

Before beginning, Jesus required of Josefa an act of conformity to the Divine Will, and in the silence of her little cell she repeated after Him the offering He deigned to teach her.

"My Lord and my God, behold me here in company with Thy Divine Son, who in spite of my unworthiness is also my Bridegroom. I submit my will to Thine and I deliver myself over to do and to suffer whatsoever Thou wilt ask of me, with the one intent of giving glory to Thy infinite Majesty and cooperating in the salvation and sanctification of souls. Receive then for this intention the merits of the Heart of Jesus Christ Thy Son who is my Saviour, my Father and my Beloved."

Josefa then kissed the ground and took up her pen in readiness.

"And now," said He, "let us carry on our work.

"Contemplate Me on the way to Calvary loaded with My heavy Cross, watch Simon carrying it behind Me and consider two things; though he was a man of good will, yet he was mercenary, and if he carried My Cross, it was for pay. So when he began to tire, he allowed the weight to bear more and more on Me, and that is how I fell twice.

261

"Secondly, this man helped Me to bear part of My Cross, but not the whole of it.

"There are many souls following in My footsteps who accept to help Me carry My Cross but they are troubled about their own rest and comfort.... Many consent to come after Me, and for that reason embrace a perfect life, but they do not give up all self-interest, which still in some cases remains their chief interest. They hesitate and let My Cross fall when it weighs too heavily on them. They try to avoid suffering, count the cost of abnegation, turn away from humiliation, work or fatigue whenever they can. They look back regretfully at what they have given up and try to obtain at least certain pleasures. In a word, their souls are so egotistical and selfish that they follow Me more for their own sake than for Mine. They accept only what they cannot avoid, or what is of strict obligation ... and so carry only a small part of My Cross and in such a way as barely to acquire the merit indispensable for salvation. In the next world they will see how far behind they lagged.

"On the other hand, there are many souls who, urged on by the hope of salvation but still more by the motive of love, are resolute in their determination to follow Me in the Way of the Cross. They eagerly embrace the perfect life and devote themselves to My service in order to carry, not part of the Cross, but the whole of it. Their one desire is to relieve and comfort Me. They offer themselves for all My Will may ask and seek out all that may give Me pleasure. They think neither of reward nor of their own merits, nor of the fatigues and sufferings that may accrue to them, their one object being to show Me their love and console My Heart.

"If My Cross comes to them in the shape of illness, if it is hidden under some employment that goes against the grain or is little adapted to their talents ... if it has all the appearance of being the result of forgetfulness or opposition from those around them, they recognize and accept it with all the submission of which their will is capable.

"Sometimes it happens that, urged by greater love and zeal for souls, they have done what seemed to them best in such or such a circumstance and things turn out differently from their expectations and there follows a whole train of humiliations and trials. These souls, moved solely by love, joyfully accept these unexpected consequences of their action, for in them they see My Cross; they worship it, offer it up, and use it to procure My greater glory.

"These are the souls that truly bear the Cross after Me. Their interests and their gain are none other than love. These are they who repose and glorify My Heart!

"Be persuaded that if your self-denial and suffering bear fruit but late or bear no fruit at all, they have not been in vain or useless. Some day you will bear abundant sheaves and reap a great reward.

"When a soul loves truly, she neither measures what she does nor weighs what she suffers; never looking for reward, and seeking only what she believes to be for God's greater glory, she never says 'enough' when labor or fatigue are in question ... and because of the purity of her aim, whatever the result, she neither excuses herself nor protests her good intentions; her motive being love, her efforts and sufferings always give glory to God. She is not troubled nor does she lose her peace of mind if she meets with contradiction or persecution or humiliation, as her sole motive is love and she leaves results in Love's hands.

"These souls are not mercenary; they only want Me to be consoled; they desire only My rest and glory. That, too, is why they have shouldered the whole of My Cross and carry its full weight."

Jesus wants generous and devoted souls to help Him carry His Cross, and their love must be loyal and disinterested.

If He has deigned to delineate the kind of cooperation His Heart loves is it not perhaps to reawaken the love of many such as were described by Saint Teresa, "one whom you know belongs wholly to you" ... souls totally abandoned to Him, ready to follow Him whithersoever He goes ... even to the death of the Cross ... resolute souls, who will carry His Cross after Him, never letting its full weight fall on Him... .

That night, when silence reigned in Les Feuillants, Jesus brought His Cross once more to Josefa. She was awaiting His coming in the tribune where she had gone to make her Holy Hour.

"Josefa! are you there? ... Come, stay with Me... ." and Jesus handed her His Cross. "Come quite close to Me to defend Me from the insults and outrages to which I was subjected in the presence of Herod."

"Contemplate the shame and the confusion with which I listened to the railleries and derision poured on Me by that man... .

"Josefa, give Me constantly loving proofs of your adoration and reparation.

"Adieu. Keep My Cross... . Tomorrow I shall prepare you for the great day of Love."

The night ended for Josefa in diabolic persecutions. Our Lord had taught her once again to recognize His Cross and help Him carry it, no matter under what aspect it was presented. She trusted His love in all these sufferings.

WEDNESDAY IN HOLY WEEK

The Crucifixion (March 28th, 1923)

"Be attentive, Angelic Spirits, and all ye who love Me."
(Our Lord to Josefa)

On the morning of Wednesday in Holy Week Our Lord was to lead Josefa after Him to Calvary.

"Kiss the ground," He said to her as He entered her cell at nine o'clock that day. "Humble yourself, for you are not worthy to hear the words I am about to speak... . But I love souls and it is for their sakes that I come to you.

"We have nearly reached Calvary. The crowd is growing excited while I drag Myself along with the utmost difficulty, and soon, worn out with fatigue, I fall for the third time.

"By My first fall I obtained for sinners rooted in evil, the grace of conversion... . By My second fall, encouragement for those weak souls blinded by sadness and anxiety, so that rising up they might make a fresh start in the way of virtue. My third fall will help souls to repent in the supreme hour of death.

"We have now reached the summit. Look at the officiousness with which these hardened sinners surround Me ... some seize hold of the Cross and lay it on the ground ... others tear My garments from Me, reopening all My wounds ... My blood flows afresh... .

"Think, dear souls, of My shame in seeing Myself thus exposed to the gaze of the mob ... what physical agony, what confusion for My soul. Think of the affliction of My Mother as she witnessed this terrible scene... . How she longs to take possession of the tunic now impregnated with My blood!

"The hour has come! The executioners stretch Me upon the Cross. They violently seize and extend My arms that My hands may reach the holes they have prepared in the wood. Every shock causes My thorn-crowned head to come into violent contact with the Cross ... the thorns are driven deeper and deeper into it. Hear the first sound of the hammer that fixes My right hand ... deep into the very earth it resounds. Listen again: they fasten My left hand. The very Heavens tremble, and the Angels fall prostrate at the sight... .

"As for Me, I keep the deepest silence - not a murmur escapes My lips.

"Having nailed My hands, they pull pitilessly at My feet; My wounds burst open afresh ... the nerves are severed ... the bones dislocated ... the torture is unspeakable! ... They pierce My feet and My blood is poured forth upon the ground!

"Stay a while and contemplate these pierced hands and feet ... this body covered with wounds ... This head pierced through and through by cruel thorns, fouled with dirt, bathed in sweat and blood.

"Wonder and marvel at My silence, patience, and resignation under such brutal treatment. Ask yourself who suffers? Who is the victim of such barbarity? It is Jesus Christ, the very Son of God, Maker of Heaven and earth and of all things ... who causes the plants to grow and every living thing to prosper... . Who created man, and whose power sustains all things... . Behold Him unable to move, an object of scorn, despoiled of all. But soon what a multitude will follow Him, throwing away fortune, comfort, honor, family and homeland ... everything that the world can give, to render Him honor and glory and the love that is His due.

"Then while the soldiers inhumanly make the air ring with their blows ...

the earth trembles ... there is silence in Heaven, angelic spirits are prostrate in adoration... . God is nailed to the Cross!

"Josefa, see thy Jesus extended on the Cross, without honor or liberty. He cannot stir hand or foot... . Nothing remains to Him.

"No one pities Him, none compassionate His sufferings, but instead fresh mockeries, new insults, more and more pain are added to what He already endures. If you love Me truly what will you do to resemble Me? Will you refuse anything My love asks? Will you spare any efforts to console Me?

"And now, Josefa, prostrate to the ground and listen to My words:

"May My Will triumph in you... .

"May My love consume you... .

"May your misery glorify Me."

Long Josefa remained prostrate on the ground. What secret intercourse passed between her and her Master? To what depth of annihilation was it not His Will to see her reduced? ... What words were exchanged between them? His words are never in vain, and in one instant are able to effect what He wills in the soul that is wholly abandoned to His divine action.

When at last she rose Jesus had departed.

It was ten o'clock when she went to the Auxiliary Chapel to follow Him to Calvary. Jesus was waiting for her. "I will accompany you in the state in which I was when I went through the streets of Jerusalem bearing My Cross."

"He was wearing a red mantle over His white tunic," she wrote; "it was soiled with blood and torn in many places. The Crown of Thorns was pressed deep on His forehead and His mournful face bore traces of the ill-treatment He had received and was all disfigured with clotted blood. He came to me and said: 'Josefa, come and contemplate Me on the sorrowful way of Calvary, adore My Blood so copiously shed and offer it to My Heavenly Father for the salvation of souls.'"

She rose and followed Him. He went before her and stopped at each Station. She on her part prostrated herself on the ground, kissed it to adore the Precious Blood and then listened to the outpourings of the Sacred Heart... . He reminded her in a few words of the measure of His sufferings and made an appeal for love to the souls whom He calls to follow Him.

Josefa spent the whole day in this atmosphere of pain and love, for her soul was penetrated through and through by it. How could it be otherwise?

Yet, as in the past and in the future to the very end, so now she allowed nothing to interfere with her daily duties which she faithfully carried out ... truly a mystery of heavenly fortitude which possessed and used her according to the Divine Will and the grace of the present moment.

In the evening of Wednesday in Holy Week whilst all slept in the great old monastery of Les Feuillants, Josefa went to the tribune where she had leave for a Holy Hour. She had hardly begun her prayer when Jesus Christ manifested Himself to her. He was resplendent in beauty, every trace of pain had disappeared, and His Sacred Heart seemed to be plunged in a sea of fire.

"Josefa," He said with vehemence, "tomorrow is the day of Love! Look at My Heart: It cannot contain the ardor with which It longs to impart Itself, and deliver Itself over, and remain always with sinners. How I long for them to open their hearts to Me, to enclose Me in them, and that the fire that consumes Mine should fortify and enkindle theirs."

"His Heart dilated in the midst of the flames. How lovely It was! No words can express it," wrote Josefa. "I asked Him to consume me with this true love which never resists Him, and He went on speaking:

" 'Let Me enter into you, work at you, consume and destroy ["self" in] you, so that it is no longer your will that acts, but Mine. Behold My Love exulting at the sight of souls who tomorrow will receive Me, accept divine grace, and console Me.

" 'Yes, tomorrow Love will flow over ... will give itself ... O happy and consoling memory ... My soul is devoured with longing ... to sacrifice Itself for them ... and that they should give themselves to Me.... You at least, Josefa, give Me all your heart, and let your littleness be no obstacle. Let Love possess and transform you.'"

Saying these words, Jesus vanished.... Josefa spent the remainder of that night in the thought of Christ's great love for souls.

LOVE'S GREAT DAY (March 29th, 1923)

"Love humbles Itself ... Love surrenders Itself."
(Our Lord to Josefa)

"Josefa, today is My great day, the day of Love.... Its feast day," said Our Lord on the morning of Holy Thursday.

She was at prayer in her cell and suddenly He came as on the preceding day, with a Heart surrounded with flames. She renewed her vows and fell on her face in adoration before Him. He spoke:

"Today is the day on which I give Myself to souls, that I may be for them just what they wish: If they will look on Me as their father I shall be a father to them.... If they desire Me as their beloved I shall be their Beloved.... If they need strength I will be their strength and if they long to console Me, I will let them console Me.... All I want is to give Myself to them ... and to fill them with graces prepared for them.... I cannot withhold them any longer. What, Josefa, shall I be to you?

"My All, Lord, for I am nothing!"

Tranquil peace and gratitude filled Josefa's heart, and so she went to Mass, then to Holy Communion. On returning to her place she at once renewed the complete offering of her whole person to her good and beloved Master, definitely abandoning herself into His hands forever. Jesus ratified the offering:

"It is on account of your nothingness and utter misery that you must let Me kindle your heart's fire, consume and destroy it. You surely know that 'nothing' and 'misery' cannot resist ... "

Josefa spent the whole day under the power of "Love that gives" ... "and Love that humbles Itself before Its own" ... She would hear these words from Our Lord's lips while in the silence and recollection of that day she lived through the ceremonies of religious life, the last actions, the last outpourings of the love of our Saviour among His own.

At about four in the afternoon Josefa was at prayer in her cell near a statue of Our Blessed Lady, and was thinking over the mysterious words of Jesus, when He Himself appeared.

"Yes, Josefa, I did indeed say that Love gives Itself to Its own and it is true.... Come, draw near My Heart and enter in, and taste and see what Its overwhelming emotions are."

" 'Love gives Itself as food to Its own and this food is the substance which gives them their life and sustains them.

" 'Love humbles Itself before Its own ... and in so doing raises them to the highest dignity.

" 'Love surrenders Itself in totality, It gives in profusion and without reserve. With enthusiasm, with vehemence It is sacrificed, It is immolated, It is given for those It loves.... The Holy Eucharist is love to the extreme of folly.'"

It looked as if Our Lord at that moment was unable to restrain the burning effusions of His Heart, then His voice changed and He spoke with gravity, saying: "This love will lead Me to My death! ... "

Then, turning to Josefa, He addressed her directly: "Today you are sustained, consoled, and strengthened by love; tomorrow, Josefa, you will accompany Me to Calvary and suffer with Me."

The somber shades of the Passion were about to descend on a day which had been all light. During the night, spent in part in the Chapel in prayer at the "Sepulchre," she was again allowed to share in the Cross, the Crown, the anguish and the sorrows of her Master, treasures she had learnt to bear and to esteem for His sake.

Towards midnight He appeared and called on her to share with Him the solitude of the dungeon. His white tunic was in shreds and stained with blood; His sacred countenance bore vivid traces of the injuries and ignominy to which it had been subjected. "Josefa," He said, "you have been My comfort ... now I come to take back My Cross."

"Keep Me company now.... Do not leave Me alone in prison.... When I raise My eyes, let Me find yours looking at Me. The presence of a sympathetic heart greatly consoles one who suffers. Do you realize this? You who have experienced the tenderness of My Heart, can gauge what My heartache is at being so outraged by My enemies and deserted by My friends... ."

Jesus then left her, saying: "No need to say adieu, for are you not always with Me?"

GOOD FRIDAY

The Seven Words (March 30th and 31st, 1923)

"Write all that you see."
(Our Lord to Josefa)

From very early on Good Friday morning Our Lord united Josefa with Himself in the scenes of the Crucifixion.

He was about to manifest His dolours to her visibly, so that they should be imprinted both on her body and on her soul. Following in His footsteps she would share the compassion of His Mother, whilst hour by hour the happenings of that dread day were unfolded before her eyes.

Who can say how intimate, intense and real, was Josefa's participation in the sufferings of Jesus Christ?

She endeavored to write down something of what she was privileged to see, to hear, and to suffer. But her power of expression broke down in the attempt. Nevertheless the simplicity of her record gives it special value.

"At about six in the morning when at prayer," she noted, "I saw Him as during the night, but a red mantle had been thrown over His white tunic. He seemed utterly spent. At once He said to me: 'Josefa, My enemies are soon going to load the Cross on My shoulders. It is so heavy.'

"I implored Him to let me carry it, for I so long to help Him... .

" 'Yes, take it,' He said, 'and may your love mitigate My pain... . I have made My sufferings known to you ... follow Me in them ... accompany Me and share in My agony.'"

In the course of the morning He returned to dictate to her the Stations of the Cross He had made with her two days before.

"His face was torn," she wrote, "His eyes swollen and filled with blood... . He let Me kiss His feet at the seventh, the eleventh and the thirteenth Stations, and before leaving He said to me: 'The hour of the Crucifixion is approaching... . I will warn you when the time comes.'

"Towards half past twelve I saw Him again," she continued. "His tunic had been wrenched off half His body.

" 'Now is the moment when the executioners are about to fasten Me to the Cross, Josefa.'

268

"Then," she wrote, "such an agonizing pain shot through my hands and feet that my whole body was shaken... . At the same time I heard the strokes of the hammer, slow and resounding afar... . In a faint and dying voice He said these words: 'Now is the hour for the world's Redemption! They are about to lift Me up as a spectacle of derision to the crowd ... but also of admiration to souls... .'

"I saw Him a few moments later. He was fastened to the Cross, and it had been lifted up erect.

" 'Peace has come to the world! ... The Cross, hitherto an instrument of torture on which criminals were made to die, is changed into the light and peace of the world and the object of the most profound veneration.

" 'Sinners will draw pardon and life from My sacred wounds ... My Blood will wash away and efface all their filth and foulness.

" 'Pure souls will come to My wounds, there to slake their thirst and kindle flames of love in their hearts ... there they will find a refuge, and forever make a home.

" 'The world has found a Redeemer, and chosen souls the Model they must copy.

" 'And as for you, Josefa, these hands are yours to give you support, these feet to follow you and never leave you alone.

" 'Write all that you see.'"

Once again Josefa attempted to describe Our Saviour as she saw Him. She knew that this manifestation was made to her for the sake of souls, that she might transmit to them the testimony of His torments. Putting all her powers to the task, she tried to omit no part in her narrative:

"He was nailed to the Cross. The Crown of Thorns encircled His brow and great spiky thorns furrowed deep into the flesh. One longer than the rest had pierced its way through His forehead and emerged near the left eye which was much swollen. His face covered with blood and filth leaned forward a little to the left. Though His eyes were very swollen and bloodshot, they were open and gazed earthwards. All over His wounded body were to be seen the weals and welts caused by the scourges which in some parts had torn away fragments of flesh and skin. Blood flowed from His head and from His other wounds. His lips were purple and His mouth slightly twisted, but when I saw Him for the last time at about half-past two, it had assumed its normal shape. The sight was so pitiful that it wrung my heart with compassion ... what caused me most sorrow was that He could not use a hand to touch His face.

"What strength this sight gave me, Jesus nailed hands and feet ... strength to leave all and to submit to His Will in everything, however costly.

"I also noticed as I gazed at Him on the Cross how they had torn away His beard. It had given such majesty to His face ... and His once beautiful hair which used to add such grace to His Person was all matted, tangled, and clotted with blood, and falling across His face."

This painful spectacle left Josefa, so to speak, annihilated, and this is not hard to understand. She seemed drowned in sorrow. She spent all the afternoon in the little cell that had witnessed so many favors, and that today by God's Will had taken on the semblance of the summit of Calvary. A silence, gripping in its intensity, reigned there, and Josefa in prayer associated herself with the sacrifice of the Redeemer.

"Towards half-past two," she wrote, "Jesus spoke again in a faint and faltering voice." Josefa listened to the Seven Words of Jesus, amplified by the last outpourings of His love.

" 'Father, forgive them for they know not what they do:

" 'They have not known Him who is their life. On His shoulders they have heaped the fury of their iniquities. But I beseech Thee, Father, heap upon them the full measure of Thy mercy.

" 'Today thou shalt be with Me in Paradise... .

" '... for thy faith in thy Saviour's mercy has wiped out all thy offenses and it will lead thee to eternal blessedness.

" 'Woman, behold thy Son!

" 'O Mother Mine! ... these are My brethren ... keep them ... love them... . You for whom I died are no longer alone; you have a Mother to whom you can have recourse in every necessity.'"

Here Josefa interrupted her narrative:

"I saw near the Cross the Blessed Virgin, standing erect. She was gazing at her Son. She wore a purple garment and veil and spoke in a voice which was firm though full of deep sadness:

" 'See, my child, the state to which His love for souls has reduced Him! ... He whom you see in so sad and pitiable a state is my Son. Love is driving Him to His death ... and it is love that constrains Him to make all men brethren by giving them all His own Mother.'

" 'My God, why hast Thou forsaken Me?

" ' ... Yes, henceforth a soul has the right to say to its God: "Why hast Thou forsaken me?" After the mystery of the Redemption was consummated, man became the son of God, Christ is his brother, eternal life his heritage.

" 'I thirst!

" 'O My Father, I thirst indeed for Thy glory, and behold now is the hour at hand! Man shall henceforth know through the fulfillment of My words that Thou indeed hast sent Me, and Thou shalt be glorified.

" 'I thirst for souls, and to appease this thirst I have given the last drop of My Blood ... and so I can say:

" 'All is consummated!

" 'Now at length is accomplished that great mystery of love in which a God delivers up His own Son to death. I came into this world to do Thy Will; O My Father, it is accomplished!

" 'Into Thy hands I commend My spirit!

" 'To Thee I give back My soul. Thus shall souls that do My Will have the right to say in all truth: "All is consummated".... My Lord and My God, receive My soul which I commit into Thy hands.

" 'Josefa, write down what you have heard. I want souls to hear and to read what is written ... so that they who thirst may drink and the hungry may be filled.'

"After these words," said Josefa, "He disappeared.

"In unspeakable sadness of heart I kept the Cross and the nails, till about six o'clock that evening; when suddenly all ceased except the pain of the Crown of Thorns."

Our Lord's very frequent visits came to an end on Good Friday evening. All Holy Saturday Josefa was weighed down by the recollection of the previous day's revelations.

At about half-past two on Easter morning Our Lady appeared, radiant in loveliness. She spoke only these words:

"Daughter, my Son and your divine Master suffers now no more, He is risen and glorious.... His wounds are a fountain from which innumerable souls will draw grace, and a shelter where the most wretched will find a home.

"Be prepared, daughter, to adore His glorious wounds!"

She vanished instantly.

"I cannot say how sad I was at seeing her go ... " wrote Josefa. "I should have loved to fly after her, so as not to remain alone - but I saw her no more... ."

The Life of Faith (April 1st-May 2nd, 1923)

"God's ways are impenetrable to the eyes of man."
(Words of Our Lady)

Easter Sunday had dawned at last, and Josefa was preparing to adore the glorious Wounds of her Master. But Our Lady's words signified a far different preparation, for only nine months separated her now from her entry into the Kingdom where forever the elect slake their thirst at the Saviour's fountains.

Here below, it was but in passing that a few drops of that saving water were to be her portion, just enough for the next phase. Jesus, who had opened His Heart to her so widely, that she might pass on the meaning of His sufferings to other souls, having strengthened her by associating her with His Passion, now left her to herself, as a tool (for the time at least) no longer required.

No doubt He had His own designs in thus abandoning her to her own limitations, and though she was unaware of it, He still carried on the great work of love. It was one which involved death and destruction, and so it would always be, that room might be made for His life and complete liberty of action in her.

Josefa's faith in this action was great, she was sure of His love, and she abandoned herself wholly to all He decreed, but there came a moment when her sensitive soul feared that the absence and silence of her Master had been caused, in some way, by herself.

"The whole of Easter Week passed by," she wrote, "and Jesus did not return.... Am I keeping Him away?"

But faithful and courageous as usual, she went back to her duties in the workroom, where indeed her Sisters had never lacked her help all during Lent.

This workroom was the center of most of her life of devotedness during this last year of her life.

It was a very large room on the first floor of the old monastery. The windows on two sides opened onto the Chapel, which at this point is separated from the main structure only by a small interior courtyard.

For many months Josefa slept in one of the cubicles there, for at one time it was a dormitory. The place where Our Lord so often appeared to her with His Cross is still venerated; it was there that in the December of 1921, she suffered the first attacks of the devil, and there too, that Our Lady bestowed on her for the first time the drops of the Precious Blood (October 16th, 1922).

This large room was somewhat remote from the rest of the house, and being light and spacious, had been transformed into a workroom, where Josefa had charge of the making of the school uniforms. There she spent the major part of her day, training the Novices and Postulants, whose work she followed up closely. From the very beginning she made of this little sphere of her influence one of prayerful industry. She and her Novice helpers rarely lost sight of the presence of God ... she taught them to turn towards the Tabernacle and unite themselves to Jesus in the Blessed Sacrament ... Surely Our Lord must have found in this busy workroom a refuge of peace and joy for His Heart, by the silent fidelity to Rule, tender charity, and mutual helpfulness to be found there.

The intentions of the Sacred Heart of Jesus, constantly in the minds of those whose horizon was nothing smaller than the whole world, stimulated adroit fingers and loving hearts to give of their best.

Josefa's thought for their fervor never allowed her to neglect the careful training of each of her Sisters.

She felt her responsibility, but also found real joy in being able to make the Novices serve the Society more usefully. She spared no pains and no labor, and with tactful discernment assigned to each of her helpers what she was fit to do, and with patient good nature repaired unskillful blunders, and corrected and finished off the work of beginners, exacting with the utmost sweetness the interest, care, and perfection that ought never to be absent from good work.

"We never saw her impatient or out of temper," was the testimony of one of them. "If work had been done carelessly, she would say: 'Don't let us ever do anything carelessly in Our Lord's service!'" Her firm and gentle ways won love and respect and her example was a constant lesson in religious life.

Josefa had a great love for children, especially the little ones, and it showed itself in all her dealings with them. The children felt her love and joy in serving them and appreciated her devotedness. How often she went through the dormitories at night to make sure that they had all that they required; she would stop to sew a button here, mend a torn garment there or come to the rescue of a little child in trouble. All was done so quietly, so unobtrusively, that it was taken as a matter of course, but the mistresses and the children too remembered the ideal of religious life wholly given to God that they noticed in this humble Sister.

Although she was so devoted, as soon as she was alone she gladly gave herself up to recollection, but without stopping her work. One evening after the Novices had left the workroom a nun came to ask a service of Sister Josefa. She was sewing energetically, but her attitude showed the direction of her thoughts. The nun watched her with respect for a few moments and then called her gently. Josefa started, turned to the speaker with an effort, Our Lord still seeming to hold her gaze; but quickly she stood up with her usual deference, though her soul seemed to have been very far away.

Many of the nuns came in contact with Sister Josefa, for she was ever ready to perform any little service that was in her power. They gladly asked her help; one would come with a seam to be done on the machine, another with a bit of needlework to be finished off or ironed, or perhaps a garment to be cut out, etc... . And on holidays she helped in dressing up the children for charades or plays. The mistresses of the needlework classes, too, could always appeal to her ingenuity and dexterity.

When the season of First Communions came round how loving was the care she put into the making of the white frocks and veils for the occasion, and when the long-expected morning dawned, one could be sure that nothing would be wanting in the little piles so carefully prepared for each child by her reverent care, and laid on tables draped in white and adorned with flowers.

These details, one may say, are mere trifles, but when they are inspired by love, and persevered in with no thought of recognition or return, they cannot but be the outward indication of a soul entirely surrendered and disinterested.

Josefa's devotedness was far from being concentrated on her workroom alone. We have already spoken of the many services she was able to render in almost every kind of housework, but what is chiefly worthy of notice is her untiring energy and invariable spirit of sacrifice, especially if we remember that her interior and hidden life was so extraordinary, and yet never prevented her from carrying out her daily and very humble duties.

Our Lord left her all through the month of April 1923 in this common and ordinary service, while He pursued His divine plans, though Josefa was unconscious of them. But surely each of her laborious days was penetrated by divine influence.

The Octave of Easter came to an end and she was still waiting for her Lord, but dark days were in store for her in the weeks that followed. The roaring lion was prowling about, seeking to devour his prey, and was never far away in the difficult moments through which Josefa had to pass. Suddenly he reappeared in full power to lay siege to her faculties by darkening her mind, inspiring her heart with crushing misgivings, and causing vacillation in her will, accompanying all this with physical persecution day and night, all aimed at shaking her fidelity. Her courage, so wonderfully renewed during Lent at the sight of her Master's Passion in which she had been so intimately associated, helped her face the assaults of the devil, but she still felt how weak she was in herself.

On the Friday of Low Week, April 13th, a soul that a few weeks previously had come from Purgatory to ask her prayers, now visited her from Heaven to give her strength. After telling Josefa who she was, she said: "I come from Him who is my eternal Beatitude and the one Object we both love, to encourage you to persevere in suffering in the path His goodness has marked out for you, for your own sanctification and that of many other souls. One day, not in time but in eternity, you will contemplate the marvels of Divine Love reserved for those He loves best. You will then understand the value of what you now endure, and will enter into bliss too great for any human being on earth to sustain.

"Courage! peace will soon return. The work of Redemption can be done only by suffering. But suffering purifies and strengthens the soul, and makes it rich in merits before God."

These words of encouragement from the other world were a great comfort to Josefa. But her trial continued till Thursday, April 19th, when Mary herself came to still the raging storm.

Josefa had not seen her since early on Easter Sunday morning, April 1st, and her heart leaped with happiness. She recommended to her intercession a soul she knew to be in danger, for her prayers and interest were ever far more centered on souls than on herself.

"Suffer ... suffer ... " was Our Lady's response. "Only at a high price can things of great value be bought."

Then she added: "That soul will be saved. Offer for her all your pain and leave the result and the glory in God's hands. But I say again, my child, that soul will not be lost."

Then tenderly and forcefully she opened out a totally new and unexpected prospect of sacrifice to Josefa. "Jesus wants you," she said, "to make the sacrifice of this house."

Josefa was struck dumb at these words. Had not Our Lady once assured her that she would die at Les Feuillants? What would become of her, frail and vulnerable as she knew herself to be, without the help Our Lord Himself had bestowed on her in her present Superiors? ... How could she, alone and unaided, bear the responsibility of the path in which she was being led? She was troubled and deeply distressed.

"Do not be astonished, my child," said Our Lady in her gentle, firm voice, infinitely reassuring. "The ways of God are impenetrable to the eyes of man... . Do not fear. This sacrifice is necessary both for your soul and for many others... . Jesus loves you ... live only for Him."

The next day Friday, April 20th, Our Lord Himself confirmed the decision that was His express will ... and in answer to her fears, He said: "Am I not always there, Josefa? And can you not confide everything to Me and talk it all over with Me? ... What is your love for Me? ... Only a shadow compared with Mine for you! I want this proof of love from you, for My work must pass through the crucible of suffering. But have no fear that the secrecy with which I have wrapped you round will be revealed ... and My work will prosper more than ever ... for I will leave traces of My passage there."

Then, giving her new courage and confidence: "A new phase in your life is about to begin. You will live in peace and in love, and we shall prepare for our eternal union. Already nothing separates us, Josefa, you love Me and I love you ... souls are being saved ... nothing else matters.

"I want you to grow," added Jesus, with tenderest compassion, "for you are so very little ... but I shall not leave you alone... ."

Unexpected as this express Will of Jesus was, it coincided with the arrangements made by Superiors. It seemed best to them that Josefa's short religious life should not be deprived of the graces brought by the changes of residence so frequent in the Society of the Sacred Heart. It was thought that others besides the habitual witnesses of her life should see and appreciate her simple and solid virtue, her detachment, her obedience, her fidelity, and her humble and total disinterestedness. Above all it was meet that the spirit by which she was led should be tried in this manner, so that it could never afterwards be doubted. These wise reasons fell in with the divine plan and it was decided that Josefa should start immediately for Marmoutier.No indication of her extraordinary life was to be given to her new Superiors. God who led her would Himself provide; Josefa belonged to Him, she was His work, more even than His instrument, and she must be committed to His sole guardianship.

The end of April found Josefa serene and ready for whatever obedience had decided in her regard.

"Though it costs me much to leave this house that I love so much, and all the rest with it, what does it matter?" she wrote. "I shall go wherever Jesus wants me to go, for He is my sole love, and I desire only to please Him."

Our Lord, who discerns the deepest thoughts of our hearts, must have looked with complaisance on Josefa's.

"Josefa, you comfort Me," He said to her on Monday, April 23rd, while she was noting down the subject of her particular examen, namely: "To multiply little acts of fidelity, and never refuse anything to Jesus."

"Yes, I like that examen. If you are faithful to these tiny details of love, I will not be outdone in generosity. Your soul will be filled to overflowing with peace, nor shall I leave you alone, and in your very littleness you will be great, for I shall live in you."

Then to give her courage, He added: "Love guides you and Love sustains you. Now you must grow and run in the way till you reach the plenitude of beatitude that I am preparing for you with so much love."

The day of departure arrived, and Josefa, who was taking very little away with her, had no great preparation to make, so, up till the last evening, she led her usual life, serene and simple. Her soul had no difficulty in embracing the Will of God, this did not prevent apprehension and heartache for the double reason that she was feeling the separation keenly, and could not entirely repress her nameless fears in bearing alone her weighty secret.

"Go," said Our Lord to her on Sunday, April 29th. "Go there and I shall meet you, so have no fear. I will tell you what to do, and I will not forsake you."

On Wednesday, May 2nd, Josefa, uniting her offering to that of Jesus in the Holy Mass, and fortified by Holy Communion, made a pilgrimage of good-bye to all the spots dear to her grateful heart ... Saint Madeleine Sophie's cell, the oratory of Our Lady in the Noviceship, the little Auxiliary Chapel she so loved ... hardly had she crossed its threshold than she met Our Lord:

"He came to me," she wrote, "with His Crown of Thorns. How glad it made me, for I had not worn it for a long time. It was indeed comforting to go away with that treasure... . Jesus placed it on my head, saying: 'Take it, and follow Me.'"

A few minutes later she left Les Feuillants.

"On the platform of the station," she wrote in the notebook in which she recorded His words during her absence, "He passed quite close to me, and said: 'I go before you.'"

He repeated the same words a little later, when the train carrying her to her new destination had started: "Yes, Josefa, I go before you and My Heart is glorified... . How many souls are going to be saved ... and what surprises I am preparing for you!"

"I saw Him no more," she added, "but I knew He was there, and in my heart we talked together. I offered myself with my whole heart to do His Will, and many times I renewed my vows, asking Him to teach me to love Him every day more and more, for I seek and love Him alone ... I delivered myself over entirely to His keeping, and it was a great joy to me on reaching my journey's end to have been able to give up for His sake the House and Mothers I so loved."

Heavenward, but in Solitude (May 8th - 20th, 1923)

"Love guides you ... and Love will sustain you... ."
(Our Lord to Josefa, May 2nd, 1923)

The grand old monastery of Marmoutier can be seen from a great distance on account of its massive bell-tower which rises over the twelfth-century gateway, and the imposing mass of its buildings standing out from the valley on the rocky hillside of Rougemont near the river Loire. It is at no great distance from the town of Tours, to which in olden times it was connected by an underground tunnel... . The site is historic and the aura of the Benedictine legends hangs over it.

It was at Marmoutier that ancient Gaul was converted to Christianity by St. Gatien, St. Leobard, and St. Patrick, whose names may still be deciphered on the rock of its ancient caves and grottos. This is the France of bishops and monks, of its great founder Saint Martin of Tours, of Saint Brice and the Seven Sleepers, and Richelieu himself was one of its Commendatory Abbots. The France of 1791 witnessed the expulsion of the Benedictines from Marmoutier, the devastations committed by the 'Bande noire,' and the final abandonment of the monastic buildings.

But there is one thing that never dies, for it consecrates holy sites, and that is sanctity. One day, Saint Madeleine Sophie on one of her apostolic journeys down the Loire, felt this mysterious spell, and in her heart of hearts resolved that she would revive its religious life. In 1847 she sent her own daughters to this spot of ancient glory where saints had once lived.

Josefa, therefore, had come on Wednesday, May 2nd, 1923, to where centuries of spiritual life had accumulated treasures of holiness, and to it she also brought her own little contribution of love, and something of the divine riches of which the Sacred Heart of Jesus had made her the Messenger. She was to spend only a month there in hidden and laborious toil such as had all along been her share.

From the first moment of her arrival she gave herself wholeheartedly to the service of the community. Nothing distinguished her in any way, unless we except what from the first was her characteristic: "fidelity in little things and eagerness to render service in the humblest employments, silence, recollection and gentle cordiality that soon endeared her to all." Such was the testimony of the Mother in charge of the Sisters.

This was not without merit on her part, for her keenly sensitive nature soon detected an undefined uncertainty which her presence aroused in the minds of those around her, discernible in spite of the charity and kindness with which she had been welcomed. The question existed though it was never openly expressed. Why had she left Les Feuillants? Why had she been sent to Marmoutier since she was not replacing any other Sister?

278

"Here," said Our Lord to her the first evening, "you will learn to love humiliations, Josefa, for they are coming to you. But they will make your soul grow, and will glorify Me." And He repeated: "But you need have no fear, for Love has brought you here, and Love will take care of you. Let love be your life, that you may die of love."

The following day, Josefa was sent to help the Portress. This was an office to which she was new, and ignorance of places and people complicated it for her. Nothing however could lessen her ardent wish to be useful. Often she could be seen going through the long corridors of the house, many a time she lost her way, but she did her best to repair the involuntary mistakes and each time she passed the chapel door, by a fervent genuflection, she renewed the spirit of joy Our Lord unfailingly recommended to her.

Again and again He repeated to her: "Do not fear. I take care of you as a mother cares for her babe. I am the joy of your soul; you will suffer, but in deep peace."

These words sum up the plans of His Sacred Heart. This stage in her life was meant to ripen her soul in suffering, while at the same time it gave a more evident proof that the work of which she was the instrument and of which the foundations were being laid was divine in its origin.

In retrospect we can see clearly God's design in its wisdom and love. Deprived of the help of her guides, Josefa experienced, not solitude of the heart, for she had given all her heart to her new surroundings and at once felt at home at Marmoutier... . but an isolation of soul, which was weighed down by the secret she must keep for God alone. By nature open and communicative with her Superiors, she felt the privation of not being able to reveal the depths of grace or of trial which lay at the very roots of her interior life, and from which she could not draw back without betraying her vocation. Our Lord willed her to undergo this ordeal in order to strengthen her faith, but even more to prepare by detachment and purification the very depths of her being of which His love would take possession. He was to meet with no obstacle in her soul. He kept her direction for Himself alone, and caused her to climb the steep ascent of suffering and of grace that her stay at Marmoutier proved to be.

Let us follow her in her pilgrimage. During her first days at Marmoutier, Our Lord kept reminding her of all His Heart was for her: His presence, all joy ... His guidance, all security. He appeared to her at her prayer, He flashed past her in the corridors. When at nightfall she was about to take her rest, He was there again, and she gathered from His sacred lips assurances that her lively faith had never doubted, but which the circumstances threw into greater relief.

"Speak to Me," He said, "for I am near you... . You are not alone, for I see you even when you do not see Me... . I follow you... . I hear you... . Speak to Me... . Smile at Me, for I am your Spouse ... your inseparable Companion."

And alluding to Les Feuillants. "You are in My Heart here, just as you were there... ."

On the First Friday of the month, May 4th, from early dawn, He opened His Sacred Heart to her:

"Come, enter in," He said, "and spend the day therein. You are in Me, Josefa, and that is why you do not always see Me... . But I see you, and that suffices."

Then, summing up for her what is in reality the whole theology of the divine presence in the soul by grace: "You in Me, I in you - could any bond of union be closer?"

Josefa noted at this time:

"I see every day more dearly that He alone is my sole Happiness, my only Love! ... O may He give me the strength to be faithful... ."

During her thanksgiving, she offered herself to this divine presence who was her All: "At once I saw Him ... O how beautiful and fatherly He was!"

That is how Josefa tried to express the feelings of security engendered by the glance of Jesus' love.

"I am in you, Josefa, supporting you, so that in the midst of pain you should never lose the peace that surpasses all earthly joys, and that nothing will ever be able to take from you. My peace ... Yes, My peace will fill you with holy joy ... it will strengthen you and bear you up under suffering."

And in answer to her cry for help - "for," as she wrote, "I so long to give Him glory and many souls" - Jesus Himself completed His thought: "Love will purify you, will consume your defects, and the very strength of that pure and ardent love will lead you to sanctity... . I will do it all."

On Saturday, May 5th, Our Lord told her of the cooperation of love that His Sacred Heart expected, and how it must feed on His good pleasure, hidden under the circumstances of the moment as they occur.

"I want you to learn to be generous," He said, "for generosity is the fruit of love. Later on I will explain this to you, but now I only give you a practical lesson in it: you will meet with many circumstances and in them you must see only Me ... and if something is done to you that pains you, or something said that wounds you, look up generously and with love as if I Myself were speaking to you, and smile."

As if to encourage her, without interrupting her work, Jesus manifested Himself to her, now here, now there ... all loving reminders of His presence.

"Suffering passes, but merit is eternal ... you are ever in My inmost Heart... . Do not lose sight of Me... . Love guides you ... leave yourself to My care ... I am your all... ."

Our Lady came to her succor while she was treading this more difficult path:

"It is the very road my Son trod," she reminded her. "Thank Him for allowing you to tread it with Him... . You will share the agonies of His Heart more than once, but in peace."

"Do not fear suffering," she said on Sunday, May 6th, "for by enduring it you can draw down new graces on souls ... But be gay, and let your whole exterior reflect the peace within."

On Wednesday, May 16th, while Josefa was thinking over the graces and trials of the ten months since her vows, Mary, her incomparable Mother, once more encouraged her to confidence:

"Jesus knows you, child; He knows what you are, and He loves you... . Your miseries will continue, that you may never be without struggle and conflict. Be humble, but do not lose courage... . You know what His Heart is! If He asks and wants your misery and nothingness, it is that His mercy and goodness may consume and transform them. He is so good... . O! if souls but knew Him better, they would love Him so much more."

Then Mary blessed her, saying: "Peace and joy, my child, humility and love."

Saint Madeleine Sophie also followed her up with vigilant affection in the old monastery so dear to her.

Every stone was known to the Saint. Her cell has been transformed into an oratory and crowns the so-called 'portail de la crosse,' a place of pilgrimage to her daughters, to which Josefa had not been slow in finding her way, there to have recourse to her motherly intercession.

"I was at a loss how to act in between the visits of Jesus," she noted in her diary, "when asked why I am here ... if I am ill... if I shall remain here, etc... . So I asked her to help me and suddenly she came herself: 'So, my child, you are here!'"

She was so understanding that Josefa trustfully poured out her troubles and the holy Mother answered: "I have but one word to say to you, and you must turn it over all day, my child: 'Love meets with no difficulties that it does not change into food for the flame of love ... later I will explain this to you, but while you are here just love ... love ... love ... "

On Monday, May 28th, to which day that year her feast had been transferred, Josefa saw her again. She had been begging her intercession regarding the unworthiness and wretchedness of which every day she became more conscious in herself. Saint Madeleine Sophie could not resist this appeal of humble trust. She showed herself to her in the Chapel, and making the Sign of the Cross on her forehead, said to her: "My own dear child! I love you as you are, little and miserable... . I, too, was just the same and as little as you, but I found means to utilize my nothingness by giving it totally to Jesus who is so great! I abandoned myself to His holy Will and sought the glory of His Heart only. I tried to live in the knowledge of my lowliness and nothingness, and He took charge of everything. So, child, live in peace and confidence. Be very humble, and deliver yourself over wholly to the Heart that is all love."

We must now return to the second week in May, when Josefa entered on a more difficult phase of her pilgrimage.

By the questions asked and the watchfulness with which she felt herself regarded, she quickly realized that her Superiors felt some uncertainty about her. Neither their kindness nor their thoughtfulness suffered any diminution, nor did the cordial charity of her Sisters change. But her soul was too sensitive not to be aware of the shadows which, though slight, were gradually descending upon her. Nothing could have given her more pain... . Her Master knew it well, and He only allowed this trial to persist and increase daily, in order to impel His child to closer union with Himself. She had to rise ever higher, leaning solely on God; but in order to help her at this stage He deigned to tell her of a desire of His Heart.

Daily He encouraged her efforts, directing them towards the realization of His wishes which were to lead her step by step to the Cross.

No doubt, poor little Josefa, alone and sorely troubled, though courageous and faithful, typified many another soul to whom He was pleased to reveal the desires of His Sacred Heart, and, with them, the secret of generous self-forgetfulness in suffering.

On Thursday, May 10th, Feast of the Ascension, He appeared to her during her thanksgiving:

"He was shining, bright," she wrote, "and all His wounds radiant in splendor. 'How beautiful Thou art, O Lord!'

" 'Today My sacred Humanity entered Heaven,' He replied with warmth... . 'Would you like Me to make of your soul another heaven in which to find My delight?'"

Josefa's answer was to humble herself to the dust.

"It matters little what your misery is, Josefa, I will make of it a throne, and I will be your King. My clemency will wipe out your ingratitude. I will both consume and destroy ['self ' in] you... . Tell Me, do you consent to give Me your heart that I may make of it a heaven of bliss?"

How could she express her complete gift of self?

"I answered," she wrote, "that my heart belongs to Him ... that with my whole soul, I give it to Him ... that He alone is my All in all ... that I love Him and that for Him, I am ready to leave everything."

Jesus seemed pleased with her loving protestations.

"I shall in very truth always live in you. I shall hide in your heart to forget the offenses of sinners ... and day by day I will entrust to you one of My Heart's desires which you will strive to realize.

"Today My wish is that you should live in My joy. You will pray that souls may learn to despise the pleasures of this world in order to acquire those that are eternal. You will rejoice at the sight of your Bridegroom entering as Man His heavenly home, accompanied by myriads of souls who have waited so eagerly and so long for the opening of this heavenly dwelling... . Adieu, keep Me, hide Me in your heart. Live in My joy... . Soon glory unending will be yours. Till that day dawns, let Me take My rest in you."

Josefa spent all that day with eyes fixed on the bliss of her Master: Heaven where He forever reigns and triumphs; on her own soul which He had deigned to make another Heaven which no shadow could cloud.

Again on Friday, May 11th, before the end of her thanksgiving Our Lord came to tell her of His next desire:

"Are you there, Josefa?" she heard Him say.

"I answered that I wanted Him more than ever.

" 'I, too, want you,' was His reply. 'Today must be a day of peace ... but peace in suffering. And as you yourself can do so little, I will see to it that many occasions of self-denial come your way. Gain advantage from them, and tonight offer Me a sheaf of them exquisitely fragrant. Have no fear, for I Myself am Peace, and as I live and reign in you, you will live in My peace.'"

Faithful to His promise, that day He spared her neither difficulties nor sacrifices. In the evening, she met Him.

"All this will pass," He said, "but Heaven will never end! So, courage! I am your All and therefore your strength... . Now, Josefa, rest in My peace."

This stage of Josefa's life was lived from one Communion to another, and each morning her Master assigned her the day's intention.

The next day, Saturday, May 12th, at the very moment when she was about to receive Communion. "Open your heart, Josefa, that I may enter in."

She could only murmur that her heart was ever open to Him:

"I know it," He answered tenderly, "but I desire and want My entry into your heart to be daily more of an event, and that your desire be so keen, your hunger for Me so great that your very soul faints ... If you only knew how much I love you ... if you could but understand it ... but you are too little... ."

Then, with all the eagerness of burning affection, He added: "Today, Josefa, must be our day of zeal! ... I will kindle in your heart a thirst for souls like that which consumes My own. Ah! souls ... souls... ."

Already Josefa felt her heart aflame. She could think of nothing, pray for nothing but these precious souls, for her whole life was consecrated to this work of redemption whose meaning she had learnt from the very Heart of Jesus.

"When He had said this," she wrote, "I began to speak to Him of those for whom I am concerned ... and He answered: 'Yes, pray ... pray ... do not grow tired nor fear to be importunate, for prayer is the key that opens every door. So, Josefa, today is a day of zeal for souls ... for souls ... for souls!'"

And He vanished.

That day the thought of souls never left her. What would she not do to assuage her Master's thirst for them?

On Sunday, May 13th, Our Lord invited her to tread the path that is redemptive par excellence.

"We shall spend a day of humility," He said to her after Communion. "You need not seek for occasions, for I will provide them... . Go on praying for souls and humbling yourself for them, and then Josefa, through it all, let Me see your smile!"

She left no record of that day, but in the evening during her adoration before the Blessed Sacrament, Jesus who read her through and through came to answer a question that was puzzling her.

"You cannot understand why I brought you here, Josefa? First and foremost to ground you in complete abandonment to My Will, in absolute detachment from all things, even from what seemed to you absolutely necessary... . Then I wanted to make you more than ever aware of how much you need support, so that the last traces of pride might expire within you... . Then, too, I wanted this parting to profit souls, and I am making out of it one of the foundation stones of the edifice of My great work."

Josefa listened in adoring love to the words that fell from her Master's lips.

"So now, Josefa," He said, as He was about to depart, "this is a day of humility, but joyous humility. I am your Happiness ... what else matters?"

Next day, Monday, May 14th, Our Lord explained to her for the second time, but with greater precision, what her part in the redemptive work of His Heart was soon to be.

"Do you belong entirely to Me?" He asked her during her prayer. "Do you want nothing but My glory? ... Have you but one desire, that My great work should be realized?"

To each of which questions she answered: "Yes, Lord." Then gravely He went on to say:

"I am going to manifest the plan of My Heart to you. I have already told you that three times before your death you will see the Bishop1... . It is necessary for the good of My work that you should entrust it to him just before your death, for I want My words to be known immediately after you die."

And though Josefa trembled, He made His Will quite clear.

"There is no need to be afraid, for I will tell you all that you have to say ...

But I want you to have now the merit of this costly act."

He comforted her after Communion:

"Today is to be a day of abandonment and confidence. I can refuse nothing to one who relies entirely on Me.

"Souls are too little conscious of how much I want to help them and how much I am glorified by their trust. Josefa, you must hope all things from Me... . Speak to Me ... ask ... trust My Heart, for you are guarded by Me."

The progressive upward steps of the week were to end in love: love that explains and enlightens all things, yet a love which in God's good time demands everything.

On Tuesday, May 15th, while at prayer, Josefa, who could not suppress a certain fear at the prospect opened out before her by Our Lord, asked earnestly for the love she knew to be the secret and the power of every offering.

"He came unexpectedly," she wrote, "and showing me His Heart in the midst of flames, He said: 'Josefa, look at My Heart, study It, and from It you will learn love... . True love is humble, generous, disinterested... . so if you want Me to teach you to love, begin by forgetting yourself. Do not stop at sacrifices. Do not be checked by what costs you ... ignore what attracts you personally, and do all things because you love.'"

It was in such wise that Our Lord encouraged the soul of His little bride: today, a day of Love; tomorrow the sign of love will light up the horizon: soon there will be a proof of true love demanded.

On Wednesday, May 16th, Josefa noted for the first time the apparition of the Cross.

"It was the Cross of Jesus," she wrote, "for I recognized it, having so often carried it. It was lit up as if a light from above was reflected onto it."

For several days the flaming Heart of Jesus and His Cross resplendent in light shone upon her path alternately, but in silence, and her Master did not appear. On Whit-Sunday, May 20th, 1923, the Cross thus lit up was before her during the whole time of her prayer; her eyes were fascinated by it and her love made more ardent, but she was nevertheless somewhat mystified.

"Lord, why is this Cross illuminated, but without Thee?" she queried.

During her thanksgiving, Jesus answered the question:

" Josefa, do you not know that I and the Cross are inseparable? If you meet Me, you meet the Cross, and when you find the Cross, it is I whom you have found. Whoever loves Me loves the Cross, and whoever loves the Cross loves Me. Only those who love the Cross and embrace it willingly for love of Me, will possess eternal life. The path of virtue and of holiness is composed of abnegation and suffering. Whoever generously accepts the Cross walks in true light, follows a straight and sure path, with no danger from steep inclines down which to slide, for there are none there.

"My Cross is the door of true life, that is why it is illuminated. And the soul that knows how to accept and love it, just as I have chosen it for her, will enter by it into the glory of life eternal.

"Do you now understand how precious the Cross is? Do not shun it... . Love it, for it comes from Me, and I shall never leave you without strength to bear it. I bore it for love of you, will you not bear it for love of Me?"

In what manner she would have to carry the Cross of her Master, Josefa was about to learn. Up to this time, the divine plan had but rarely admitted anything in the nature of suspicion or mistrust on the part of Superiors. Our Lord had Himself foreseen and guaranteed to Josefa the security of their support as also of their control over her in the extraordinary ways in which it pleased Him to guide her. The attacks of Satan had necessitated such support, and their help had hitherto never failed her. The grace of opposition was, however, too precious for God to withhold it from one so dearly loved by Him. The hour had come when she was to experience it, and it was to be laid on her shoulders by the gentle and strong hands of Jesus Himself, who let it sink, too, deeply into her heart.

The Cross and Many Graces (May 20th-June 2nd, 1923)

"Though this hour seems dark to you, My power dominates it, and My
work will gain by it."
(Our Lord to Josefa, May 20th, 1923)

May 20th was a Sunday and Josefa, finding she had a little leisure, sat
down to write to Les Feuillants, since she had permission.

It gave her great joy and comfort to write to her friends there, though, of
course, she could not trust to a letter the secret of all that had happened
since her departure from Poitiers.

But as soon as she had begun her letter, Our Blessed Lord appeared and
charged her with a message to be delivered in His Name to the Mothers at
Poitiers. Josefa was seized with dismay at the very thought, and at first
refused, protesting that it would be impossible for her to pass such a
missive through the censorship of her Superior, who was entirely ignorant
of the communications it had pleased Our Lord to make to her. But Jesus
insisted: "What have you to fear, if it is I who order you to do this?"

Josefa implored Him to have compassion on her and let her off so costly
an act, which was sure not to pass unnoticed, and would but add to the
misgivings with which she felt she was already regarded. Had He not
promised her that the secret of her life should remain undivulged? ... That
He Himself would guarantee its secrecy? ... But Our Lord was inflexible
this time, and His Will imposed on Josefa obedience and abandonment.
"Love," He said to her, "will give you strength to do what I ask."

Her distress was extreme; poor Josefa hesitated and could not make up her
mind to an act whose consequences she rightly fore-saw. On the other
hand, it was impossible for her to stand out against Our Lord's express
wish ... At last, with many heart-searchings, she slipped the message in, in
terms as veiled as she could devise.

The evening went by without incident, but not without the most wearing
disquiet of mind for Josefa, and her forebodings proved to be well
founded. The watchful solicitude of Superiors quickly took alarm, and
with good reason, at what in their eyes seemed a way of acting beyond the
competence of a humble Sister. Fearing that there might be something
abnormal about the matter, and alarmed at what, at first sight, struck her
as a venture into perilous and foolhardy flights of fancy, her Superior sent
for Josefa the very next day.

She began by questioning her kindly, and then represented to her in very
forcible terms the dangers of illusion, explaining how easily she could
thereby become the sport of an overexcited imagination... . Josefa listened
humbly to this strongly-worded advice, intended to put her on her guard
against herself and the devil. But her soul was profoundly disturbed, and
silent tears began to flow, while there revived within her all her previous

fears of illusion and the apprehension and repugnance which she had fought against so long, and conquered with such hardly-won victories.

"I have resisted this course so long," she wrote in her notebook that evening, "and my greatest temptation still is to escape from it... .

"O! how happy I should be if I could walk in the simple and common way of my dear religious life! ... What anxiety ... what anguish ... what conflict! ... O my God, what am I to do? ... Must I again resist Thee, as I have done for too long already? ... "

That evening, Monday in Whit-week, May 21st, after a day of sad uncertainty, she begged her Master to forgive her if she had failed in prudence, and had caused in any way the reproaches which she had accepted in all sincerity. In order to tranquilize her misery and find assurance, she went to the chapel where the Blessed Sacrament was exposed.

"Jesus came instantly," she wrote, "with burning Heart, and bearing on His right arm the Cross all bright and resplendent, as I have seen it all these days."

"You only did My bidding, Josefa," He said. "Have no anxiety concerning your Superiors. Cannot you see how I have helped you hitherto? Have I changed? I loved you before and My love is just the same now. I am your Father, your Saviour, and your Spouse, but I am likewise your God, and you are Mine. The Creator has supreme mastery over His creature, and that is why you are Mine."

He then appealed to her spirit of faith:

"Do you think that anything happens without My permission? I dispose all things for the good of each and every soul. Though this hour seems dark to you, My power dominates it and My work will gain by it. I am your All, Josefa, so do not be afraid, for you are not alone. I have not brought you here for your ruin, but from love, and because it is fitting that all this should happen."

These words soothed Josefa's troubled heart, though the pain remained. The Cross still rose up before her, but its light was quenched. She embraced it, nevertheless, with all the love of her heart, and no change was visible in her outward life. Always simple and confiding, it seemed that there could not exist even a shadow between her and her Mothers. Her perfect religious spirit was already proof to their minds of the spirit by which she was animated, and in it they discerned tokens of a divine influence.

A few months later the Superior of Marmoutier gave a moving testimony of the impression made on her by Josefa's gentle and humble acceptance of the strongly-worded reproof which she thought it her duty to administer. She was not afraid to add, that as she watched Josefa leave her room, there came over her a singular intuition that the little Sister's soul was the object of divine predilection.

All this time the other Sisters, who knew nothing of what had happened, found her always forgetful of self, obliging, friendly and even merry at recreation, while they could not but be influenced by her virtue. God alone knew the mental and moral suffering of the remainder of that Whit-week.

"Your heart has not yet suffered as Mine has," said Our Lord to her on Tuesday, May 22nd.

And as Josefa explained that there could be no comparison between His Heart and her stingy little one: "Nevertheless," He answered, "in the measure of your strength I want yours to be a reflection of Mine.... . But do not be afraid; I love you and I will never forsake you."

This was the hour when Jesus planned to flood with grace her soul now deepened by humiliation.

Josefa already knew by experience much of the Fatherhood of God, but on Friday, May 25th, this knowledge was, as it were, confirmed by such assurances that her childlike, filial spirit gained that sense of immense security and of abandonment which are its specific fruit.

"That evening," she noted, "as I was about to go to bed and was kissing my crucifix and renewing my vows with all the love of my heart, suddenly my Jesus was there, so beautiful ... but above all so fatherly."

She could not find words to express all that this meant to her. "Do not be afraid," He said. "I am watching over you.... . I am guiding you ... and I love you."

How can the Fatherhood of God be better expressed? "As He is so good," she wrote, "I called Him Father, and I tried to say how tenderly I love Him."

"When you call Me Father," He replied, "it pleases Me, Josefa, and when you give Me that name I feel bound to take care of you. When here below a little child begins to talk and utters the sweet name of Father, with what joy parents press their child to their hearts, for the world holds no greater pleasure for them. If this is true of an earthly father and mother, how much truer of Me, for I am your Father, Mother, God, Creator, Saviour and Bridegroom! ... And none equals My Heart in loving-kindness.

"Yes, Josefa, when you feel oppressed and sad, hasten to call on your Father, and rest in His Heart.

"If on account of your work you cannot throw yourself at My feet as you would like, only murmur the one word Father and I will help, sustain, guide, and comfort you.

"Now go in peace to your rest. Another day is over and it will count for all eternity."

Great was the impression left on Josefa's mind by this first grace, but it was to be followed by others still greater.

On the eve of Trinity Sunday, May 26th, Josefa's relations with her Lord reached what one might almost call the peak of divine intimacy. Yet Josefa's simple statements of the signal graces she received make us realize to what an extent in her humility she ignored herself. We give what follows without commentary:

"After Communion," she wrote, "I saw Jesus. He looked like a poor man, and as if afraid to say anything. I renewed my vows and asked Him why He looked so... . He stretched out a hand: 'You ask Me what I want, Josefa? ... Do you not know? ... I want nothing less than your heart... .'

" 'But, Lord, Thou knowest that it is Thine already ... long ago I gave it to Thee, and Thou art my only love.'

"His Heart glowed like fire while He said eagerly: 'I know it! But today I will take it! ... and in its place I will place a spark of My own which at every moment will fire and devour you.' Then, with increasing eagerness: 'Yes, you will live on love, and your soul will suffer unslakable thirst to possess Me, to glorify Me, and to give Me souls! Your heart will be burnt up in a flame of love ... a flame which will kindle you with zeal for souls... . Then, nothing will prevent your entering on the path which My Heart has prepared for you with so much love.'

"I answered that I want to love Him without measure, but I should be so happy if, as tiny children do, I could love without reflecting on the fact, without seeking occasions or proofs, but always, and quite simply, just love. That is how I should like to be: loving Him and giving Him souls, but in small and hidden ways, so that my responsibility would not be so great.

" 'Do not fear, Josefa; there is nothing to prevent this, for you will no longer act by your own power, but guided and impelled by Me.

" 'I, too, want you to be like a little child. But I want to make use of this littleness. Just because you are so little you must let yourself be led by My fatherly hand, which is all-powerful and infinitely strong. So, if there is anything good in you, you will never attribute it to yourself, for little children know and can do absolutely nothing. But if they are docile and obedient, it is their father's wisdom that leads them, and his prudence.

" 'Josefa, let Me take your heart!'

"Before I could reply, Jesus had taken it from me," she went on. "I felt a violent pain, and instantly, snatching a burning spark of fire from His Heart, He let it fall upon my breast. Ah! my Jesus ... this is too much... .

"But He went on: 'Let Me do it ... let Me do it ... this is love. The flame of My love will take the place of your heart, but it will in no wise prevent you from feeling and loving; on the contrary, the stronger love is, the more intimate it is... . And now let us spend a day of zeal, ardor and intimacy, I for you and you for Me.'"

"And He went away," wrote Josefa, "taking my heart with Him."

What had taken place in this mysterious exchange, so simply and objectively recorded? ...

That evening, Josefa, overwhelmed by what had happened and unable to speak of it to anyone, attempted to commit some of her thoughts to writing. In the lines that follow one must not look for more than a forthright and unpretentious record of what she neither understood nor tried to explain.

"From that time on I have felt in my breast so ardent a flame that at times I can hardly bear it. Then, too, everything now seems to fall short of my desires. I long to be rid of my body ... to attract innumerable souls to His Heart ... to give Him very great glory... . I so hunger to possess Him that it is a veritable martyrdom to be still far from Him... . I cannot explain it... but there is in me now such a consuming flame of desire for Him. How I yearn to love Him and see Him loved!"

Earth had now become a place of exile to her longing soul, and it was in vain that she tried to express this; hitherto she had not felt its utter emptiness. Yet, wonderful to relate, no outward sign betrayed the consuming fire within, while all alone she bore the weight of this stupendous grace which annihilated her faculties in adoration and love.

The next day, May 27th, Feast of the Blessed Trinity, a new grace was added, reminiscent of one she had already received during her Noviceship. The Three Divine Persons were manifested to her in a vision of resplendent loveliness. Then Josefa heard these words: "Three, but We are One in Sanctity, in Wisdom, in Power and in Love. Man, whose human nature is divinized by grace, becomes one with God. Thus does God reside in souls that are in a state of grace. Thus do the Three Divine Persons take up their abode in them, making these souls their habitation of delight."

After recording the words that she had heard, Josefa continued:

"Then I saw no one but Jesus alone, extending His hand, He said, with eyes raised to Heaven: 'May men adore the Father. May they love the Son. May they let themselves be possessed by the Holy Spirit, and may the Blessed Trinity abide in them.'"

Then, He fixed His eyes on Josefa: "O! if you could but see the beauty of a soul in grace. But such beauty is invisible to mortal eyes, Josefa. Look rather with eyes of faith, and realizing the value of souls, consecrate yourself to giving this glory to the Blessed Trinity, by gaining many souls in which the Triune God may find a dwelling."

Jesus continued instructing her in very simple language: "Every soul can be instrumental in this sublime work... . Nothing great is required, the smallest acts suffice: a step taken, a straw picked up, a glance restrained, a service rendered, a cordial smile ... all these offered to Love are in reality of great profit to souls and draw down floods of grace on them. No need to remind you of the fruits of prayer, of sacrifice, of any act offered to expiate the sins of mankind ... to obtain for them the grace of purification, that they too may become fitting sanctuaries for the indwelling of the Blessed Trinity."

Then Josefa prayed for the apostolic Orders, who work for that end, and begged Jesus to inflame them with zeal and to bless their toil and sufferings. He, in reply, made her understand how pleasing to Him is disinterestedness in apostolic laborers, and how dear it makes them to His Heart.

"If a man devotes his life," He said, "to working either directly or indirectly for the salvation of souls, and reaches such a degree of detachment from self that without neglecting his own perfection he leaves to others the merit of his actions, prayers and sufferings ... that man draws down abundant graces on the world ... he himself reaches a high degree of sanctity, far higher than he would have attained had he sought only his own advancement."

Such teachings concerning faith were carefully noted by Josefa, since, falling from the lips of Jesus, they acquired in her eyes an importance to which her heart attached great value.

"Then He went away," she added. "Ah! how sad I feel when I am left all alone after such a contemplation! ... I who am so insignificant can hardly bear such happiness... . How trivial the things of earth appear... . I am so indifferent to them... . I wish I could explain this: I see in such a vivid light the meaning of God alone that I feel detached from everything here below.

"Today after that communion with what ardor I renewed my vows, and handed myself over to Him again. He has already taken my heart, but I renewed the donation I had made of it to Him, and together with it of all I love most: homeland, family, Les Feuillants ... everything! He is all I desire and if I must needs suffer more, that, too, I offer Him. How my soul thirsts for Him!"

The solitude and sadness in which her soul had been plunged for the last week, increased this thirst. She continued to bear it religiously and in silence, but obedient to her Superiors, she endeavored to enter into their views, by more constant prayer and, if possible, greater vigilance.

On Monday, May 28th, transferred Feast of Saint Madeleine Sophie, a day of great solemnity in all convents of the Sacred Heart, Our Lord was about to crown her faithful service by adding to the signal graces of the last days one which became a veritable foretaste of Heaven.

"After Holy Communion," wrote Josefa, "it seemed to me that Heaven itself was in my soul. Suddenly I saw Jesus in all His beauty ... with His Heart resplendent and shining as a very sun. It was surmounted by a cross of fire... . He said: 'She that eats My Flesh possesses God, Author of Life ... and of Life Eternal... . That is how this soul becomes My heaven. Nothing can compare with her in beauty. The angels are in admiration and, as God is within that soul, they fall down in adoration... . O soul, didst thou but know thy dignity... . Your soul, Josefa, is My heaven and every time you receive Me in Holy Communion My grace augments both your dignity and your beauty."

Josefa could do nothing but humble herself at her Master's feet and confess her sins, her miseries and weakness, knowing herself unworthy of the infinite Sanctity that, descending to her nothingness, went to the length of making her in reality His heavenly place of repose.

"Lord," she said, "I give Thee my heart, my life, my liberty ... all.

"I desire nothing else," He answered. "What does all the rest matter? ... Your sins? Why, I can wipe them out.... Your miseries? I consume them.... Your weakness? I will be its support.... Let us remain united."

God's eternal purpose for this stage of Josefa's life seemed now to have been accomplished in every detail, and was to end with the month of May. She had given a true proof of her love; she had been detached, separated and purified by the loneliness in which her divine Master's Will had been her only support. She had entered with entire docility into His designs, which step by step had led her to a fresh experience of the Cross. This Cross she had embraced with wholehearted loyalty, in a spirit of faith and generous love.... God used the freedom she thus left Him to pour into her soul a full measure of choice graces which transformed her and in a very short time raised her to heights she never could have attained by her own efforts. It was the work of Love realized in her person before being carried out in the world.

The radiance that had illuminated the close of the month of May little by little waned, like the sunset of a glorious summer day. Only the Cross still appeared to Josefa from time to time. Though she continued to help in the house in whatever way she could, from now on she suffered violent pain, but she did not try to find out its cause, though she was exhausted each evening. She never complained, for she had long been accustomed to bear extreme physical pain. But what was far more painful to her was her moral isolation, and this, too, she bore in silence.

"I who so love my Superiors and have learnt to have no secrets from them," she wrote sadly, "not to be able to speak to them nor tell them all is my greatest privation.... If my Jesus did not support me, how could I bear it? But when I feel most tormented by it I offer it all to Him in sacrifice and that strengthens me."

This complete sacrifice of herself, of her reputation, of help from her Superiors, of an ultimate return to Poitiers, Jesus knew how keenly she felt it all and how sincere she was. With one gesture of love He was about to restore it all to her.

On June 1st she wrote this brief note: "I have just been told that tomorrow I am to go back to Poitiers. I have thanked Jesus, for I had completely given it up, and never thought to return there."

A few moments later, Jesus appeared to her and confirmed the news:

"I have accepted the sacrifice of all you gave Me, Josefa. Today I give it back to you. And now I shall go on telling you My secrets.... The devil will attack you again and often try to deceive you and hurt you. But have no fear, I will defend you.

"May your heart keep the flame of love and zeal in joy and abandonment.... I love you and am entirely yours."

Return to Poitiers, Feast of the Sacred Heart (June 2nd - 10th, 1923)

"I will speak in you, and My words will reach souls and will not pass away. I will love you, and by that love souls will discover My love for them. I will forgive you, and souls will recognize My mercy by that with which I have wrapped you round."
(Our Lord to Josefa, Feast of the Sacred Heart, 1923)

On Saturday, June 2nd, Josefa returned to Poitiers. It was for her a totally unexpected event which filled her with gratitude, and the whole community rejoiced with her, for she had their love, such true love as is found in religious houses. But in her case there was something quite indefinable which attracted their respect and affection, and made her return among them a real feast day. At once she resumed her place among the Sisters and claimed for herself the large share in daily devotedness that had always been hers. The following Monday saw her back, too, at the head of the Novices' workroom, and soon it seemed as if she had never been away.

Superiors were much struck by her spiritual progress during the month's absence. She had come back to them invested, so to speak, by a supernatural influence.

"How God has worked in that soul," wrote her Superior to the Very Reverend Mother General. "I cannot say how changed we find her ... and in so short a time! What a distance between her and us! ... We are so impressed by her. God seems to have begun the crowning of His graces in her, the loftiness of which is beyond us, but her attitude of simplicity, obedience, and detachment are unchanged and must be very pleasing to our Blessed Mother Foundress. Our Lord seems to be hastening on her transformation with truly giant strides. She has resumed her life of silence and humble labor, but her body is exhausted by suffering and more so by the interior fire consuming her day by day."

Josefa, on her side, wrote on Monday, June 4th:

"Since May 20th, when Our Lord took my heart, I feel in myself such burning fervor ... such a longing to love Him ... and console Him... and give Him souls ... that all the rest fades into nothingness, and though I have no difficulty in loving, yet I feel a sort of detachment from all things ... such a desire for Jesus, that my only longing is to die in order to go to Him ... and my soul seems imprisoned ... a state impossible to express... ."

The realization of her own nothingness at times overpowered her. She continued:

"I feel disconcerted and ashamed to see myself such as I am ... anybody overwhelmed with graces such as mine would be a saint ... and I become daily more unworthy, more ungrateful, and perhaps, God knows, sinful, too! It is very painful to realize this, and though I do not lose my peace of mind over it, it is nevertheless very grievous to bear."

Whilst she was kneeling in the cell where, in accordance with obedience, she had once more begun to write her daily notes, Jesus appeared:

" 'You must not be troubled, Josefa,' He said gently. 'I want you to be nothing, that I may be All.

" 'The smaller a thing is the more easily it can be handled. It is just because you are so paltry a thing that I can use you as I like. You know well that I need nothing ... and all I ask of you is to be plastic in My hands... . Your misery is of little account in My eyes... . Remain as you are, nothing ... but look, and you will see what I who am All can fashion out of your nothingness!'

"Then," Josefa's notes continue, "I saw a multitude of souls pass before Him, so many that I could not reckon the number, and Jesus said: 'All of them will come to Me.'"

That evening, June 4th, Our Lord renewed for the first time the mysterious grace of the 26th of May.

During night prayers He showed her His Heart in a veritable sea of fire, and taking a flame from this furnace, He said: "This flame will replace the one I have already placed in your heart."

She assured her Master that the first still burnt her with desire to be united to Him in love, and was her greatest suffering.

"For," she wrote, "my will yearns ... but I believe that I do not know how to love.

" 'Ah! Josefa,' came the ready response, 'that is nothing to what will be some day... . I will set you on fire ... I will utterly consume you.'"

Letting the flame fall on Josefa, He vanished. She still perceived His Heart for a short time ... and from the wound came a fiery ray. "O! my God," she wrote, "what suffering that I cannot love Thee as I would!"

Such wonderful graces were repeated several times during the month of June 1923. Josefa noted them down with the same unimaginative simplicity, never succeeding in expressing adequately the state of her soul, thus consumed by divine fire.

"I know of no pain in the world I would not be ready to endure for Him," she wrote on June 5th. "My soul is full of peace, but its hunger is unsated... . I believe it is from Jesus ... that I may never be separated from Him, that I may love Him... . These are things too lofty for me to understand ... all I know is that there are moments when I cannot restrain my soul... ."

This Tuesday, June 5th, was the third anniversary of the day when the Heart of Our Saviour appeared to her for the first time (1920). During her prayer Jesus again manifested Himself to her, and kept her long immersed in the fiery rays of love that issued from His wounded Heart. Josefa could scarcely endure their ardor, and they did not cease when she went to Mass.

"The more I see how great and good He is, the more unworthy I feel," she wrote, "and never would I dare approach Him if I had not Our Blessed Lady to help and guide me.

"I saw Him again after Communion, my Jesus, so gentle, gracious and fatherly, no word can describe Him ... and opening His Heart to me, He said: 'The less there is of you, the more I shall be your life, and you will be My heaven of rest.'

" 'How can I, Lord, miserable as I am?'

" 'Do you not know, Josefa, that on earth My heaven is in souls?'"

Then her apostolic heart thrilled:

"I asked Him how to win many souls to knowledge and love, a burning love of Himself.

" 'Pray, Josefa, pray intensely... . Yes, beg for souls this burning love!'"

Though the Master drew her so powerfully to His Heart, He did not allow her to forget her great natural weakness. He left her the repugnances and difficulties of her character, and wanted her to reproach herself with even her smallest imperfections. "Yes, I see how weak you are," He said to her that evening, when at her night prayers she recalled some feelings for which she was sorry.

"He told me all my failings," she wrote, "and then said: 'What are you, Josefa, after all? A mere pinch of dust that one blows away with a breath.'"

From the bottom of her heart she begged His forgiveness.

"You know that I always forgive you. If I tell you of your faults, this is because of My love for you, that your 'self' may disappear and I may live in you. And now, I will change the flame in your heart and kindle it afresh to give you new vigor for the work of your own effacement."

"Then," wrote Josefa, "He did as yesterday, and left me in great pain. For some time past my body seems to have lost all power and I suffer in every limb. Over my soul hangs an oppression that I cannot understand, but it leaves me in an ever deepening peace."

"I shall return every evening," said Our Lord to her on Wednesday, June 6th, "to consume all your failings, and rekindle the flame which I have put in place of your heart."

And so He did that very evening, and after listening in all tenderness to the recital of her failings and miseries, He said: "You know that it is the property of fire to destroy and to enkindle. In the same way My Heart's property is to pardon, love, and purify. Never think that I shall cease to love you because of your miseries. No, My Heart loves you and will never forsake you."

Then Jesus, grasping a flame from His burning Heart, let it fall on her. As the flame of Divine Love struck her Josefa's whole being quivered; she clasped her hands over her heart as if to restrain its fire, her eyes were fixed with indescribable longing on the Heart of her Master, which remained visible to her for some moments longer while gradually she regained her panting breath. It was a moving scene, and was repeated on several successive days in her poor cell.

A quarter of an hour or so later Josefa, under the eyes of the Mothers who were kneeling in prayer by her side, was seen slowly to come out of her rapture. Her breathing became normal once more; she joined her hands and lowered her eyes. All had disappeared, but her soul remained for some time yet plunged in that all-consuming fire, her body a prey to excruciating pain that sometimes lasted all night till early dawn.

Those who were present and saw these happenings have thus described them, but how depict what each of these divine intrusions into her inmost being left of capacity for love and suffering and union with the redemptive work of the Sacred Heart of her Lord... .

It was in the midst of these exceptional favors, now, as ever, silently kept from all but the two aforesaid witnesses, that the triduum of preparation before the Feast of the Sacred Heart ran its course. They were days of recollection and intense prayer, when the nuns, without interrupting their usual apostolic work, were preparing for the renovation of their vows.

On the evening of the vigil, Thursday, June 7th, the whole household was gathered in the Chapel for a Holy Hour before the Blessed Sacrament. Josefa was there, lost amid the throng of her Sisters. In the silence of prayer, Our Lord, looking on her with special love, deigned to manifest Himself to her.

Josefa noted next day:

"I should have liked to comfort Him, but the consciousness of my unworthiness filled me with confusion as well as with grief. I told Him of my desires, and how I dared not ask pardon for the sins of the world, considering I have committed so many sins myself! ...

"Suddenly He came, and said compassionately: 'Why these fears? Have I not told you that My one desire is to forgive? Do you think that I have chosen you because of your virtues? I know well that you have nothing but misery and weakness, but as I am a purifying fire, I will wrap you round in the flame of My Heart and consume you. Ah! Josefa, how often I have told you that My one longing is for souls to bring Me their miseries! Come ... and let Love consume you.'

"Then, as on the preceding day, a flame escaped from His Sacred Heart, and falling on mine, set it all aglow."

A moment or two passed in the unspeakable ardor which Josefa had now experienced several times, but which she could never express.

"After that," she wrote, "I prayed to Him for several souls that require His help, and He answered me:

" 'When a king espouses the daughter of a subject he assumes the obligation of providing all that the new rank to which he has raised her requires.

" 'I have chosen you and have undertaken thus to provide for your every want.... I require nothing of you beyond what is already yours. Give Me an empty heart and I will fill it ... give me a heart destitute of all adornment and I will make it beautiful. Give it Me with all its miseries and I will consume them. What is hidden from you I will reveal, and all that you lack, I take on myself to supply.'

"By this He made clear to me how He helps souls who desire only to please Him, and how He supplies their every want, and all they lack."

Then reminding Josefa once more of her incapacity and weakness, He repeated:

"You know well, Josefa, that had I been able to find anywhere a creature more miserable than you, I would assuredly have chosen her, in order to manifest the longings of My Heart through her, but not finding one, I chose you.

"You know, too, what happens when an insignificant little flower devoid of charm or fragrance springs up on a high-road full of traffic. It quickly gets trampled underfoot by the passers-by, who pay not the slightest attention to it, nor so much as notice its existence. And think, Josefa, what would have become of you if I had left you, frail and miserable as you are, to the cold of winter, the heat of summer, to be the sport of wind and rain; assuredly you would have died. But because I want you to live, I transplanted you into the garden of My Sacred Heart, tending you with My own hands, that you may grow up under the beams of the Sun with Its vivifying and restoring power, whose strength is tempered in your regard, that no injury may come to you. Ah! Josefa, leave yourself, such as you are, to My care, and let the sight of your nothingness never lessen your trust, but only confirm you in humility."

Josefa reaffirmed her entire confidence, and asked Him to prepare her for the renovation of her vows by cleansing her in His sacred blood.

Eagerly Our Lord rejoined: "If your desire is so great Mine far exceeds it! I will purge and cleanse you in the fires of love.... What glory I shall be given here tomorrow!"

Surprised, Josefa questioned this assertion and Jesus answered: "Do you not know what store I set on the complete donation made in public to Me by a soul?

"Remain in peace and live in My love."

Early on the morning of the Feast of the Sacred Heart, Friday, June 8th,

1923, Josefa's divine Master Himself prepared her for the renovation of vows.

This ceremony of solemn renovation, which with the Sacred Host held before her at the moment of Communion, each nun makes individually, is not in the Society of the Sacred Heart the remaking of a promise that has lapsed. The First Vows as the Last are made forever. Rather is the ceremony an act of devotion, signifying the reaffirmation of a promise that will last till death, and that is made by each religious in the joy of her heart.

Our Lord began the day by showing Josefa His Heart, all aflame, and during her prayer, He plunged her into its fiery depths.

She wrote: "I implored Him to give me true contrition for my sins ... for the greater the graces He gives me, the more unworthy I know myself to be... . On the one hand, my soul is urged by love to unite itself to Him, and on the other, the consciousness of my sins keeps me away and makes me fear to approach Him ... with all the intensity of which I am capable I begged Him to purify me before I renew my vows."

A little later, when Mass had begun, and the chapel was filled with the whole assembled household, Jesus showed Himself to her. "Open your soul," He said, "for I Myself have come to purify you."

Then He drew Josefa's attention to what each of the vows implied and to the plenitude of self-sacrifice which is demanded by each.

"Despoil yourself of all things," He said, "keeping back no desire, no attraction, no personal judgment... . Then, submit yourself wholeheartedly to the Will of your Beloved. Let Me do with you what I like, and not what you desire. You ought so to conform yourself to Me that My Will in you becomes your own, by total submission to My good pleasure. You have given over to Me all your rights by the vow of obedience.

"Would that souls understood that never are they more free than when they have thus given themselves up to Me, and that never am I more inclined to grant their desires than when they are ready to do My Will in everything... . Clasp tight those chains that sweetly bind you to Me. Go and renew the vows that bind you to My feet, to My hands, and introduce you into My Heart."

Josefa went up to the altar-rails, and when the Sacred Host was held before her, she renewed her loved vows, then received Communion and returned to her place. Then Jesus once more manifested Himself to her and with overwhelming love said: "Josefa, you have just told Me that you love Me alone ... that you have voluntarily despoiled yourself of everything for My sake ... that you will never have any other liberty or will than Mine ... My Will is yours, your will is Mine ... I shall be Master of your thoughts, of your words and of your actions. If you have nothing, I will provide everything for you. I will live in you, speak in you, love you, and forgive you."

Taking up each of these words, Our Lord made His thought clear:

"I will live in you and you in Me.

"I will speak in you, and My words will reach souls and will not pass away.

"I will love you, and by that love souls will discover My love for them.

"I will forgive you, and souls will recognize My mercy by that with which I have wrapped you round.

"Many believe in Me, but few believe in My love ... and among those who do, too few rely on My mercy... . Many know Me as their God, but how few trust in Me as their Father.

"I will manifest Myself ... especially to those who are the objects of My predilection. I will show them through you that I ask nothing of them that they do not possess. But I do ask that all they have they should give Me, for all is Mine.

"If they possess nothing but miseries and weaknesses, these I desire ... even if they have only faults and sins ... I desire them also. I beg them to give them to Me. Give them to Me; yes, give all to Me and keep nothing, but trust My Heart: I forgive you, I love you, I will sanctify you Myself."

Such graces from Our Lord ought surely to have anchored Josefa in the great work for souls in which she found herself more and more involved, as its destined messenger.

Yet, strange to say, in the little notebook where she put down her personal and secret thoughts, we find how to the very end of her life she had to fight in order to accept the role assigned to her. Our Lord allowed her to feel the repugnance in order that the generosity of her will should constantly have to be brought into play, adhering to His Will. It kept her humble, and the unremitting struggle was in itself a very sure sign that this mission, none of her seeking, was of divine origin.

That very day she wrote: "Yes, my Jesus, I accept all. I will do and say all thou askest of me, disregarding my own likes and dislikes. I accept the path Thou hast chosen for me solely because I know it is Thy Will... . With all my heart I renew the offering have made to Thee of all my tastes, inclinations, person and life."

These same loyal and generous protestations recur repeatedly in her notes. Her Master accepted and appreciated their value, and read in every line of them Josefa's wholly given and ardent soul.

But she had become more pliant, and Jesus was once more to use her as His instrument, and by her send His Message to the world.

"Tomorrow," He said to her on the evening of Saturday, June 9th, "I will go on telling you My secrets for souls, for I want them all to come to Me. O! pray for souls, you especially who are the privileged ones of My Heart... . More than others you must console Me and make reparation. Yes, pray earnestly for souls."

Before the end of the Octave of the Sacred Heart, Saint Madeleine Sophie gave Josefa some valuable teaching about the motto she had previously given her at Marmoutier: "Love knows no obstacles."

On Sunday, June 10th, she appeared at Josefa's side during Mass, and blessing her, said:

"Daughter, I have come today to tell you how to love, so that true love may find no opposition in you.

"The basis of love is humility; for it is often necessary to submit and sacrifice our likes and dislikes, our comfort and our self-love if we wish to give proof of true love ... and this act of submission is none other than one of humility, for it is abnegation, self-denial, generosity and adoration in one. In fact, to prove this love in something that costs us very much we have to think in this way: 'If it were not for Thee, O my God, I would not do it. But as it is for Thee, I cannot say no; I love Thee and I submit to Thy Will. It is my God who asks this of me, so I must obey. I do not know why He asks it, but He knows.' And so because of love we humble ourselves, and with submission do what we do not understand and do not like, unless with a supernatural love and solely because it is the Will of God.

"Daughter, it is by loving that you will change interior resistance and any difficulties that occur into love that is humble, strong and generous. Let them be an act of perpetual adoration of the one Lord and God who is Master of all souls. Never resist, never question, never falter. Do what He asks of you; say what He wants you to say, without fear or vacillation or omission. He is All-holy and Wisdom itself, Master and Lord and Love. Adieu, my child."

Do Men Know? (June 10th - 14th, 1923)

"All My longing is to set hearts on fire ... to set the whole world on fire."
(Our Lord to Josefa, June 12th, 1923)

The time has now come, when according to the Divine Will, Josefa was to transmit the desires of the Sacred Heart to the Bishop of Poitiers. Very gravely Our Lord prepared her for the continuation of His Message on Sunday, June 10th. It looked as if He wanted all possible security for His words, while at the same time He reassured and strengthened His frail intermediary, Josefa.

"While I was writing in my cell this morning Jesus came," noted Josefa. "His wonderful beauty was enhanced by the majesty and sovereign power that the tone of His voice expressed. 'Josefa,' He said, 'humble yourself, and make an act of entire submission to God's holy Will.'

"I prostrated myself in adoration before Him and He continued: 'Offer My Heart the profound, tender, and generous love of yours.'

"This I did from the very depths of my being. Then He was silent, as if waiting for something further... .

"I renewed my vows. I told Him that I belong to Him and that I am ready to do whatever He wills. I think that was what He was waiting for, for then He said: 'As I have triumphed over your heart and your love, you will not refuse Me anything, will you?'

" 'No, dear Lord, I am Thine forevermore.'

" 'Then tomorrow I will come and tell you what in the first place you are to communicate to the Bishop.'"

Josefa was filled with fear. "I was unable to hide it," she wrote, "and I told Him how frightened I feel at the mere thought of it."

"You need have no fear," He replied. "My Heart is watching over you, and besides, it is for souls."

This assurance somewhat allayed her anxiety.

"When I think of having to speak of all those things to His Lordship the Bishop, I am very frightened," she noted, "but I am certain that Jesus will give me the courage I need.

"That evening, when Jesus came to forgive my sins, I again told Him of my fear.

" 'You will have to suffer, Josefa, but it is for souls, and did I not suffer Myself to redeem and save them?'"

Our Blessed Lord stimulated her generosity by laying such motives before her, and her close union with His Sacred Heart also helped her to accept all that was to be demanded of her.

On Monday, June 11th, in the quiet of her thanksgiving after Communion, something of the vastness of His plans was revealed to Josefa.

"Why are you afraid?" He said. "Do you not know that I love you and am watching over you? It is all for souls... . They must know Me ... they must love Me more... . Children ought to make their father known. You are My well-loved daughter specially chosen, that through you I may be revealed and that My Heart may be glorified. You need not fear, for I am strong and will make you strong; I am Love and will sustain you... . I will not abandon you."

A few minutes later Our Lord rejoined her in her cell. "I am now about to tell you, Josefa, the first thing that you are to tell the Bishop. Kiss the ground!"

She renewed her vows and prostrated herself at His feet. Then Jesus began to speak and Josefa wrote:

"I am Love! My Heart can no longer contain its devouring flames. I love souls so dearly that I have sacrificed My life for them.

"It is this love that keeps Me a prisoner in the Tabernacle. For nearly twenty centuries I have dwelt there, night and day, veiled under the species of Bread and concealed in the small white Host, bearing through love, neglect, solitude, contempt, blasphemies, outrages, sacrileges... .

"For love of souls, I instituted the Sacrament of Penance, that I might forgive them, not once or twice, but as often as they need to recover grace. There I wait for them, longing to wash away their sins, not in water, but in My blood.

"How often in the course of the ages have I, in one way or another, made known My love for men: I have shown them how ardently I desire their salvation. I have revealed My Heart to them. This devotion has been as light cast over the whole earth, and today is a powerful means of gaining souls, and so of extending My kingdom.

"Now, I want something more, for if I long for love in response to My own, this is not the only return I desire from souls: I want them all to have confidence in My mercy, to expect all from My clemency, and never to doubt My readiness to forgive.

"I am God, but a God of love! I am a Father, but a Father full of compassion and never harsh. My Heart is infinitely holy but also infinitely wise, and knowing human frailty and infirmity stoops to poor sinners with infinite mercy.

"I love those who after a first fall come to Me for pardon... . I love them still more when they beg pardon for their second sin, and should this happen again, I do not say a million times but a million million times, I still love them and pardon them, and I will wash in My blood their last as

303

fully as their first sin.

"Never shall I weary of repentant sinners, nor cease from hoping for their return, and the greater their distress, the greater My welcome. Does not a father love a sick child with special affection? Are not his care and solicitude greater? So is the tenderness and compassion of My Heart more abundant for sinners than for the just.

"This is what I wish all to know. I will teach sinners that the mercy of My Heart is inexhaustible. Let the callous and indifferent know that My Heart is a fire which will enkindle them, because I love them. To devout and saintly souls I would be the Way, that making great strides in perfection, they may safely reach the harbor of eternal beatitude. Lastly, of consecrated souls, priests and religious, My elect and chosen ones, I ask, once more, all their love and that they should not doubt Mine, but above all that they should trust Me and never doubt My mercy. It is so easy to trust completely in My Heart!"

Here Jesus ended His appeal. He gave Josefa a few indications to be transmitted to her director, who was to lay the whole matter before the Bishop, and reading in Josefa's soul all the anxiety she felt: "Why, why do you fear?" and tenderly He soothed her. "You know that I love you... . You know, too, that it is for souls and for My glory. Do not be troubled... . Just carry out My directions and give Me all the time that I want."

The following day, Tuesday, June 12th, on entering her cell at about eight in the morning, she found her Master already there, and waiting for her. After a few moments spent in adoration, she renewed her vows and once more offered herself to His Will. Jesus then continued from where He had stopped the day before.

"I want to forgive. I want to reign over souls and pardon all nations. I want to rule souls, nations, the whole world. My peace must be extended over the entire universe, but in a special way over this dear country where devotion to My Heart first took root... . O that I might be its peace, its life, its King. I am Wisdom and Beatitude! I am Love and Mercy! I am Peace, I shall reign! I will shower My mercies on the world to wipe out its ingratitude. To make reparation for its crimes, I will choose victims who will obtain pardon ... for there are in the world many whose desire is to please Me ... and there are moreover generous souls who will sacrifice everything they possess, that I may use them according to My Will and good pleasure.

"My reign will be one of peace and love and I shall inaugurate it by compassion on all: such is the end I have in view and this is the great work of My love."

Then with divinest condescension Our Lord explained to Josefa, that she might tell the Bishop the reasons that caused His choice of the Society of the Sacred Heart to be the intermediary to the world of His designs. "It is founded on love, its end is love, its life is love ... and what is love but My Heart?"

Thus did Our Lord outline in a few brief words the bond that was to exist between His work and the Society.

"As for you," He said to Josefa, "I have chosen you as a useless and incapable being, so that it may be clearly I who speak, who ask, who act.

"My appeal is addressed to all: to those consecrated in religion and to those living in the world, to the good and to sinners, to the learned and to the illiterate, to those in authority and to those who obey. To each of them I come to say: if you seek happiness you will find it in Me. If riches, I am infinite Wealth. If you desire peace, in Me alone is peace to be found. I am Mercy and Love! and I must be sovereign King... ."

Then, turning to Josefa, who was kneeling and had just transcribed the last burning words of her Master: "This is what you will first give the Bishop to read."

There followed again a few brief words, a personal communication for His Lordship. Our Lord then continued: "Let him not be surprised at the kind of instruments I use, for My power is infinite and self-sufficient. Let him trust Me. I will bless his undertakings... . And now, Josefa, I shall begin to speak direct to the world, and I desire that My words be made known after your death. As regards yourself, you will live in the most complete and the deepest obscurity, and because I have chosen you as My victim you will suffer, and overwhelmed with pain, you will die! Do not look for rest or alleviation; you will find none, for so have I disposed things. But My love will uphold you, and never shall I fail you!"

In these few moments, Jesus revealed to Josefa the last stage of her life: her meeting with the ecclesiastical authority whose control was to be an assurance of God's blessing ... the Message that she was charged to deliver to all souls thirsting for mercy, peace, and happiness ... her mission as a victim inseparable from the Message and the source from which it would draw its fruitfulness ... the hiddenness which would continue to veil her suffering days and nights ... and finally her death, overwhelmed by pain. All this, down to the minutest details He Himself arranged; her part was full adherence to His work of love, which so soon now He would complete in her and by her means.

That night Our Lord once more renewed the gift of a flame from His Heart: "I come to consume you with fire and set you alight," He told her. "All My longing is to set souls on fire ... those of the entire world... . Alas! they turn from the flame, but I shall triumph, they will be Mine, and I shall be their King. Suffer with Me, that the world may know Me, and that souls may come to Me. It is by suffering that love will triumph."

It was on Wednesday, June 13th, that, as He had said, Our Lord gave a direct Message to the crowd of souls on whom He had compassion ... the throng of the hungry and thirsty, of those in labor and strife, who suffer and weep in hopeless misery ... who seek, want, long for, but do not find the security and happiness they so eagerly desire. To all of them Jesus opened His Heart.

"Mankind must know Me," He said. "I want men to know My love. Do they know what I have done for them?"

And this was precisely what He was about to explain to them.

It almost seemed as if the days in Galilee had returned, when Jesus, seated in the midst of a great concourse of people on the peaceful hillsides, taught them in parables and held them fascinated by the wisdom of His words, and absorbed by the radiance of truth. Then all alike, high and low, sinners and sinless, the lettered and the ignorant, all listened to Him. Some were stirred to their souls' depths, others were rebellious to the secret pleadings of Love ... some drawn by the simplicity of His parables, and others again subdued by the clarity of His instructions. "The sower went forth to sow the seed," He said, "and it fell abundantly." He watched, as He alone could, able to penetrate into the depths of each soul, and see the answer it would give.

So now once again Jesus spoke to the world in a parable, this time to make known the vastness of His all-embracing love.

"So now, Josefa, write.

"A father had an only son.

"They were rich and powerful, served by devoted retainers, and surrounded by all that makes for honor, comfort and pleasure in life, and nothing, neither person nor thing, was wanting to their good fortune. The son was all in all to the father, and the father to the son, and each found in the other perfect contentment, though not so as to exclude others, for such noble and generous hearts felt sympathy for anyone in distress, however slight it might be.

"Now it came to pass that one of the servants of this good master fell ill, and as the danger increased, the only hope of saving his life lay in the application of powerful remedies and most careful nursing.

"But this servant lay at his poor and lonely home. At which the master felt alarm, for if left deserted, the man would certainly die. What was to be done? True, a fellow servant could be sent to minister to him; but such service, done for gain rather than love, gave no assurance against possible neglect.

"So, moved with compassion, the master called his son, and told him of his anxiety. He explained how near death the poor man was, and that the most unremitting care alone could save him.

"Like father, like son! The offer to go himself to succor the dying man is made at once. He will spare neither trouble, fatigue nor night watches until the servant's health is fully re-established.

"The father accepts his son's offer, and willingly allows him to take on the likeness of a servant, that he may serve him who is his slave.

"Many months go by, months of anxious watching by the sick-bed, till at length health is restored, for nothing has been spared that could not only cure his sickness, but also ensure his complete well-being. And what of the servant? With a heart overflowing with gratitude, he asks what he can do in return for such marvelous charity.

" 'Go,' said the son, 'seek out my father and with restored health offer yourself to become his most faithful servant in return for his liberality.'

"Overwhelmed by his obligations, the man stands in humble gratitude before his benefactor and proffers his services gratis, forever. What need has he of remuneration from such a master, who has treated him not as a servant, but as a son.

"This parable is but a pale image of the love I bear to mankind, and of the loving return I look for from them. I will explain it so that all men may know My Heart."

There was a moment's silence ... then Jesus turned to Josefa. With ardor He urged: "Help Me, Josefa; help Me to let men know how I love them! For this am I come, that they may know that they will never find true happiness except in Me ... suffer, Josefa, and love, for we two are out to conquer souls!"

The remainder of that day she passed in humble labor and fidelity like that of the other Sisters, but her mind was preoccupied and absorbed in her Master. When night came, again Jesus exchanged the flame for her heart, leaving her on fire with love. Before leaving, He said: "I thirst ... yes, I thirst for a soul that must die tonight."

Josefa asked if it was a sinner to be rescued... . No, it was a soul very much loved by His Heart. "But I want your suffering to make up for the graces which, owing to her frailty, she has neglected, so that in the short span of life that remains to her she may attain a higher degree of glory."

We can but wonder at Our Lord's all-powerful goodness to the souls He loves! He watches over them, to increase, if possible, their perfection, even to their last breath. Who would not be touched at the thoughtful kindness with which such an intention is presented to apostolic prayer and sacrifice! We know that sinners need the prayers that are to save them from eternal damnation, but cooperation in prayer for saintly souls who are about to die is no less important in His eyes, for in the last and supreme hour He puts the finishing touch to His handiwork.

For Josefa, after a day of labor the night was full of pain, till suddenly a bright light broke in on the darkness of her cell, and a deep peace overwhelmed her soul. Every vestige of suffering disappeared.

"That soul has entered into glory," Our Lady told her next day after her Communion. Such were the apostolic victories that more than made up to Josefa for whatever she had to expend in prayer and suffering, and attached her more deeply than ever to the interests of the Sacred Heart.

On Thursday, June 14th, when she was awaiting Our Lord in her cell, "He appeared," she wrote, "vested in extraordinary majesty."

"Josefa," He said, "humble yourself to the very ground. Adore your God, to make reparation for the contempt and offenses He receives from the greater part of mankind... . Love Him, to make up for their ingratitude... . And now write."

Our Lord then explained the parable of yesterday:

"God created man out of pure love. He placed him on the earth in circumstances that ensured his happiness until the day of eternal bliss should dawn for him. But to have a right to such felicity he is bound to keep the sweet and wise laws laid down by his Maker.

"Man, unfaithful to this law, fell grievously sick; sin was committed by our first parents, and all mankind, their descendants, contracted this guilt and lost their right to the perfect beatitude promised them by God; and pain, suffering and death became henceforth their lot.

"Now God, in perfect bliss, has no need of man or of his services. He is sufficient unto Himself. Infinite is His glory and nothing can diminish it.

"Infinite in power, He is also infinite in goodness; hence He will not allow man, created out of love, to perish; instead, He met the grave evil of sin with a remedy infinite in price: one of the divine Persons of the Blessed Trinity, assuming human nature, will repair in a godlike manner the evil of the Fall.

"The Father gives His Son, the Son sacrifices His glory. He comes to earth not as an all-powerful Lord and Master, but in poverty as a servant and as a child.

"The life He led on earth is known to you all.

"You know how from the first moment of the Incarnation I submitted to all human afflictions. In My childhood I endured cold, hunger, poverty, and persecution.

"In My life of labor, how often humiliation and contempt were meted out to the carpenter's son. How often after a hard day's work we, My foster-father and I, found that we had earned hardly sufficient to support us... . and this I continued for thirty long years.

"Then, forgoing the sweet company of My Mother, I devoted Myself to the task of making My heavenly Father known. I went about teaching men that God is Love.

"I went about doing good to bodies as well as souls: to the sick I gave back their health; the dead I raised to life; and to souls? ... Ah! to souls I restored liberty ... that liberty which they had lost through sin, and I opened to them the gates of their everlasting home - Heaven.

"Then came the hour when to win salvation for them the Son of God willed to surrender life itself.

"And how did He die? ... Was He surrounded by friends? ... Acclaimed as a benefactor? ... Beloved ones, you know that the Son of God did not will to die thus. He who had preached nothing but love was the victim of hatred... . He who had brought peace to the world was treated most cruelly... . He who came to bring men freedom was imprisoned, bound, ill-used, calumniated, and finally died on a cross between two thieves ... contemned, abandoned, abject and despoiled of everything.

"It was thus He surrendered Himself for man's salvation. It was thus He accomplished the work for which He had voluntarily left His Father's glory. Man was sick and wounded, and the Son of God came down to him. He not only restored fallen man to life, but earned for him both strength and power to acquire in this life the treasures of eternal beatitude.

"And what was man's response?

"Did he, like the grateful servant, offer his ministrations gratis and renounce any other but his Master's interests? ...

"Let us consider and distinguish ... for there are different ways in which a response has been made by man.

"But this is enough for today. Remain in My peace, Josefa, and do not forget that you are My victim. Love, and leave all the rest to Me."

The Response Made by Mankind (June 15th - 19th, 1923)

"My words will have such power and be accompanied by such grace that even the most obdurate will be won by love."
(Our Lord to Josefa, June 19th, 1923)

The whole of Friday, June 15th, Our Lord did not appear. As usual Josefa had awaited His coming. "He did not come," she wrote, and, ever fearful, she examined the inmost recesses of her heart, and thought to have discovered a momentary yielding to the never-absent distaste she could not completely overcome for all that was extraordinary in her life.

"Jesus had made me understand very clearly, that not only is His Heart saddened, but souls, waiting for the grace these little acts win for them, are left without the help they need. So when He came in the evening, I begged Him to forgive my want of generosity.

"Very tenderly, He replied: 'Yes, Josefa, open your heart to the light. Nothing that is done in love is small. No, there are no small things in My sight, for the very force of love makes them great.'"

This was a lesson that we have heard from His lips before, and He was never tired of reiterating it that souls might, on their side, never tire of offering Him their smallest efforts.

After her return from Marmoutier, Josefa never had a full night's rest. She spent them in moral and physical pain - for when Our Lord left her after renewing the gift of the flame of His Heart, she generally remained a long time under its influence. These sufferings of body and soul made it impossible for her to forget the crucifying fact that she had been chosen as God's victim for the work of His Heart's love.

However, each morning she was at meditation with the other Sisters and also at Holy Mass, after which she went through the whole round of her daily occupations about the house. Her energy was unconquerable and her smile endeavored to hide, not always successfully, the utter exhaustion of her body.

"Today," she noted, Saturday, June 16th, "Our Lord came at eight o'clock, and showing me His Heart, said: 'Behold this Heart; It is that of a Father, and is consumed with love for His sons; would that they knew It!'"

Then He explained to Josefa the different responses of mankind to God's offer of love.

"Some have truly known Me, and urged by love, have ardently desired to make an entire sacrifice of themselves to My service, which is that of My Father. They begged to be told the greatest thing they could do for Him, and My Father answered thus: 'Leave your home, give up your possessions, and having surrendered self, come, follow Me, and do whatever I tell you.'

"Others, moved by all that the Son of God had done for their salvation, offered themselves to Him, endeavoring with good will to make a return for His goodness, by working for His interests, but without entire renunciation of their own. To these My Father says: 'Observe the law which the Lord your God has given you. Keep His commandments, and erring neither to right nor left, live in the peace which belongs to faithful servants.'

"There are others again who have little understanding of God's great love, yet they have an upright will and live under the law, but without love.

"These servants have not volunteered to carry out all God's orders ... yet a slight indication of His Will is often enough to enlist their service, since they are men of good will.

"There are yet others who submit to their God, not so much through love as through self-interest, and only fulfill the law as far as is necessary to ensure their salvation.

"Yet, do all men offer God their service? Are there any who through ignorance of the great love of which they are the object, make no response to all that the Son of God has suffered for them?

"Alas! ... there are many who know and despise it ... but a far greater number are entirely ignorant of it... ."

For each of these Jesus Christ has a word of love:

"I will speak in the first place to those who do not know Me:

"My sons, who from infancy have lived apart from your Father, come, I will tell you why you do not know Me ... for once you realize the affection I bear you, you will not resist My love.

"It is often the case that those brought up far from their parents have little affection for them; but when by chance the sweet love of father or mother is manifested to them, there awakens a keener appreciation of this warm devotion than is found in those who have never left home.

"To you, who not only do not love, but hate and persecute Me, I say: 'Why this hatred? ... What have I done to deserve persecution at your hands? ... There are many who have never asked themselves this question. Today when I ask it, they will perhaps say: 'We do not know.' Behold, I will answer for you: 'If from childhood you have never known Me, it is because no one has ever taught you about Me; and as you grew up, nature also was developing in you love of pleasure and enjoyment, a longing for wealth and freedom. Then came the day when first you heard of Me, and how to live according to My Will; that to do so you must love and bear with your neighbor, respect his rights and his goods and gain a mastery of your own nature, in a word, live subject to a law. Hitherto, subject only to your own natural inclinations, if not to your passions, not knowing even of what law there was question, to you I say, is it to be wondered at that you should protest, should wish to enjoy life, to be free, and to be a law

311

unto yourself?

"In this lies the beginning of your hatred and persecution of Me. But I, your Father, love you, and even as I see your blind revolt, My Heart is filled with tenderness for you.

"So the years in which you led this life sped by, and they were, perhaps, many... .

"Today I can no longer restrain My love for you, and the sight of you at war with your best friend compels Me to enlighten you as to Who I am.

"Dearly loved son, I am Jesus, which name signifies Saviour! why else are My hands transfixed with nails which fasten them to a cross? On it, for love of you, I died. My feet are wounded, My Heart wide open, riven by the lance after death... . Thus do I stand before you that you may know Who I am and what My law is. But do not fear - My law is one of love ... and in knowing Me you will find peace and joy. It is sad to live as an orphan: come, My sons, come to your Father.

"Let us stop here, Josefa; we shall continue tomorrow, and do you, meanwhile, love your Father, and live by this love."

At these words Our Lord disappeared, but Josefa, under the impression of the divine presence, remained for some time longer in silent recollection. After which she rose and, handing to the Mothers the notebook in which she had rapidly written Our Lord's words for the whole world, she went back to the active labors of her workroom, no one there so much as suspecting the stupendous happenings of the morning.

But her strength was wearing out. Though sustained by her love, she was no longer able to withstand the overpowering lassitude which took possession of her at times, and which she condemned in herself with characteristic self-reproach as cowardice.

"Have no fear," said Our Lord, when He came to her that evening. "If your weakness is great, My love for you is immense, and My strength will work on this very weakness."

Again He tenderly addressed her on Sunday, June 17th:

"Josefa, if you knew that a sick person was about to die, would you not do your utmost to restore her to health? ... Yet, what is the life of the body when compared to that of the soul? ... And many, so many, will recover their life, thanks to the words I am confiding to you... . Think no more of yourself... ."

He then resumed the subject of the preceding day.

"Let us return to the souls who persecute Me because they do not know Me. I want to tell them Who I am and what they are:

"I am your God and your Father, your Creator and your Saviour. You are My creatures, My sons, bought at the price of My life and Heart's blood, which I shed to free you from slavery and the tyranny of sin.

"You have souls great and immortal, destined for eternal happiness, wills capable of all good, hearts made both to give and receive affection... .

"The thirst for contentment and love can never be appeased by earthly and fleeting gains, which will always leave you hungry and unsatisfied. Perpetual conflict, sadness, anxiety, and affliction will still be your portion.

"If you are poor and have to earn a living by work, the miseries of life will embitter you; you will be hostile to your employers, and may even wish them ill, that like yourselves they may experience the hard grind of daily toil.

"Fatigue, disgust, even despair will weigh heavily on your spirits, for the way is rough and in the end comes death! ...

"O! how great are these calamities when viewed from a human standpoint. But I come to show you life under a different aspect.

"All you who are deprived of this world's goods and obliged to labor for your daily bread under a master, reflect that you are not slaves, but created for the freedom of eternity... .

"All you whose craving for affection is unsatisfied, remember that you were made to love that which is eternal, not that which passes with time.

"You who love your homes and labor to support your families and provide them with comforts and happiness, do not forget that though death will one day sever every tie, this is only for a time... .

"You who serve a master, and owe him respect, love, care for his interests, hard work and fidelity, forget not that he is your master only for the short span of a lifetime. How soon this will pass away and give place to an eternity, where you will no longer be workers but reign as kings forever and ever.

"Your souls, created by a loving Father who bears you a limitless and eternal affection, will find one day in the bliss of Heaven prepared for you a final answer to all your aspirations.

"There, every labor will be rewarded... .

"There, you will find your family for whom you worked so hard on earth.

"There, you will live eternally, for earth is but a passing shadow, Heaven will never pass away.

"There, you will be united to your God and Father... . O! if you but knew how great is the beatitude that awaits you... .

"Perhaps you will answer Me: 'I have no faith, nor do I believe in a future happiness.'

"Have you no faith? Then how is it that you persecute Me? ... Why do you rebel against My laws, and war against those who love Me? ... And since you desire freedom for yourselves, why not grant it to others?

"You say you do not believe in a future life? ... Tell Me, are you perfectly contented here and do you never feel a yearning for that which it is not possible to obtain here below?

"If after seeking for enjoyment, you succeed in obtaining it, does it satisfy your cravings? ...

"If after pursuing riches, you at last possess them, have you ever enough? ... If you feel the need of affection, and one day find it, are you not soon tired of it? ...

"None of these things is what you long for, and here below you will never obtain all that your heart desires. Your craving is peace, not the peace of this world, but that of the children of God; and how do you expect to find it in the midst of rebellion? ...

"That is why I have come to show you where true peace and happiness are to be found, and where you can slake the thirst that for so long has consumed you.

"Do not rebel when I tell you that all these things are to be found in accomplishing My law. Do not fear this word law, for My law is no tyranny but a law of love, because I am your God and your Father.

"Listen while I explain this law to you, and the kind of Heart that imposes it on you; a Heart that you do not know and so often wound. You pursue Me to give Me death, while I seek you out to impart life. Which of us will prevail? And will your souls continue to harden themselves against Me who have laid down My life for you and given you all My love?

"Adieu, Josefa, love this Father who is your Saviour and your God."

Josefa had no difficulties in that direction... . All through her long day's work the thought of the souls who suffer through ignorance, error, or ingratitude, pursued her.

She had gone to rest at length, but had hardly laid her head upon her pillow, when Our Lord stood by her side on that Sunday night. She quickly rose and prostrated herself in adoration at His feet, renewing her vows:

"His wounds," she wrote, "were open and from them issued flames. In one hand He carried the Crown of Thorns and the Nails; with the other He held up His Cross.

" 'Josefa, are you willing to listen to My desires? See My wounds! O! that I could draw in all sinners!

" 'Yes, into these wounds many sinners must be drawn this night... . Take My Cross, My Crown and the Nails ... I go in search of sinners and I shall enlighten them when they are on the point of falling into the bottomless pit, that they may find their way home.

" 'Take My Cross, guard it well... . You know that it is a great treasure.'

"At the same moment," she wrote, "I felt the heavy weight of the Cross on my shoulder.

" 'My Crown,' and He pressed it down upon my head. 'I crown you Myself, and the wounds caused by its thorns will obtain enlightenment for blind souls.'

" 'Take, too, the Nails... . See how I trust you; but then you are My beloved, so I have no fear in confiding them to your care. I know they will be safe.

" 'And now I go in search of souls, for I want them all to know and love Me!'

"And as He uttered these words, His Heart shone with incomparable brilliancy ... and He continued speaking with the same vehemence:

" 'I cannot any longer restrain My love for them ... love so strong must triumph over their callousness. O yes, they must love Me! I want to be their King. Let us draw them all into My wounds... . I go in search of them, and when I have found them I will return and take back My Cross. Suffer for Me, Josefa! ... but wait, before I go, let Me sink the arrow of purifying love into you ... for pure you must be, like all who are My victims.'

"The same flame issued from His Heart as on previous evenings; then I saw only His Sacred Heart, till gradually all faded away."

Long hours of unutterable torment followed; her head, hands and feet, her whole body suffered from the Crown, the Nails and the weight of the Cross.

"The night seemed interminable," wrote Josefa. "I was even under the impression that it had lasted for more than one... .

"Suddenly, He appeared in great radiance. Behind Him, on each side, in the light from His hands, came many souls.

" 'See,' He said, 'all these have followed Me.'

" 'They all recognized Me. Poor, poor, souls! They would have been lost had I not been at hand... . But I was there to cast light on their gloom. Now they will follow Me ... and be faithful sheep in My fold.

" 'And now, give Me back My treasures and rest a while in My Heart... .'

"He took the Cross and the Nails, but left me the Crown of Thorns."

What energy Josefa needed when after such a night she threw herself into her usual work. None knew of the splendors which lighted up her poor cell that night, when she guarded her Master's treasures, whilst He went in search of souls. What grace must have upheld her, so utterly worn out as she was!

Our Lord again sought her out in her cell, on Monday, June 18th, for another, by no means the last of her redemptive ventures. There was once more question of a soul to be saved.

"He appeared as one begging," she wrote. "I cried out, 'Lord, what has happened? Why art Thou like that?' ... I renewed my vows with fervor, and He replied: 'Comfort Me, for I must give up a priest's soul, a soul consecrated to Me!'

" 'O no, that is not possible, dear Lord... . Remember what Thou didst say about sinners ... that Thou lovest them and art ever ready to forgive.'

" 'Look, though, and see the state to which he has reduced My Heart. I am about to leave him to his own efforts.'

"I was so sorely grieved to see His Heart covered with wounds, and above all to think that a poor sinner was to be given up, that I implored Him to be mindful of His mercy and love.

" 'If you can bear the pain," He replied, "that this soul causes Me, I will entrust his soul to you.'

"I answered: 'Gladly, if Thou wilt help me.' And I did my best to console Him. I offered Him all the love He receives in this house, in the whole world, from holy souls, and from priests ... then I kissed the ground many times, and recited the Miserere ... and as I could think of nothing else, I begged of Him to tell me what I could do.

" 'Yes, I will tell you. Spare nothing to comfort Me,' He answered, 'since he spares Me nothing that wounds Me.'

"I went on offering Him whatever I thought might lighten His grief, and little by little He seemed to throw off His extreme sadness.

" 'The obstinacy of a guilty soul wounds My Heart deeply,' He said. 'But the tender affection of one who loves Me not only heals the wound, but turns away the effects of My Father's Justice.'

"Then He vanished, and I endured great pain of body and soul all day."

The succeeding night was one of the worst in Josefa's long experience of making reparation for sinners. When at nightfall Jesus came, as was His wont, to purify her soul, He brought His Crown, His Cross, and the Nails:

" 'I will not only purify you," He said, "but kindle in you the zeal that consumes My Heart.

" 'This night we shall have to suffer again for that priest's soul, for he is flying from Me... . Take My Cross, My Crown and the Nails. Keep united to Me while I go once more in pursuit of him.'

"He left me ... and when a long time after, He returned, He said: 'You are in pain, Josefa, and that soul is still resisting... . I call him ... he despises My love!'

"Then there was silence, and as if to Himself, I heard Him murmur:

" 'It is not so much an actual sin that wounds Me, but his obduracy. If he continues deaf to My appeals, I shall have to leave him to himself.

" 'Rest now, Josefa, while I make yet another appeal.'

"He took away His Cross, but how could I sleep, haunted as I was with the thought of His grief, and of that soul?"

While the next day, Tuesday, June 19th, she was making her thanksgiving, Our Lord showed Himself to her, resplendently beautiful, and said: 'That soul is going to listen to My pleading, and though his mind is not yet quite made up, he is beginning to turn to Me ... You are charged not only with his conversion but with his sanctity... . I want him to realize that no goods here below are comparable to those of eternity... . You must obtain him the grace to embrace all the mortifications of the hard way I want him to tread. Otherwise his peril will be very great. Poor, poor soul, he needs light."

Josefa renewed the offering of herself for this soul so precious to Our Lord's Heart. Emboldened by His kindness, she confided to Him her deepest aspirations. Since He had begun to transmit to her His Message for the world, she had often questioned in prayer if souls, all souls would respond to His appeals as He hoped. And the thought of possible heedlessness was a cruel torment to her loving heart. Jesus, she felt, must not be subjected to such a disappointment.

She had been for some days anxiously trying to find a solution, but had not dared to ask Him about it. Today, however, she could hide this trouble no longer.

Then in a voice of such grave and majestic dignity that she could not find words to express it, Jesus answered her:

"Have no fear, Josefa. You know what happens when a volcano is in eruption? So great is the force of the flowing lava, that it is capable of removing mountains and destroying them. Do men then need to be told that a devastating power has been unloosed? Such will be My words, accompanied by grace; a strength that will conquer even the most obdurate by love. Society becomes perverted, when those in authority do not act according to truth and justice. But if the ruling power knows how to govern, the majority will see and follow the light, though no doubt some will still fail to keep straight... . I tell you once more that grace will accompany My words and those who make them known. Truth will triumph and peace will reign over souls and the world ... and My kingdom will come!"

Josefa was struck by the energy with which Our Lord uttered these words, her doubts were dispelled and her trust greatly reinforced. She knew that His promises would be accomplished, and each day she realized better that nothing would be able to hinder Love's work with all its vast implications. No opposition could finally break the impetus of Divine Mercy, which would soon inundate the whole world... .

A few minutes later Our Lord dictated to her the final paragraphs of His appeal to souls:

"Josefa, do you love Me?" He asked earnestly, when He rejoined her in her cell.

"Lord, this is my only desire."

Then, with ineffable tenderness, He replied:

"I, too, love you, because your lowliness is wholly Mine."

Then: "Write:

"Come; My sons, and hear what your Father asks of you as proof of your love:

"You know that in a well-regulated army discipline must be maintained, just as in a household there must be established customs. So in the great family of Jesus Christ there must be law, albeit a law of love.

"In the order of nature sons are not recognized as such unless they bear their father's name; so My sons bear the name of Christian given them at their birth in Baptism. All ye who bear this name are My sons, and as such have a right to your Father's estate.

"I realize that you do not know Me or love Me, but rather detest and persecute Me. On My part, I love you with an infinite tenderness, and I want you to know this heritage which is yours by right, and know also the means to acquire it:

"Believe in My love and My mercy.

"You have sinned against Me; I forgive you.

"You have persecuted Me; I love you.

"You have wounded Me both by word and deed; still I wish to do you good and to let you share all My treasures.

"Do not imagine that I am ignorant of your state of soul. I know that you have despised my grace, perhaps even profaned My Sacraments. Yet you have from Me a full pardon.

"If then you would be happy in this world and at the same time secure your eternal salvation, do as I tell you:

"If you are poor, do the work that necessity forces on you with submission, and remember that I, too, lived for thirty years in subjection to the self-same law, for I was needy and poor.

"Do not consider your masters as tyrants. Banish all hatred from your hearts... . Never wish them ill, but further their interests and be faithful to them.

"If, however, you possess this world's goods and employ workers and servants, be fair to them in all your dealings; pay them a just wage, and show them both gentleness and kindness. If you have an immortal soul, so too have they, and if you abound in wealth, it is not for your sole comfort and enjoyment, but that you may administer it wisely and practice charity to your neighbor. Both employer and employed must accept the law of labor with submission, acknowledging a Supreme Being over all created things, who is both your God and your Father.

"As God, He demands of you the accomplishment of His divine law.

"As your Father, He asks you to accept His commandments in a spirit of filial piety.

"Thus, when you have spent a week in the pursuit of work, business or sport, He claims but one half-hour, that you may fulfill your Sunday duty. Is this excessive?

"Go then to your Father's House, where day and night He awaits your coming, and as Sundays and Holy Days recur, give Him the homage of this half hour by assisting at the Mystery of Love and Mercy, that is, Holy Mass.

"Tell Him about everything: about your families, your children, your business, your desires... . Lay at His feet your sorrows, difficulties and sufferings ... believe in the interest and love with which He listens to your prayer.

"You may perhaps say to Me: 'I have not entered a church for so many years that I have forgotten how to hear Mass.' Do not be afraid on that account... . Come, spend this half-hour with Me; your conscience will tell you what to do, and be docile to its voice... . Open your soul wide to grace, and it will inspire you... . Gradually it will teach you how to act in a given circumstance, how to treat with your family, what to do in regard to your business ... how to bring up your children, love those who depend on you, and honor those in authority over you... . It may make you feel that such and such a concern must be given up, such a friendship relinquished, or such a meeting avoided... . Again, it may tell you that you are hating a certain person quite unreasonably; or it may put it into your mind to sever your connection with some person you feel drawn to and whose advice is doing you harm. Only give grace a chance, and gradually its power will grow stronger in you, for just as evil increases insensibly, once it is given in to, so will each new grace prepare your soul for a still greater one. If today you listen to My voice and let grace act, tomorrow its influence will be stronger and so steadily increase as time goes on; light will grow in your soul, peace envelop you, and the reward will be eternal bliss.

"Man was not created to live forever here below. He was made for eternity... . If then he is immortal, he should live, not for the passing things of time, but for that which will never die.

"Youth, wealth, wisdom, human glory, all that is nothing, it will all end with this life; God only will endure forever.

"The world is full of hate, races are in perpetual conflict with one another, so are nations, and even individuals, and all this is due to the decay of faith. Only let faith reign once more over the world and peace and charity will return to it.

"Faith in no way impedes civilization and progress. The more it is rooted in individuals and peoples, the more wisdom and learning increase, for God is infinite in wisdom and knowledge. But whenever faith is completely lacking, peace, civilization and true progress likewise vanish ... for God is not in war ... and in their place come enmities, clash of opinions, class wars, and within man himself, rebellion of passions against duty. All that is noble in humanity is exchanged for revolt, insubordination and warfare... .

"Let yourselves be convinced by faith and you will be great. Let yourselves be ruled by faith, and you will be free; live by faith, and you will escape eternal death."

Such were the last words of Christ's Message to the world.

Then He looked down at Josefa and said: "Adieu. You know that I expect reparation and love from you all. Love is proved by deeds, so let all your works prove your love. Be messengers of love in things great and small. Do all for love. Live by love."

He vanished.

Anniversary of First Vows (June 20th-July 16th, 1923)

"Tell Me once more your joy in being My bride."
(Our Lord to Josefa, July 16th, 1923)

The parting from Our Lord was to last a long while, and the devil who for a space had been restrained, was once more granted freedom. He was beginning to gauge how stupendous was the divine plan which was to shatter his kingdom of darkness. His hatred broke out in the vain hope of countering it, and God allowed this to deepen still more the nothingness of His instrument.

On June 20th, Josefa avowed humbly that she had yielded to the repugnance for the extraordinary in her life, which sometimes seemed invincible ... Her Lord no longer visited her ... His absence reawakened in her soul the clear realization that she could not now withdraw herself from His divine Will, to which she so completely surrendered herself.

In spite of these momentary weaknesses which she so sincerely deplored she took back nothing of her surrender. Her Master knew this well, and though He allowed her to be tempted by her enemy, He nevertheless defended and hid her in the very depths of His Heart.

But the knowledge of this, and so the consolation, was hidden from her, and while the fiend as of old haunted her path, she struggled and fought in utter desolation.

So the month of June, which had opened so luminously for her, faded away in the dark of a cheerless night.

But with the first days of July it seemed to her that on the distant horizon a dim light was beginning to glimmer, for July 16th was the anniversary of her First Vows.

She concentrated, therefore, all her efforts on preparing this renewal of the total donation she had made of herself, and brought to it all the trust, courage and generosity she could muster. How it must have touched and glorified the Heart of her Master who knew that no tribulation or distress could diminish her oblation.

On July 13th, after a night of terrible ordeal, she suddenly found herself in the presence of her Lord ... and hardly dared to believe the evidence of her senses.

"Fear not. Come, Josefa... ."

And as she hesitated: "If you dare not come to Me, then I will go to you... . You cannot possibly measure My love for you ... and however great is the number of your frailties, far greater are the mercies of My Heart."

Did she not know it? ... All doubt and diffidence vanished. "O! how loving and kind He is," she wrote. "I begged Him to forgive me, to save sinners and not to allow me to hinder His great work."

This is ever her first preoccupation, even in the midst of temptation and suffering.

"You are more than forgiven, Josefa, and none of the graces I have prepared for sinners will be lost ... they will not remain hidden, and I shall pour them out over the world. Do not, however, refuse Me anything. Leave Me free to train you and use all necessary means, even the most drastic, to destroy ['self' in] you. Do and say all I tell you, and never fear. I loved you before this trial, and I still love you. My love never changes."

Such words imparted a divine fortitude to Josefa. Let the devil assault her again ... his rage would always break on the rock of her faith in love. He suggested too that he would somehow prevent the coming of the Bishop of the Diocese, and "stop," as he said, "that important advance" in Our Lord's work. But this did not shake her trust.

On Saturday, July 15th, eve of Josefa's renovation, Our Lady herself came during Mass to preside at her vigil of recollection. It was nearly a month since last she had seen that Blessed Mother, and her joy can be imagined. Her first impulse as always was to tell her how weak she felt. She would like to promise, so much ... for her desire to be faithful to the work of Jesus was utterly sincere and deep. But what could be expected of her? ... especially when He asked her to transmit messages and declare His wishes? ...

" 'Do not be afraid, my child,' Our Lady said in tender pity. 'He will never ask anything of you without giving you grace. Then try to overcome your repugnance by remembering that all His commissions are given you because of His goodness and love for souls.'

"I told her then of the horror that the sights and sounds of Hell inspire in me."

Then gently, with a mother's love, Our Blessed Lady explained the meaning of these mysterious happenings and the part they played in her Son's work of love.

" 'You must not be afraid,' she told me, 'for every time Jesus allows you to endure those torments He means you to draw from them a three-fold fruit: First: Great love and deep gratitude to the Divine Majesty who in spite of your faults prevents you from falling eternally into Hell. Secondly: Boundless generosity and ardent zeal for the salvation of souls, with the desire of saving many for Him by your sacrifices and even your tiniest acts, for you know how much these please Him. Thirdly: The sight of such innumerable crowds of souls lost forever ... of souls, of which not one can so much as make an act of love, ought to make you who can love, send up unceasingly to Him echoes of love's clamor to drown the blasphemous vociferations of that impious abode.

" 'Therefore, great generosity for the salvation of souls, daughter, and much love... . Let my Son use you as He wills... . Let Him finish His work.'

"She blessed me, I kissed her hand, and she disappeared."

It was certainly in a spirit of generosity and love that Josefa spent her day of retreat. "I took my resolutions," she wrote, "and God helping, I will be faithful to them unto death."

Henceforth this anticipation of death was clear. She mentioned it explicitly in the little notebook in which at every stage of her life she wrote her resolutions and desires.

On July 15th, 1923:

"Eve of the first anniversary of my Vows:

"I am the miserable creature that it has pleased Jesus to use for His work of love. It matters not at all how much it costs me, I owe Him entire submission.... If He tells me to write, I will write, if to speak, I will speak, and so with all the rest.... O my Jesus, what sorrow that I have responded so badly to Thy love.

"But I mean to do better, and with Thy grace I will try to live the few months that remain to me without allowing myself to be troubled or refuse Thee anything whatsoever. I will say anything Thou willest at once, even if it is to His Lordship the Bishop, and I will do everything Thou askest of me. That is my first resolution. The second is to obey my Mothers in everything, especially when it is to write, which always costs me so much. The third is to make immediate avowal of my temptations1 and the devil's threats, for these often begin by quite small things, and when I keep them to myself, they end by worrying me. The fourth is to make many acts of humility and loving service, because I know this is pleasing to Thee.

"Thou wilt see, O my Jesus, how hard I am going to try to be faithful till death ... four or five months will soon pass ... and I hope Thou wilt take me to Heaven for Christmas, or at latest for the Epiphany.I am glad to die, for this world is a very sad one and I am afraid of my weakness. In Heaven, I will still save souls for Thee and help them. That is why I ask today with all my heart, that during these few months I may repair for all the failings of my life, and as I am so little, and Thou art my Beloved, I take Thy Heart and Thy merits and plunge everything I do in them, so that they may acquire a value so great that, while repairing my own sins, they may likewise save many souls.

"Adieu, my Jesus; ask whatever Thou wilt of me, and hide me in Thy Heart until Thou takest me to Heaven. Do not forget my littleness and please never forsake me who am

"Your helpless little bride,

"JOSEFA."

Sunday, July 16th, dawned on her humble and fervent hopes:

"I repeated the formula of my vows before Communion, just as I did a year ago," she wrote, "with the firm determination of being faithful until death. A moment afterwards, Jesus stood by me and showing me His burning Heart:

"Josefa,' He said, 'and I? ... I have never ceased being faithful to you, have I?

" 'Have no fear about your wretchedness and misery, your carelessness or even your faults... . I Myself will supply for all. My Heart is the repairer par excellence. How, then, could it not be so for you?'"

Then Josefa repeated to Him her loving promises, and begged Him, in spite of her weakness, to complete His great work for the salvation of the world.

"Even if I did not do so for love of you, Josefa, I would do it for souls, for I love them. Nothing, indeed, is wanting to My heavenly beatitude, which is infinite, but I yearn for souls ... I thirst for them, and want to save them."

Long ago, Jesus had endowed Josefa with something of His own love for souls but every day it seemed to grow stronger. "I asked Him that there might be many saints among His consecrated souls, and in the world as well ... many souls to console and glorify Him. How I wish that I were better, so as to obtain this grace."

" 'Do not worry, Josefa, about what you can and what you cannot do. You know very well that you can do nothing. But I am He who can and will do all. Yes, I will do all, even what seems to you impossible. Only let Me make use of you to transmit My words and hopes to souls. I will see to the rest, and supply for all that you lack or cannot do. I ask you only for your liberty.'"

Then bending towards her: "Tell Me once again your joy in being My bride!"

How could she express her happiness? ... She could find no adequate words.

Our Lord continued: "Still, all that is nothing, you have not yet tasted true happiness. But you shall do so soon ... and then you will possess it without fear of ever losing it. Meanwhile, let us go on with our secrets!"

The prospect of the Bishop's visit remained in spite of all a grave anxiety for Josefa. She entreated her Master to help her and to explain exactly what she had to say, for she could not overcome her fear.

"I will tell you all that you have to do," Our Lord answered patiently. "Do not be frightened. I will tell you all and help you in it all. Let Me work."

"Then," she wrote, "I told Him of the resolutions I had taken yesterday in my monthly retreat. He listened attentively, and had a little comment to make on each. Then He added: 'I bless these resolutions, Josefa, and if at times you are too weak to carry them out, come to Me... . Tell Me what troubles you ... and what you fear ... and I will give you strength, I will give you peace. Go now, remain in My love and abandon yourself to My Will.'"

Thus ended a radiant day for Josefa, in the peace and joy of belonging wholly to Him.

"I am so happy," she wrote. "I have now but one desire, to refuse nothing to Him during the few remaining months of my life. But I never cease entreating Him for His strength and His love, for I am afraid of myself."

Yet another grace awaited Josefa that evening; she wrote:

"I had gone at about seven o'clock to the oratory of our Holy Mother, when suddenly I saw her there, simple and humble as ever. I had hardly time to renew my vows, when she said to me: 'So, my child, it is already a year since you made them!'"

Josefa, whose trust in this best of Mothers was unbounded, poured out her joy at belonging to Our Lord forever, but also told her of her sorrow for what she termed her "ingratitude."

"But, my child, surely you know that His Heart is a blazing furnace, and its fire exists only to consume our miseries. As soon as you have owned them to Jesus, He remembers them no more. And if, in exchange, He has already granted you so many graces, He is prepared to grant you others greater still. His Heart is an inexhaustible Fountain: the more He gives, the more He desires to give. The more He forgives, the more He wants to pardon."

As Josefa told her of her promises of fidelity until death, death which she knew was near, our Holy Mother encouraged her:

" 'Believe me, child, Jesus has forgiven and forgotten all your failings and all your strivings against His Will, but He never forgets your good resolutions and He takes pleasure in them. His Heart is an abyss of mercy, and it will never fail you. It is, too, an abyss of riches which will never diminish, however largely distributed. Love Him as much as you can. He cares for nothing else. Acknowledge your littleness, and be submissive and ready to surrender to His Will in all things.

" 'Let Him rest in you and do you rest in Him. When you receive His graces, then you repose in Him; when He tries you in one way or another, then He reposes in you.

" 'Thank Him with your whole heart for the singular favor He has done you in choosing you to be the bride of His Heart; and while you recognize how unworthy you are to belong to Him, love the Society of His Heart which is so particularly His own choice... .

" 'Adieu. Be generous, be humble. Do not forget your nothingness. Only mercy like His could so love you in spite of it. But trust Him always, and as you of yourself can do nothing let yourself be guided, and live full of gratitude, peace and love. Adieu, my child.'

"She gave me her blessing, I kissed her hand, and she was gone."

Would Our Blessed Lady allow the anniversary to pass by unnoticed? Josefa's hopes ran high, but it was already night, and the last bell had rung. Alone in her cell, as she knelt before the statue of her Immaculate Mother into whose virginal hands she committed the keeping of her soul, suddenly she was surrounded with a luminous radiance; it was Mary herself who appeared to her child.

"I am always with you," she said.

And in response to the prayer Josefa had just made:

"Yes, daughter, you will be faithful to the end, if you never rely on yourself, but only on Jesus. He will be your strength and will help you ... and so shall I... ."

Josefa never could keep any of her most secret thoughts from this incomparable Mother, and she poured out her heart to her, entreating her not to abandon her in face of the devil's wiles and the long and terrible trials of Hell, the very remembrance of which filled her with apprehension and anxiety.

" 'Do not forget what your Holy Mother Foundress said to you,' answered Our Lady. 'When you suffer, it is Jesus who reposes in you, so what is there to fear? Abandon yourself to His Will. You cannot imagine now what your joy will be for all eternity in Heaven, when you see the many souls saved by your little acts and sacrifices. Life is of no account, and yours will pass like a flash! Use every moment of it to merit, by giving your Heavenly Bridegroom the glory of complete surrender to His good pleasure. Live in His peace and love, and above all leave Him free to use you.'

"She stretched out her hand to bless me and vanished."

Trials (July 16th-August 24th, 1923)

"Have no fear, all is arranged and controlled by My love."
(Our Lord to Josefa, August 30th, 1923)

We rarely find in Josefa's life long hours of radiant happiness which were not the forerunners of pain, and though Our Lord's own privileged one was never free from suffering at any time, yet there were moments of greater trial bringing with them greater love.

As Josefa's death drew near, the law of God's dealings with her could be seen more clearly. She must fulfill in herself that which was wanting to the Passion of Christ. Victim she must be in every sense of the word, and the Message she was to pass on to the world, must be given no otherwise than through her pain and anguish.

The devil remained to the very end the scourge that belabored her. No human opposition or persecution, however severe, could have equaled his in intensity, or as surely reached the very depths of her being which it was God's intention to sanctify by suffering.

So we must not be surprised at the somber days about to break upon her, for they were part of a design of love, quite as much as the ecstatic joys of the months of May and June had been. They call for our admiration of God's secret ways of dealing with souls which, though hidden from themselves, lead through darkest night to brilliant dawn.

So it was with Josefa from the close of the month of July 1923. The anniversary of her First Vows, when Our Blessed Lady's hand had rested in blessing on her head, had scarcely gone, when the devil suddenly once more crossed her path. He had never left her in peace for any length of time, but at this stage, like the saintly Curé d'Ars, she constantly saw him under the guise of a huge black dog, of hideous and furious appearance, which attacked her, without however succeeding in overthrowing her. At the same time, long sojourns in Hell occupied the major part of her nights, and there her mind was racked with acute distress by all she saw and heard.... . As if it depended on his efforts to wreck God's designs, Satan vaunted with insolent effrontery his counter-plans to prevent the intervention of the Bishop of Poitiers, which he presumed all important. Josefa, who had formerly shown herself vulnerable enough to his lying boasts, never flinched this time, and as she had promised Our Lord, she sought and obtained the courage she needed, by humbly admitting her frailty.

The last days of July, however, brought her some alleviation and an assurance, doubly welcome, that God's great work was progressing, and that she herself was safely in His keeping. On Friday, July 27th, St. John the Evangelist appeared to her while she was praying before the Blessed Sacrament:

"Majestic beauty enveloped him," she wrote. "I renewed my vows, and he said: 'Soul whom Jesus loves, as the Lord intends you to make His mercy and His love known to many souls, prepare the way for His coming.

" 'May you be docile and entirely submissive to His holy Will. May the flame of His Heart purify and consume you. And when He deigns to visit you, receive His words with all reverence and love, for He who speaks to you is none other than He before whom the whole heavenly court forever sings a canticle of praise and love.'

"Then, joining his hands: 'May the Lord guard you and fill your soul with the heavenly delights of His Heart.'

"He disappeared," said Josefa, "and a minute later I saw the Heart of Jesus alone... . Its wound opened wide and emitted a flame which fell upon my own heart, as it used to when He came every evening to consume my sins... . This fire is a scorching flame and it fills me with such longing for Him that the whole world appears to me to be but dust and ashes."

Two days later Our Lady came, in the evening of July 29th, to bring her the glad tidings of the speedy return of Our Lord. She held the Crown of Thorns in her hand, and placing it on Josefa's forehead said:

"Daughter, I bring you the jewels of your Beloved, so as to adorn you myself for His coming... . As soon as you have finished your adoration, go up to your cell. He will be there. Meanwhile prepare for His coming by acts of humility, surrender and love."

And as if sensing her child's apprehension at what new sacrifices would be required of her:

"Adieu," she said as she blessed her. "He will help you, for it is His own work. Trust Him and be of good courage ... and remember: submission, humility, love and surrender."

Josefa had no doubts about the importance of a meeting prepared with such unusual solemnity. A few minutes later, Our Lord appeared. She fell on her knees in adoring love, and offered herself unreservedly to His sovereign Will.

"Yes, Josefa," He said, "it is I; have no fear, for I have disposed all things, and they are ruled by love."

In the impressive silence Josefa wrote, while Jesus dictated all that she was to say and do to make the Bishop of Poitiers acquainted with His Will. Every contingency was foreseen and provided for; nothing was left to chance, so that it might be clear - clearer even than in any of the incidents that had preceded it, that here grace was at work.

As He ended, Jesus reiterated: "Have no fear, I will help you, I will guide you. Love and trust My Heart, for I will never abandon you."

On Monday, July 30th, at the request of Fr. Boyer O.P., Josefa's director, the Bishop granted him what proved to be a most friendly interview, and received the first personal message from Our Lord's Sacred Heart.

The last graces and the last trials that Josefa was to undergo henceforth had his most valuable and reassuring support. So notable a step forward was followed, as was only to be expected, by a recrudescence of diabolic fury and persecution.

Did the devil think he could hinder the plans of the Almighty? Reading Josefa's notes from July 30th to August 12th, one almost fancies it might be so, for the assaults of the devil increased both in number and intensity ... his beatings, his lying affirmations ... his apparent assurance that he was about to triumph, not only over Josefa and the Bishop, but in thwarting the very plans of God.

Thus it was that, tossed by storms, she resolutely kept loyally on her way, doing her share of Love's great work. "You are not alone," Our Lord said to her on Sunday, August 12th, "for I am your life, your support, and without Me you never could bear such a weight of tribulation. Surely you know this!"

The next day, August 13th, He again appeared to tell her in detail all He wished transmitted to the Bishop.

We are led to conjecture, from the words of Our Lord, the detailed directions He gave His messenger, and the care with which this first interview was prepared, how great were the results He expected for the realization of His plans. At the same time His gentle kindness reassured Josefa, who still feared the prospect, not only of issuing from her carefully guarded obscurity to discuss the things that were the very soul of her soul with a stranger, but also of giving so grave a message from her Master to the Bishop. She felt such a trial to be beyond her strength, and greater than any that had hitherto been asked of her generosity, unless Our Lord gave her an exceptional grace of strength and of peace.

"Do not fear," He said before leaving her that morning. "Love will always lead and bear you up. I will tell you what to say and I will help you... . There is nothing to fear; I am sheltering you in the depths of My Heart. I love you; surely that will give you courage!"

The feast of the Assumption of Our Blessed Lady, August 15th, 1923, brought another short interval of radiant happiness to Josefa, for towards evening on that glorious day Our Lady appeared in all her beauty. With motherly love, she listened to Josefa's troubles, to her fears for the future on account of her frailty and weakness.

"Daughter," she replied, "do not be discouraged by your weakness, acknowledge it in all humility, but always with confidence, because you know well that Jesus made choice of you for the very reason of your misery and worthlessness ... so be humble, but also very trustful."

And alluding to the devil's increasing persecutions: "Do not be afraid, for he can only do one thing, that is, give you opportunities of increasing your merit. Do you not know that I am watching over you and that Jesus will never abandon you?"

So Josefa threw off the burden of her personal preoccupations to rejoice in the bliss of her Heavenly Mother, of whom the whole world was celebrating the Assumption into Heaven.

A thrill of joy transfused the face of Our Lady, as she recalled the beatitude of the eternal present she now possessed.

" 'Today,' she said, 'in very truth, there began for me a beatitude which was perfect and unalloyed, for during the whole of my life in this world my soul was transpierced by a sword of grief.'

" 'I asked her,' wrote Josefa naively, 'if the presence of the Child Jesus, so small and so lovely, had not been the best of consolations?'

" 'Listen, child,' Our Lady went on. 'From childhood I knew of divine things and the hopes centered in the coming of the Messiah. So when the Angel declared the mystery of the Incarnation to me, and I found myself chosen as the Mother of the Redeemer of mankind, though my heart adhered to the Divine Will with entire submission, it was drowned in a sea of bitterness and woe. For I knew all that this tender and heavenly Child was destined to endure, and Simeon's prophecy only confirmed the anguish of my mother's heart.

" 'Can you, then, imagine how I felt while contemplating my Son's charms, His heavenly countenance, His hands and feet which I knew were to be so cruelly ill-treated?

" 'I kissed those little hands, and felt my lips already stained with the Precious Blood that one day would gush from their wounds.

" 'I kissed His feet, and already saw them nailed to the Cross.

" 'And as I carefully tended His hair, I pictured it all clotted with blood and entangled in the cruel thorns.

" 'And when at Nazareth, He first ventured on a few steps, hastening with outstretched arms to meet me, my tears fell as I pictured them extended on the Cross on which He was to die.

" 'When He reached boyhood, He was so divinely beautiful that none could contemplate Him unmoved ... yet in my heart, the heart of a mother, the sword was turned at the thought of the tortures that were to be inflicted on Him, of which I felt beforehand the savage recoil.

" 'Then He left me for three years during His apostolic life, and there followed the terrible hours of His Passion and death. What a martyrdom!

" 'When after three days I saw Him in the glory of His risen life the trial changed, for I knew that He could suffer no more ... but O! how sad it was to part from Him! My sole relief then lay in consoling Him, by repairing for the sins of men. And my long exile began... . How I sighed for the hour of everlasting union... . What was life without Him? ... How dim was my light! ... How ardent my desires! ... How long, long, He was in coming!

" 'I was about to enter my seventy-third year, when my soul passed like a flash from earth to Heaven. At the end of three days the Angels fetched my body and brought it in triumph and jubilation to reunite it to my soul... . What adoration! ... What admiration! ... What sweetness, when at long last my eyes beheld in glory His Majesty surrounded by the angelic choirs ... my Son ... my God!

" 'And how, daughter, can I express the amazement of my lowliness when I was crowned with such gifts and overwhelmed with jubilations and rejoicings? ... Sorrow had indeed passed away, never to return... . For all eternity, glory, sweetness and love were mine.'"

Our Lady spoke with enthusiasm, Josefa remarked later, yet all her words still mirrored sweetest humility.

There was silence for a short time, for Our Lady seemed absorbed by the recollection of that marvelous entry into Heaven. Then once more turning to Josefa, and looking lovingly upon her, she said: "All things pass away, daughter, and bliss is everlasting. Suffer and love. My Son will soon crown your efforts and labors. Do not fear, He and I both love you!"

Then, after giving her a few motherly counsels, Our Lady said as she left: "Be faithful to Him and refuse Him nothing. Pave the way for His coming by the little acts He so loves, for He will come soon. Courage, courage, generosity and love... . Life's winter is short, and its springtide eternal."

Josefa noted down that she could not recall Our Lady's exact words.

"On Friday, August 17th," she wrote, "when I went to my cell to try to write it all out, Our Lady herself came, radiant and lovely, and smiling gently, repeated all she had said on the evening of her feast. Then, after allowing me to kiss her hand, she blessed me and disappeared."

A few more days of peace were granted her till Monday, August 20th. Josefa was making her prayer on "Jesus is the Light of the world" -

"When suddenly I saw before me a great wooden cross all in light. In the center was the glowing Heart of Jesus, wounded and surrounded with a thorny crown. A vivid flame issued from the wound, and I heard a voice which said: 'Lo! the Heart that gives life to the world ... but from the Cross. So must the victims whom I have chosen to aid Me spread this life and light over the world allow themselves to be nailed to the Cross in utter surrender, after the example of their Master and Saviour.'"

To the very end, therefore, the Cross was to be her light and safety. Josefa knew it and she made the offering required. That evening Our Blessed Lady came to encourage and strengthen her in her generous resolve.

Josefa had gone to the oratory of the Novitiate, and was kneeling before the statue of Our Lady, when she appeared:

"Yes, Josefa, give me your heart and I will guard it; give me all your activities and I will transform them; give me your love, your life ... and I will pass them on to Jesus for you."

Drawing near, she blessed her, saying: "With all a Mother's love, I bless you. May this blessing give you courage and generosity to accomplish to the full all that Jesus expects of you. What is there to fear, my child, if your trust is in Him? You know well that He is Almighty ... that He is Good ... that He is all Love!"

Josefa did know it, but her soul shrank from her mission in spite of herself. She had, however, centered great hopes on the retreat which was about to open. This she told Our Lady, entreating her help, for she knew that it was the opening phase of the last days of her life.

Our Lady answered: "If you want your soul to profit fully by the retreat, prepare for it by often repeating the prayer that my son St. Ignatius used to say so fervently... . 'Take, O Lord, and receive all my liberty, my memory, my understanding and my will... .' Offer everything to Jesus that He may make use of you according to His good pleasure. Make many little acts of humility, of mortification, and generosity... . That is how you can make your soul ready to receive the graces Our Lord destines for you during these days. Do not forget that these are the last Spiritual Exercises of your life, so let Jesus work and prepare you as He pleases for the union which will be eternal."

Then reminding her of the secret of generous self-surrender: "And as you love souls, think of them, and let yourself be ground to powder, as their salvation may demand."

These last words made Josefa pensive. And as Our Lady looked long and lovingly at her, she felt that some new sacrifice was about to be asked of her.

"Bear in mind, daughter, how unworthy you are of the graces God bestows on you. Yet thank Him that He has chosen you in your worthlessness and nothingness to be the means of saving many souls, by manifesting to them the greatness of His mercy."

Then in a tone of maternal authority, she disclosed to Josefa what the immediate future held in store for her: she was to go to Rome, in order to carry a secret, personal message to the Mother General.

Josefa was struck with consternation. The meeting with the Bishop had already filled her with fear which it had taken all her fortitude to overcome... . Was she then to be brought still further into the open out of her hitherto well-guarded obscurity and silence? ... It involved a journey abroad ... and worse than all was the prospect of having to make known herself things that she found hard to tell even the Mothers at Les Feuillants.

For the moment Josefa was seized with panic, but Our Lady kept her long at her feet, and little by little calmed the storm that had swept over her soul. Her inmost will all along adhered to God's Will, and a powerful grace enabled her finally to triumph over her reluctance, and accept blindly all that Love's great work could demand of her.

Our Lady concluded with these parting words:

"Have no fear. Jesus who loves you so specially will Himself tell you His wishes ... and all will be carried out easily, simply and humbly.... . It is a very great grace for all of you, my dear daughter, to be God's instrument in this great work."

Our Lady had gone. "How shall this be done?" Josefa did not even ask the question.... . Our Lord who was Himself training her in abandonment had now caused her to make a giant stride. She handed over Our Lord's project to her Superiors and until the moment of departure never so much as asked a question about it. As on the day of her first arrival, so now, but with how much deeper significance, her motto remained: "God is leading me."

On Friday, August 24th, during her thanksgiving, Our Lord confirmed this offering which only love could warrant: "Tell Me, Josefa, all you would say if you did not see Me. For though you love listening to Me, I, too, rejoice and am pleased to listen to you."

"Then," she wrote, "I told Him how I longed to love Him, to be faithful and never refuse Him anything. But He knows better than anyone what a weakling I am.... . He was gazing at me all the time with such a look of affection that this beautiful and kind gaze filled me with trust."

" 'Give Me that proof of your love, Josefa,' He said, 'for love makes all things easy. Do as you see My Heart does; for having created souls out of love, I want to save them by love. Let them in their turn show Me their love. And if I so ardently long for the love of every soul ... how much more do I yearn for that of those consecrated to Me by vow.... . Love can only be paid in the same coin, so love Me in return! And show it by your acts.'

" 'My acts, Lord! How wretched and small they are! ... '

" 'Never mind, give Me your misery and I will enrich it ... and for every sacrifice you offer Me, I will pay you back with the love of My Heart.'"

But heavenly barter is of a different kind from this earth's exchanges. Josefa had experienced this and would make further discoveries in the near future. Her faith, however, would recognize, under the ever-deepening shadow of the Cross, the return of love, infinitely strong and yet tender, of the Heart of Jesus.

Before the journey to Rome took place another painful phase had to be gone through which, in God's own way, prepared her for the graces that awaited her.

A Suffering Retreat (August 25th-October 2nd, 1923)

"My work is wrought in the dark, but when it sees the light, all will wonder at its every detail."
(Our Lord to Josefa, August 30th, 1923)

There were still nine days to wait before Josefa entered on her much-longed-for retreat ... the last of her life ... they were nine days of deepening cloud, on which no glimmer of light shone. "I cannot find words in which to say how I suffered till August 29th, on which day the retreat began," she wrote.

The days of agony which she had just gone through so depressed her spirit that she hardly felt equal to any new effort. In her private notes we read:

"O Jesus, hast Thou forsaken me? ... Do look at me... . Yet I love Thee... . Yes, I love Thee more than all the world... . I long to do all Thou requirest of me, but I am unsettled ... full of doubts as to how I shall act next... . I place my trust in Thee, I surrender myself to Thee... . I know Thou wilt support and forgive me. I am sure of Thy love for me."

Again we read a little later:

"Thou alone, O my Jesus, knowest the anguish of my soul ... This cross seems too heavy ... more than I can bear... . Lord, come to my assistance ... raise me up ... give me light.

"On that same evening of August 29th," she wrote, "Jesus came for an instant. I saw His Heart and once more understood that His love for me is immeasurable. His very glance told me. I threw myself at His feet and there unburthened my heart into His.

" 'What does it all matter?' He said. 'I am rich, powerful, loving and faithful. How often have I not told you that it is your utter misery and frailty that attracts My love. Believe what I say ... and remain in peace... . Use this retreat to respond with great love to the graces with which I have loaded you. Every day you will say the Miserere five times and add a Pater, to honor My Five Wounds... . Hide in these Wounds ... let them ever be your shelter. Be humble and do not fear. I am your support and life, and I will always defend you.'

"Ah!" she wrote, "such words would make a saint of anybody except me ... and my soul is cold as stone ... O God! how I suffer... . Thou alone knowest and yet I yearn to love Thee... . Do not let me be separated from Thee!"

Jesus could not resist such appeals and on the morning of Thursday, August 30th, suddenly she was herself again. "Behold me at Thy feet, Lord, just as I am, miserable, sinful, ungrateful and worthy only of the deepest contempt; but I see Thee as Thou art - all mercy, love and kindness."

Jesus loved to hear such protestations, and He was attracted, too, by such humble trust in Him.

"Suddenly He appeared before me," she wrote, "so beautiful and so kind!

" 'Do not fear. Do you not know that My Heart has only one desire: to consume your wretchedness and to consume you yourself... . I know you, and love you ... and I shall never grow tired of you.'

"The nearer I get to Him," she went on to say, "the more I grieve at not knowing how to love Him; I can only beg His forgiveness."

" 'You know very well,' He answered, 'that I am ready to forgive you, not once, but every time that, through frailty, you fall. If you are feeble, I am strong; if you are misery itself, I am consuming fire. Draw near with trust and let me purify your soul.'

" 'And now, take My Crown as proof of My love and forgiveness. Follow the guidance that is given you, be very humble and faithful. I am leading you ... and My action is ruling you.'

"I gave humble thanks and asked Him never to allow me to become a hindrance to Love's work."

Jesus then encouraged her with words which only He could say: "Fear nothing. My work is wrought in the dark, but when it sees the light, all will wonder at its every detail."

The peace brought to Josefa through Our Lord's intervention proved to be no more than a breathing-space. With her characteristic simplicity, she threw herself into the meditations of the first days of the Retreat, and noted down her reflections:

"I made the meditation on death," she wrote on September 1st, "and was filled with awe, on reflecting how near it is for me, but I took courage and was even consoled to think that I should be taking that definite step in four or five months' time. Why should I fear it? True, I have no merits of my own, but those of Jesus are mine... . I must count on Him who is all power and all mercy. Yes, how good He is ... how merciful, and He is my Spouse. If I live in Him, I shall die in Him, and then there will be no fear of ever losing Him. O come, divine and eternal union! Even while I call for it, I feel no desire ... my nature is full of fears ... and my heart may betray me... . O God, Thou knowest this heart of mine, and how it loves and gets attached ... but no, I leave all in Thy hands... . Thou alone, my Jesus ... Thy Heart alone... ."

It was in very truth the moment to lean on Him alone, for that Saturday, September 1st, brought notification from His Lordship the Bishop that, in response to the communication he had received, he would call at the Convent on the following day, and would be pleased to have a few minutes' interview with Sister Josefa.

The visit was well timed, for owing to the whole household being in retreat, the desired incognito and silence would be assured.

Our Lord Himself was directing all things through human happenings, and for the time being the powers of darkness themselves, subject to His divine Will, were held in abeyance. "You are in My hands, so have no fear," Jesus said to Josefa during Holy Hour. "Act simply. I shall be with you, and will tell you all you have to say."

"Today, September 2nd," she wrote, after the Bishop's visit, "I spoke for the first time to His Lordship. I was, at first, rather intimidated, but after a while I acted just as I would had it been Our Lord, and my peace of mind was very great. I told him how repugnant that path was to me, how I was tempted to escape from it, of my weakness in resisting, and then of the distress that takes hold of me when I see how weak I am in keeping my resolutions. His Lordship spoke so kindly that his words strengthened and comforted me very much."

Josefa added nothing more about the interview which was to have such an effect on the work of Love. She had faithfully followed the directions of her Master, she had given the Bishop the message intended for himself alone, and which had remained secret. She told him of Our Lord's plans for the world, then answering all his questions very simply, she poured out her whole soul to him who stood to her as the very paternity of God Himself.

That same day her Superior wrote the following letter to the Mother General in Rome:

"This morning's interview was simple and consoling. His Lordship came alone and said Mass in the oratory of Saint Stanislaus for the community in retreat. The Polish novices sang very nicely,1 and he then addressed a few words to them all, truly a great grace. We then followed point by point the line of conduct drawn up by Our Lord so clearly and with such love. How faithful His Heart has been to us! His Lordship in a most fatherly and kind way - Father Boyer had prepared him for what was to come - saw Josefa privately for about forty minutes... . After the interview he kindly told us how moved he had been by the artless candor of the child who had talked to him without the slightest pose, in her picturesque French, but as one full of God. He took away with him the words personally addressed to him on June 11th and 12th, and asked us to pray very much, telling us that he intended to enter fully into God's plans. He will certainly return before November... . But what reassur ance and peace this first visit has left to us!"

Once again Our Lord's words had been literally fulfilled. "I will do all," He had said.

Josefa was to see the Bishop again several times. Mgr. Durfort had become and remained a sure support to her to the end of her life. He read all her notes and was good enough to interrogate and encourage her.

From his hands she received the last anointing, and he presided when she made her final vows of Religious Profession. More than that, he spoke with her and blessed her several times in those last hours before her death, and when her offering had been consummated, it was he who performed

336

the last rites over her body.

But for the moment, her divine Master seemed jealous of her humility and her complete obscurity. These few hours of respite were meant only to tide over a grave and important step, and already on the third day of the retreat, Monday, September 3rd, dark night once more enveloped Josefa's soul. Dryness, abandonment, desolation, temptations to despair ... nothing was spared her ... and it was in this state of suffering that she continued to follow the Spiritual Exercises... . Her little notebook has but one more record, a cry of anguish: "Sixth day: I have lost my Jesus... . How have I made this retreat? ... God knows!"

Yes, surely, He knew, and it was through such sufferings that Love's work was accomplished, and His victim's whole-burnt offering consummated. By His permission she descended to the very depths of human destitution of spirit ... He crushed her under the weight of divine severity. He made her realize most vividly her approaching death, the emptiness of her life, the overwhelming responsibility of the graces which she had received, and all the while He reduced her to complete helplessness, and brimmed her chalice with an insatiable thirst of love for Him.

Josefa could not express this distress, to which was added the complete wearing out of her physical powers.

"On Friday, September 14th," she wrote, "I saw Father Boyer and he helped me to regain confidence, although I am suffering much because I cannot love Jesus as I long to. But I am at peace, for I expect nothing of myself, but everything from His merits and mercy."

The infinitely compassionate Heart of Jesus who had all along sustained and upheld her, though unfelt and unknown by her, suddenly appeared to her on the morning of September 18th.

"During my thanksgiving," she wrote that Tuesday, "I was adoring and loving Him by the Heart of His Mother, since I myself can do nothing, when suddenly I saw Him in His beauty, His Heart aflame. With incomparable sweetness He said to me: 'Come, Josefa - draw near this furnace of love. Bring to It all your miseries that they may be consumed in Its fires.'

"I asked Him to have pity on me, for every day I grow more unworthy, not only of His graces, but of His pardon and of His mercy.

" 'Why fear? The more miseries I find in you, the more love you will find in Me.'

"Then I told Him all my longings ... and my sins, too, that He may forgive them.

" 'I know your wretchedness, Josefa,' He said, 'and I take on Myself to make reparation for it; you on your part, make reparation for souls.'"

So convinced was she of her unworthiness and nothingness that it came as a surprise to her to find that He still counted on her cooperation. "Have I not told you that I have taken charge of everything? I will make reparation for you, and you for souls."

After He had revivified her confidence, and once again directed her eyes towards the vast horizon of souls, He told her that He had a new mission to entrust to her:

"Listen attentively," He said. "I have several things to tell you for the Bishop and for your Mother General... . No doubt you are unworthy to be the messenger of My words, but I use you because of My love for souls.

"Meanwhile," He added, "you know what I like best ... many little acts of humility. Let Love choose them, and you, be generous."

On two more occasions - Friday, September 21st and 28th - the obscurity of her path was enlightened by the radiance of her Lord's presence. He came to make her write under His direction the Message reserved for the Society of the Sacred Heart, which she was to hand over to the Very Reverend Mother General. "I want you to tell her yourself," He insisted.

These were grave happenings, and Josefa fully realized their importance. They so far surpassed, in the greatness of their design, both her thoughts and even her fears and forebodings, that her own nothingness as an instrument was more than a palpable reality to her. Complete surrender in the blindness of faith was all that she could contribute, and this consummation, so desired by her Master, she seemed now to have reached.

"Let yourself be led blindfolded," He said to her on September 18th. "My eyes are wide open to lead you, and am I not your Father?"

The Mother House - Divine Pledges (October 2nd - 26th 1923)

"Just as the sun shines with greater splendor after a dark day, so after such intense suffering shall My work appear in all its brightness."
(Our Lord to Josefa, October 14th, 1923)

Josefa was about to leave Les Feuillants for the second time, but now for a more distant destination.

Since the day when Our Lady had intimated that it was Our Lord's will that she should personally convey a message concerning the great work of Love to the Mother General in Rome, and Jesus Himself had confirmed it (August 20th, 1923), much correspondence with the Mother-House and a great deal of anxious prayer had prepared for the realization of Our Lord's wish.

For a considerable time the Mother General had wanted to meet and speak with this distant little member of the Society. From Rome she had followed Josefa's history, controlling with maternal solicitude and enlightened prudence her guidance and direction, and now guided as are God's friends, by the supernatural wisdom He imparts, she was on the look-out for any providential sign that would favor the project of a short stay for her at the Mother-House.

A retreat for Superiors was about to open at the Via Nomentana, and a large number of Reverend Mothers from Europe had been invited to take part in it, that the spirit of unity and fervor might receive fresh impetus. This seemed the providential sign. Josefa would accompany her Superior to Rome to help with the extra household work at the Mother-House. The journey was therefore decided upon and the day of departure fixed.

Such changes of house, while looked upon as a matter of course in the Society of the Sacred Heart and unhesitatingly made, are nevertheless keenly felt offerings. Josefa's heart was too closely conformed to the Heart of Jesus not to be sensitively alive to anything in the way of partings from all she loved ... her Mothers, her Sisters, the cell of Our Mother Foundress, the chapel, the very cloisters ... all scenes of signal graces. She quite believed that this time her departure was for good, and one of the Mothers whom she had helped for the last two years wrote after Josefa had gone:

"I met her in the little Auxiliary Chapel which she loved so much and to which she was paying a parting visit. There on the threshold where we had so often met in prayer, we made a pact together to remain united in His Heart. 'What shall we ask for each other?' I said. She was silent, and I proposed 'that Jesus should be able to carry out His designs on our souls perfectly.' 'Oh, yes,' she answered at once. 'His Will - everything is in that. We must leave Him perfectly free in us.' And she went on: 'However great the suffering of each day, the grace of the day will never be wanting.' By the expression of her face, I guessed that a very intense suffering was at the moment God's Will for her, as well as the proof of her love for Him.

"As she was leaving, she said to me: 'I am so happy to be able to make Our Lord the sacrifice of this house. It cost me to leave Spain, now it costs to leave France, the home of my soul and the cradle of my religious life. But it is God's Will.'"

On Tuesday, October 2nd, at midday Josefa and her Superior left for Rome.

Jesus was to make Himself their Companion on this first stage of the route. No sooner had the train started, than in recollected silence, though the carriage was very full, Josefa was deep in prayer. So many conflicting emotions filled her heart that they could only be stilled in silent contact with the inward Guest. No need for her to strive to find Him; her heart went straight to the inner solitude that no outward commotion could interrupt, and soon she was absorbed in the presence that was everything to her.

Suddenly, Jesus appeared. Which of the travelers in that crowded carriage would have guessed what the closed eyes of the humble little Sister beheld?

"Look at My Heart," He said, and from the wound there issued fiery sparks. "Souls do not know how to come to this Heart and to find the graces I wish to pour out on them. There are so many who will not let themselves be drawn by the loadstone of My love. That is why I need My chosen souls. They must spread these magnetic sparks the whole world over. You cannot think, Josefa, how much glory your faith, your trust and submission have given Me. I bless you, and will make use of you to pour My graces and My love on the world."

Jesus disappeared ... but towards evening, a little before they arrived in Paris, He returned once more, and reassured her about His plans for this particular stage of her life's journey. "I want to save the world," He said, "and use you, poor and miserable creature, by passing on to you My desires, that many souls may know of My mercy and love through you."

And to her reiterated query about what she was to say and do "over there," for that "over there" was a formidable unknown to her mind -

"Do not be afraid," He said. "I will tell you Myself... . I am leading you... . You will speak fearlessly, Josefa, for this is the means by which My desires will begin to be realized."

Later He again insisted on this, and repeated: "Do not fear, though My footsteps seem at times made on sand so that they leave no trace... . It is not really so. You, on your part, have only to be docile and not to worry about anything nor about what people may say or think of you. I am taking full charge and I know what conduces to the good of My work."

Greatly comforted, Josefa was encouraged to tell Our Lord of yet other things that moved and troubled her:

"If you had no faith, I should understand your fears," answered Our Lord, "but if you believe in Me, why be anxious? Remember these words: 'I work in darkness, yet I am Light.' I have warned you more than once that the day will come when everything will seem lost, and My great work brought to nothing. But today I tell you 'The light will return, stronger than ever!'"

These predictions surely pointed to some happenings in Rome, affecting not only herself but the precious enterprise of which she carried the secret in her heart. No doubt she must suffer much, but she must also trust Him absolutely.

What could this clearly predicted suffering be? ... There was no hint of it when at about midday they reached the Eternal City on October 5th, a First Friday of the month.

Many Superiors were already there, and as the day went on, there were fresh arrivals. In this happy gathering nobody noticed the little Spanish Sister who had come to help with the housework. She quietly slipped into the shade she so coveted and loved, and very soon she had blended with the Italian Sisters, and found her way about the big Mother-House.

At once she felt at home and her soul was filled with happiness and a deep sense of security. She loved all the Mothers so much ... and her first interview with her Mother General was proof enough that, as Our Lord had told her, He was paving the way for her.

The kindness of her reception filled her with gratitude and confusion. Already she looked forward to spending herself in helping everywhere in the house so soon to become a Cenacle of prayer. She met several of the Spanish Mothers she had known and other religious with whom it gave her great pleasure to talk in her own tongue, and thus to make contact once more with her beloved Spain. This she had not expected, and no shadow came to darken this deep happiness so well known in religious houses, and prized all the more because so rarely granted.

Josefa delighted in her new-found joy. It seemed to her that for once all clouds had been swept from her sky, dispersed by the warm Southern sun, and that she herself was nothing more than a happy little Sister of the Society she so loved.

But God's ways are not our ways. Soon He reminded His messenger that it was not for her personal enjoyment that she was there, but to help Him in Love's great work.

On Saturday, October 6th, He told her where to meet Him, because, He explained, she must write down His wishes for the Mother General.

Faithful always, she reassumed the heavy burden of the divine demands so contrary to her attractions, and while the Mother-House on the eve of the opening of the Retreat was filling with joyful new arrivals, she was busy writing the Message which Jesus entrusted to her. The secrets that these pages contained cannot be published; they remain the cherished inheritance of the Society of the Sacred Heart. But brought thus suddenly back to her mission, Josefa's fears were re-awakened, and there arose in her soul a flood of nameless terror.

Our Lord appeared to her again during her thanksgiving the next day, Sunday, October 7th, and, as once to the Disciples of Emmaus, He asked her: "Why are you sad?"

"Lord," she answered, "I feel sad to find myself in this path of extraordinary happenings, in which sometimes I fear I may be lost forever."

"Do you not realize, Josefa, that I never leave you alone? My one desire is to reveal to souls the love, the mercy, and the pardon of My Heart, and I have chosen you to do it for Me, wretched as you undoubtedly are. But do not be anxious, I love you, and your misery is the very reason of My love. I want you for Myself, and because you are so miserable I have worked miracles to guard you carefully.... Yes, I love all souls, but with very special affection those who are the most weak and little."

Then very gravely Jesus continued:

"I have loved and watched over you, Josefa. I still love and watch over you, and will love and watch over you to the very end. Hide Me in your heart lovingly, for I hold you in Mine, tenderly and mercifully."

A few minutes later, during the nine o'clock Mass, Jesus deigned once more to manifest Himself. Nothing betrayed the divine presence. Josefa was kneeling among the Sisters, she renewed her vows and adored Him of whom her heart could only say "He was so beautiful." She heard these words: "I am looking for love from My beloved ones, and I come to tell them that what I yearn for, what I implore them to give Me, is love, nothing but love! As for you, Josefa, be very faithful and obedient; gradually I will make all known to you, and soon I shall take you to eternal beatitude. Then My words will be read, and My love known."

That Sunday afternoon Jesus returned, as He had said He would, to continue the dictation of His Message.

How profound was the silence, here as at Poitiers, that surrounded these marvels of Divine Love.

When He had gone, Josefa went humbly and simply back to her household duties, handing over to the prudent care of her Superiors the secrets of which she knew herself to be only the frail and profitless intermediary. Several times she herself took to the Mother General the papers on which she had transcribed the Master's plans. These visits, necessarily kept secret, filled Josefa with confusion. She was reserved and respectful as always, but this did not prevent her from expressing in her own tactful and self-forgetting manner the loving and childlike feelings that filled her grateful heart. Yet Our Lord kept her soul in a lowly and painful awareness of her nothingness. It had all along been His way with her; and what human opposition or humiliation could equal the depths of annihilation to which God can reduce His creature, when it so pleases Him? ... Josefa acquiesced wholly, allowing herself to be destroyed by that all-powerful and ever growing possession.

She wrote on Monday, October 8th:

"I told Our Lord during my thanksgiving how my soul trembles at the thought of His judgments, now that I see myself on the brink of death and my life laid bare before Him... .

"He came quite suddenly and looked at me long and sweetly, with immense tenderness... ."

Josefa loved to dwell on Our Lord's look, which of itself gave her such peace. How many souls, when they read of that divine glance of Jesus, will feel faith in His tenderness revivified, for it penetrates, purifies, calms and strengthens. The eyes of Jesus will surely rest on them too; none who believe can doubt this.

When He had, as it were, read Josefa through and through, He said:

"All that is true, if you merely look at what you have done. But, Josefa, I shall Myself introduce you to the citizens of Heaven. I am preparing the robe I destine for you. It is woven of the precious flax of My merits and dyed in the purple of My blood. My lips will seal your soul with the kiss of peace and love. So do not fear, I will not forsake you till I have led you where your soul will rest in everlasting Light."

Josefa's simple comment was: "Jesus has taken away all my fear of death."

As this history has already shown many times, such hours of bliss usually presaged a coming storm, and Josefa was about to face the worst that had ever befallen her.

That same morning, when helping the other Sisters in the laundry, she felt the first symptoms of an attack that nothing hitherto had led her to foresee. She had a slight hemorrhage from the lungs, which she tried to make nothing of, but her pallor revealed that some accident had occurred.

The doctor who was consulted was not alarmed. But after careful examination, he asked her age. She was thirty-three. He expressed his astonishment, saying: "She is worn out." It would have needed less than the mystery of her daily and nightly dolorous persecutions to explain her loss of strength. But this could not be revealed, and steps were taken to afford her some extra rest during the days that followed, though she did not completely give up her work or common life. When one of the Assistants General kindly inquired how she was, she answered naively: "As I am going to die, I must have something the matter."

However this physical lassitude was as nothing to the trial that awaited her. The arch-fiend made his appearance unexpectedly on that same October 8th. With specious cunning he succeeded in deceiving Josefa. He appeared with the features of Our Lord, and tried to alter His plan.

But the very excess of this infernal craft made clear who he really was, for this was not the first time he had attempted to pose as an angel of light. Seeing himself unmasked, he changed aspect, threatened, blasphemed, and finally vanished in a whirl of smoke, leaving Josefa in a terrified and confused uncertainty.

She wrote afterwards: "I am so full of genuine doubts, that I believe that I have all along been the sport of the devil, and feel convinced that everything I have seen and written is his doing, and now I can only implore Our Lord to enlighten my Superiors, that they too may see the truth."

On the following day, Tuesday, October 9th, she continued in the same strain: "The same awful anxiety and sorrow ... the thought that all those things have never been Our Lord's doing, but the devil's, is causing me the most terrible distress! The only grace I implore is that my Superiors may see the truth as I now do."

A gleam of peace and truth lighted up her overwhelming tribulations. Our Lady came in response to her agonized supplications. Josefa, however, was so unbalanced for the moment that she did not believe that she really saw her. After listening to the renewal of her vows and repeating with her the Divine Praises, Our Lady reassured her:

"Daughter, it really is myself, the Mother of God, the Mother of Jesus, who is Purity and eternal Light itself... . It is your Mother who speaks to you and who has come to calm your troubled soul. Be not afraid, Jesus will defend you and will so order events that the craft of the enemy will always be unmasked, every time he tries to deceive you. If you are in doubt, say bravely: 'Begone, Satan; I will have nothing to do with you who are delusion and falsehood. I belong to Jesus who is Truth and Life.' Fear nothing; the Heart of Jesus guides and loves you all, always. I too love you, Josefa, and I bless you ... be at peace."

These words comforted her for the time being. But the hour of darkness had come. Satan so powerfully deluded her, that she was convinced that she had been deceived for the last three years. Evidence to the contrary only increased her anxiety, for it added the further certainty that unknowingly she had deceived all those who had helped her up to this time.

So poignant was her distress, that never before had she experienced the like. God alone can gauge the sharp suffering of a soul that has, so to speak, lost its footing, and knows not where to turn for support... . But He alone also can gauge the value of a faith and abandonment that have reached the heights of heroism; Josefa had but tried to be faithful to the truth. Her detachment from the path which she had hitherto believed to be God's own, the humility with which in the midst of darkest night she faced and accepted the consequences of what she termed her 'mental aberrations' ... the piteous fidelity and sorrowful peace that anchored her, in spite of everything, to God's Will, the giving up of herself to that mysterious chain of events, of which she could not now see even a trace, the simplicity of an obedience which hoped and looked for no other security than the word of Superiors: are not all these authentic signs of the Spirit of God?

While the devil was using the power granted him, and while his efforts seemed to be triumphing over Love's great work, the watchful eyes that guarded Josefa were able to discern in the storm the luminous action of Jesus who, in Josefa herself, was giving indubitable proofs of His presence and His plans. Jesus had said "I work in the dark, yet I am Light." Never before had these words seemed so true.

As for Josefa, judging herself to be beneath compassion and worthy only of contempt, she humbly went on with her work, in spite of the fatigue that was wearing her out. The devil never stopped hurling his false accusations at her, but she relaxed neither her faith nor her energy.

God did not allow the assurances given by her Superiors to allay her moral anguish, He Himself seemed to have abandoned her, and her prayer which was rather a cry of distress remained unheard. A long week passed, and not a ray of light pierced through the gloom. Josefa bore her cross in silence, and not for an instant betrayed her intense suffering. But there were moments when her features were quite altered, and she felt the trial to be beyond her strength. In vain the kindness of the Mother General endeavored to distract her and bring some alleviation to her tribulation by sending her to visit Mater Admirabilis, the miraculous Madonna of the Trinita, and again allowing her to take part in one of the public audiences of H. H. Pope Pius XI, who blessed her and gave her his hand to kiss. Her faith was strengthened by this grace and as a true daughter of the Church she appreciated the favor, and from it drew strength to go on bearing her cross, which was not, however, for an instant less heavy on her exhausted shoulders.

He whose wisdom disposes all things knew at what moment He would intervene.

On Sunday, October 14th, during her thanksgiving, Josefa suddenly found herself in the presence of the Master who stilled the storm and calmed the winds and the sea. She hesitated, feared, and tried to doubt and repulse far from her the vision she believed to be false.

"Fear not."

It was the strong sweet voice of Jesus, a challenge to all Satan's craft. And as, after renewing her vows, she persisted in her refusal and energetically protested with her whole will against the trickery:

"Fear not," reiterated her Master. "I am Jesus, I am the Spouse to whom you are united by those vows of Poverty, Chastity and Obedience which you have just renewed. I am the God of Peace!"

These words brought with them such conviction and security that all hesitation was at an end. "Without my willing it," she wrote, "so great a light came to my understanding, that I felt convinced that it was indeed He... ."

A few hours later, the devil tried, but in vain, to persuade her that she was mistaken. But at the time of her adoration that evening:

"He," she said, "whom I took to be Jesus came back. I asked Him to assert with me that He was indeed the Son of the Immaculate Virgin. Then with peace radiant on His countenance as in His voice, He said: 'Yes, Josefa, I am the Son of the Immaculate Virgin, the Second Person of the most Holy Trinity, Jesus, the Son of God and God Himself. I clothed Myself

345

with human nature that I might give My blood and My life for souls. I love them, Josefa, and I love you... . Now I am searching for them to manifest My love and mercy to them, and for this reason I abased Myself and came down to you. Fear nothing, for My power protects you.'"

Then with sovereign authority came the words: "No, you are not mistaken."

The thick mist that had enveloped Josefa was torn asunder at these words and Jesus continued: "Tell your Mothers that I want you to write. And just as the sun shines with greater splendor after a dark day, so after such intense suffering shall My work appear in all its brightness."

Peace now succeeded to the storm, though gradually, as to a tempest-tossed sea which has been lashed to its very depths.

On Monday, October 15th, as she was passing the oratory of Saint Madeleine Sophie she heard herself called by a well-known voice. Fearful still, she tried to run away, but her Mother Foundress drew her to trust and peace.

"I am your Mother, Josefa," she said to her, and to reassure her completely, she added: "I want to tell you only that all during my life I sought nothing but the glory of the Divine Heart. And now that I live in Him and by Him, my only desire is to see His Kingdom come. That is why I pray that for many souls this little Society may be a means by which He may be known and loved ever more and more.

"... Fear nothing. For if the devil tries to harm it, it is because the Heart of Jesus loves it with such a special love. But Our Divine Master will not allow it to fall a victim to the snares of the enemy.

"Go now, child, to your work; I bless you."

That evening in the silence of the retreat which had been going on while Josefa had been the victim of such terrible happenings, Our Lord came to continue giving the Message which had been so painfully interrupted.

"Do not imagine that I am going to speak to you of anything but My Cross. By it I saved the world; by it I will bring the world back to the truths of the Faith and to the Way of Love... .

"I will manifest My Will to you: I saved the world from the Cross, that is to say through suffering. You know that sin is an infinite offense and needs infinite reparation ... that is why I ask you to offer up your sufferings and labors in union with the infinite merits of My Heart. You know that My Heart is yours. Take It, therefore, and repair by It... . Instill love and trust into the souls that come in contact with you. Bathe them in love - bathe them in confidence in the goodness and mercy of My Heart. Whenever you can speak of Me and make Me known, tell them always not to fear, for I am a God of Love.

"I recommend three practices very specially to you:

"First: The practice of the Holy Hour, because it is one of the ways by

346

which an infinite reparation can be offered up to God the Father, through the mediation of Jesus Christ His Divine Son.

"Second: The devotion of the five Paters in honor of My Wounds, since through them the world was saved.

"Third: Constant union, or rather daily offering of the merits of My Heart, because by so doing you will give to all your actions an infinite value.

"Unceasingly use My life, My blood, My Heart ... confide constantly and without any fear in this Heart: this secret is known to few; I want you to know it and to profit by it."

Then after a few definite requests addressed to the Society1 Our Lord added: "Rest in My peace. I love you, I guide you, I defend you, so never have any doubts of My loving kindness."

After the storm, peace had come to Josefa who, ignoring herself as usual, had little idea of how greatly the work of Love had progressed during the tempest through which she had passed. The Mother General, who had been a close observer of the confusion of mind into which her child had been thrown, had been able to gauge the depth of Josefa's virtue, and the sincerity of her detachment. The supernatural and spiritual had never been more evident or authentic than in those awful hours when drowned in anguish, she had accepted in peace and complete abandonment the apparent destruction of the work of Love, which she had believed in, and for which she had sacrificed her life and surrendered her whole being.

The visit to Rome was about to end; Our Lord had carried out His plan in full. There followed a few more happy days filled with graces, and on Friday, October 19th, Saint Madeleine Sophie, speaking to Josefa of the work which was nearing completion, reminded her child of the function of the Cross in it:

"Have no fear," she said, "for the Sacred Heart has always Himself directed and guided this little Society, though it is not always easy to recognize His action. Faith is much wanting in the world, and Jesus looks to His religious to repair this lack by their acts of trust. You must not be afraid or worried when light is not granted you, Jesus will give it to you when you need it, and will do everything to bring about the full accomplishment of His wishes. Your part is to obey and surrender your will to His. True, there are moments when all is dark; the Cross rises stark before us and prevents our seeing Jesus Himself. But then it is that He says to us: 'Fear not, it is I.' Yes, indeed it is His very self and He will guide and finish the work He has begun. Have no fear, be faithful and remain in peace."

The feast of Mater Admirabilis, one very dear to the Society of the Sacred Heart, fell on Saturday, October 20th. It was not to pass without the Mother of God coming to reassure Josefa. "I am your Mother, the Mother of Jesus and the Mother of Mercy," she said, so making Josefa sure of her identity.

At once Josefa told her all her troubles, for she still could not completely dominate them.

"Let bygones be bygones, my daughter. Let Jesus gather glory from your littleness and misery, it is thus that His power and mercy shine forth the more... . Do you not see how His Fatherly hand has led and guarded you here? Have no fear, He will continue helping you to the end. Be very simple, for you will have no other glory in Heaven than your simplicity. Little children have no acquired merits, and so it is with you. You are the beloved of His Heart without having done anything to merit it. He it is who does everything in you, who pardons you, who loves you."

The following day, Sunday, October 21st, whilst she was at prayer, Jesus showed her His Heart all ablaze and said to her:

"Behold this Heart! It is the Open Book wherein you must meditate. It will teach you all virtues, especially zeal for My glory and for the salvation of souls.

"Gaze well and long on this Heart. It is the Sanctuary of the miserable, hence yours, for who is more miserable than you? Look deep down into My Heart. It is the Crucible in which the most defiled are purified, and afterwards inflamed with love. Come, draw near this Furnace, cast your miseries and sins into it; have confidence and believe in Me who am your Saviour. Once more fix your eyes attentively on My Heart. It is a Fountain of Living Water. Throw yourself into its depths and appease your thirst. I desire, I long that all may come and find refreshment at this source. As for you, I have found a hidden place for you in the depths of My Heart ... you are so lowly that you could not attain to It alone. Use well the graces I have there stored for you... . Let My love have free play in you, and always remain little."

That same evening, Saint Madeleine Sophie appeared to Josefa, and her motherly counsels ended on this note: "May Jesus be loved and glorified in a special way by all the souls that are in the Society of His Heart!"

"I asked her to bless me," wrote Josefa, "since she is my Mother. This was the last time I saw her in Rome. The following days were full of peace and true joy, and on Wednesday, the 24th, we left Rome and reached Poitiers on the 26th."

Last Days at Poitiers: Purification (October 26th-November 30th, 1923)

"Hitherto My Cross has rested on you. My Will now is that you should rest on it."
(Our Lord to Josefa, October 27th, 1923)

Genoa ... Paris ... Poitiers! The rapid if uneventful journey home ended on October 26th, at five o'clock in the evening, when the travelers found the expectant Community waiting to welcome them. As in the preceding June, after the first burst of joyous inquiries and the questions at recreations about all that had happened in Rome, Josefa sank into the shadow, and silence deepened around her. It was thus that Jesus had all along been pleased to veil His familiar intercourse with her, and so to the end He would hide His last messages, as well as the sufferings and trials which would complete His work.

The last stage was to be a short one, and Josefa knew it. The exhaustion which was wearing out her whole being was sufficient warning of her approaching end. Side by side with it was the strong call of love, detaching and irresistible in its appeal.

On Saturday, October 27th, after a restful night, she wrote her thanks to the Mother General. It was a very simple, unstudied and spontaneous little letter, which we quote, for in it was revealed her fresh and naïve soul, which knew nothing of striving for effect.

"Very Reverend Mother,

"I write to you today with great joy to thank you for all the kindness you have shown me.

"May Jesus repay you for it all.... . I have been asking this of Him with my whole heart, and to you, Very Reverend Mother, I promise to do my utmost to be very faithful during the four or five months of life that remain to me. I will do and say whatever Jesus tells me, and will try to be a little more humble. I think that is what costs me most ... that is why I promise it in all sincerity, and it will be by such efforts that I shall try to repair a little for my past life.

"For the moment, I am in great peace and very happy, although I have not seen either Jesus or Our Lady or our Holy Mother again.

"I am glad to be back at Poitiers, but I shall never forget the days spent at the Mother-House, and the maternal affection I found there. I shall not forget you in my prayers either, and when I get to Heaven I will try to scatter many 'regalitos' (little gifts) on the Mothers whom I love so much, and to obtain for them little joys in those things they need.

"Bless me, Very Reverend Mother, I remain always

"Your little and humble child in the Heart of Jesus,

"JOSEFA MENÉNDEZ."

Our Lord did not long delay His return, He seemed in haste to tell her His plans for the last days of her life. On the evening of October 27th, she wrote:

"He came all beautiful, with His Crown of Thorns in His hand. I was delighted, for I had not seen Him since I left Rome, So I told Him all that fills my heart, and He answered so tenderly. 'Why, Josefa, do you suppose that I do not know that you are here again? ... It was I that brought you back!'"

"Now do not be afraid," He continued, as He read in her soul's depths the ever-present fear of Satan's snares. "It really is I Myself, Jesus, the Son of the Immaculate Virgin, your Saviour and Beloved."

Then with grave kindness, He added: "Hitherto, My Cross has rested on you. My Will now is that you should rest on it. You know that the Cross is the patrimony of My chosen souls."

It was impossible for Josefa not to surrender to a love that solicited her suffering so graciously. At once she offered herself, and looking longingly at the Crown, she ventured to beg Him to leave it in her keeping.

"Yes," was His reply, "today My Crown of Thorns, and soon My Crown of Glory... . Leave it all to Me... . Let Me work in you and through you for souls. I love you ... love Me."

The work of love, mysterious and divine, was about to receive its consummation.

The next day, October 28th, Josefa resumed her ordinary occupations. As was her custom, she went toward nightfall to make the Stations of the Cross in the little Auxiliary Chapel she so loved, and of which she had again been given the charge, to her extreme satisfaction.

"After I had finished the Stations," she wrote, "I recited the five Our Fathers in honor of His wounds. I had hardly begun the first when He appeared. He stretched out His right hand, then His left, and as I recited the five Paters, a ray of light shone from each of His wounds. I renewed my vows, and at the end He said to me: 'I am Jesus, Josefa, the Son of the Immaculate Virgin. Behold the wounds that were opened on the Cross to redeem the world from eternal death and give it life! They obtain forgiveness and mercy for so many who incense the Father, and they, henceforth, will bestow on them light, strength and love.'

"Then, pointing to His wounded Heart: 'This wound is the fiery furnace to which chosen souls, especially the brides of My Heart, must come to enkindle theirs. This wound is theirs; It belongs to them with all the graces it contains, that they may distribute them to the world, to the many souls who do not know where to seek them, and to so many others who despise them.'

"Then," wrote Josefa, "I asked Him to teach these souls how to make Him known and loved.

" 'I will give them all the light they need, that they may know how to utilize their treasure, and not only to make Me known and loved, but also to repair the outrages with which sinners overwhelm Me. Alas! The world offends Me, but it will be saved by the reparation of My chosen souls.

" 'Farewell, Josefa. Love, for love is reparation and reparation is love.'"

The following days were to be a response to this appeal.

On the first day of the week Josefa had returned to her work-room where everyone welcomed her with joy. Much needlework had been done during October, for a large increase in the school necessitated a great deal of industry to finish the uniforms for all. It gave her great pleasure to see how her Sisters had worked, and above all she was delighted to think that her death would not cause much inconvenience, now that she was so ably replaced by those she had trained. She felt that they must gradually take over all responsibility in the workroom; and though she continued to spend long hours at her needle, for the most part she mended and darned, leaving the initiative and management to the young nun who was her substitute, just guiding her by an encouraging look when occasion demanded it.

This effacement, which so entirely detached her from the employment she had loved, was in itself precious to her soul. Though her attraction for it never changed, she became if possible more kindly and helpful and her smile more radiant, in spite of her exhaustion.

In the midst of these last efforts, the secret chiseling by which Our Lord conformed her to His Passion and Cross was continued. November had hardly begun than the devil once more tried the same wiles that had caused her such agony in Rome. He appeared to her under the lineaments of Our Lord and allowed her to renew her vows, but when asked to repeat the Divine Praises and the words that Jesus so exultingly gloried in saying: "I am Jesus, the Son of the Immaculate Virgin... ." "Say it yourself; that will do," was the answer he gave her. In vain he tried to simulate the words Jesus used, but Josefa repulsed him with indignation. But her soul was troubled by this and by the thought of her approaching death, and day after day went by in painful anguish of spirit.

"And so," she wrote, "from October 28th to November 13th I did not see Our Lord again."

On the feast of Saint Stanislaus, Patron of the Novices, light once more shone on her troubled path.

"This morning after Communion," she wrote, "Jesus came. He was beautiful, in His wounds were shining flames, and before I could say a single word He said: 'Do not fear; I am Jesus, the Son of the Immaculate Virgin.'"

Then He gently repeated the Divine Praises with her, and in order to reassure her fully, He said: "Yes, I am Love, I am the Son of the Immaculate Virgin, I am the Bridegroom of virgin souls, the Strength of the feeble, the Light of souls, their Life, their Reward and their End. My Blood cleanses all their sins; I make reparation for them, I am their Redeemer."

Josefa was fully reassured by such kindness, and told Jesus of all the sufferings of the last days, especially of her lassitude, which made work impossible and gave her a presentiment that her end was near.

"But Josefa," was His tender reply, "do you not long to possess Me and enjoy Me without end? ... I, on My part, long for you! I glory in those who do My Will always and in all things, and for that reason I chose you. Leave Me free to do with you what I know will be both for My glory and for your good. The winter of this life is about to end... . I am your Beatitude!"

Then Jesus arranged to give her the second message which she was soon to pass on to the Bishop of Poitiers. A little later He rejoined Josefa in her cell. He began by dictating His message for the Bishop; after which He spoke for a wider following:

"I desire that My love should be the sun to enlighten, and the heat to reanimate souls. That is why My words must reach them. I want all the world to recognize in Me a God of mercy and of love. I wish that everywhere My desire to forgive and save souls should be read, and that not even the most wretched be kept back by fear ... nor the most guilty fly from Me... . Let them all come. I await them with open arms like the most affectionate of fathers in order to impart life and true happiness to them.

"That the world may know My clemency, I need apostles who will reveal My Heart ... but first these must know It themselves ...

otherwise how can they teach others?

"So for the next few days, I will speak for My priests, My religious and My nuns, that all may clearly understand what I require: I want them to form a league of love in order to teach and publish the love and mercy of My Heart to all men, even to the extremities of the world. I want the need and desire for reparation to be re-awakened and grow among faithful and chosen souls, for the world is full of sin ... and at this present moment nations are arousing the wrath of God. But He desires His reign to be one of love, hence this appeal to chosen souls, especially those of this nationality. He asks them to repair, to obtain pardon, and above all to draw down grace on this country which was the first to know My Heart and spread devotion to It.

"I want the world to be saved ... peace and union to prevail everywhere. It is My Will to reign, and reign I shall, through reparation made by chosen souls, and through a new realization by all men of My kindness, My mercy and My love.

"My words will be light and life for an incalculable number of souls. They will all be printed, read, and preached, and I will grant very special grace, that by them souls may be enlightened and transformed."

Her Master had spoken with such ardor and force that Josefa was greatly struck. Now He was silent, and she adored the Divine Will which in affirming its plans removed her last fears.

"I begged Him to forgive my still doubting," she wrote, "though He better than any understands the snares of the evil one... . With the utmost kindness, He answered me: 'Do you suppose that I would give you over to be the sport of that cruel enemy? I love you and I will never let you be deceived. You must not fear, but trust Me who am Love.'"

Such messages could hardly be bought but at a high price ... and this price was first to be paid by their messenger through intense suffering. She was fully aware of it, and day by day her oblation deepened.

Since the beginning of November, Josefa's physical sufferings by day and principally by night had been destroying her, while intolerable pains, the cause of which could not be ascertained, increased in severity every Friday.

She was forced to spend November 9th stretched on a bed of pain; she was practically unable to stir, her head, chest and limbs worn out by excruciating agonies... . A renewal of the hemorrhage seemed to bring her to death's door, and the doctors in consultation were not able to diagnose the cause. On Thursday, the 15th, towards eight in the evening, she had a most painful attack which seemed to presage death. It was renewed during the night, but when the morning of the 16th dawned Our Lord was brought to her in Holy Communion, and He appeared to her during her thanksgiving. These were moments of bliss and they gave Josefa strength to continue her ascent of Calvary.

"Have no anxiety," He said to her. "I am your Life and your Strength. I am your All, and I will not forsake you."

Then He reminded her of the visit of the Bishop which was to take place in the near future:

"As to yourself, remain in My hands, for I want to speak to My chosen ones. Leave Me entirely free. Thus shall I glorify Myself."

This liberty was expressed chiefly in the gift of suffering. Three times that same Friday: at nine, at midday, and again between three and four, Jesus meant to associate her closely with the suffering of His Passion. As soon as she recovered a little she would rise and with incredible energy make an effort to resume her work. Thus it was that from day to day Josefa offered up to Him who was immolating her the sacrifice of a life which was going forward to its consummation.

On Tuesday, November 21st, Feast of Our Lady's Presentation, she publicly renewed her vows with all the other young Sisters. She had prepared herself for this feast of oblation with a love that suffering had but stirred into a flame. She knew it was the last time that her voice would be heard in the Chapel renewing the vows that bound her to the Heart of

Jesus and to the work of love.

During her thanksgiving Jesus appeared and said to her: "I, too, Josefa, renew the promise that I have made to you to love you and be faithful to you. Though I have made you suffer, this is not because I love you less: I do love you, and will love you to the end, but I need suffering to heal the wounds of sin. Farewell, stay with Me, as I with you."

A few days later, on November 24th, Mgr. de Durfort paid Josefa a long and most kind visit. This was a great comfort to her, and she received it gratefully and simply as an immense grace.

Her complete unawareness of the importance of the role she was being called upon to play struck the holy old man very much. Her one preoccupation was the furtherance of Our Lord's interests. Her share in the work of love, her personal sufferings, shown only too evidently by the exhaustion of her frame, were of no account to her, when compared with the plans and desires of her Master. She transmitted these to the Bishop with such exactness and objective clarity that no detail was lost, even in her halting French. And just as simply as she had for the moment come out of the shade, so did she once more step back into the way of suffering and purification which was more than ever hers.

Once more as November drew to a close, Tuesday, the 27th, Our Lord showed Himself to her as a blissful vision of peace, which she thus described:

"While I was making my adoration this evening before the Blessed Sacrament, I could find nothing to say to Him, so, that I might not lose my time, I read the Litany of the Sacred Heart very slowly. Then as there was still a little time over, I took the invocations of the First Friday Novena1 and when I got to the words 'To Thy close union with the Heavenly Father, I unite myself,' He suddenly appeared in radiant beauty. His raiment seemed to be woven of gold, His Heart was a blazing furnace and from the wound in It came dazzling light. I renewed my vows and begged Him to pardon me for being so cold in His presence. It seemed to me though that it was not from want of love, because I love Him more than anything on earth ... He listened to me and looked at me, and then said: 'Do you know, Josefa, that that prayer is so pleasing to Me and is of such worth, that it far surpasses the most eloquent and sublime ones that could be offered Me. What is of greater value than My Heart's union with My Heavenly Father? ... When souls say this prayer they penetrate, as it were, into My Heart, unite themselves to My good pleasure for them. They unite themselves to God, and this is the most supernatural act that can be done here below, for by it they begin to live a heavenly life which consists of nothing else than the perfect and intimate union of the creature with its God and Creator.

" 'Continue your prayer, Josefa, for by it you adore, repair, merit and love. Yes, go on with that prayer, and I will continue the work of love.'

"Then I committed all my distresses to His Heart," she wrote, "and He replied: 'Be not disquieted... It is I Myself who am directing everything.'"

Blind faith in the guidance of Love was Josefa's loadstone in these hours of darkness and obscurity. Overwhelmed by physical suffering she seemed to be thrown on her own unaided resources. She suffered deep dejection of soul which reduced her to a kind of moral agony. Yet her faith in Him who permitted it all never wavered; it sufficed that it was His permissive will, and, impotent but trustful, she gave herself up to the purifying action of Love.

God Sets the Seal on His Work

"The sign that I shall give will be in you yourself."
(Our Lord to Josefa, September 20th, 1920)

We have reached December 1923, Josefa's last month on earth. All was peace, order, wisdom, power, and sovereign liberty, such as belongs only to the King of Love in the great work that He was about to complete through the frail instrument of His choice.

It would seem to be a fitting moment to pause and consider Josefa's soul in order to seek out the divine seal which might authenticate her mission.

"By their fruits ye shall know them," Our Lord had once said to His disciples, and the principle holds good for all that is supernatural in virtue here below.

Answering one day the urgent but secret prayer of Josefa's guides Our Lord had said to her (though she had no suspicion of their anxieties): "Let no one ask Me for any sign, Josefa. The sign that I shall give will be in you yourself." A divine answer indeed, imprinted on every day of the four years of Josefa's short religious life, marking it with what seems an unmistakable stamp.

It showed itself first and foremost in her childlike simplicity. She was one of those single-minded, lowly souls that truly delight the Heart of God and to whom He reveals His secrets. There was in her a total absence of self-consciousness, a confiding simplicity, a straightforward spontaneity; nothing 'precious' about her devotion nor anything the least complicated in her attitude of mind. Her faith was too firm to admit of exaggerations or fantastic imaginings... . She went straight as an arrow to God. It was this simplicity that engendered her effortless approach to the divine, and enabled her to endure trials without so much as suspecting their extraordinary character, and to return quickly and with ease to her ordinary life.

Her way of giving an account of herself to Superiors was devoid of pretentiousness; deferential, but also ingenuous and candid, the very style and handwriting of her notes leave an impression of one who was artless and simple, concentrated wholly on God.

Humility and charity, the two characteristics of the Heart of Jesus, recognized by the Church as peculiarly those of the Foundress, Saint Madeleine Sophie Barat, were likewise distinctive of Josefa's virtue.

There was something grave and mature about her, resulting from the lowly opinion she had of herself. Proud and vivacious by nature, she found in religious life many occasions on which she might practice love in the smallest things, and realizing her own weakness, genuinely judged herself to be the last in the house. But her sincere humility showed itself also in other ways: forgetfulness and habitual sacrifice of self were the logical result of this conviction of her nothingness, itself a source of struggles to accept God's Will for her. There were times when submission to the Divine Will reached the heights of heroism, so opposed was it to her natural inclinations; hence each step she took increased in her detachment from her own views and humble trust in authority.

Her humility seemed all the more genuine because its outward manifestation was charity, a charity so supernatural that it bound her every day more closely to the Heart of Jesus.

A humility less real might have taken advantage of her exceptional favors to stand aside from common life, enwrapped in a kind of self-complacency; but there was no trace of this in Josefa. The more the Sacred Heart made her the confidant of His secrets and filled her with His spirit, the greater became the evidence of her sweet charity; the closer her contact with the divine, the more simply helpful and kindly she grew towards others - her interest in them, her gift of self, and her ready prayers on their behalf never failing them. The whole world, nothing less, to be gained for Christ, such was the sole boundary of her horizon ... yet no tiny service was allowed to escape her watchful attention for each and all. Over and above the world of souls, and of her community, there was plenty of space in her heart for God's beautiful nature, the birds, flowers and insects ... the starry sky ... she embraced them all in her wide, strong, yet simple and naïve affection - an affection that must have delighted the Heart of her Master, since it was but an aspect of her love for Him.

Obedience, in the long run, is the great sign of Our Lord's choice. The witnesses of her daily life note this virtue as characteristic of her. Her submission to the control over her actions and spirit was perfect: a submission both of judgment and of heart. Not a wish or attachment to one way of acting rather than another, and never a reason for or against decisions taken in her regard; she submitted herself simply and wholly to whatever line of conduct was prescribed, and so free was she from self, that she refrained even from comment on the graces she had received, much less expressed any sort of complaisance. Josefa's notes, written only for the sake of obedience and with great reluctance, she never asked to read again. She just handed them over to her Superiors. This she had learned from Our Lord's own mouth; He demanded of her complete dependence on authority. "I have drawn you to My Heart that obedience may be your very breath ... know this, that if I should ask one thing of you and your Superiors another, I prefer you to obey them rather than Me." "Go and ask leave ... " He would say to her. He Himself explained to her how far and in what degree she was to be docile and pliant and as it were transparent in openness with Superiors. Again and again He came back to the point, impressing on Josefa the importance of this paramount virtue of religious life. "Seek Me in your Superiors. Listen to their words as if they fell from My lips; I am in them for your guidance." Josefa adhered faithfully to this line of conduct.

Her love of Rule and of Common Life played a conspicuous part in defending her against the snares of the devil and against illusion. Many a time, her love of Common Life would have made her choose rather to follow it than the way marked out for her by Our Lord Himself, had not He given her a clear assurance of His divine Will. The Rule which she kept so carefully sometimes demanded heroic acts of courage and will by which she defied the evil one, when he threatened her with dire consequences if, for instance, she obeyed the first sound of the bell; yet though she dreaded the conflict and moral agony involved, love made her overcome her fear and brave the fiend. (Who would not have feared such an antagonist?)

Finally may we not see God's seal on Josefa's way of life in the perfect agreement of the teaching she received from the Sacred Heart of Our Lord, with the Rule she so loved and the spirit bequeathed by the Foundress St. Madeleine-Sophie to her daughters? That spirit is one of love and generosity, of reparation and zeal, and should mark each member of the Society of the Sacred Heart as spouse, victim, and apostle. Josefa, who possessed this spirit so deeply, was further rooted in it by Our Lord Himself. In the light of God, her special graces never seemed to her comparable in importance with that of her vocation, the guidance of obedience and the security of the Rule.

And so the promised sign was given in her, day by day and hour by hour, in every tiny detail of her religious life, while, enveloped in silence and obscurity, the unsuspected intensity of her love was hidden in her generous self-oblation.

There were, notwithstanding, hours, days, even months, when obedience, love of duty, courage and submission to God's Will, faith and abandonment to His guidance, required sheer heroism on Josefa's part. How often the passive witnesses of her superhuman struggles and anguish were amazed at her gallant fight, at the fidelity, liberty of spirit and overmastering grace displayed in the conduct of this simple child of the people, so unconscious of the grandeur of her destiny, and giving such unequivocal signs of genuine virtue... .

The story of her short life in religion is about to end with a further sign: death came as it had been predicted by Our Lord and Our Lady, who, while keeping her utterly submissive to the Divine Will, had told her clearly both the time and circumstances.

Josefa, counting only on the words of Jesus, warned her Superiors that she would not see the close of the year 1923. The Master of life and death came on the date and in the manner He had announced, and in His own way put His seal on the work of His Heart.

The Final Message (December 1st - 9th, 1923)

"It is My Will to speak now to My consecrated religious."
(Our Lord to Josefa, December 4th, 1923)

This last Advent, the most wonderful and significant of Josefa's life, opened soon after the beginning of December. She was waiting in the true sense of the word. And the dark night of her soul was pierced from time to time by a ray of light at the thought of the bliss that was soon to be hers forever. How thrilled she was in such moments at the thought of the great day for which she longed so vehemently. Then the horizon grew dark again, all the darker indeed, for the fleeting ray of light that had preceded it.

The last lines of the Message were to be written in the first week of this same month. On Monday, December 3rd, Saint Madeleine Sophie came to prepare her for this completion of her mission.

"Come to my cell," she said to her that morning - and Josefa went. Our Holy Mother was already there, and said reassuringly: "Yes, I am your Mother, the poor creature whom God chose to be the foundation stone of this little Society."

After these opening words which calmed Josefa's misgivings, she continued: "Jesus is coming! Await Him with great humility, but with joy and trust. He is the Father of mercies, always ready to pour out His loving-kindness on all His creatures, but especially on those who are very little and abject. Listen with great reverence to His wishes, His commands, and all His words, and may the Society preserve them carefully."

Then our Holy Mother stressed what was the authentic sign for each of its members: "Tell them not to be afraid of suffering; they must never recoil from suffering, and above all (and this is a message from their Mother,) never let the graces showered on the Society lessen their humility, the most precious of all treasures. The more humble the Society is, the more Our Lord will favor it."

Jesus was about to make His last appeal to these chosen souls consecrated to His Sacred Heart.

On Tuesday, December 4th, Josefa, occupied with her needlework, was sitting in her cell, when Our Lady appeared to her, the dawn before sunrise. Josefa renewed her vows and asked her to repeat with her what Satan had never been able to say: "My God, I love Thee and I want the whole world to know and love Thee."

With motherly affection and enthusiasm Our Lady complied.

"She repeated the words," said Josefa, "and added: '... because Thou art infinitely good and merciful. Yes, daughter, Jesus is full of compassion for little and abject souls. He forgives them and He loves them dearly. His goodness makes Him incline to the lowly, and His strength sustains the feeble. Let your littleness lose itself in His greatness. And now wait for Him lovingly, for He is coming... .'"

"She disappeared, and a very few moments later Our Lord was present. I renewed my vows and at once He said: 'It is I, Josefa, so do not be afraid. I am Love, Goodness, and Mercy... . I am the Son of the Immaculate Virgin, the Son of God ... and God Himself!'"

After these assurances which banished every trace of doubt, He spoke and she wrote:

"I wish to speak today to My consecrated religious, that they may make Me known to sinners and to the whole world.

"There are many among them who as yet are unable to understand My true feelings. They treat Me as One far away ... known only slightly, and in whom they have too little confidence. I want them to rekindle their faith and love, and live trustfully in My intimacy, loving and loved.

"It is usually the eldest son of the family who knows best the mind and secret affairs of his father. In him the father is wont to confide more than in the younger ones, who as yet are unable to interest themselves in serious matters, or penetrate below the surface of things. So when the father comes to die, it behooves the eldest brother to transmit his wishes and will to these the younger ones.

"In My Church, too, I have elder sons: they are those whom I Myself have chosen, consecrated by the priesthood or by the vows of religion. They live nearest to Me; they share in My choicest graces, and to them I confide My secrets, My desires ... and My sufferings also. I have committed to them the care of My little children, their brothers, and through their ministry they must, directly or indirectly, guide them and transmit My teaching to them.

"If these chosen souls know Me truly, they will make Me known to others; if they love Me, they will make others love Me. But how can they teach their brethren if they hardly know Me themselves? ... I ask you: Can there be much love in the heart for One who is barely known? Or what intimate converse can be exchanged with One who is avoided ... or in whom one has little confidence? ...

"This is precisely what I wish to recall to the minds of My chosen ones. Nothing new, doubtless, but they have need to reanimate their faith, their love and their trust.

"I look for greater intimacy and confidence in the way they treat Me. Let them seek Me within their own hearts, for they know that a soul in a state of grace is the tabernacle of the Holy Spirit. And there, let them consider Me as I truly am, their God, but a God of love. Let love triumph over fear, and above all let them never forget that I love them. Many are convinced that it was because of this love that they were chosen, but when they are cast down at the sight of their miseries, of their faults even, then they grow sad at the thought that I have changed and love them less than before."

Here Josefa stopped, for her strength was giving out. She humbly asked leave to sit down, and Jesus, full of compassion, gave her permission. He comforted her, as He alone can, and then disappeared.

At the same hour the following day, Wednesday, December 5th, Jesus rejoined Josefa in her cell. At once she took up her pen, and on her knees before her small table, wrote while He went on:

"I was telling you yesterday how little such souls really know Me. They have not understood My Heart. For it is their very destitution and failings that incline My goodness towards them. And when, acknowledging their helplessness and weakness, they humble themselves and have recourse to Me trustfully, then indeed they give Me more glory than before their fault.

"It is the same when they pray, either for themselves or for others; if they waver and doubt, they do not glorify My Heart, but they do glorify It, if they are sure that I shall give them what they ask, knowing that I refuse them nothing that is good for their souls.

"When the Centurion came to beg Me to cure his servant, he said very humbly: 'I am not worthy that Thou shouldst enter under my roof' ... and, faith and trust prevailing, he added: 'Say but the word, and my servant shall be healed.' This man knew My Heart. He knew that I could not resist the prayer of one who trusted Me absolutely. He gave Me much glory, for to humility he joined confidence. Yes, this man knew My Heart, yet I had made no manifestations to him as I have to My chosen ones.

"Hope obtains innumerable graces for self and for others. I want this to be thoroughly understood, so that My Heart's goodness may be revealed to those poor souls who as yet do not know Me."

Here the Master interrupted His appeal, and with much emphasis insisted:

"I once again repeat what I have already said, and it is nothing new: As a flame needs to be fed, if it is not to be extinguished, so souls need constant fresh urging to make them advance, and new warmth to renew their fervor.

"Few among the souls that are consecrated to Me possess this unshakable confidence, because there are few that live in intimate union with Me. I want them to know that I love them as they are. I know that through frailty they will fall more than once, I know that they will often break the promises they have made Me. But their will to do better glorifies Me, their humble avowals after their falls, their trust in the forgiveness I will grant, glorify My Heart so much, that I will shed abundant graces on them.

"I want them all to know too how greatly I desire a renewal of their union and intimacy with Me. Let them not be satisfied with merely conversing with Me in church, where doubtless I am truly present, but remember that I abide in them, and delight in this union.

"Let them speak to Me of all their concerns ... consult Me at every turn ... ask favors of Me... . I live in them to be their life... . I abide in them to be their strength. Yes, I repeat, let them remember that I delight in being one with them ... remember that I am in them ... and that there I see them, hear them, love them. There I look for a return from them.

"Many are accustomed to a daily meditation; but for how many it becomes a mere formality, instead of a loving interview... . They say or assist at Mass and receive Me in Holy Communion, but on leaving the church become once more absorbed in their own interests to such an extent that they scarcely say a word to Me.

"I am in that soul as in a desert, she neither speaks to Me nor asks anything of Me ... and when in need of comfort, she solicits it from creatures whom she must search out rather than from Me her Creator who abides and lives within her... . Is not this want of union, want of interior spirit, in other words, want of love?

"Further, let Me once more tell those who are consecrated to Me how I specially chose them, that they might live in union with Me, to comfort Me and repair for the sins of those who offend Me.

"I want them to remember that it is their duty to study My Heart, in order to share in Its feelings and, as far as is in their power, to realize Its desires.

"When a man works at his own field, how hard he toils at weeding it of all noxious growths, sparing neither trouble nor fatigue till he has attained his object. In like manner, as soon as My chosen ones know My desires, they should labor with zeal and ardor, undeterred by difficulty or suffering, that My glory may be increased and the sins of the world repaired.

"Tomorrow I shall come back on this. Go now in peace."

Here Josefa's notes ended that day with a very simple little tale:

"Yesterday," she wrote, "after a day of great pain of soul and body, I went through such intense agony that I thought I was dying. All the sins of my life came up before my eyes in the most startling way and I was unable to make the smallest act of trust or love."

She often experienced these feelings of helplessness by which Satan tried to paralyze her and drive her to despair.

"The suffering was so intense that I thought my last hour had come. Suddenly I saw high up in my cell a little white dove whose head was aureoled with light. She was vainly trying to take flight, but one of her wings, still a little grey, seemed to be tied. She remained for a short space like that, then, beating her wings, flew away... . I think it must have been the one I had seen once before of which Jesus had said 'this dove is the picture of your soul.'

"When He came this morning, I told Him how I long to die on the 12th of this month, the feast of Our Lady of Guadalupe1 and our Holy Mother's birthday. It is also a Wednesday, so consecrated to my holy Patron Saint Joseph. Jesus answered me so kindly: "And what about that little wing which is still grey? ... "

Josefa then told Him how afraid she was of offending Him and parting from Him, for the devil's temptations had reached such a pitch of vindictiveness.

"Look, Josefa," He answered, "you must be further purified in love. Surrender yourself and desire nothing but to do My Will. You know very well that I love you, what more do you want?"

So this December 5th, like the preceding day, was spent in very great distress of soul and the obscure temptations of the arch-enemy.

Courageous and docile as Josefa was, she did her very best to maintain herself in a spirit of faith and love. These awful hours of dereliction which, as she well knew, were speeding her to her end left her nevertheless in a state of affliction and completely helpless. Obedience remained her one ark of safety, and it was touching to see how she clung to its observances in the minutest particulars.

Thursday, December 6th, found her in the little cell where she had so often waited for the Master. Faithful to the rendezvous, He listened patiently and tenderly to her desires and to the hope she could not hide from Him - that of dying on December 12th under the protection of the three great loves of her religious life.

" 'What have you done, Josefa, to merit Heaven?'

" 'Nothing, Lord, but Thou hast promised me Thy merits.'

" 'Are you not content, then, to live in My Heart?'

"Of course," wrote Josefa, "but that does not prevent my longing for Heaven; once there, I shall see Him forever, and shall never offend Him any more."

"Let Me choose the hour.

"And now write for My consecrated souls."

It was the last time that Josefa would transcribe the burning desires of the Heart of Jesus for them:

"I call them all - My priests, My religious, and My nuns - to live a life of intimate union with Me.

"It is their privilege to know My longings and to share in My joys and sorrows.

"Theirs, to labor at My interests, never sparing themselves trouble or pain.

"Theirs, by prayer and penance, to make reparation for many, many souls.

"Theirs, above all, to become more and more closely united to Me and never to abandon Me, never to leave Me alone! Some do not understand and forget that it is for them to give Me companionship and consolation...
.

"And finally, it is for them to combine together in a league of love making but one in My Heart, to implore for souls the knowledge of truth, light and pardon. And when they see with deep sorrow the outrages I receive, My chosen souls will offer themselves to make reparation and to labor at My work; let their trust be unhesitating, for I shall not refuse their supplications, and all they ask will be granted them.

"Let them all, then, apply themselves to the study of My Heart and to understand My feelings, striving to live in union with Me, to converse with Me and to consult Me. Let them clothe their actions in My merits, bathe them in My blood, and consecrate their lives to the saving of souls and the extension of My glory.

"Let them not descend to personal reflections which belittle them, but rejoice at seeing themselves clothed with the power of My blood and of My merits. If they rely on self, they will do little or nothing, but if they labor with Me, in My Name and for My glory, they will be powerful.

"Let these consecrated souls revive their desire for reparation, and beg confidently for the advent of the divine King: that is, for My universal Sovereignty.

"Let them have no fear, let them hope in Me, let them trust in Me.

"Let them be burnt up with zeal and charity for sinners ... praying for them with compassionate hearts and treating them with all gentleness.

"Let the world hear from their lips how great is My kindness, My love and My mercy.

"Armed with prayer, penance, and reliance on Me, never on self, let them go forward to their apostolic labors in the power and goodness of My Heart which is ever with them... .

"My Apostles were poor and ignorant men, but rich and wise in the wealth and wisdom of God, and their watchword was: In Thy Name, O Lord, I shall labor and be all-powerful.

"I ask three things of My consecrated souls:

"Reparation, that is a life of union with Him who makes Divine Reparation: to work for Him, with Him, in Him, in a spirit of reparation, in close union with His feelings and desires.

"Love, that is intimacy with Him who is all Love, and who humbles Himself to ask His creatures not to leave Him alone, but to give Him their love.

"Confidence, that is trust in Him who is Goodness and Mercy ... in Him with whom I live day and night ... who knows Me and whom I know ...

who loves Me and whom I love ... in Him who calls His chosen souls in a special way to live with Him, to know His Heart and so to trust Him for everything."

The last lines of the Message were written... . Josefa noted down what her Master wished her to communicate from Him to the Bishop of Poitiers, whom she was expecting shortly, then she laid down her pen. A few instants passed in love's embrace ... God's secret... . How solemn was the hour which marked the termination of Our Lord's Appeal to souls.

It is a never-to-be-forgotten date in the annals of infinite Love. It is a new light thrown, in our time, on the "unfathomable riches of the Heart of Jesus," it is a turning-point on the road of Redemption. It is the hidden source from which a torrent of mercy will, before long, overwhelm the iniquities of the world.

It is a volcano from which the flame that is to give new life and spirit to the world will issue.

It is the beginning of the dawn, before the sunrise that is to shine on the "great day of the Divine King."

Jesus had vanished. Josefa closed her notebook and quietly resumed her needlework. Only a few pages would be added to it, for the end was almost in sight.

On Friday, December 7th, Mgr. de Durfort was kind enough to come to receive Our Lord's last words written down for him by Josefa. Simply and with burning words Josefa spoke to him of her yearning for Heaven and of her approaching death. It was very moving to listen to her, for though her face showed traces of the suffering she was undergoing, her speaking eyes and vehemence gave such animation to her talk that it did not seem likely that the end was really at hand. She was perfectly sure of it, however, and spoke of her coming death to the Bishop with a conviction that her perfect submission to God's Will made all the more striking.

All was joy on Saturday, December 8th, and Josefa spent her last remnants of strength in helping to prepare for the traditional procession in honor of Our Lady. She put her whole soul into the decoration of the little oratory of the Noviceship for this feast of her Immaculate Mother. She was, however, unable to take part in the procession herself, but hidden in a corner of the infirmary corridor, she watched the long files of children in white, each carrying the lily she was to lay at Our Lady's feet.

In the afternoon she wrote farewell letters to her mother and sister, moving letters that were to be kept as precious relics, and which at her request were to be sent only after her death. They may fitly find a place here, for they show how tender and supernatural her affection was, transformed and vivified by her love for her Lord.

To her mother she wrote: "I am glad to die, because I know it is the Will of Him whom I love. Then, too, I long to see His face unveiled, and that is impossible here below. Do not be sad on my account, for death is the beginning of life, if we love and wait for His coming... . We shall not be parted for very long, for life is so short and we shall be together for all eternity. From Heaven I will take care of you and I shall pray God to give you all you need, and to give you, too, a happy death in the peace of Him who is Our End, our Joy and our God. Do not go into mourning for me, but pray much for me to go to Heaven quickly. I do not know the day of my death, but I hope it will be on 12th of this month. Does Jesus want it then? I want only His Will. Do not think that I am sad. These four years of religious life have been just Heaven to me, and my one desire for my sisters is that they may be as happy as I have been and may know that this lies in doing God's Will. You must not think either, that I am dying from pain and distress... . I think it is just from love. I do not feel ill, but something makes me long for Heaven and I cannot live without Our Lord and Our Blessed Lady... ."

To her sister Mercedes,1 who was, like herself, a Sister in the Society of the Sacred Heart, she wrote more intimately: "I am dying in great happiness, and what gives me this joy is the knowledge that I have done God's Will. It is true that He has led me through paths that were none of my choosing, but now at the end He is rewarding me and I feel only peace. I beg you to serve Our Lord and the Society gladly and fervently in whatever occupation and house, and under whatever Superiors He puts you ... do not take any notice of your likes and dislikes. Nothing gives such peace at the hour of death as to have denied oneself in order to do the Will of God. Do not let your wretchedness distress you; Our Lord is so good, and loves us as we are. I have experienced this. Have perfect trust in His goodness, love and mercy. I am dying in great happiness... . The Society has, indeed, been a true and tender mother to me. Jesus has given me Superiors who have treated me with wonderful consideration and kindness; I cannot repay them here, but I shall obtain all I ask for them from Our Lady when I get to Heaven. I have been very happy in France; it has been the home of my soul, and in it Our Lord has given me innumerable graces. We have always loved each other very much, dear Sister, and now after our separation for awhile, we shall be united again, more intimately and strongly than ever. I shall be waiting for you in Heaven where we shall be united not only as sisters, but as fellow religious. Adieu."

Though she felt these farewells deeply they did not unman her, and when she had finished writing them, she went confidently to Our Lord, exposed in the Chapel, to offer them to Him, and there spent nearly all the rest of that day.

Then Our Lady was awaiting her to give her a foretaste of the heavenly meeting. Could she have resisted her child's longings? Josefa thus recorded the vision; they were the last lines in her little notebook.

"This evening, while I was in the Chapel, suddenly Our Blessed Lady came. She was clothed as usual, but surrounded with dazzling light and standing on a crescent of azure blue clouds which were very airy and ethereal. On her head she wore a long pale blue veil, transparent as gossamer, which was lost in the clouds on which her feet rested. She was so lovely that I dared say nothing to her. My soul melted as I gazed on her beauty.

"At last I managed to renew my vows, and she said to me in a voice both sweet and grave: 'My child, the Church honors me today by contemplating My Immaculate Conception. Men admire in me the wonders wrought by God, and the beauty with which He clothed me even before original sin could stain my soul. He who is the Eternal God chose me for His Mother and overwhelmed my soul with graces greater than any bestowed on a creature. All the beauty you see in me is a reflection of the Divine Perfections, and the praises given me glorify Him who, being my Creator, willed to make me His Mother.

" 'My choicest title to glory is that of being Immaculate at the same time as being Mother of God. But my greatest joy is to add to this title that of Mother of Mercy, and Mother of Sinners.'

"When she had said this she vanished, and I have not seen her again."

Here end Josefa's notes. In Our Lady's last statement, she, as it were, signed the divine Message given by her Son... . It was an echo of the work of love, from the lips of His Virgin Mother... . Her Immaculate Heart as Mother of Mercy and of sinners leads the world to the Sacred Heart of Him who is Love and Mercy.

Union Through Crucifixion
(December 9th - 16th, 1923)

"Soon the never-ending day will dawn."
(Our Lord to Josefa, December 12th, 1923)

Josefa's last days had come; only twenty still separated her from the end, and they were to be days of suffering, of grace, and of trial, during which her earthly mission was consummated.

She wrote nothing more, if we except the personal messages dictated by her Master and the last recommendations that our holy Foundress addressed to her Order through Josefa's means. Always faithful, she confided the secret of the supernatural conversations between herself and her Lord to her Superiors after each visit, so that not one word should be lost. Fervor caused her often to pray aloud, and her words, unknown to herself, were lovingly recorded. So, from day to day, the riches imparted by the Heart of Jesus, and hidden in the soul of His messenger, were made known for the whole world.

The Feast of the Immaculate Conception had ended for Josefa in a night of extreme bodily pain. So great was her agony that she had lost consciousness repeatedly, a truly mysterious state, in which she still could and did suffer, as the expression of her face only too evidently showed. She lingered on for three weeks more, and at no time was there any lightening of the pain, nor could any alleviation be afforded her.

On Sunday, December 9th, she succeeded by dint of extraordinary courage in attending Mass and going to Holy Communion for which she longed. On her return to her cell, however, she fell into a long faint which left her completely exhausted. But so used was she to bearing pain, and so great was her power of overcoming herself, that she spent the greater part of the afternoon before the Blessed Sacrament exposed. This was her farewell to the Tabernacle and Chapel which had witnessed so many graces and such costly offerings on her part.

After Benediction that evening, Josefa was worn out; she gave in and went to the infirmary where she was to die.

An attack of agonizing pain began and lasted the whole night. In the rare intervals in which she was conscious of those around her, she smiled and kissed the crucifix that never left her hand. She spoke only with difficulty, so that one guessed rather than heard what she said. She lifted her hand painfully and pointing with three fingers murmured slowly: "Three days ... only three days more." The hope of soon meeting with the Beloved for an instant illuminated her face which was contracted by pain.

"Are you sure?"

"No, but I hope... . I am waiting for Him... . Jesus is so good, and it is such a coincidence that one day should bring together my three loves: Our

Lady, St. Joseph, and our Holy Mother."

Then she relapsed into silence, the better to suffer.

On the morning of Monday, December 10th, she was very weak and though she attempted to rise at the cost of heroic efforts, in hopes of being able to communicate, she could not and fell back inert, the tears of disappointment trickling down her cheeks, so hungry was she for her Lord. She could not speak, nor swallow even a drop of water, and again and again she lost consciousness... . Was the end near, as near as she hoped, and would the 12th open Heaven to her?

Towards the end of the morning there was a slight improvement, which made it possible for Holy Communion to be taken to her. To the very end Our Lord so disposed all things that she was not deprived of It. Could she without that Bread of Strength have gone through the darkness of those last hours of struggle?

Our Lord manifested Himself to her during her thanksgiving that day and she was scarcely able to express her grateful love.

"Josefa," He said to her. "I have come Myself to prepare you for your entrance into My celestial Home."

"Will it be on the 12th, Lord?" she asked naïvely.

"If you wish it, I will give you that joy," He answered, "but will you not be generous enough to grant Me a few more days? I want them for certain souls."

Such a question roused in Josefa a love that had no personal desires.

"Thou knowest that I am Thine, and that all that I have is Thine."

"Yes," Our Lord continued in a voice of unspeakable tenderness. "I am watching over you, I am taking care of you, let Me do as I think best and choose the hour."

He then added: "I shall return tonight and you will write, here."

At half-past two that afternoon He came. Josefa, propped up with pillows, for she had no strength left, was waiting for Him.

"He has come," she murmured a few moments later. "Oh! so beautiful! His Heart open wide is as a furnace of fire."

"See the dwelling that I am preparing for you forever and ever," He said, "and what are you preparing for Me, Josefa?"

"Ah! Lord - my sins ... my miseries ... my sorrow to have done so little for Thee."

"Never mind that," He replied. "Give it all to Me and I will consume everything in the fire of My Heart; and now write."

With trembling fingers she wrote under His dictation a message to be sent after her death to Fr. Rubio, S. J., who had been her father and director in childhood.

"Tomorrow I shall return," He added, and soon afterwards departed.

That same evening there came upon Josefa an attack of terrible pain; she was alone, she felt life slipping away from her, she had no voice left to call for help ... but Heaven was on the watch. Suddenly Saint Madeleine-Sophie stood by her side, and more motherly than ever, took her in her arms, comforted and supported her. Then she revealed Our Lord's wishes to her.

"You are not to die on the 12th," she said, "but Jesus Himself will come to you and will unite you to Himself by the closest of bonds, and that for all eternity, my child."

Then our Holy Mother explained to Josefa that she would be anointed and make her religious profession on that happy day.

"I come to tell you this from Him," she said. Josefa was to prepare herself in joy. "Jesus Himself is arranging everything, and difficult as it may appear to creatures, He ordains each event in the way best for His plan."

In response to Josefa's question, she said: "Yes, I shall be there with Our Lady, and Jesus never leaves you alone... . We shall all three be there... . Courage! Only a few days more to spend here below to merit your heavenly reward. Remain in peace, for I am watching over you."

And she vanished.

A few minutes of much-needed sleep followed on this visit of our Holy Mother, and though the respite was a short one, the thought of the graces awaiting her on December 12th gave Josefa the peace of self-surrender throughout the pain of the day and night that followed.

On the afternoon of Tuesday, December 11th, Our Lord, faithful to His promise, returned. This time He was to dictate a last word for the Mother General. The message ended with these words: "I love My Society. I shall guide My work."

The heavenly directions given to Josefa required the sanction of Superiors in what regarded her final vows.

On the morning of Wednesday, December 12th, there was a slight improvement in her condition, and the Mothers wondered whether the danger was sufficient to warrant the administration of the Last Sacraments and Profession 'in articulo mortis.' Josefa was somewhat troubled at this uncertainty, but her director reassured her, by letting her make after Communion an act of total submission to whatever should be decided about her. Meanwhile the doctor was consulted, and once more Our Lord allowed His plans to receive human ratification, though those He employed for this were quite unaware of it.

After a thorough examination, as on several previous occasions, the doctor's verdict was that he could diagnose no disease, but that he felt a certain anxiety. This was not to be wondered at, as he was ignorant of the extraordinary graces that had ruled Josefa's life. He decided, however, on account of her extreme weakness and long fainting fits, that it would be advisable to administer the Last Sacraments at once.

Do we not see in this the intervention of Him who leads and governs all the events of our lives, relieves uncertainties and obliges His creatures to follow blindly the supernatural guidance of His love?

The day was passed in expectation, but in peace, recollection, and fervor. Mgr. de Durfort had decided that he himself would preside at the little ceremony which was to give Josefa a double consecration.

The whole religious household, knowing of her precarious state of health, was asked to pray very specially for her, and preparations for the ceremony were made in her little cell which had witnessed so many divine favors.

The moving ceremony began at about five o'clock that evening. Josefa was radiantly happy and quietly recollected. The nuns crowded in the adjacent corridor and neighboring rooms, as her own was too small to contain them. Only the Bishop, Canon de Castries, our chaplain, and Fr. Boyer, O.P., were in the cell itself near Josefa's bed. The tiny room had become a sanctuary.

Beside Our Lady's statue, the tall Profession candle was burning, the Blessed Sacrament was placed on an improvised altar, and in the silence Josefa humbly accused herself of the faults of her religious life, asking pardon of her Mothers and Sisters. Then the Bishop began the prayers of the last anointing; but nothing of all this was present to Josefa's consciousness, for Our Lady and our Holy Mother had taken their stand by her bedside, and while the sacred unctions were being given, Josefa though aware of the rites of the Church, saw nothing beyond her heavenly visitors who clothed her in a white tunic that had been brought by angels.

"See, daughter," said Our Lady, "what Jesus in His infinite mercy has done for His little bride, not because of your merits, but because of those of His Heart. And now that you are clothed with this very pure garment, your Bridegroom will give you the kiss of peace and love. Surrender yourself wholly into His hands, for in these divine hands you are safe. He will accompany you to your eternal home, and Himself will present you to the citizens of Heaven."

When the anointings were concluded, the Bishop addressed a few fervent words to Josefa, but she knew nothing of them, for she was still in deep ecstasy, though her attitude barely betrayed the fact. The Veni Creator and liturgical prayers by which the Church blesses the cross and ring followed, but she remained unconscious of all.

Jesus then joined Our Lady and Saint Madeleine Sophie, and it was in their presence that the newly Professed answered the questions of the Ritual in a firm voice.

"Do you consent to take Jesus Christ Crucified for your Spouse?"

"Yes, Father, with all my heart."

"Receive, then, this ring as a sign of the eternal alliance you are about to contract with Him."

And handing her the little cross which she was henceforth to wear upon her heart: "Receive, my child, this precious pledge of the love of Jesus Christ, and remember that in becoming His Spouse you must live henceforth in union and conformity with His Divine Heart.

"May your Beloved be to you as a bundle of myrrh;

"May it rest on your breast as a mark of love and of an eternal alliance."

In the silence surrounding the sickbed now become an altar, the Bishop drew near, holding the sacred Host. Josefa read the formula of her perpetual vows, and received Holy Communion.

As Our Lady and Saint Madeleine Sophie went away, they left her these words of farewell:

"We shall both come back to fetch you and take you to Heaven."

Jesus, the Divine Bridegroom of her soul, alone remained.

"Josefa, why do you love Me?"

"Lord, because Thou art so good."

"And I love you because you are so wretched and so lowly. That is why I have clothed you with My merits and covered you with My Precious Blood, that so I may present you to the Elect in Heaven. Your littleness has given place to My greatness ... your misery, and even your sins, to My mercy ... your trust to My love and tenderness.

"Come, lean upon My Heart and rest there, since you are My bride. Soon you will enter this abode never to leave it."

Josefa's heart overflowed - she told Him of her yearnings, her happiness, her desire, that the goodness of His Heart might be known to the ends of the earth, for men do not know it enough.

"Yes, it is true. I am good. To understand this souls need one thing, union and interior life. If My chosen souls lived more united to Me, they would know Me better."

"Lord," answered Josefa ingenuously, "it is difficult ... for sometimes they are so busy working for Thee."

"Yes, I know, and that is why I go and search them out when they wander away from Me.

"That will be our work in Heaven, Josefa; to teach souls how to live united to Me, not as if I were far away, but in them, because by grace I dwell in them.

"If My chosen ones lived thus united to Me and really knew Me how much good they would be able to do to many poor souls who are far from Me and do not know Me.

"When My chosen ones are closely united to My Heart, they will realize how often I am offended ... they will understand My feelings... . Then they will comfort Me and repair for sinners, and full of trust in Me, they will ask pardon and obtain grace for the world."

Our Lord stopped as if to leave so glorious a prospect of mercy and salvation before Josefa's mind. Then He said as before: "Josefa, why do you love Me?"

"Lord, because Thou art so good!"

"And I love you because you are so lowly and have given me your lowliness. I have cared for you tenderly ... I have guarded you faithfully. Let nothing affright you; the eternal Sun is about to rise. Farewell. Abide in Me!"

And He was gone.

During these divine colloquies the ceremony had come to an end. After the Te Deum the nuns had sung one of Josefa's favorite hymns. The priests had gone. Only His Lordship the Bishop stayed on in the room that seemed the ante-chamber of Heaven itself. Half-seated, with closed eyes, ardently pressing her crucifix to her heart, Josefa, her face smiling and full of repose, remained in ecstasy... . The Bishop blessed her, and then he, too, went away. He was deeply moved, and with difficulty hid his feelings... .

Little by little the nuns also dispersed, carrying with them a vivid impression of the supernatural, but unaware of the mysterious truth.

Only the two Mothers remained in prayer beside Josefa for another quarter of an hour. When she came back to consciousness the calm joy and radiance of the heavenly visitation still filled her soul. Her cross and ring remained as testimony of the mutual everlasting love between herself and the Beloved.

Her last oblation was still to be a crucifixion, for that very night her critical state returned, leaving her apparently in a desperate condition and unconscious from sheer agony. She was still able to communicate on December 13th, and as so often before, Our Lord became manifest to her during her thanksgiving, and showed her, plunged in the flame of His Heart, her own small heart. How minute it appeared to her!

"I took it, you remember, Josefa, and with it all your affections. Trust them to Me, for I love whatever you love, and I take care of all you love here below."

Then she spoke to Him of her mother and sisters, of the Society of the Sacred Heart, the Mothers of Les Feuillants, and all those she loved. To all Jesus replied with divine condescension, then before going away, He said: "Wait for Me just a few days longer, Josefa."

And alluding to the little dove: "We have still to break the cords that bind its wings, though now it is all white."

And He vanished.

This allusion to the dove was a great joy to her in the sufferings which had become much worse, yet spiritual joy exceeds all the pains of earth and Josefa lovingly kissed the hand of her crucifix, which she playfully said would cut those cords and free the Palomita forever.

The community had not all been able to say good-bye to her the day before and were now invited to do so. Little groups succeeded one another and came out delighted with their short visit. Little was known of Josefa except her fidelity, and hidden, silent work, but today she appeared so simple and happy that all felt the better for seeing her. The Kingdom of God was shining from within.

There were moments when she could hardly contain her overflowing sense of happiness, and when alone with the Mothers, she threw off all constraint and revealed herself in exclamations and fervent, loving words which, though she was not aware of it, were carefully written down, for they were a revelation of the depth of her inner life and her childlike simplicity. We quote some of them:

"Jesus is waiting for me.... I am all ready to go, I have reached the station.... I am on the platform ... my ticket has been paid for ... and my luggage registered ... this luggage consists of the merits of His Heart.

"I know where I am going.... I have no fear at all.... I want nothing.... I have given Him everything."

And remembering the little dove, she wrote in pencil what she called her "versitos," in which the freshness and poetry of her soul were expressed:

"Poor little dove, she thirsts ...

But her wing is tied, and she cannot fly to the water course to slake her thirst ...

Jesus in His goodness has come Himself to fetch her ...

And she has drunk His Precious Blood!

Poor little dove, she cannot fly ...

And Jesus has said: 'you must wait ...

And He does what He wills, and she is glad ...

Except that she fears He may forget her ...

So without appearing to, she whispers

'Come my Jesus! break these bonds that your little dove

May fly to flowery orchards ... '

Come, O come and fetch her ... her eyes are straining after Thee

And on the day and at the hour when Thou shalt free her,

How delighted she will be to contemplate Thee forever."

That evening she had the further joy of a visit from Fr. Boyer, who spent a long time with her, and left in admiration of God's work in her soul, for her surrender to His good pleasure was perfect. The end was approaching and apparently without any impediment whatever.

The night, however, brought back great suffering and she seemed to be dying. Yet she was able to receive Holy Communion in the morning, and this grace was given her each day to the end.

On Friday, December 14th, her soul was illumined, in spite of pain, with a peace and joy that were more of Heaven than of this earth.

Josefa was silent, she was anxious to avoid giving trouble to her Mothers who sat by her in turns so that she was never alone. At moments she broke out into fervent and very simple ejaculations of love. She seemed to be thinking out loud ... She recalled the thought of her entrance, of her noviceship, of her struggles to be faithful to her vocation, and all with a deep feeling of gratitude. She would stop, recollect herself, kiss her crucifix, or gaze lovingly at the statue of Our Lady which faced her bed and seemed to be watching over her, after presiding over so many of the happenings in that little cell ... then she rambled on:

"I am glad I feel worse, for I know that God's Will is being done. Nothing gives such peace and consolation as God's Will. I am dying because it is His Will... . I have never done my own since I entered here ... for all those things were none of my choice. But what gives me so much peace now is to have struggled and suffered to do God's Will, and to die faithful."

A number of intentions were confided to her for Heaven - vocations, sinners, etc... . This roused her ardent nature.

"I do so love work," she said. "I shall go here, there and everywhere and obtain many graces."

When France was spoken of:

"Yes, indeed," she answered. "France is the home of my soul, because it is the home of my religious life ... this house too, which belongs to our Holy Mother ... this little corner of the earth is indeed one to live and die in!"

Then once more she returned to the main thought occupying her mind at the moment:

"If only they knew ... they would never seek for anything on earth but God's Will ... no one can imagine what a joy it is ... it is the only thing that gives peace... . Ah! to die a nun, and in such peace, repays a thousand times all, and much more, than I have suffered."

This thought was one she lingered on lovingly:

"One never need be anxious, because Jesus is so kind - He supplies for everything... ." And lovingly she kissed her crucifix.

"His sacred feet ... His hands, so fatherly ... yes, fatherly ... His Heart! O! how good Jesus is, it fills me with such happiness... . He forgives, He repairs, He loves... . As soon as trouble comes, I feel Him saying 'Do not fear ... I am good, and I love you.'

"He is so good, because I am the last and least, by far the most wretched... . Yes, I am glad to be ... just nothing."

"Jesus is good, that word fills my heart... . I might be feeling great remorse for my sins ... but no, I am only filled with gratitude, because He has forgiven me.

"My Jesus!" she suddenly exclaimed ... "it is twenty-three years since Thou didst say to me 'I want you to be all Mine ... ' I loved Him then without knowing Him ... I did not know Him yet, but I loved Him already... . He was always with me... . I know very well what I am... but above all I know what He is... . He has given me His Heart... . It is true."

After a long silence she exclaimed: "My God, I make Thee the offering of my life in union with the Heart of Jesus, in submission and in joy because I love Thee. I want all that Thou desirest ... if it is life, then I will to live, if it is death, then I say 'yes' again... . Thirty-three years ... how many graces! Especially during the last four in religion. O! how happy I am ... to die fully conscious ... to know that the moment of death is near... . O! what joy ... what a happy death ... How faithful my Jesus is... ."

So the hours passed. Fr. Boyer paid her a kindly visit and gave her another absolution. Her door remained open and many of the nuns entrusted to her their special intentions. In her delicate charity she even found enough strength to help her successor in the workroom, for propped up in bed she cut out, with all her usual dexterity, a garment that was wanted.

When evening came and silence filled the house, alone with the two Mothers she went over the various phases of her life, and these memories which filled her with grateful thoughts were less of a conversation than a prayer and hymn of thanksgiving.

Her strength was now rapidly declining and she was unable to take any nourishment, except a few drops of water, and even these caused her violent pain.

Early on Saturday, December 15th, Jesus came once more during her thanksgiving:

"You see," He said, "that I never leave you alone."

His tone was unspeakably kind. "I have been your strength in life, and I will be your consolation in death. And after that, forever and ever. And as I have taken delight in your littleness, you will find in Me everlasting bliss."

Josefa could not restrain her desire to go to Heaven to see Him forever.

"And then," she added, just like a child in her simplicity, "I shall have so many intentions to confide to Thee.... I have been given so many commissions these days!"

"Yes, yes," said the Divine Master - ardent yet so kindly; "we shall contrive little surprises for them, you and I, what they call here 'petits plaisirs.' Let Me rest in you, Josefa, a little longer; soon it will be your turn to rest in Me. Farewell, I am with you all the time."

A few minutes later another violent attack came on which reduced her almost to agony. She lost consciousness, but the contraction of her face showed that there was no diminution of the excruciating pain. When at last she returned to life once more, her deep joy had in no wise been affected. She coaxingly caressed the wound in the right hand of her crucifix, and murmured in an almost inaudible voice: "This is the hand that will break the cords that bind the Palomita, and set it free," and she covered the wound in His sacred side with burning kisses.

"I was very happy on the day of my First Vows," she said, "but I did not know whether I should be faithful to the end. Today Jesus has united me to Himself forever, and He will not allow me to be separated from Him."

During the morning Father Boyer conferred the grace of the indulgence 'in articulo mortis' on her, for she seemed very near death.

At ten o'clock our Holy Mother appeared. With infinite pains Josefa managed to write the message under her dictation. It ended thus:

"May all the members of this dear Society live united to the Heart which has bestowed Itself on them out of love. May they work unceasingly, and never forget that they are His consecrated brides and victims.

"Now one more soul will protect the Society on earth, for those who are humble and little find favor in His sight."

The afternoon began in peace, but suddenly the dear little Sister seemed worse. Her face changed, she gasped for breath, her eyes grew misty though wide open, and her agony began, though she was still quite present to all that was going on around her. Was it really the end? ... Would Our Lady come to call her home on this lovely Saturday afternoon? The Community assembled in the rooms nearby to pray. Josefa was beside herself with joy at the thought of the beatitude that was at hand.

With eyes closed now to things of earth, she joined in the prayers and asked for her favorite ones. The litanies of Loreto and of the Sacred Heart, the invocations of the First Friday novena, the Miserere, the five Paters in honor of the Five Wounds and seven Aves for Our Lady's sorrows, all were recited one after the other, whilst she pressed her cross of Profession on her burning heart. Then she asked for her favorite hymns.

"No," said Josefa, "you must not sing 'J'irai la voir un jour' ... but 'J'irai la voir ce soir'!"

Father Boyer said the prayers for the dying, Josefa interrupting them with her own childlike and fervent aspirations. In broken words she told of her joy at dying all for Jesus, her trust which knew no shadow, her happiness at being nothing and nobody and poor, her faith in His mercy, her assurance of pardon and of the merits of Him whose love was to her full and entire security.

The hours passed by... . Josefa consumed with fever, was in joy unalloyed. She spoke of Heaven and of those she would see again there, and she promised to be busy about sinners, vocations and the many intentions entrusted to her prayers.

A fervent conversation went on between herself and Father Boyer and those who came in one by one; a conversation all the simpler because, with her eyes almost sightless, she did not notice the emotion, and admiration of those around her.

At five o'clock her veiled eyes seemed suddenly to fix themselves on some object passing before them:

"Poor little Palomita," she repeated twice. "She is all pure and spotless now"; and whispering to the Mothers: "The Cross is shining on her breast and she is trying hard to fly away, but her wing is still held by two little cords.

"Must she wait much longer? ... "

A few minutes later Our Lady stood beside her.

"Not yet, not yet, Josefa," she said. "You must suffer now, but soon the time for suffering will be past."

Three hours had gone by, they had seemed but a flash, and reluctantly those present in that happy room went away. There was such a sense of peace ... such a mysterious interchange between earth and Heaven that they could not account for; they were far from divining the real truth. The whole house seemed under the hush of this influx of grace.

In Josefa's cell the Cross was about to succeed to the joys of Thabor: Love's work! ... The comparative calm of the day was followed by paroxysms of intense suffering. Josefa was again in agony, apparently unconscious of all except her suffering and the stifled groans which were drawn from her brave endurance. With difficulty she drew each labored breath, her eyes remained dimmed but wide open, her poor body racked with fever, and the sweat of death covering her face. There was no change all night, and it was not possible to foresee when the end would come.

Sunday, December 16th, was the seventeenth month since her First Vows. About six o'clock she was able to swallow a few drops of water, to her intense joy, for it meant that she would be able to receive Holy Communion.

Jesus Himself did not wait for that moment of union, but came to soothe His little victim with spiritual comfort. Had He come to fetch her?

"No - not yet," He answered; "you will not die till Reverend Mother has received from the Mother General in Rome directions as to what is to be done after your death." And He added, to leave her the merit of abandonment: "It will not be today or tomorrow."

Josefa asked Him humbly if her moans when in pain were a cause of displeasure to Him.

"No," He answered promptly and with compassion, "I know what you are suffering, and I make your pain Mine."

"Your sufferings are as a precious balm to My Heart. They heal My wounds, they are as sweetest honey to My lips, and fill Me with delight, Palomita Mia.It is My love that binds and imprisons you, both for your good and that of many souls. But it is Love too that will intoxicate you with the pure joys of Paradise. Love is clothing you with My merits and will make you taste the beatitude reserved for virgin souls.

"Yes, Palomita Mia; during your life I fed you with little wild flowers which I Myself had sown for you. In Eternity I will feed you on the most pure flowers that adorn the gardens of the pure-in-heart. Farewell, we shall not be separated for long, for you know how I delight in your littleness."

And Jesus vanished.... . This was the last vision she had of Him on this earth.

Consummatum Est! (December 16th - 29th, 1923)

From now on Josefa would wait in darkness ... a few more days of peace, and then the formidable powers of Hell would gather in a last supreme effort against her. But the audacity of Satan would serve only to bring into greater relief God's victory, and her last sufferings set the seal on her union with her Master for all eternity. When the hour marked by God had struck, Jesus in the sovereign liberty of His love would break the last bonds: "Arise, My dove, My love, and come," He would say, and in the deep and silent solitude of her last oblation, Josefa would die; the work of Love on earth was done... . But this was to be at the same time the dawning of a new day.

All Sunday morning, December 16th, Josefa suffered much, but the pain diminished in the course of the afternoon and she slowly regained her sight. At nightfall she grew worse and became unconscious, and it was thus, that the Bishop, who kindly called, found her. For a long while he remained in prayer at her bedside which seemed to be the altar of sacrifice on which a pure victim was being immolated.

That night and the following days were spent in alternations of relative calm and acute distress, so that both Josefa and those about her remained in the uncertainty of abandonment which the Heart of Jesus so loves.

She was devoured by thirst, yet every drop of water she managed to swallow seemed to burn and scorch her, instead of relieving her.

"It feels," she said, "as if that little drop of water fell where a fire was raging and everything falling to pieces." So painful and distressing was the impression it left on her. Jesus was associating her with His thirst and with the bitter vinegar and gall which was given Him on the Cross. She had lost all strength, and the slightest movement, even when two or three nuns together changed her position with the utmost care, made her pant for breath. At times she was seized with a sort of general torpor but without the relief of sleep, while at other times she was tortured in every member of her body.

However, though in the throes of such terrible physical agony, she had lost none of her self-forgetfulness and childlike joyousness, nor her delicate thoughtfulness for others and expansive abandonment. No sooner did she find comparative relief from pain than she resumed her inspiring colloquies in radiant peace.

"I am so happy to know that Jesus is making me ready, for I have done nothing, I owe everything to His merits and merciful love... . I no longer have the strength to pray, but I just tell Him over and over again how glad I am to be going to Him."

A letter from Spain, just at this time, reawakened thoughts of her mother and sisters.

"There was a time," she said, "when news from home moved me deeply, but I am happy about them, I feel sure that all will be well, for Jesus is so good; He loves them and will care for them and console them ... I know His Heart so well. Yet I do love them with all my heart - Mama, Mercedes and Angela. They hardly realize how much I love them.... . It is this that makes me understand what the Heart of Jesus feels when He sees that souls do not realize how much He loves them."

The same thought ran through her head on Wednesday, December 19th.

"Souls do not understand how much Jesus loves them," she murmured, as if talking to herself. "The more they have lived in the obscurity of faith," she said at another time, "the more Jesus will help them and reward them at the hour of death.

"I have never been so happy, I am in such peace, my joy is perfect ... there is not the smallest shadow on it. I am absolutely certain of His forgiveness and tenderness.... . I have no desires.... . I leave it all to Him. I cannot speak to Him anymore with my lips, but my heart repeats how good He is, and how I love Him."

The thought of the children always delighted her, and as the sound of their merry voices reached her, she would exclaim: "How I love them!"

The ardent tone of her voice betrayed her zeal, she was so little occupied about herself, so interested in souls.

His Lordship the Bishop paid her another visit on Thursday, December 20th. After a long talk of which he said nothing, and some time spent in praying out loud with her, he went away much moved.

Nothing but peace and tranquil calm was felt at that bedside, for in spite of the suffering there was so much love. Josefa was waiting; complete submission to God's Will was no doubt paying the price of souls whom she would go on helping from Heaven, winning souls for the Heart of Jesus, usque ad finem!

The testimony of the Sister Infirmarian who nursed her in these last days of her life is worth quoting:

"I had to guess what could relieve her pain or give her pleasure; she had only one desire: Heaven and the accomplishment of God's will. She was so grateful for the smallest attentions and was most anxious that no one should be late for any community exercise on her account."

Another writes: "I cannot say what her example meant to me during those three weeks. She must have been very mortified and very close to Our Lord, to have remained so tranquil, happy and abandoned to God's good pleasure. She never alluded to her sufferings, never asked for water, though her thirst was very great, for she seemed on fire interiorly; if anything was offered to her, she accepted it, but never complained.

The nun who helped her so long in the care of the little oratory wrote: "I was granted the grace of a visit to her once during her illness. She received me with such a smile of welcome, for the sight of me recalled to her mind the memory of our dear little chapel.

" 'How well one understands,' she said, 'when the end comes, how God is everything and all the rest nothing ... how quickly these four years of religious life have passed, it seems as if I arrived only yesterday as a postulant ... then there was my noviceship ... I had much to bear at that time, oh! how I suffered, and I almost feared I should be forced to leave, yet I loved the Society so much.'

"I remember then how, on the day of her vows, she looked triumphantly at her crucifix. The look she gave me, and the expressive gesture that accompanied it, seemed to speak of a victory won. I have never forgotten them.

"Then she came back naturally to thoughts of her childhood:

" 'When I was small,' she said, 'I wanted to love Jesus very much... . There seemed to be something urging me to love and give myself to Him. On the day of my First Communion, when they gave us an instruction on "Jesus Sponsus Virginum" ... though I did not quite understand, I was simply carried away ... the call was growing stronger and stronger.'

"On the evening of her anointing and Profession, she recognized my voice and calling me to her: 'In Heaven I will pray for your intentions ... '

"Then again and again she repeated: 'Our Lord is so good, so kind when we do all we can, which of course is really nothing, He takes charge of the rest; it matters so little whether we feel we are getting better or not.'"

The Mistress General of the school at Les Feuillants, who died shortly after Josefa, left the following notes about her:

"Her cell was less of a sickroom than an oratory, and lying there on a bed of pain, she seemed radiant with heavenly peace. Without understanding why, one felt something great and supernatural in the atmosphere of that infirmary cell. I saw her several times on the following days, and asked her to pray for the children's retreat which was about to take place.

" 'I love them so much,' she said. 'I am so happy when I hear them at their games but more especially when I see them at Holy Communion and know that Our Lord is in each one's heart. O! yes, indeed, I shall pray for them and I shall go on praying for them when I get to Heaven... . God has given me,' she continued, as if speaking to herself, 'a heart that loves very much... . I love the Society and all the Mothers and Sisters ... and the children; I do love them so!'

"One cannot reproduce the tone of sincere and deep love in her words. Another day she said:

" 'The Novices must be very fervent and energetic in their vocation. I myself had to fight so hard that sometimes I felt as if I could not go on. When this happened, I used to go to the Mother Assistant, and then I felt strengthened. It cost me much to leave Spain, but what was that in comparison to my vocation? Yes, I did it with all my heart. What we have to learn above all else in the Noviceship and never forget is obedience. If we only really valued obedience in a spirit of faith ... ' and this she repeated several times, recollecting herself, as it were, and seeing in her own soul the safety of this way of obedience.

"Another day when she seemed to be in great pain, she said: 'Our Lord wants us to suffer in many ways... .'

"She was silent for a few minutes, and then went on: 'I have suffered much, but' - and here her voice took on a firmness that was quite unforgettable - 'but one forgets it, one forgets the suffering ... and now Our Lord is about to ... ' For a moment she stopped, as if ashamed of what she had almost said. 'O! no, not reward me, for I have done nothing... . He is going to make me happy forever.' She was silent in the contemplation of such bliss. Then, 'How good God is, O! how good,' and she seemed to relish the words which she repeated again and again."

This tranquil calm in happiness was to be brusquely interrupted. The powers of Hell were allowed to seize Josefa and crush her as the grape in the winepress. For a time Satan would even imagine that he had at long last vanquished her and ruined God's plan for the world.

This last assault, the most redoubtable of all, was made both on her soul and on her body, which became possessed and dominated by an unyielding force.

On Friday evening, December 21st, the shadow began to fall. A sudden weariness of suffering seized upon Josefa. She longed to die, but regained sufficient self-possession to cling blindly to the Will of God, which in any case was the habitual attitude of her soul. On Saturday, the 22nd, the letter promised by Our Lord arrived from Rome, and the blessing of her Mother General braced her, as the dark tunnel opened before her.

That evening a terrible attack brought her to death's door and deprived her of consciousness for a long time. What passed during the mysterious dark night into which her soul had passed?

Josefa would say later that during this night the devil was given a strange power. A realization whose origin was not from within herself, suddenly imposed itself upon her mind so clearly, that she could not reject it:

"... Death was the result of the extraordinary life she was leading. Who was forcing it on her? She could be faithful without agreeing to be led in such a way... . If she refused she would get well... ."

Instantly all her pain left her and she felt physical ease. But this time under this diabolic obsession, the evil spirit walled her up in so absolute a silence that she could not break through it except to say that she was cured and free to walk no more in those ways. Never before had Josefa suffered so grievously in this way, yet at the very summit of her soul she never ceased loving Him who allowed so terrible a trial to befall her.

For a short space on Christmas Day she recovered enough liberty to explain to Father Boyer what had happened and was happening in her. These were but a few moments of painful relief in which she realized the truth, and the Father comforted her as best he could... . But the flash of light soon passed and the evil spirit would not give way. One could feel the interior struggle that must be going on, and that made her silence more painful still. What prayers and supplications arose to Heaven for her enlightenment and deliverance! Nothing counted in that terrible trial, but suffering.

Christmas Day passed, and Wednesday, December 26th, dragged on slowly, with no change. Father Boyer was following the course of this diabolic attack closely, and said the prayers prescribed for exorcisms several times, but in vain.

Faith in Him whose love is faithful and strong, confidence in the intercession of Mary, His Mother, were the very sure support of all during these tragic hours. How could one doubt the ultimate accomplishments of God's great work ... or the power of Him who directs all things ... or the love of the Sacred Heart, incapable of abandoning His frail instrument on the brink of Hell?

It was when the Mother of Sorrows was invoked that in His own time He intervened. That Wednesday evening, kneeling near Josefa's bed, the Mothers were invoking the Dolours of the most pure heart of Mary, and repeating Aves in a low voice. No sound was to be heard but the low murmur of prayers - God knows how intense - rising up to the Mother of Sorrows, whom none ever invoke in vain.

Suddenly Josefa's body began to relax ... she lowered her eyes ... crossed her hands ... her lips parted ... and gradually she joined in the prayers which rose so insistently to Heaven. A quarter of an hour charged with feeling went by. After the Aves came a Pater ... "Thy kingdom come, Thy will be done on earth as it is in Heaven... ."

Josefa's tears flowed silently and with her whole soul she repeated the words of a much-loved prayer by Saint Madeleine-Sophie:

"O Sacred Heart of Jesus, I hasten, I come to Thee, throwing myself into the arms of Thy tender mercy! Thou art my sure refuge, my unfailing and only hope. Thou hast a remedy for all my evils, relief for all my miseries, reparation for all my faults. Thou canst supply for what is wanting to me in order to obtain fully the graces that I ask for myself and others. Thou art for me the infallible, inexhaustible Source of light, of strength, of perseverance, peace and consolation. I am certain, too, that Thou wilt never cease to aid, to protect, to love me, because Thy love for me, O Divine Heart, is infinite. Have mercy on me then, O Heart of Jesus, and on all that I recommend to Thee, according to Thine own mercy; and do with me, in me and for me, whatsoever Thou wilt, for I abandon myself to Thee with the full, entire confidence and conviction that Thou wilt never abandon me either in time or eternity. Amen."

As these last words were said, affirming total and entire surrender to Our Lord, the evil spirit fled away forever... . The Virgin had once more crushed his head, and his power over Josefa was at an end.

In a moment, suffering returned to every member of Josefa's body and she was stretched once more upon the Cross of her Saviour... . Who could

384

doubt that it was Mary's intervention and the all-powerful fidelity of her Son's Sacred Heart that in one moment had effected so tangible and sudden a deliverance?

The night was spent in acts of intense thanksgiving. Josefa's body was racked and broken, but her spirit had regained contact with the graces of that blessed pain.... with the Mothers, too, who never left her for a moment, and to whom only with her eyes as yet she could express the humility, thanksgiving and abandonment reawakened in her, as gradually the remembrance of these terrible days faded away.

On Thursday, the 27th, she received Holy Communion, in a peace that nothing could again impair.

It was the Feast of Saint John, the friend of virgin souls, who had often come to her as Messenger of the Heart of Jesus. She could not forget it. Father Boyer saw and spoke at length with her after her thanksgiving.... Clearly, and with remarkable lucidity, Josefa gave him an account of the mysterious state in which she had been conscious of her will-power. Her soul seemed to have touched the very depths of distress and also of humiliation, and annihilation, which were, in very truth, the depths of love... .

But these things were passed and gone ... and the Magnificat best expressed the feelings uppermost in every heart. It was recited again and again by her bedside, while she lay radiant on her cross. All the old suffering had come back, the fictitious cure of the last days was gone, and the day passed in the joy of suffering and surrender reconquered.

On Friday, the 28th, an early visit from Father Boyer brought her the grace of another absolution. Duty took him away from Poitiers that day, but he left reassured, as Josefa had regained peace and unclouded joy. At about one o'clock in the afternoon a long attack of intense suffering seemed to bring her close to death. Until three o'clock she was so overcome by pain that she remained unconscious of those around her. Towards evening, however, she gradually revived, and in pity for her poor emaciated body, they did all that could be done for her, which was to moisten her lips with water and try to ease her breathing, by lifting her very gently into another position. But as always, she was quite forgetful of self and only anxious to spare trouble to others, and words of thanks were constantly on her lips.

The night, her last on earth, was spent in these vicissitudes, and on the morning of Saturday, the 29th, the Blessed Sacrament was brought to her for the last time. What must have been the love-meeting which so closely preceded that of eternity? Josefa, no doubt, had a presentiment of her approaching end, but her thoughtfulness for others which had grown so delicate through her union and conformity with the Heart of Jesus did not allow her to dwell on the separation which would cast such a gloom around her. So in deep recollection and silence she suffered on, more intensely as the hours passed, a warning perhaps, yet no clear indication, that death was drawing near, since she was praying, too, in perfect peace today as yesterday. She kept looking lovingly at a tiny statue of the Infant Jesus asleep in the crib. The beads of her rosary slipped through her fingers as her eyes expressed what she no longer had the power to say.

In the afternoon, propped up in bed, she read her favorite Chapter of the Imitation (Bk. iii, X), and was able to say a few words of grateful affection to the Mothers. One felt that she was thinking solely of Jesus and of souls; her face alone showed how severe was the pain she was enduring.

The day was beginning to darken; it was the fall of the evening, and the deepest silence reigned in her room... . It was so like many other evenings, that even the Mothers who watched her carefully did not suspect that the end was near. Jesus allowed this that He might keep for Himself the secret of the last preparation, completion, and supreme consummation.

It was half-past seven, and the Sister Infirmarian asked if she could do anything for her. Night had now fallen. "I am all right," she said; "you can leave me alone," for the Angelus was ringing and she knew it was time for community supper.

O mystery of God's adorable will! By a chain of unforeseen circumstances, Josefa, who had never once been alone, either day or night, since December 9th, now remained alone!

And it was in this solitude, this abandonment willed by God, that the Master came swiftly and fetched His privileged little victim home; allowing her to die, like Himself in dereliction, forsaken by all... .

When a few minutes later the Sister Infirmarian returned, Josefa was dead... . She was lying with her head slightly tilted back, her eyes half closed and an expression of intense pain on her face, reminding one of Him who had died on the Cross, abandoned by His Father.

"Let Me choose the day and the hour," He had said to her.

Our Lady and Saint Madeleine-Sophie had told her: "We two together will be there to lead you to Heaven." Was not this the hundredfold of the hour, when in loneliness, solitude, perhaps distress, Our Lord's words found their realization?

"You will suffer and in the depths of suffering, you will die." This journey to Paradise from her lonely cell Our Lord deigned to signalize by a sign, an unmistakable testimony of His incomparable love... .

When at about eleven o'clock that night the Mothers went to clothe the little Sister in the religious habit, what was their astonishment to find that "Someone" had forestalled them! Under the blankets, which were tucked in to the very top, and better than any human hands could have done, Josefa was lying, her arms by her sides, clothed in her grey petticoat which was carefully tied at the waist and covered her down to her feet. When? How? Who had done it? No one had entered the room since her death, as her next-door neighbor in the infirmary testified, and the little Sister, who had been incapable of the slightest movement, could not have done it, nor did she even know where the petticoat had been put away.

The fact, however, could not be denied and is moreover quite in harmony with Josefa's known modesty; she always dreaded being handled after death. Perhaps we may surmise that Our Lady and Saint Madeleine Sophie, who had both promised to come and take her soul to Paradise, had themselves wished to give this proof of their maternal presence, a proof which was absolutely convincing to the witnesses.

The little grey petticoat was therefore left untouched just as it had been arranged and Josefa carried it with her to the tomb. Thus ends the story of a very faithful love, Saturday, December 29th, 1923.

Almost at once the expression of Josefa's countenance changed to one of peace and serenity, and the whole house was filled with a sense of the supernatural and much grace.

On the morning of Sunday, December 30th, the community heard with indescribable emotion the divine secret of the last four years, of which not one had so much as suspected the existence. A letter from the Mother General said: "It is only just that they should be the first to receive the tidings of this grace."

The most absolute discretion was imposed on all, since no one outside Les Feuillants was for the moment to know the favors or the mission given to the humble little Sister.

But what graces of fervor, of thanksgiving and generosity were poured out on the house... . The cell where Josefa's body lay among lilies became a sanctuary. Heaven seemed close, and all came to pray and venerate her. There was a majesty about the beautiful countenance that reflected something of the serene tranquility of eternity.

"It seemed that I was not kneeling by a deathbed," wrote one of the nuns who watched by her the next night, "but before a spotless white altar, and that around her the triumph of her oblation was being chanted by the very palms and lilies. I tried to make my prayer an echo of hers. She embraced the whole world in hers ... souls, sinners, our dear Society, and deep gratitude mingled with my prayer during those silent hours of the night."

So it seemed as if already Our Lord was pleased to lift the veil that had shrouded so completely the little instrument of His love and to discover to souls the burning appeals of that love.

"The night she died, not knowing that she was worse," wrote the Sister in charge of the kitchen, "I saw her in a dream. She was most lovely, and lay on a bed adorned with flowers. She made me a sign to come near and said to me: 'Oh! Sister, do not be afraid of suffering, and do not lose the smallest particle that God may send you. If you could but understand what a privilege it is to suffer for Him ... you must make a prayer of your work. Say to Him as each occasion arises: "For Thee, dear Jesus, I offer it to Thee" - so that He may see that you want to be with Him and to love Him. Oh! if you only knew how much He wants to be loved!' She spoke impressively, so that I was very much moved, all the more, that on coming down to Mass that Sunday morning I heard that she had died in the night."

That same Sunday evening the Bishop of Poitiers came to pray beside her remains. He stayed in deep silence for a long while, then blessed the little Sister who had been confided to his care by Our Lord Himself, and went away with evident reluctance, unable to restrain his tears. After signing the Act of Profession, he declared that he would himself perform the last rites after the Requiem Mass which was to take place on the following Tuesday, January 1st, 1924.

So the year 1923 ended in an outpouring of graces from Josefa's little cell. It acted as a magnet to the household and there went up to Heaven from it thanksgiving, offerings, and desires that must have consoled and glorified the Heart of Our Lord. Already the work of His love had begun.

At about half-past four that evening Josefa's body was enclosed in the plain wood coffin that was to hide her from every eye. The restful face still bore the expression of a gentleness and peace that one could not tire of gazing on. She was taken along the cloister to the very place in the chapel where eighteen months before Jesus had said to her: "See how faithful I have been to you."

These two faithful loves met here for the last time.

Whilst the Community spent the night before the Blessed Sacrament exposed in the oratory of Saint Stanislaus, so to close a year of singular graces, Josefa's body alone kept guard before the Tabernacle where she had made her first vows.

On Tuesday, January 1st, the funeral took place. In a letter to the Mother General written by the Superior of Les Feuillants who knew how closely she was united by thought and prayer to all that was happening, we read: "I had feared that the Chapel would be very empty, considering the day and the absence of the School away for their holidays, but it was not so: His Lordship and six priests filled the sanctuary, nuns of various Orders, the little girls from the Good Shepherd Convent, the children of the day-school, Children of Mary and friends made a gallant escort to our humble little Sister after the long file of her Mothers and Sisters.

"The Requiem was sung with great devotion, and about it all was a sense of recollection which the circumstances made very moving. The Bishop gave the solemn absolution, and the procession started, while the In Paradisum led us in thought to where our dear little Sister now rejoices.

"It was raining, and the gloomy sky on that January 1st formed a contrast to the serene peace of our souls. We crossed the garden and passed the oratory of St. Joseph and our Mother Foundress' 'solitude' where she used to make her retreat. Here the hearse was stopped unexpectedly beneath the Crucifix that dominates the place where the paths cross, and it was as if Saint Madeleine Sophie was giving a last blessing to her child.

"Then we reached the great gates at the entrance. Josefa was leaving Les Feuillants.... How deep was our emotion as the hearse disappeared."

The nuns' burying-place is a reserved part of the public cemetery at the end of the town, and here numerous graves are grouped round a Cross. Facing the entrance, in a vault which had been prepared with care a few weeks before Josefa's death her precious body was laid to rest. There is nothing to distinguish her grave from that of the other nuns, but it is close to the statue of Our Blessed Lady.

There rests the humble and privileged Messenger of the Sacred Heart.

Conclusion

It is not fitting that I should write a conclusion to these wonderful conversations between Our Lord and the little Sister of the Society of the Sacred Heart, but finding myself no longer able to refuse the repeated and urgent requests to express my opinions about these new appeals of God's mercy, I can only beg my readers to forgive me for offering here only the response of a "poor sinner." They will have the good sense to take it, not as the judgment of a connoisseur, but as a proof of my gratitude to Jesus Christ, Victim of Love for us, and to the Society of the Sacred Heart which has allowed us all to share in the most intimate thoughts of the Heart of Jesus.

In the unassuming and simple narrative of facts that we have read, it seems to me that the eminent virtues of the chosen bride of Christ so intimately associated with Himself have been sufficiently brought into relief, and it is therefore of set purpose, though with some reluctance, that I propose to pass over what relates to her personal holiness. Privileged as she was, and she will yet be glorified on earth as in Heaven, it seems best to me to allow her to remain completely in the background in these concluding remarks.

Our Lord's aim was never to set her as an example to be imitated. He did not speak so much to her in order to draw down upon her the admiring gaze of the world. She was a voice ... nothing more. She existed for the Message, the Message did not exist for her. Christ Our Lord willed that she should be a mere nothing. He never drew her out of her littleness; in fact, He continually and purposely laid stress on her nothingness, and that even when He showed Himself with the greatest radiance. Lux lucebat in tenebris.

Josefa's one desire was to retire into completest obscurity. Nothing would please her more than if she were treated as an outcast today. It is because of this that the Message has some chance of reaching us untouched, as she hoped.

I will not hide the fact that when, following the instructions of the Master and of Josefa herself, I put her personality completely out of the picture I was overpowered by the Presence of the Living Christ. At once I was convinced that Our Lord Himself was speaking here. There was no possibility of mistake, no need for discernment of spirits; one had only to note the Voice of Jesus. In its clear simplicity I recognized it as the same Voice that souls hear at times of great grace, and above all the same that the Gospels and the Saints have let us hear throughout the ages.

Mistake is impossible. The Voice that entrusted to Josefa the secrets of the merciful Heart of Jesus is exactly the same as that of the Saviour in the Gospels and of the God of Love heard from all eternity. Deus Caritas est. From the beginning of time He has never ceased His Appeal of Love. Prior dilexit nos. If the Law proclaimed "Thou shalt love the Lord Thy God with thy whole heart, with thy whole soul and with all thy strength" (Deut. 6:5), it was He Himself, first, who urged us with infinite persistence to respond to His infinite love for each one of us. How often He has assured us that His love surpasses that of a mother. Was it only yesterday that we heard from His divine lips the almost foolish avowal: "Thou art My Spouse, and I thy Bridegroom." "A voice of joy ... the voice of the Bride and the Bridegroom, the voice of them that shall say: Give ye glory to the Lord of Hosts, for the Lord is good and His mercy endureth forever" (Jer. 33:11). When Our Blessed Lord tells the little Sister that He loves us "to folly," we have already heard the Bridegroom of souls, par excellence, repeat the old prophecy in words that all can understand.

And what of His mercy? Ought we not, since it is the Voice of God, to realize that it surpasses our wildest imaginings? Yes, Lord, "The earth is full of Thy mercies" (Ps. 118:64). Holy Scripture abounds in instances of God's goodness to sinners, and the secret history of souls is a continuous record of forgiveness that nothing can discourage. Has not the world already received messages more eloquent perhaps than Josefa has conveyed to us? Witness the parable of the vintners of the "House of Israel." When they had rid themselves of servants sent by the Father of the family, beating one, killing another, and stoning a third, the Master sent other servants in greater numbers, but they treated them in the same way. Then He sent them His Son, saying, "they will respect My Son." But when these wicked men saw the Son, they exclaimed: "Here is the heir; let us kill him and the inheritance will be ours." What was the message brought by the Son? That God is charity, that He so loves these sinners that He is sending them His well-beloved Son. And behold, we have crucified Him, because we have not understood His testimony. But before dying and sending His Holy Spirit (the substantial bond of the Blessed Trinity) this only Son revealed to us the depths of God. His Gospel overflows with acts of mercy and kindness, and is in reality from beginning to end the Gospel of mercy to sinners. Everywhere repentance is exalted. His preferences are clear: for the Publican, the Prodigal Son, the lost sheep, the sick, the woman taken in adultery, Mary Magdalen, all the humbled and contrite. In the Beatitudes, everlasting mercy is promised to the poor, the persecuted, victims of injustice, and mourners both for their sins and for their sorrows. Miracles, too numerous to count, are worked on the infirm and ailing multitude who from the depths of their misery call on Christ for help, and what more poignant than the appeal of Jesus in the marketplace, where, as a beggar among beggars who hunger for happiness and justice, He cried out on the last day of the feast, "If any man thirst, let him come to Me and drink; He that believeth in Me, as the Scripture saith: Out of his belly shall flow rivers of living water." "Now this He said of the Spirit (that is the love of the Father and of the Son), which they should receive who believed in Him, for as yet the Spirit was not given, because Jesus was not yet glorified." (John 7:37-39).

He calls to Him the workers and the oppressed: "Come to Me all ye who labor and are heavy-burdened and I will refresh you" (Matt. 11:28). "I am come that they may have life and have it more abundantly" (John 10:10). And before dying at our hands, He sends forth a last cry of distress: "Sitio" - "I thirst."

How seldom is this call, which should resound at all times and in all places, and above all in the depths of Christian hearts, accepted as a personal appeal! Some, indeed, have responded not only in words, but by their life and death "et nos credimus caritati" ... but a great number of Christians and especially multitudes of sinners have closed their ears to the entreaties of Love.

Following these heralds of God - Doctors, Martyrs, Confessors, Virgins, even children, comes Josefa Menéndez with a message more moving than ever. She is heir to an open secret, which throughout the ages has remained unaltered. This actual fact I am anxious to bring into relief. As I read the familiar talks she has with Our Lord, I seem to hear not only Margaret Mary and those like her, but the most illustrious Doctors and classical saints (if I may so name them) of the New Dispensation.

Was the Message delivered by the little Sister or by Saint Augustine? From the contents we could not tell, for the great Doctor also spoke of the goodness and mercy of God for sinners, only in his inflamed and more eloquent words: "O immense and Fatherly tenderness! O inestimable charity! that the sinner might go free, Thou hast delivered up Thine only Son... . O ineffable love! O charity supreme! Who hath heard the like? Who would not be dumbfounded at the depths of Thy mercy, at Thy loving-kindness? Who would not sing the excess of Thy tenderness?"

"I love Thee, O my God, I love Thee and would that I could love Thee more. Grant that I may desire Thee, that I may love Thee as much as I want and as I ought. O Thou who art Immensity, men should love Thee without measure, for Thou hast loved them without measure, hast saved them with a measureless love and hast given such boundless proofs of Thy charity."

These are the passionate tones of a mind in delirium, nay, intoxicated by grace, and we find more of them in the writings of Saint Augustine, perhaps, than in any other of the mystics.

If I read the lofty "Elevations" of Saint Bernard on the love of God or his commentary on the Canticle of Canticles, or the best known mystical writers of the Middle Ages, and immediately after open the little Sister's book The Way of Divine Love, the disparity I find is only as it might be between a large consecrated Host and a small one!

It is the self-same Heart of Jesus who has loved, sought, appealed, pardoned, and filled with benefits the most miserable sinners. I have no hesitation in saying that it is indubitably His Voice that has been calling to us across the ages, inviting us to His Banquet, offering us closest union with Himself, and the ineffable joy of espousals to His Heart.

I will give but one example among a thousand:

Josefa spoke with special love, not only of the Passion of Our Lord in general, but particularly of His Five Wounds.

"Behold these wounds," Our Lord said to her one day, "pierced on the Cross to redeem the world from eternal death and give it life. It is they that win pardon and mercy for so many souls who rouse My Father's wrath. It is they that, henceforth, will give them light, strength and love...
.

"The wound of My Heart is the glowing brazier at which I want My chosen ones to be enkindled."

But Saint Augustine had heard the same cry, for he writes: "The wounds of Jesus are brimming with mercy, full of tenderness, sweetness and charity. They have pierced His hands and His feet and opened His side with the thrust of the lance; through these channels I am permitted to taste how sweet is the Lord my God... . A copious Redemption is given us in the wounds of Jesus Christ our Saviour! A great immensity of sweetness, fullness of grace and perfection of virtues!"

Not once, but hundreds of times does this great convert, this Doctor of God's mercy, summon sinful souls, especially those who are tempted to despair, to trust in God's compassionate forgiveness.

And who has not read the tender supplications of Saint Bernard? "Never say in thy desperation, my sin is too great for forgiveness! No, no, however great it is, much greater is the fatherly loving-kindness of thy God."

"As for me, trustfully I fly to the Heart of my Jesus, there shall I find mercy, for grace flows from every one of His wounds. They have pierced His hands and His feet, they have opened His side; so now I can, by these Wounds, draw honey from the flint and oil from the stony rock, that is, taste and see how sweet is the Lord. His thoughts were thoughts of peace and I knew it not ... the nails cry out, His wounds are clamorous. How truly in Christ, God is reconciling the world with Himself. Open is the sanctuary of His Heart whither all these bleeding wounds lead us. Open wide is the great sacrament of the love of the Father ... draw near, and enter into this seat of mercy! It is visible through these wounds. Where, if not through these openings, could we have learnt the truth of how sweet the Lord is, how tender and rich in mercy? Who can show greater pity than to die for criminal man, condemned as a criminal to perish? Therefore, my merit is the mercy of the Lord."

In quoting these beautiful passages, I want to remind the reader of the wealth that is available in the Church's treasury; and there are an infinity of other passages as poignant, as moving, as those whose secret is divulged to us today. We are apt to forget them, as we forget the dead. They are now once more brought to our memory.

The disclosures of lowly Sister Josefa are the literal echo of a great and divine Voice, which in every age, with divine condescension and adorable patience reiterates for our benefit the old, old truth that He is love, disinterested love, liberal and merciful love, love divinely impatient to see all men one Body in Christ Jesus. When shall we realize this craving of His Heart?

By repeating what we hold from tradition, my object is not merely to attest the authenticity of the Message of the Heart of Jesus. I testify not for Sister Josefa, but against all of us. The perseverance of Christ shows us our spiritual deafness, our hardness of heart, our levity, ingratitude and tepidity, which are in reality astounding, terrifying!

By means of His little bride, Jesus bewails our indifference, as many a time before; as He did over the disciples of Emmaus: "O foolish and slow of heart to believe in all things which the prophets have spoken." (Luke 24:25).

This indifference ought to be a subject of deep concern to us. Possibly under the pretext that "idle tales" are not to be believed, that private revelations are not matters of faith, that imagination may have had a large share in the Message; or again, under the pretext that the diabolical apparitions render the heavenly ones suspect; or finally, that it is not possible to distinguish between what is true and what is false in mystical phenomena ... it may happen, I say, that some are reluctant to spread abroad and give a world-wide diffusion to the revelations of Sister Josefa.

The Samaritan woman hastened to tell her compatriots what she had heard from the Master (John 4:28). Mary Magdalen ran to tell the disciples that she had seen the Lord and that He had entrusted a message to her (John 20:18). How can we allow ourselves to keep back from hungry souls the unfathomable riches of the Heart of Jesus?

It is no excuse to say that there is nothing new in these private revelations, for it is precisely because Our Lord lets us hear once more the age-long clamor of His love and mercy, that we are under obligation, today more than yesterday, not to allow their sound to be suppressed by doubts and superfluous discussions.

Shall we claim to put our hand into the wound of His side before we believe in His love? Rather let us remember the Master's words: "Blessed are they that have not seen and have believed."

The validity of Josefa's Message does not depend only on its intimate connection with the eternal revelation of God's infinite tenderness towards man, but also on its manifest timeliness, and this is a point that I should like to stress again for those who read this book.

The perfect harmony in thought between the Message of the Heart of Jesus and the recent encyclical of our Holy Father Pius XII on the Mystical Body of Christ, Mystici Corporis Christi, is most striking. The Message dates from 1922-3, the Encyclical, June 29th, 1943. In the course of the twenty years that have elapsed between the two, Pius XI has condemned modern heresies, the Second World War has set the globe on fire, Cardinal Pacelli has been elected to the See of Peter, and more than once His Holiness Pope Pius XII has condemned errors and enlightened the faith of Christians. What God prompts His Vicar to say in 1943 palpably confirms the desires expressed by Jesus Christ in the intimacy of a convent to His humble servant in 1923. The teaching of the two shows perfect consonance, harmony and congruity, by which the present tendency of the Holy Spirit's guidance in the Church can clearly be discerned.

Whether we meditate on the words transmitted to us by the untaught little Sister, or on those of the Sovereign Pontiff, we find that both invite us to rebuild a crumbling Christian civilization on the foundations of Charity. This fact seems to me to lend great weight to the Message. Christians everywhere are to be convened to a more perfect restoration of the world. God wills the inauguration of a stage of progress in the development of the doctrine of the Mystical Body of Christ.

Let me here show this harmony in at least a few points:

1) Our Lord seems to recommend devotion to the Sacred Heart more urgently than ever. The Revelations at Paray had dispelled the heresies of fear, especially Jansenism and Calvinism. We all know the incomparable and magnificent promises by which Our Lord had endeavored to attract timid souls. There is no doubt that, all over the world, the Church has gradually responded to His appeal. But it has taken two hundred years of persevering effort on the part of apostles of the Sacred Heart to make people, who for so long had regarded the devotion with misgivings, not only understand it, but love and appreciate it. Such are the difficulties which the love of Jesus meets with in stubborn man! And now He comes once more to let us know that He is far from satisfied with our grudging adoration and our niggardly sacrifices. His thirst is not slaked, far from it; He longs for ever more love and more trust. And He now solicits our affection in such passionate terms that we cannot doubt that He holds this devotion very dear, and that the Blessed Trinity Itself, which is pleased to take delight in it, considers it the most efficacious means of glorifying God and saving souls. The Message is new only in Christ's insistence on the revelation of His love. Who has ever spoken of what he loves most with such force as Jesus does in telling us of His mercy? The only possible conclusion we can draw is that, alas, we do not show enough eagerness to listen to His pleadings!

Christianity today is being dragged into a catastrophe which threatens to overwhelm humanity with something akin to despair. Who will save us? Who can give an assurance that in the end faith will prevail? But once again, in the hour of stress, Christ makes Himself known to pure hearts, and tells us through them: "Respond confidently to the appeals of the Heart of Jesus, and salvation and victory will be yours."

In his Encyclical Annum Sacrum of May 25th, 1899, H.H. Leo XIII, speaking of the signal victory expected by Constantine, of which the portent was the apparition of the Cross in the sky, said: "Today there is another divine symbol, a happy portent visible to our eyes: it is the Heart of Jesus, surmounted by the cross, and shining with incomparable effulgence in the midst of flames; from It we must expect salvation, and in It is our only hope." Pius XII tells us in his last encyclical Mystici Corporis with what joy he has noticed an increase in devotion to the Sacred Heart, and the eagerness displayed by many to "meditate more profoundly on the unfathomable riches of Christ to be found in the Church," for all our hope is in it.

2) Past ages have gone through periods of danger, and the bark of Peter has many a time been on the point of foundering. What then has happened that is extraordinary in our times that Our Blessed Lord should have sent us a new Message? This has happened: our age is one of blood and iron. It attacks charity directly, and is trying to set up a new idol, Force, in the place of its late one, Science.

Wild and lawless propaganda tries to persuade men that they will become as gods by armed force, for charity, they say, is paralyzing in its effects; they must treat it with contempt, as degrading, and leading mankind to a state of decadence. Happily the Law of the Jungle, in vogue among some today, is not God's Law, for what could be easier for the Almighty than to banish humanity from the earth, as once our First Parents from the Garden of Eden, and condemn them to destruction or hell-fire for all eternity. But God's strength lies in His love for erring men. He wants to have mercy on them, to forgive them and make them happy. Josefa Menéndez was charged to repeat His Message of love to them on the very eve of the disastrous war, into which we have fallen. Through her, Jesus speaks to those who have lost belief in Love. That is why He repeats hundreds of times: "Come to Me" - "Trust" - "I love you" - "I am Mercy itself."

Likewise the Holy Father, at the same time and for the same cause, makes himself the echo of Christ's voice, reminding us that charity is man's supreme title to nobility and his highest endowment. If love is a very excellent thing in nature and the source of true friendship, what can be said of heavenly love, which God Himself has implanted in our souls? "God is charity, and he that abideth in charity abideth in God and God in him" (1 John 4:16). Consequently, according to God's law, the effect of love is to establish him who loves in heavenly love, as He said: "If anyone love Me, My Father will love him, and we will come to him, and will make our abode with him" (John 14:23). Thus only shall we become, not merely "as gods," but one God with Himself in Christ Jesus. In the same way shall we overcome the nations and the whole of this lower world, and even the domain of the spirits of darkness, for thus we shall possess the strength not only of the super-man, but of the Holy Spirit Himself. The Holy Father continues: "It is in the glow of this heavenly flame that so many sons of the Church have rejoiced to suffer contempt, and to brave and overcome every danger even to their last breath and the shedding of their blood." "O admirable condescension of divine tenderness! O incomprehensible plan of so immense a charity!"

It is at this critical moment, in order to thwart the machinations of Satan, that the Message reaches us. It invites us to imitate the tenderness of Our Saviour for sinners, for the sick, the infirm, the wounded, and for children whom He so particularly loves. It reminds us of the saying of Saint Paul whose words the Holy Father quotes: "It is those parts of our body which seem most contemptible, that are necessary to it; what seems base in our bodies we surround with special honor, treating with special seemliness that which is unseemly in us." (1 Cor. 12:22, 23).

"This, says Pius XII, is a very grave affirmation, and we remind you of it with a heart full of sorrow, aware as we are of our compelling obligation towards many hapless beings, for do we not see that the deformed, the demented, and those afflicted with hereditary diseases are being considered as a burden to society. This is not the way of Jesus who wished the law of charity to govern the mutual intercourse of men in the same way as He Himself dealt with them."

3) That is why at the solemn moment when, amid the ruins of a society that seemed utterly destroyed, hope awakened in the hearts of the sons of God that a more lasting and solid civilization would take its place, it was

a matter of urgency that Christ should reanimate our faith through Sister Josefa. We needed to hear the call of His Love, to remind us that the true society of men must be founded on a "very glorious fellowship of love," and that Christian brotherhood must exist between nations. Mere justice, divorced from charity, will never solve international and social problems, so varied and obscure. There is but one solution for all these questions, one that removes all obstacles: it is faith in charity.

There is only one barrier that prevents the happy and fruitful understanding that should exist between workers and employers, races and their home countries; it is egoism, and so strong is this passion of egoism, that it can be overcome only by the love of Christ, by the union of all the members in one Body, whose Head is Jesus Christ.

Pius XII again tells us, following the trend of the Message of the Sacred Heart of Jesus: "The love of the divine Spouse is so widespread that it embraces as its spouse the whole human race. If Our Saviour shed His Blood on the Cross it was to reconcile to God all mankind, even if they were separated by nationality and blood, and to unite them into one single body." And the Holy Father is not afraid of including in this charity the very enemies of the Church. "True love ... demands that in other men not yet united to us in the body of the Church, we should recognize brothers of Christ, called to the same eternal salvation as ourselves. Doubtless there are plenty of men, especially today, who proudly vaunt war, hatred and jealousy as a means of exalting the dignity and the strength of man. But we, seeing with sorrow the wretched results of this theory, follow our King of peace who teaches us to love not only those who do not belong to the same nation (Luke 6:33-37), but even our enemies (Luke 6:27-35; Matt. 5:44-48). Convinced by this doctrine of love, let us rejoice with Saint Paul in the breadth and length and height and depth of the love of Christ (Eph. 3:18): A love whose bonds no difference in race or customs can break, no distance set by the immensity of oceans lessen, no wars, or undertakings be they just or unjust diminish.

4) But this charity which is to reconcile all men, even those whose antagonisms are most deeply rooted, can only act efficaciously by blood shed in a Spirit of Reparation. One of the most important points of the Message, the most important, perhaps, is the appeal of the Sacred Heart for collaboration through suffering in union with His Passion, to fill up what is wanting to the fruits of His Passion. By means of Josefa, Our Lord returns repeatedly to the necessity and power of our reparation.

"How much suffering must go to the saving of a soul... . Men rush to perdition and My Blood is wasted for them! But those who love Me and offer themselves as victims of reparation, draw down God's mercy. That is what saves the world! ... Glorify Me through My Heart. Make reparation and satisfy God's justice with It. Offer It up as a victim of love for souls, and especially for those that are consecrated to Me. Live with Me as I live with you... . Your suffering will be Mine, and Mine will be yours."

Words like these are said a hundred times to Josefa, as if it was too easy to forget them. Anyone who reads the revelations attentively will note how Our Lord appeals to His little victim to sacrifice herself with Him for the redemption of the world, or for the salvation of certain specified sinners who are placed by Him in her charge. These words, which recur time after time in the confidential communications He made her, express a very important doctrine which cannot be sufficiently meditated on or made known. We do not live, we do not suffer, we do not die for ourselves alone: Christ, our Head has established a solidarity of the closest and profoundest kind between the members of His Mystical Body, and the inter-communication of prayer and immolation is so perfect that we can, if we please, draw our own profit from the redemption of Jesus, and anyone, no matter who, can avail himself of the mercy and grace gained for him by a voluntary victim, united to the one unique Victim of Calvary. Here indeed we can see the originality and supereminence of Christianity. Now, the Sovereign Pontiff enunciates the same doctrine, and makes the same pressing supplications. His encyclical on the Mystical Body which is reminiscent of Pius XI's Miserentissimus teaches that reparation is an urgent duty for the salvation of nations at war. He begs us to follow in the bloodstained footsteps of our King, to die with Him that we may live with Him, to share devoutly, daily, if possible, in the Eucharistic Sacrifice, to lighten, when we can, the misfortunes of so many who are very poor, to subdue our flesh by voluntary penance, in short, to "fulfill what is wanting in the Passion of Christ in our own bodies, for His Body the Church." "His Body the Church" includes all sinners, be it this or that one in particular, for, by reason of our inter-dependence, there is none which is beyond being revivified, restored and saved by those who suffer in Christ Jesus for their salvation.

5) To Reparation, which ought to be a veritable obsession with us, is united both in the Message of Jesus and in the Pope's Encyclical on the Mystical Body, the idea of constant recourse to Mary, Co-Redemptrix. This concordance of thought in both is striking and very significant.

In the familiar converse between Jesus and His little bride, Our Lady constantly intervenes, to console Josefa when she is sad, or to reassure her when afraid, to prepare her to receive Jesus, to guide her when she wanders from the right path, to strengthen her in timidity, to encourage her when her weakness overwhelms her, to give her fresh confidence in her hesitations, to help her against the attacks of the devil, and above all to teach her to follow the way of the Cross when some fresh object of compassion or reparation is presented to her. In a word, the Message taught this lesson, that the word of God will not bear fruit in a human soul unless it be by the help of the Blessed Virgin. Her intercession is at all times necessary.

The Holy Father says: "If we really have at heart the salvation of mankind which has been redeemed by Christ's Blood, we must put into Mary's hands the desires we hold dear." There are so many reasons for confidence in her intercession! "Did she not, exempt from every personal and hereditary sin and ever closely united to her Son, as a new Eve, present Him on Calvary to God the Father, sacrificing her own rights and making a holocaust of her love, offering Him for all the sons of Adam who have been corrupted by original sin? Therefore, she who was His Mother in the flesh, becomes spiritually the Mother of all who are His members, and that by a new title acquired by suffering and glory." Reparation is easier when the example of Mary and her prayers support us.

6) Had not directors and militant members of Catholic Action special need to study these doctrines? One of the reasons which induced the Holy Father to publish an encyclical on the Mystical Body of Christ on June 29th, 1943, notwithstanding the fact that war, at that very moment, threatened not only Italy but even Rome itself, was that "erroneous ideas were beginning to spread" and had become a danger to the faithful. The Pope warned the members of Catholic Action to guard against such mental aberrations, all the more that owing to the sublime doctrine of the Mystical Body, they were united to all Christians, to the ecclesiastical Hierarchy, and to the Holy Father himself.

Militant members of Catholic Action who study the Message of the Sacred Heart, will find that they are able to obtain a marvelous grip of modern errors and of the doctrinal truths on which the encyclical throws so much light. A more and more trustful recourse to the merciful Heart of Jesus, a conviction that Christ's love is the source of all spiritual good, and that we must not count on our own merits, nor despair on account of our demerits (for divine love uses our very faults to extend His reign but is hindered by our pretentious pride) ... lively faith in the constructive power of charity to establish among men a society founded on love ... incontrovertible hope, that one day all that exists on earth and in Heaven will be brought into the unity of the Mystical Body ... the urge of the Holy Spirit, directing our cooperation by prayer, sacrifice, penance, mortification, disinterested and generous efforts to the redemption of guilty humanity ... filial piety towards the Mediatrix of all graces - these and many other benefits shall we draw from meditating on the words of Christ, and they will at the same time guard us against false mysticism, which instead of humbling man and glorifying Christ, tends rather to clothe man in divine attributes which of right belong to God; guard us too against false quietism, which leaves to Christ alone the salvation of the world, excluding and neglecting man's cooperation; against naturalism which places its faith in the social and juridical force of the Church and human action, instead of in the divine assistance of the Holy Spirit - and lastly all those systems that disparage supernatural means, such as prayer, Confession, suffering, charity to the poor, and laud instead, man-made means, discounting the communion of Saints and of all the members of the Mystical Body of Jesus Christ.

Christ's Message contains the antidote to all the errors that, according to the warning of the Pope, threaten the faithful.

Its opportuneness, its novelty, therefore, become self-evident. All who are not blind to the evils of our times will realize that The Way of Divine Love is by no means a mere edifying biography. On the contrary (unless we are deaf to His voice), it will stand out in the history of spirituality in France and of apostolic Catholicity.

There remains for me only to state my own private reflections, suggested by Josefa's Message, concerning the future of the Society of the Sacred Heart:

When Our Blessed Lady visited her cousin Saint Elizabeth, this holy woman exclaimed loudly: "Exclamavit voce Magna." "Blessed art thou," she said, "amongst women, and blessed is the fruit of thy womb." And she added these words, which were a prelude to the Magnificat: "Blessed art thou who hast believed, for those things shall be accomplished that were spoken to thee by the Lord."

I should be wanting in faith did I not believe that the Message is inaugurating a new era of sanctity and apostolic fruitfulness in the Society of the Sacred Heart. It is undoubtedly true that however liberal God's Will may be, it produces results of mercy only under certain conditions. His wishes must be responded to with confidence and entire generosity, if even the firmest promises are not to fall short of accomplishment. Is it possible that anyone will not do all he can to carry out God's plan which has been designed with so much love by the Bridegroom of souls, and which I have tried to sketch in outline?

Ah! who would not love with a measureless love Him who has so loved mankind? How could any religious of the Sacred Heart fail to engrave on her heart the great words written large in letters of fire in the Message: Devotion to the Sacred Heart, charity, kindness, confidence, abandonment, total gift of self, humility, compassion, reparation, the salvation of souls, and the mediation of Mary? How could these virtues, so characteristic of Saint Madeleine-Sophie and her supernatural family not be practiced by them with heroic fidelity?

The mission of the Society of the Sacred Heart in the Church and in Catholic Action, depends on its trust in the Sacred Heart of Jesus, and consequently on the importance it will give to His Message.

Christ could have addressed souls by means of a contemplative. He chose - in order the better to attain His object - to seek for the collaboration of an Order devoted to the education of youth. This was no mere chance election. Doctrines with a moral and a spiritual bearing can only penetrate the body and soul of humanity by the education of the young generation who will be leavened by its strong principles, for it takes leaven to make the dough rise! I reflect with immense gratitude on the grace received by the Society of the Sacred Heart ... that of training militant members of Catholic Action and future mothers of families, who, in this age of diabolic terror when some are crushed by fear and others exalted by presumption, will find in their unshakable Faith courage to win back many souls by their reparation in union with the pierced Heart of Jesus. The Message has been confided first of all to this Society. God grant that it may in no way minimize its grave importance at the present moment, but that through its means the seed may bear fruit a hundredfold!

REV. FATHER FR. CHARMOT, S. J.

Appendix-

SISTER Josefa wrote with great reticence on this subject. She did it only to conform to Our Blessed Lord's wishes, Our Lady having told her on the October 25th, 1922: "Everything that Jesus allows you to see and to suffer of the torments of Hell, is ... that you may make it known to your Mothers. So forget yourself entirely, and think only of the glory of the Heart of Jesus and the salvation of souls."

Some extracts of her notes have been quoted in a former Chapter (V) and a few more are added here:

She repeatedly dwelt on the greatest torment of Hell, namely, the soul's inability to love.

One of these damned souls cried out: "This is my torture ... that I want to love and cannot; there is nothing left me but hatred and despair. If one of us could so much as make a single act of love ... this would no longer be Hell... But we cannot, we live on hatred and malevolence ... " (March 23rd, 1922).

Another of these unfortunates said: "The greatest of our torments here is that we are not able to love Him whom we are bound to hate. Oh! how we hunger for love, we are consumed with desire of it, but it is too late... . You too will feel this same devouring hunger, but you will only be able to hate, to abhor, and to long for the loss of souls ... nothing else do we care for now!" (March 26th, 1922).

The following passage was written by obedience, though it was extremely repugnant to Josefa's humility:

"Every day now, when I am dragged down to Hell and the devil orders them to torture me, they answer: 'We cannot, for her members have undergone torture for Him ... ' (then they blasphemously name Our Blessed Lord) ... then he orders them to give me a draught of sulfur ... and again the reply is: 'She has voluntarily deprived herself of drink... .' 'Try to find some part of her body to which she has given satisfaction and pleasure.'

"I have also noted that when they shackle me to take me down to Hell, they never can bind me where I have worn instruments of penance. I write all this simply out of obedience." (April 1st, 1922).

She records, too, the accusations made against themselves by these unhappy souls: "Some yell because of the martyrdom of their hands. Perhaps they were thieves, for they say: 'Where is our loot now? ... Cursed hands... . Why did I want to possess what did not belong to me ... and what in any case I could keep only for a few days ... ?'

"Others curse their tongues, their eyes ... whatever was the occasion of their sin... . 'Now, O body, you are paying the price of the delights you granted yourself! ... and you did it of your own free will ... '" (April 2nd, 1922).

"It seemed to me that the majority accused themselves of sins of impurity, of stealing, of unjust trading; and that most of the damned are in Hell for these sins." (April 6th, 1922).

"I saw many worldly people fall into Hell, and no words can render their horrible and terrifying cries: 'Damned forever... . I deceived myself; I am lost... . I am here forever... . There is no remedy possible ... a curse on me... .'

"Some accused people, others circumstances, and all execrated the occasions of their damnation." (September 1922).

"Today, I saw a vast number of people fall into the fiery pit ... they seemed to be worldlings and a demon cried vociferously: 'The world is ripe for me... . I know that the best way to get hold of souls is to rouse their desire for enjoyment... . Put me first ... me before the rest ... no humility for me! but let me enjoy myself... . This sort of thing assures victory to me ... and they tumble headlong into Hell.'" (October 4th, 1922).

"I heard a demon, from whom a soul had escaped, forced to confess his powerlessness. 'Confound it all ... how do so many manage to escape me? They were mine' (and he rattled off their sins) ... 'I work hard enough, yet they slip through my fingers ... Someone must be suffering and repairing for them.'" (January 15th, 1923).

"Tonight," wrote Josefa, "I did not go down into Hell, but was transported to a place where all was obscure, but in the center was a red smoldering fire. They had laid me flat and so bound me that I could not make the slightest movement. Around me were seven or eight people; their black bodies were unclothed, and I could see them only by the reflections of the fire. They were seated and were talking together.

"One said: 'We'll have to be very careful not to be found out, for we might easily be discovered.'

"The devil answered: 'Insinuate yourselves by inducing carelessness in them ... but keep in the background, so that you are not found out ... by degrees they will become callous, and you will be able to incline them to evil. Tempt these others to ambition, to self-interest, to acquiring wealth without working, whether it be lawful or not. Excite some to sensuality and love of pleasure. Let vice blind them ... ' (Here they used obscene words.)

" 'As to the remainder ... get in through the heart ... you know the inclinations of their hearts ... make them love ... love passionately... work thoroughly ... take no rest ... have no pity; the world must go to damnation ... and these souls must not be allowed to escape me.'

"From time to time Satan's satellites answered: 'We are your slaves ... we shall labor unceasingly, and in spite of the many who war against us, we shall work night and day. We know your power!'

"They all spoke together and he whom I took to be Satan used words full of horror. In the distance I could hear a clamor as of feasting, the clinking of glasses ... and he cried: 'Let them cram themselves with food! It will make it all the easier for us.... Let them get on with their banqueting. Love of pleasure is the door through which you will reach them... .'

"He added such horrible things that they can neither be written nor said. Then, as if engulfed in a whirl of smoke, they vanished." (February 3rd, 1923).

"The evil one was bewailing the escape of a soul: 'Fill her soul with fear, drive her to despair. All will be lost if she puts her trust in the mercy of that ... ' (here they used blasphemous words of Our Lord). 'I am lost; but no, drive her to despair; do not leave her for an instant; above all, make her despair.'

"Then Hell re-echoed with frenzied cries, and when finally the devil cast me out of the abyss he went on threatening me. Among other things he said: 'Is it possible that such weaklings have more power than I, who am mighty.... I must conceal my presence, work in the dark; any corner will do from which to tempt them ... close to an ear ... in the leaves of a book ... under a bed ... some pay no attention to me, but I shall talk and talk ... and by dint of suggestion, something will remain.... Yes, I must hide in unsuspected places'" (February 7th-8th, 1923).

Josefa, on her return from Hell, noted the following: "I saw several souls fall into Hell, and among them was a child of fifteen, cursing her parents for not having taught her to fear God nor that there was a Hell. Her life had been a short one, she said, but full of sin, for she had given in to all that her body and passions demanded in the way of satisfaction. Especially she had read bad books." (March 22nd, 1923).

Again, she wrote:" ... Souls were cursing the vocation they had received, but not followed ... the vocation they had lost, because they were unwilling to live a hidden and mortified life ... " (March 18th, 1922).

"On one occasion when I was in Hell I saw a great many priests, religious and nuns, cursing their vows, their Order, their Superiors and everything that could have given them the light and the grace they had lost... .

"I saw, too, some prelates. One accused himself of having used the goods belonging to the Church illicitly ... " (September 28th, 1922).

"Priests were calling down maledictions on their tongues which had consecrated, on their fingers that had held Our Lord's sacred Body, on the absolutions they had given while they were losing their own souls and on the occasion through which they had fallen into Hell." (April 6th, 1922).

"One priest said: 'I ate poison, for I used money that was not my own ... the money given me for Masses which I did not offer.'

"Another said he belonged to a secret society which had betrayed the Church and religion, and he had been bribed to connive at terrible profanations and sacrileges.

"Yet another said that he was damned for assisting at profane plays, after which he ought not to have said Mass ... and that he had spent about seven years thus."

Josefa noted that the greater number of religious plunged into hell-fire were there for abominable sins against Chastity ... and for sins against the vow of Poverty ... for the unauthorized use of the goods of the Community ... for passions against charity (jealousy, antipathies, hatred, etc.), for tepidity and relaxation; also for comforts they had allowed themselves and which had led to graver sins ... for bad Confessions through human respect and want of sincerity and courage, etc.

Here, finally, is the full text of Josefa's notes on "the Hell of consecrated souls" (Biography: Ch. VII-September 4th, 1922).

"The meditation of the day was on the particular judgment of religious souls. I could not free my mind of the thought of it, in spite of the oppression which I felt. Suddenly, I felt myself bound and overwhelmed by a crushing weight, so that in an instant I saw more clearly than ever before how stupendous is the sanctity of God and His detestation of sin.

"I saw in a flash my whole life since my first Confession to this day. All was vividly present to me: my sins, the graces I had received, the day I entered religion, my clothing as a novice, my first vows, my spiritual readings, and times of prayer, the advice given me, and all the helps of religious life. Impossible to describe the confusion and shame a soul feels at that moment, when it realizes: 'All is lost, and I am damned forever.'"

As in her former descents into Hell, Josefa never accused herself of any specific sin that might have led to such a calamity. Our Lord meant her only to feel what the consequences would have been, if she had merited such a punishment. She wrote:

"Instantly I found myself in Hell, but not dragged there as before. The soul precipitates itself there, as if to hide from God in order to be free to hate and curse Him.

"My soul fell into abysmal depths, the bottom of which cannot be seen, for it is immense... . At once, I heard other souls jeering and rejoicing at seeing me share their torments. It was martyrdom enough to hear the terrible imprecations on all sides, but what can be compared to the thirst to curse that seizes on a soul, and the more one curses, the more one wants to. Never had I felt the like before. Formerly my soul had been oppressed with grief at hearing these horrible blasphemies, though unable to produce even one act of love. But today it was otherwise.

"I saw Hell as always before, the long dark corridors, the cavities, the flames... . I heard the same execrations and imprecations, for - and of this I have already written before - although no corporeal forms are visible, the torments are felt as if they were present, and souls recognize each other. Some called out, 'Hullo! you here? And are you like us? We were free to take those vows or not ... but now! ... ' and they cursed their vows.

"Then I was pushed into one of those fiery cavities and pressed, as it were, between burning planks, and sharp nails and red-hot irons seemed to be piercing my flesh."

Here Josefa repeated the multiple tortures from which no single member of the body is excluded:

"I felt as if they were endeavoring to pull out my tongue, but could not. This torture reduced me to such agony that my very eyes seemed to be starting out of their sockets. I think this was because of the fire which burns, burns ... not a fingernail escapes the terrifying torments, and all the time one cannot move even a finger to gain some relief, nor change posture, for the body seems flattened out and doubled in two.

"Sounds of confusion and blasphemy cease not for an instant. A sickening stench asphyxiates and corrupts everything, it is like the burning of putrefied flesh, mingled with tar and sulfur ... a mixture to which nothing on earth can be compared.

"All this I felt as before, and although those tortures were terrific, they would be bearable if the soul were at peace. But it suffers indescribably. Until now, when I went down into Hell, I thought that I had been damned for abandoning religious life. But this time it was different. I bore a special mark, a sign that I was a religious, a soul who had known and loved God, and there were others who bore the same sign. I cannot say how I recognized it, perhaps because of the specially insulting manner in which the evil spirits and other damned souls treated them. There were many priests there, too. This particular suffering I am unable to explain. It was quite different from what I had experienced at other times, for if the souls of those who lived in the world suffer terribly, infinitely worse are the torments of religious. Unceasingly the three words Poverty, Chastity and Obedience are imprinted on the soul with poignant remorse.

"Poverty: You were free and you promised! Why, then, did you seek that comfort? Why hold on to that object which did not belong to you? Why did you give that pleasure to your body? Why allow yourself to dispose of the property of the Community? Did you not know that you no longer had the right to possess anything whatsoever? that you had freely renounced the use of those things... . Why did you murmur when anything was wanting to you or when you fancied yourself less well treated than others? Why?

"Chastity: You yourself vowed it freely and with full knowledge of its implications ... you bound yourself ... you willed it ... and how have you observed it? That being so, why did you not remain where it would have been lawful for you to grant yourself pleasures and enjoyment?

"And the tortured soul responds: 'Yes, I vowed it, I was free... . I could have not taken the vow, but I took it and I was free... .' What words can express the martyrdom of such remorse?" wrote Josefa, "and all the time the jibes and insults of other damned souls continue.

"Obedience: Did you not fully engage yourself to obey your Rule and your Superiors? Why, then, did you pass judgment on the orders that were given you? Why did you disobey the Rule? Why did you dispense yourself from common life? Remember how sweet was the Rule ... and you would not keep it ... and now," vociferate satanic voices, "you will have to obey us not for a day, or a year, or a century, but forever and ever, for all eternity... . It is your own doing ... you were free.

"The soul constantly recalls how she had chosen her God for her Spouse, and that once she loved Him above all things ... that for Him she had renounced the most legitimate pleasures and all she held dearest on earth, that in the beginning of her religious life she had felt all the purity, sweetness and strength of this divine love, and that for an inordinate passion ... now she must eternally hate the God who had chosen her to love Him.

"This forced hatred is a thirst that consumes her ... no past joys can afford her the slightest relief.

"One of her greatest torments is shame," added Josefa. "It seems to her that all the damned surrounding her continually taunt her by saying: 'That we should be lost who never had the helps that you enjoyed is not surprising ... but you ... what did you lack? You who lived in the palace of the King ... who feasted at the board of the elect.'

"All I have written," she concluded, "is but a shadow of what the soul suffers, for no words can express such dire torments." (September 4th, 1922).

THE TEACHINGS OF PURGATORY

Josefa never went down into Purgatory, but she saw and spoke with a number of souls who came to solicit her prayers, and some told her that, thanks to her sufferings, they had escaped Hell.

These souls, as a rule, humbly accused themselves of the faults for which they were in Purgatory (see Ch. V. of Biography). A few facts are here added.

" ... I had a vocation, but lost it by reading bad books; I also had discarded my scapular, out of contempt" (July 27th, 1921).

" ... I was given up to a great deal of vanity and on the point of marrying. Our Lord made use of very severe measures to prevent my falling into Hell." (April 10th, 1921).

"My religious life was wanting in fervor... ."

"I had a long religious life, but I spent my last years rather in taking care of my health than in loving Our Lord. Thanks to the merits of a sacrifice you made, I was able to make a fervent death, and I owe it to you that I escaped the long years in Purgatory I had deserved. The important thing is not so much entrance into religion ... as entrance into eternity." (April 7th, 1922).

"... I have been a year and three months in Purgatory, and were it not for your little acts I should have remained there long years. A woman of the world has less responsibility than a religious, for how great are the graces the latter receives, and what liabilities she incurs if she does not profit by them... . How little nuns suspect the way their faults are expiated here ... a tongue horribly tortured expiates faults against silence ... a dried-up throat, those against charity ... and the constraints of this prison, the repugnance in obeying! In my Order, pleasures were few and comforts still fewer, but one can always manage to secure some ... and the smallest immortifications have to be expiated here. To restrain one's eyes, to refuse oneself the gratification of a little curiosity may at times cost a big effort ... and here ... the eyes are tormented by the impossibility of seeing God." (April 10th, 1922).

"Another nun accused herself of failings against charity, and of having murmured at the election of one of her Superiors." (April 12th, 1922).

"... I have been in Purgatory till now ... because during my religious life I talked a great deal and with little prudence. I often communicated my impressions and complaints, and these indiscretions were the cause of faults against charity which my Sisters then committed."

"Let all learn from this," commented Our Lady, who was present at the apparition, "for many souls fall into this danger."

Our Lord stressed this grave warning by these words: "That soul is in Purgatory because of her faults against silence, for this kind of fault leads to many others: first, the Rule is broken; secondly, there often occur in such failings sins against charity or religious spirit, personal satisfaction, outpourings of heart that are ill-placed among religious, and all this, without a feeling of responsibility not only for oneself but for one or many others who are led into the same faults. That is why this soul is in Purgatory, and burning with desire to see My face." (February 22nd, 1923).

"I am in Purgatory because I did not care enough about the souls confided to me, and because I did not sufficiently realize their value and the devotedness called for by so precious a charge." (August 1922).

... I was in Purgatory a little under an hour and a half to expiate a certain want of confidence in God. True, I always loved Him very much, but not without fear. It is true also that the judgments of religious are severe and rigorous, for we are judged not by our Spouse, but by our God. Nevertheless, during life our confidence in His mercy ought to be boundless, and we should trust His goodness. How many graces are lost by religious who have not enough trust in God." (September 1922).

"... I am in Purgatory because I did not treat the souls that Jesus entrusted to me with the care they deserved... . I allowed myself to be influenced by human motives and natural likes, not seeing in them God, as I should have, and as all Superiors must. For if it is true that all religious should see in their Superior the Person of God Our Lord, the Superior also ought to see Him in her daughters... ."

"Thanks be to you who have helped to free me from Purgatory... . O! if nuns realized how far they can be led by unruly feelings ... how vigorously they would strive to conquer themselves and master their nature and passions." (April 1923).

"My Purgatory will be a long one, for I did not accept God's Will for me, nor make the sacrifice of my life generously enough during my illness. Illness is a great grace of purification, it is true, but unless one is careful, it may cause one to stray away from religious spirit ... to forget that one has made vows of Poverty, Chastity and Obedience, and that one is consecrated to God as a victim. Our Lord is all love, certainly, but also all justice." (November 1923).

www.ingramcontent.com/pod-product-compliance
Lightning Source LLC
LaVergne TN
LVHW091757040125
800529LV00038B/492